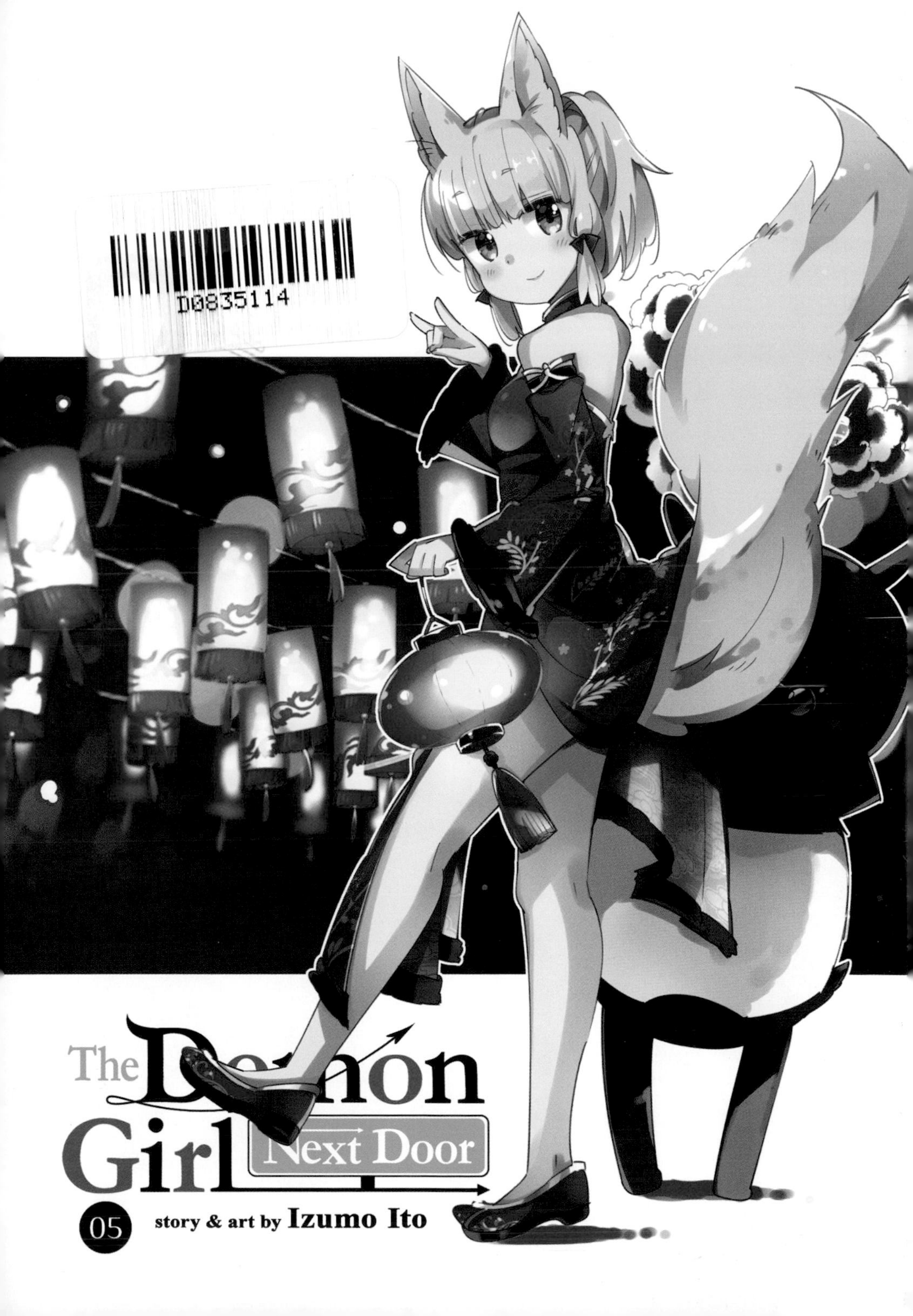

The Demon Girl Next Door

05

story & art by Izumo Ito

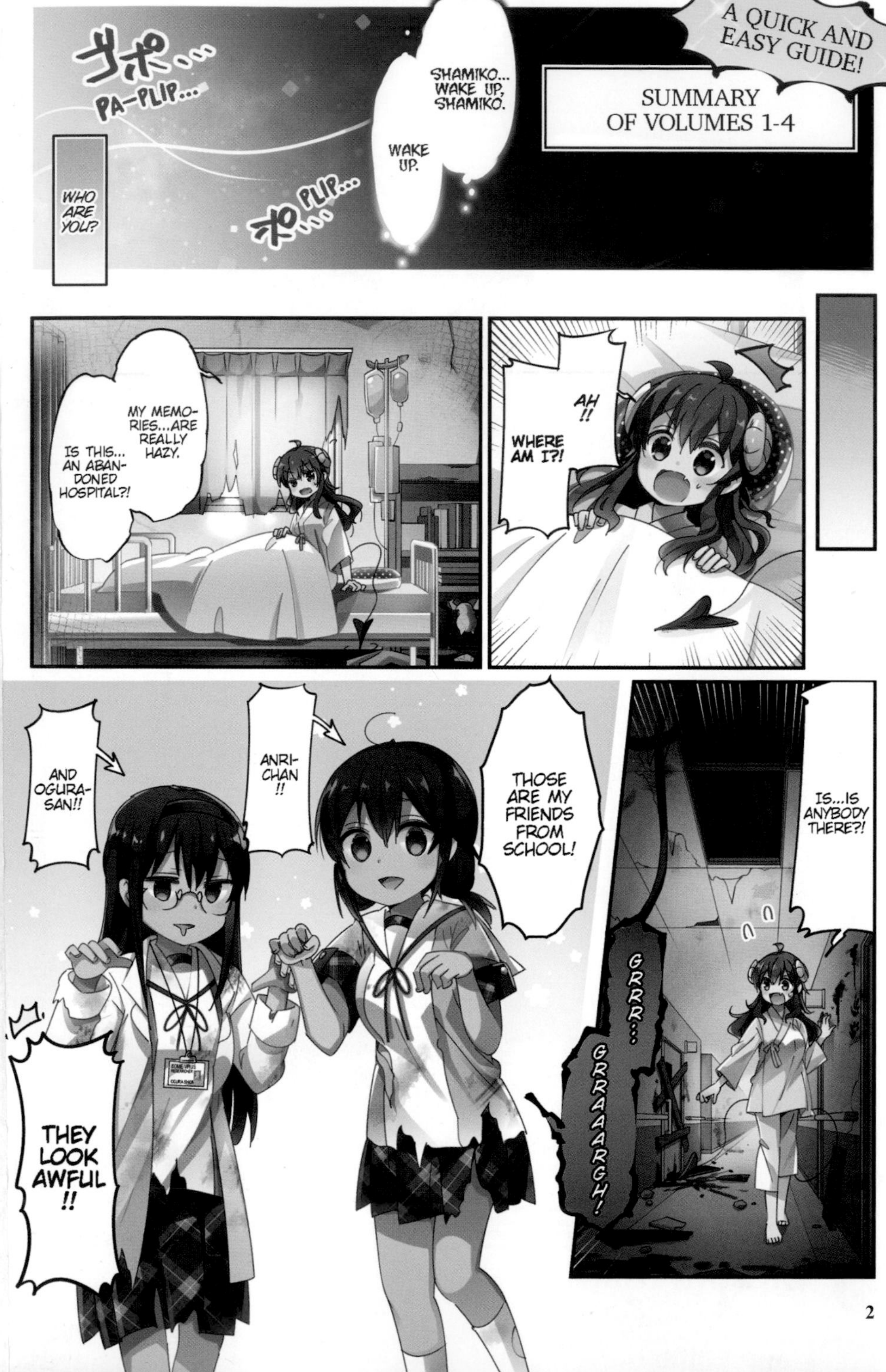
A QUICK AND EASY GUIDE!
SUMMARY OF VOLUMES 1-4
SHAMIKO... WAKE UP, SHAMIKO.
WAKE UP.
ゴポ...
PA-PLIP...
PLIP...
WHO ARE YOU?
AH !!
WHERE AM I?!
MY MEMO-RIES...ARE REALLY HAZY.
IS THIS... AN ABAN-DONED HOSPITAL?!
IS...IS ANYBODY THERE?!
GRRR...
GRRAAAARGH!
THOSE ARE MY FRIENDS FROM SCHOOL!
ANRI-CHAN !!
AND OGURA-SAN!!
THEY LOOK AWFUL !!

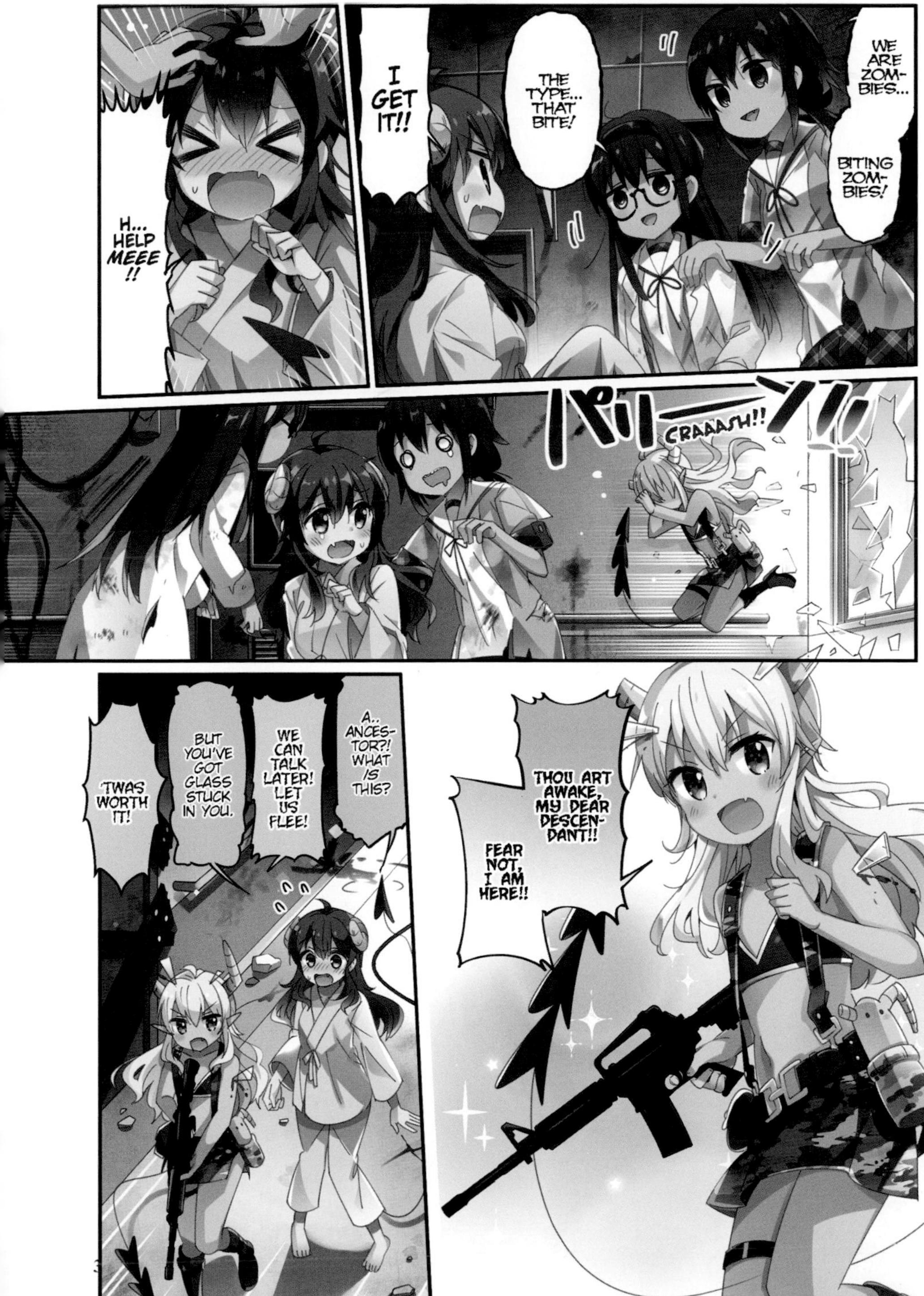
WE ARE ZOMBIES...
BITING ZOMBIES!
THE TYPE... THAT BITE!
I GET IT!!
H... HELP MEEE!!
パリーン!!
CRAAASH!!
THOU ART AWAKE, MY DEAR DESCENDANT!!
FEAR NOT, I AM HERE!!
A.. ANCESTOR?! WHAT IS THIS?
WE CAN TALK LATER! LET US FLEE!
BUT YOU'VE GOT GLASS STUCK IN YOU.
'TWAS WORTH IT!

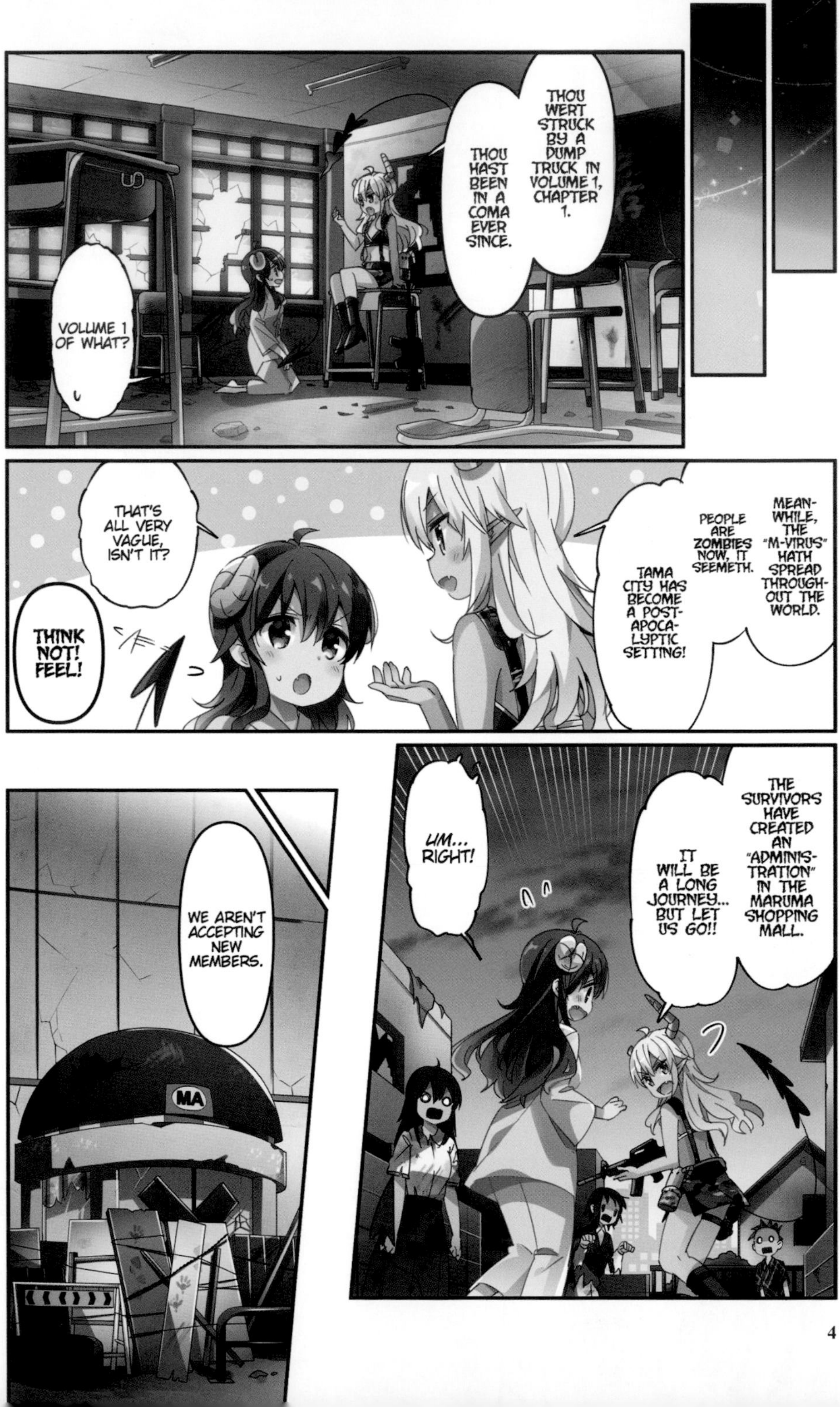
THOU WERT STRUCK BY A DUMP TRUCK IN VOLUME 1, CHAPTER 1.
THOU HAST BEEN IN A COMA EVER SINCE.
VOLUME 1 OF WHAT?
MEANWHILE, THE "M-VIRUS" HATH SPREAD THROUGHOUT THE WORLD.
PEOPLE ARE ZOMBIES NOW, IT SEEMETH.
TAMA CITY HAS BECOME A POST-APOCALYPTIC SETTING!
THAT'S ALL VERY VAGUE, ISN'T IT?
THINK NOT! FEEL!
THE SURVIVORS HAVE CREATED AN "ADMINISTRATION" IN THE MARUMA SHOPPING MALL.
IT WILL BE A LONG JOURNEY... BUT LET US GO!!
UM... RIGHT!
WE AREN'T ACCEPTING NEW MEMBERS.
MA

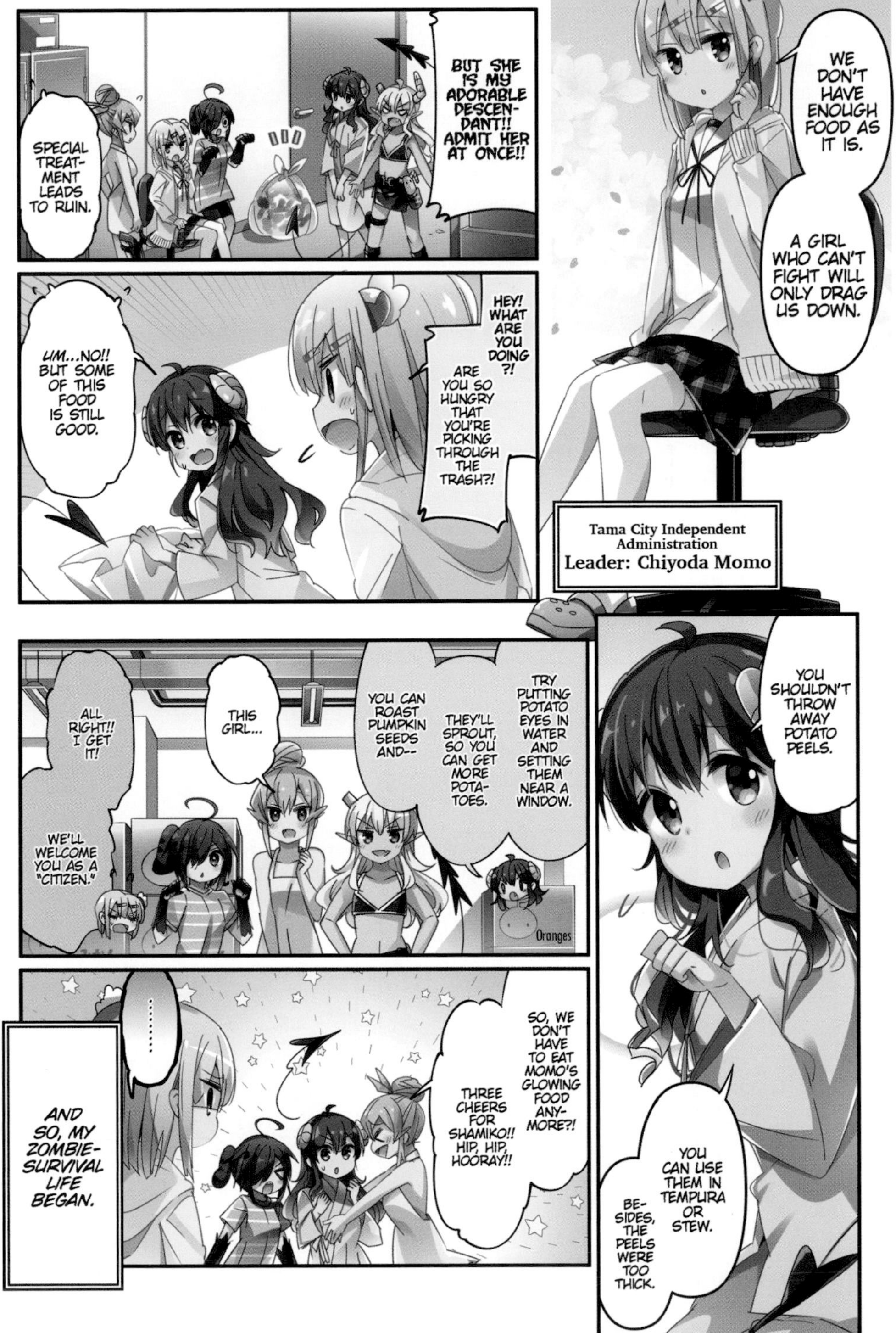
WE DON'T HAVE ENOUGH FOOD AS IT IS.
A GIRL WHO CAN'T FIGHT WILL ONLY DRAG US DOWN.
Tama City Independent Administration
Leader: Chiyoda Momo
BUT SHE IS MY ADORABLE DESCENDANT!! ADMIT HER AT ONCE!!
SPECIAL TREATMENT LEADS TO RUIN.
HEY! WHAT ARE YOU DOING?!
ARE YOU SO HUNGRY THAT YOU'RE PICKING THROUGH THE TRASH?!
UM...NO!! BUT SOME OF THIS FOOD IS STILL GOOD.
YOU SHOULDN'T THROW AWAY POTATO PEELS.
YOU CAN USE THEM IN TEMPURA OR STEW.
BESIDES, THE PEELS WERE TOO THICK.
TRY PUTTING POTATO EYES IN WATER AND SETTING THEM NEAR A WINDOW.
THEY'LL SPROUT, SO YOU CAN GET MORE POTATOES.
YOU CAN ROAST PUMPKIN SEEDS AND--
THIS GIRL...
ALL RIGHT!! I GET IT!
WE'LL WELCOME YOU AS A "CITIZEN."
Oranges
SO, WE DON'T HAVE TO EAT MOMO'S GLOWING FOOD ANYMORE?!
THREE CHEERS FOR SHAMIKO!! HIP, HIP, HOORAY!!
......
AND SO, MY ZOMBIE-SURVIVAL LIFE BEGAN.

People who ignore zombies and argue!!

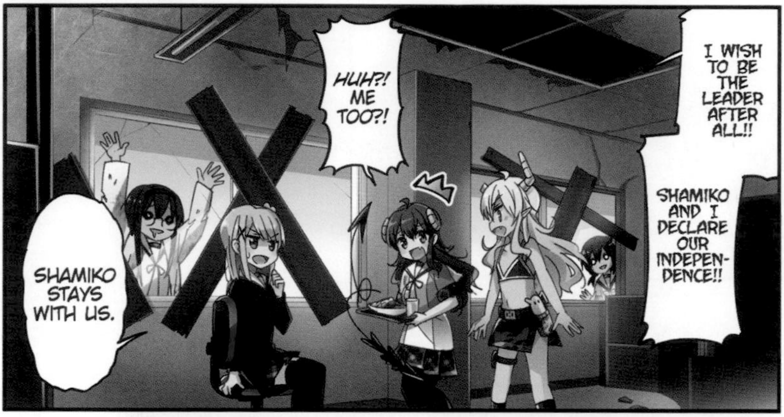
I WISH TO BE THE LEADER AFTER ALL!!
SHAMIKO AND I DECLARE OUR INDEPENDENCE!!
HUH?! ME TOO?!
SHAMIKO STAYS WITH US.

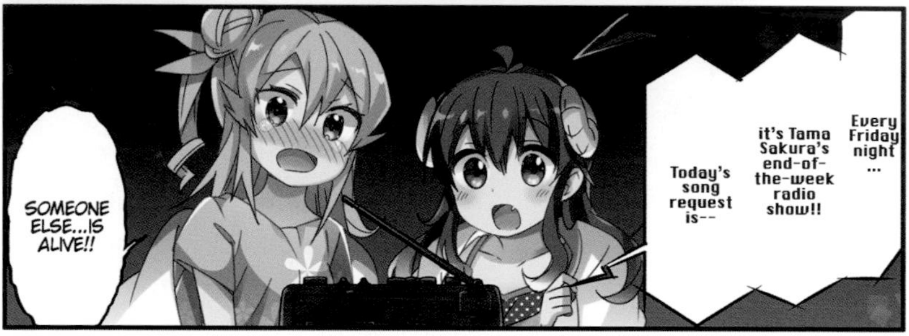
Every Friday night ...
it's Tama Sakura's end-of-the-week radio show!!
Today's song request is--
SOMEONE ELSE...IS ALIVE!!

An end-of-the-week DJ appears!

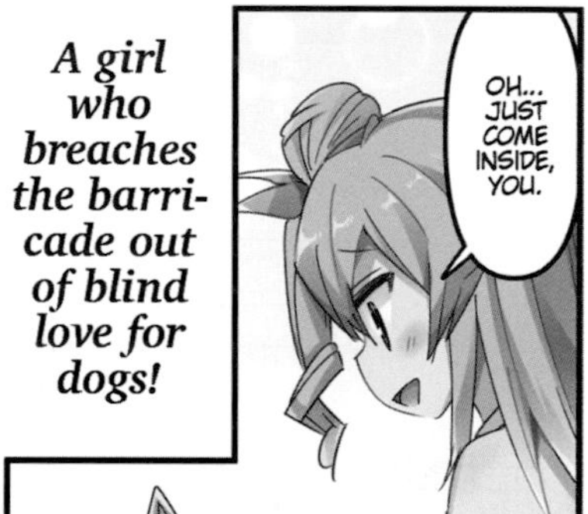
OH... JUST COME INSIDE, YOU.

A girl who breaches the barricade out of blind love for dogs!

A beloved mistress turned into a zombie!

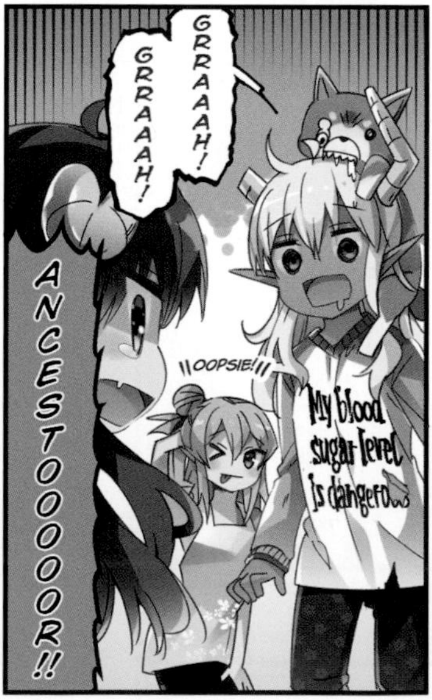
GRRAAAAH!
GRRAAAH!
ANCESTOOOOOOR!!
OOPSIE!
My blood sugar level is dangerous

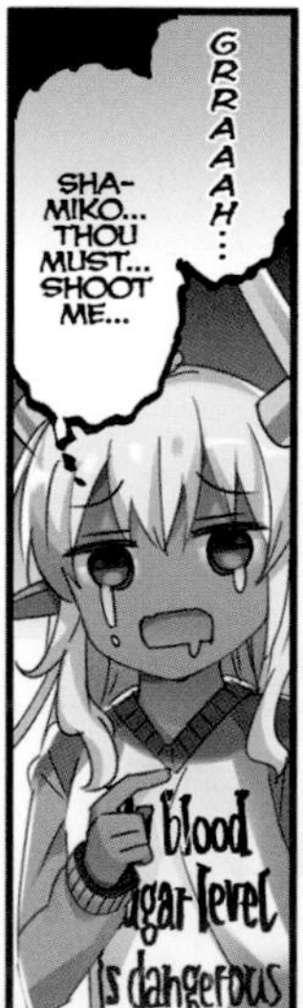
GRRAAAAH...
SHA-MIKO... THOU MUST... SHOOT ME...

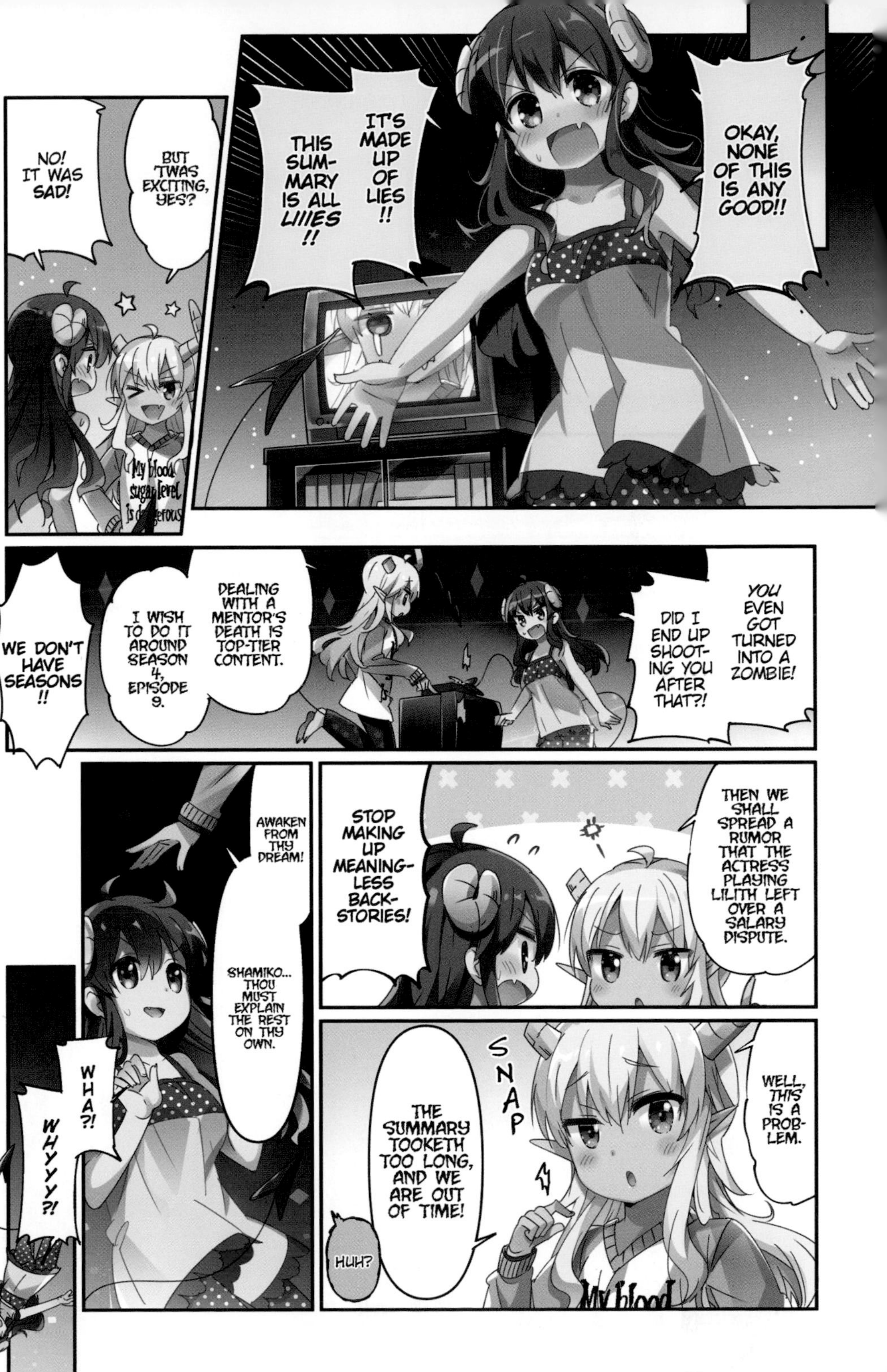
OKAY, NONE OF THIS IS ANY GOOD!!
IT'S MADE UP OF LIES!!
THIS SUMMARY IS ALL LIIIES!!
BUT 'TWAS EXCITING, YES?
NO! IT WAS SAD!
My blood sugar level is dangerous
YOU EVEN GOT TURNED INTO A ZOMBIE!
DID I END UP SHOOTING YOU AFTER THAT?!
DEALING WITH A MENTOR'S DEATH IS TOP-TIER CONTENT.
I WISH TO DO IT AROUND SEASON 4, EPISODE 9.
WE DON'T HAVE SEASONS!!
THEN WE SHALL SPREAD A RUMOR THAT THE ACTRESS PLAYING LILITH LEFT OVER A SALARY DISPUTE.
STOP MAKING UP MEANINGLESS BACK-STORIES!
WELL, THIS IS A PROBLEM.
SNAP
THE SUMMARY TOOKETH TOO LONG, AND WE ARE OUT OF TIME!
HUH?
My blood
AWAKEN FROM THY DREAM!
SHAMIKO... THOU MUST EXPLAIN THE REST ON THY OWN.
WHA?!
WHYYYY?!

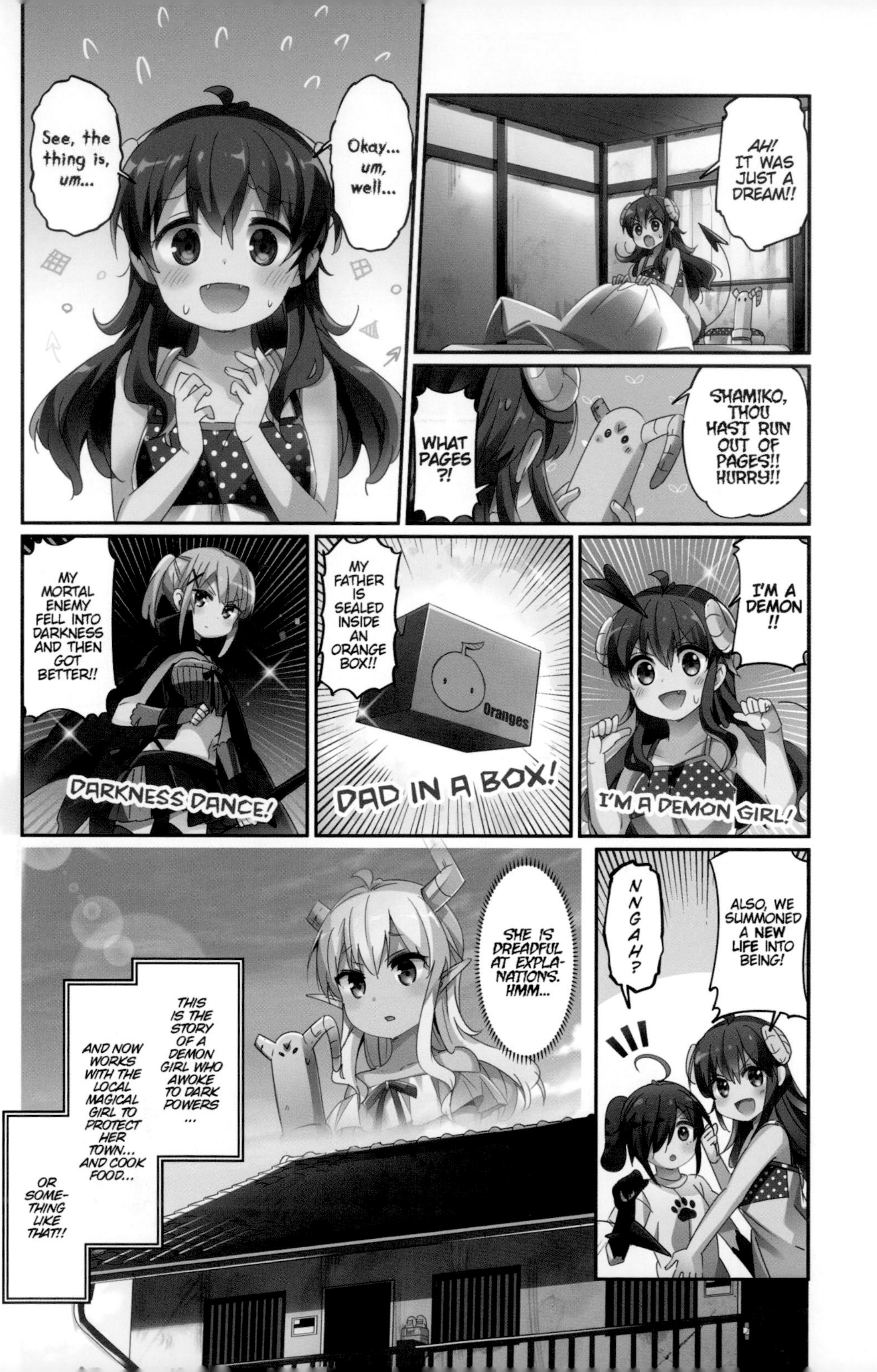
AH! IT WAS JUST A DREAM!!
SHAMIKO, THOU HAST RUN OUT OF PAGES!! HURRY!!
WHAT PAGES?!
Okay... um, well...
See, the thing is, um...
I'M A DEMON!!
I'M A DEMON GIRL!
MY FATHER IS SEALED INSIDE AN ORANGE BOX!!
Oranges
DAD IN A BOX!
MY MORTAL ENEMY FELL INTO DARKNESS AND THEN GOT BETTER!!
DARKNESS DANCE!
ALSO, WE SUMMONED A NEW LIFE INTO BEING!
NNGAH?
SHE IS DREADFUL AT EXPLANATIONS. HMM...
THIS IS THE STORY OF A DEMON GIRL WHO AWOKE TO DARK POWERS...
AND NOW WORKS WITH THE LOCAL MAGICAL GIRL TO PROTECT HER TOWN... AND COOK FOOD...
OR SOMETHING LIKE THAT!!

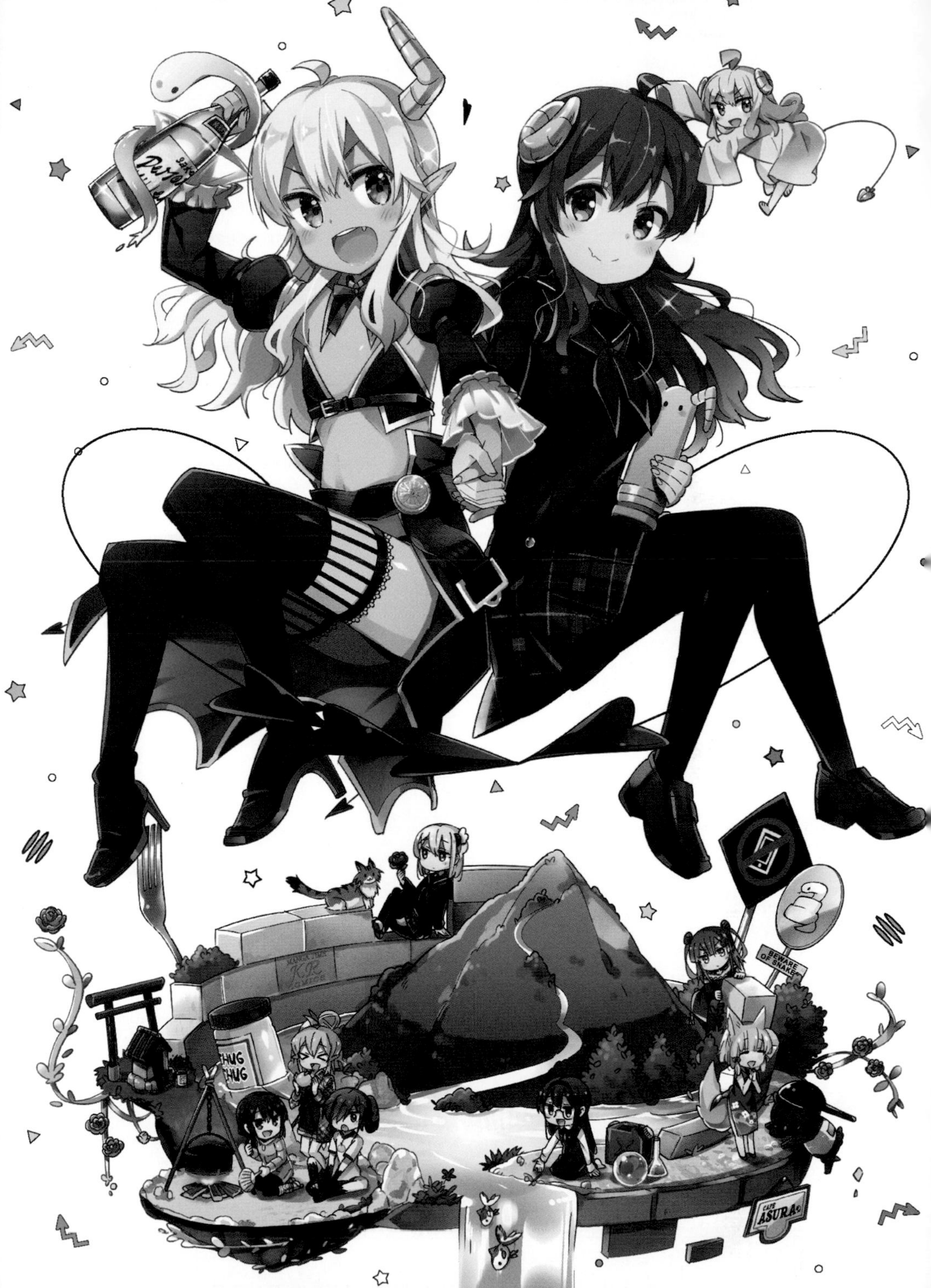
THUG
THUG
BEWARE
OF SNAKES
CAFE
ASURA

THE DEMON GIRL NEXT DOOR 05

< 120

KIRARA

SHAMIKO, ARE YOU GETTING THE HANG OF YOUR SMARTPHONE?

SHAMIKO

OF COURSE I AM!

CHIYODA MOMO

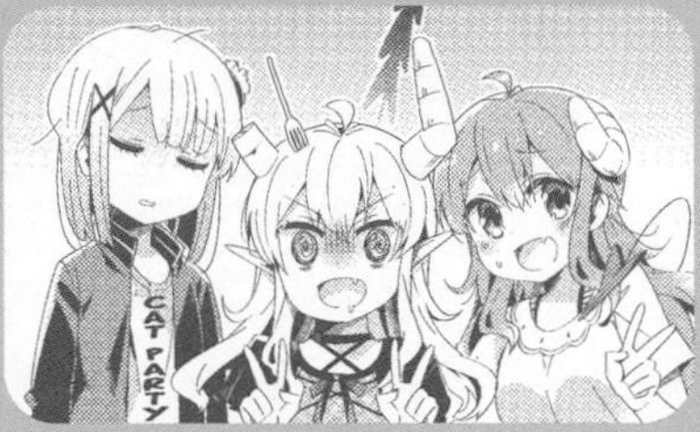
CAT PARTY

HERE'S A PHOTO.

MIKAN

IT WAS HECTIC, BUT STILL FUN!

SATA ANRI

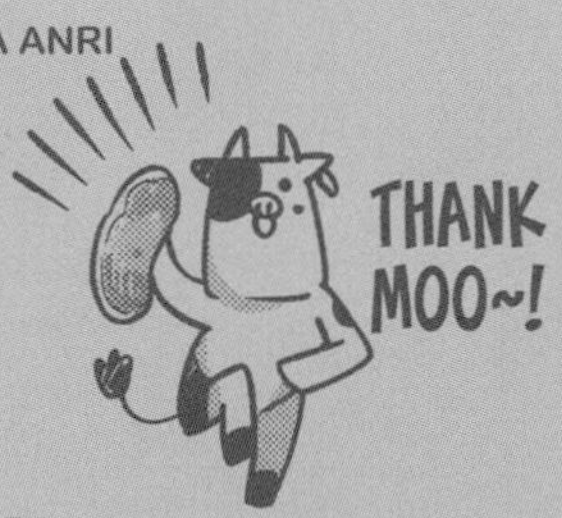
THANK MOO~!

OGURA

DO YOU THINK I'VE BECOME MORE OF A BOSS?

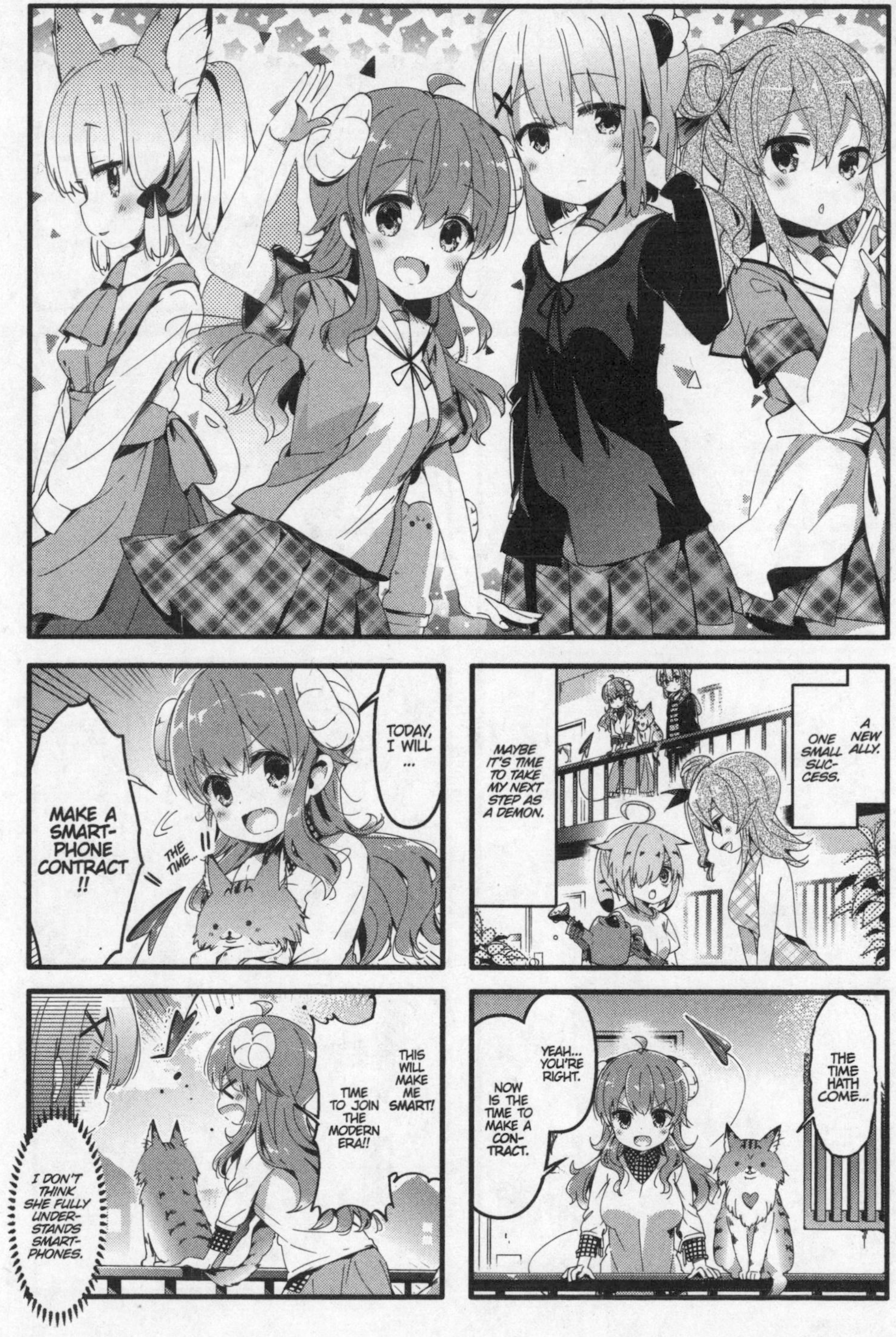
A NEW ALLY.
ONE SMALL SUCCESS.
MAYBE IT'S TIME TO TAKE MY NEXT STEP AS A DEMON.
TODAY, I WILL ...
THE TIME...!!
MAKE A SMARTPHONE CONTRACT !!
THE TIME HATH COME...
YEAH... YOU'RE RIGHT.
NOW IS THE TIME TO MAKE A CONTRACT.
THIS WILL MAKE ME SMART!
TIME TO JOIN THE MODERN ERA!!
I DON'T THINK SHE FULLY UNDERSTANDS SMARTPHONES.

NOT THAT KIND OF SMART

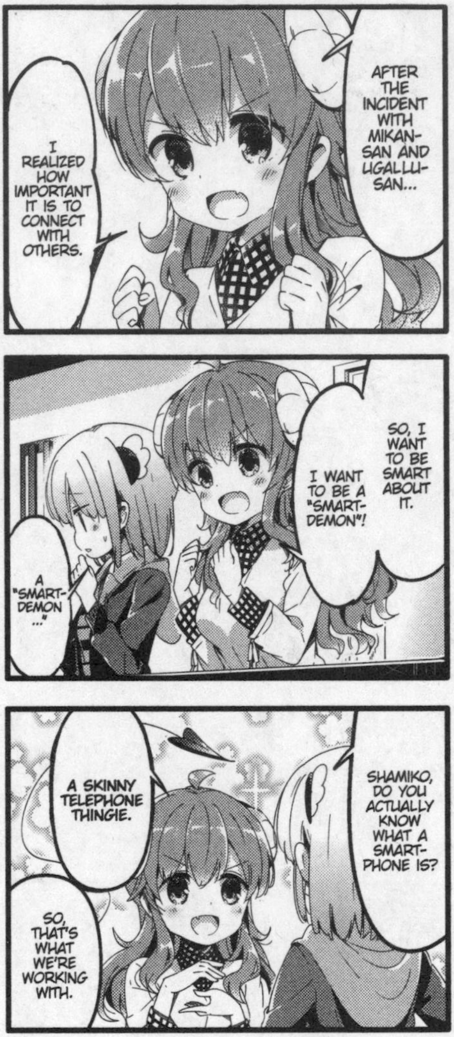
AFTER THE INCIDENT WITH MIKAN-SAN AND UGALLU-SAN...
I REALIZED HOW IMPORTANT IT IS TO CONNECT WITH OTHERS.
SO, I WANT TO BE SMART ABOUT IT.
I WANT TO BE A "SMART-DEMON"!
A "SMART-DEMON"..."
SHAMIKO, DO YOU ACTUALLY KNOW WHAT A SMARTPHONE IS?
A SKINNY TELEPHONE THINGIE.
SO, THAT'S WHAT WE'RE WORKING WITH.
I WANT TO TEACH YOU A FEW THINGS. COME BY MY PLACE, OKAY?
HUH?! NO WAY!! TOO MUCH PRESSURE!!
JUST DO IT.
NO! THANK! YOU!

DEMONS AND TECHNOLOGY DON'T MIX

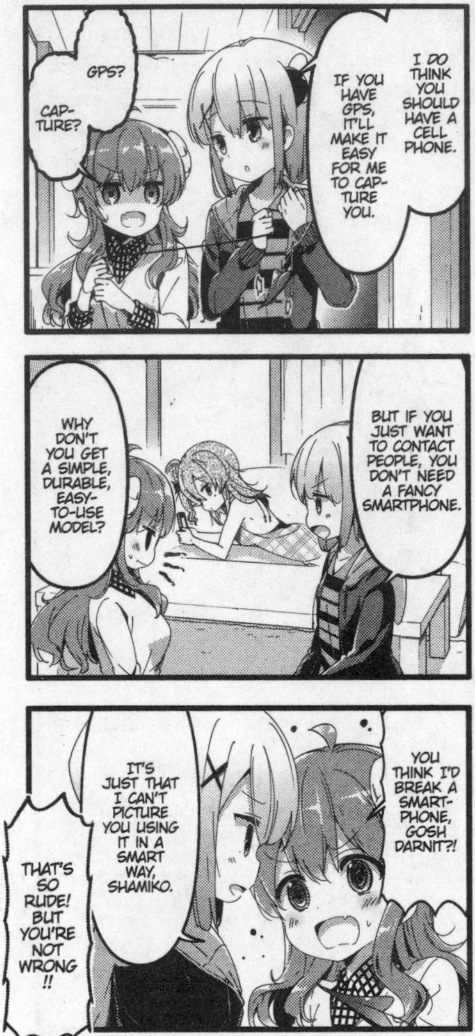
I DO THINK YOU SHOULD HAVE A CELL PHONE.
IF YOU HAVE GPS, IT'LL MAKE IT EASY FOR ME TO CAPTURE YOU.
GPS?
CAPTURE?
BUT IF YOU JUST WANT TO CONTACT PEOPLE, YOU DON'T NEED A FANCY SMARTPHONE.
WHY DON'T YOU GET A SIMPLE, DURABLE, EASY-TO-USE MODEL?
YOU THINK I'D BREAK A SMARTPHONE, GOSH DARNIT?!
IT'S JUST THAT I CAN'T PICTURE YOU USING IT IN A SMART WAY, SHAMIKO.
THAT'S SO RUDE! BUT YOU'RE NOT WRONG!!
WAIT A MINUTE, DIDN'T YOU BREAK *YOUR* SMARTPHONE, MOMO?!
CRAAACKED!!
AAH!! BUT... THAT... WASN'T MY FAULT.
YOU'RE JUST AS BAD AS ME!!
DON'T GET SO SHAKEN UP ABOUT IT!!

SURVIVAL-ORIENTED MODEL

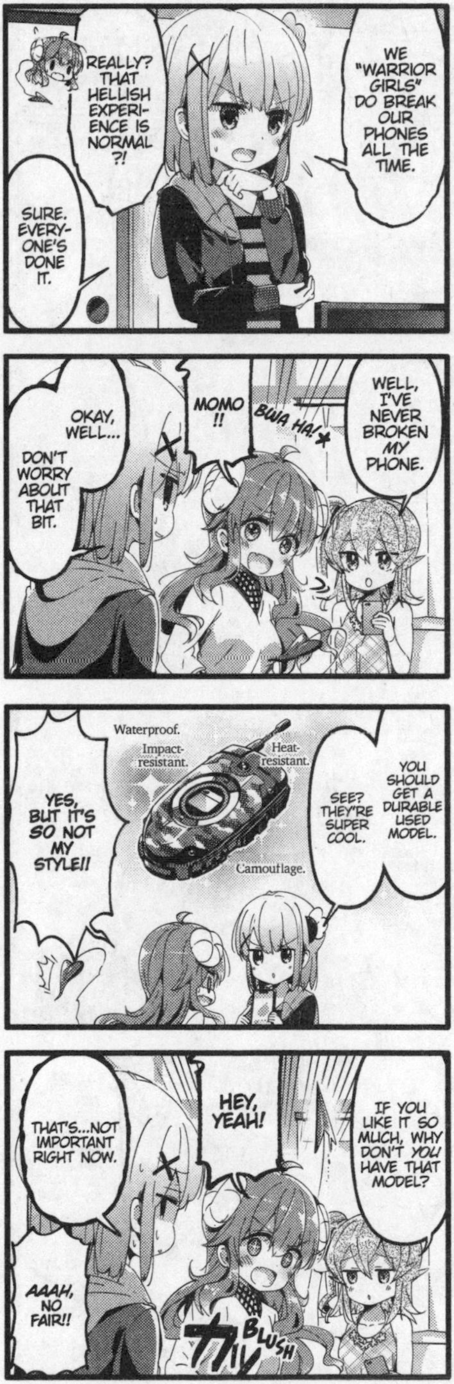
WE "WARRIOR GIRLS" DO BREAK OUR PHONES ALL THE TIME.
REALLY? THAT HELLISH EXPERIENCE IS NORMAL ?!
SURE. EVERYONE'S DONE IT.
WELL, I'VE NEVER BROKEN *MY* PHONE.
BWA HA!
MOMO !!
OKAY, WELL... DON'T WORRY ABOUT THAT BIT.
YOU SHOULD GET A DURABLE USED MODEL.
SEE? THEY'RE SUPER COOL.
Heat-resistant.
Waterproof.
Impact-resistant.
Camouflage.
YES, BUT IT'S SO NOT MY STYLE!!
IF YOU LIKE IT SO MUCH, WHY DON'T *YOU* HAVE THAT MODEL?
HEY, YEAH!
THAT'S...NOT IMPORTANT RIGHT NOW.
BLUSH
AAAH, NO FAIR!!

MIKAN-CHAN'S ON FIRE TODAY

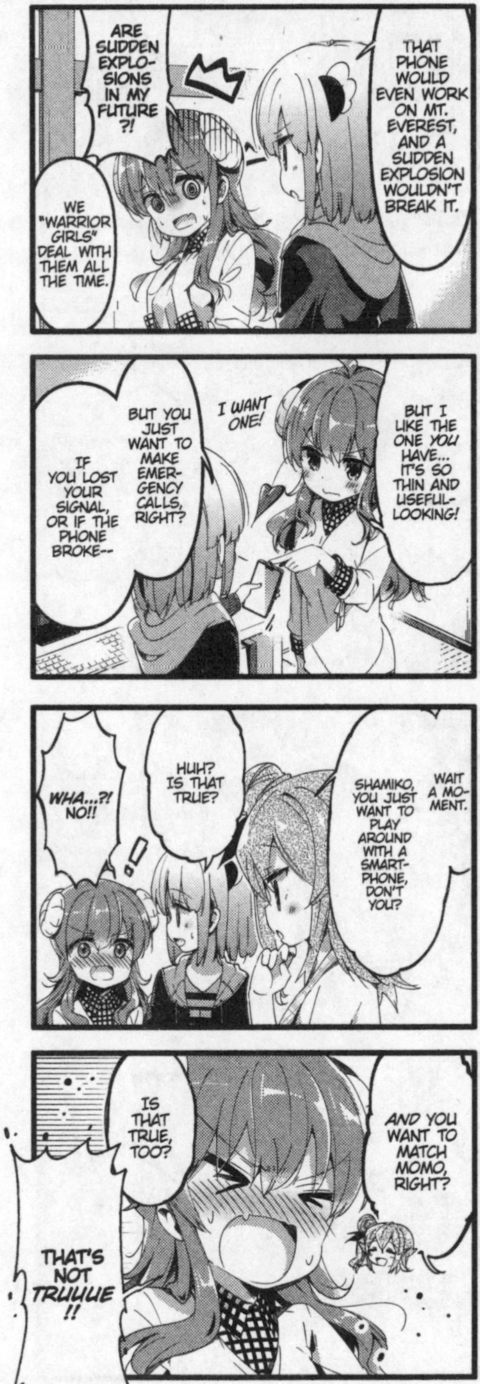
THAT PHONE WOULD EVEN WORK ON MT. EVEREST, AND A SUDDEN EXPLOSION WOULDN'T BREAK IT.
ARE SUDDEN EXPLOSIONS IN MY FUTURE ?!
WE "WARRIOR GIRLS" DEAL WITH THEM ALL THE TIME.
BUT I LIKE THE ONE *YOU* HAVE... IT'S SO THIN AND USEFUL-LOOKING!
I WANT ONE!
BUT YOU JUST WANT TO MAKE EMERGENCY CALLS, RIGHT?
IF YOU LOST YOUR SIGNAL, OR IF THE PHONE BROKE--
WAIT A MOMENT.
SHAMIKO, YOU JUST WANT TO PLAY AROUND WITH A SMARTPHONE, DON'T YOU?
HUH? IS THAT TRUE?
WHA...?! NO!!
AND YOU WANT TO MATCH MOMO, RIGHT?
IS THAT TRUE, TOO?
THAT'S NOT TRUUUE !!

I WANT IT

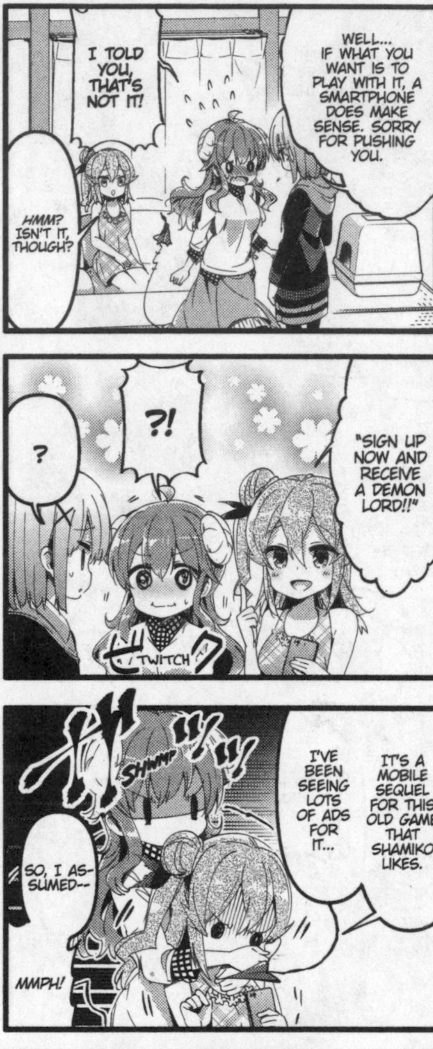
WELL... IF WHAT YOU WANT IS TO PLAY WITH IT, A SMARTPHONE DOES MAKE SENSE. SORRY FOR PUSHING YOU.
I TOLD YOU, THAT'S NOT IT!
HMM? ISN'T IT, THOUGH?
"SIGN UP NOW AND RECEIVE A DEMON LORD!!"
?!
?
TWITCH
IT'S A MOBILE SEQUEL FOR THIS OLD GAME THAT SHAMIKO LIKES.
I'VE BEEN SEEING LOTS OF ADS FOR IT...
SHWMP
SO, I AS-SUMED--
MMPH!
I ONLY WANT A SMART-PHONE TO BECOME A BETTER DEMON!!
NOT SO I CAN MATCH MY MORTAL ENEMY...
OR GET MY FAVORITE CHARAC-TER FROM THE BEST GAME EVEEER!!

PEACH-COLORED GOOD INTENTIONS

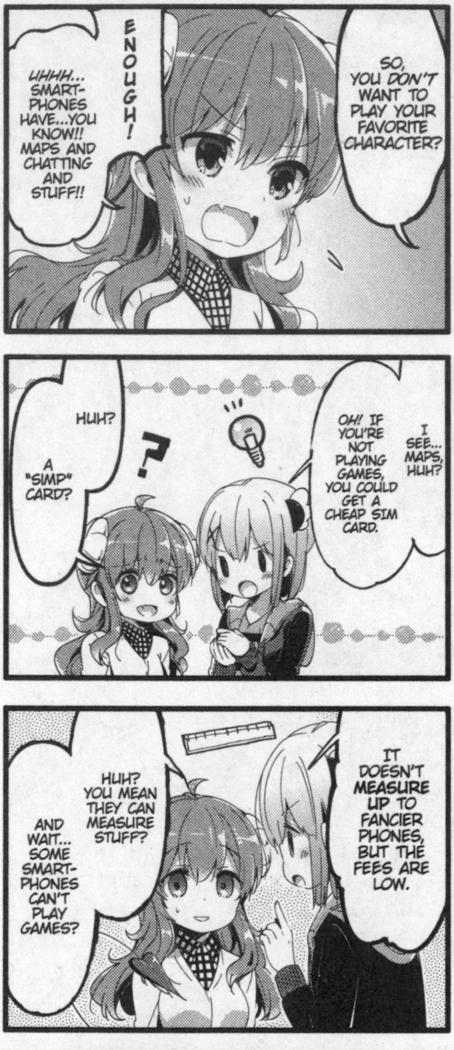
SO, YOU DON'T WANT TO PLAY YOUR FAVORITE CHARACTER?
ENOUGH!
UHHH... SMART-PHONES HAVE...YOU KNOW!! MAPS AND CHATTING AND STUFF!!
I SEE... MAPS, HUH?
OH! IF YOU'RE NOT PLAYING GAMES, YOU COULD GET A CHEAP SIM CARD.
HUH?
A "SIMP" CARD?
?
IT DOESN'T MEASURE UP TO FANCIER PHONES, BUT THE FEES ARE LOW.
HUH? YOU MEAN THEY CAN MEASURE STUFF?
AND WAIT... SOME SMART-PHONES CAN'T PLAY GAMES?
I THOUGHT YOU JUST WANTED TO USE MAPS AND CHAT?
ARRGH! Y-YEAH... BUT STILL...

A SCREAM FROM A DEMON'S SOUL

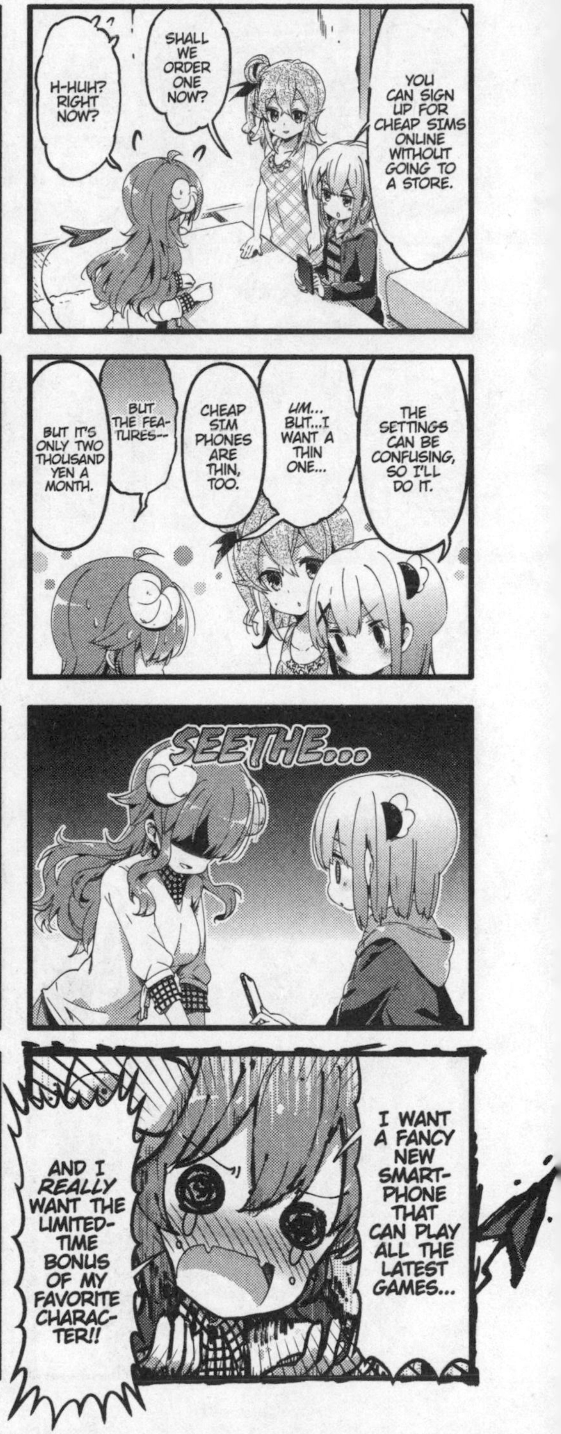
YOU CAN SIGN UP FOR CHEAP SIMS ONLINE WITHOUT GOING TO A STORE.
SHALL WE ORDER ONE NOW?
H-HUH? RIGHT NOW?
THE SETTINGS CAN BE CONFUSING, SO I'LL DO IT.
UM... BUT...I WANT A THIN ONE...
CHEAP SIM PHONES ARE THIN, TOO.
BUT THE FEATURES--
BUT IT'S ONLY TWO THOUSAND YEN A MONTH.
SEETHE...
I WANT A FANCY NEW SMARTPHONE THAT CAN PLAY ALL THE LATEST GAMES...
AND I *REALLY* WANT THE LIMITED-TIME BONUS OF MY FAVORITE CHARACTER!!

THE DEMON RAN AWAY!!

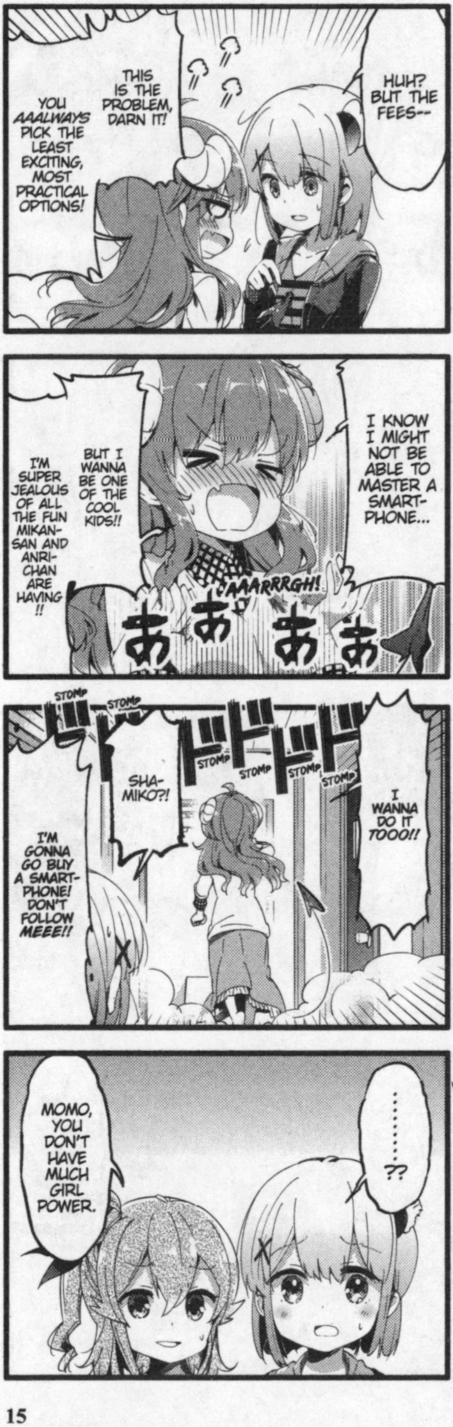
HUH? BUT THE FEES--
THIS IS THE PROBLEM, DARN IT!
YOU *AAALWAYS* PICK THE LEAST EXCITING, MOST PRACTICAL OPTIONS!
I KNOW I MIGHT NOT BE ABLE TO MASTER A SMARTPHONE...
AAARRRGH!
ああああ
BUT I WANNA BE ONE OF THE COOL KIDS!!
I'M SUPER JEALOUS OF ALL THE FUN MIKAN-SAN AND ANRI-CHAN ARE HAVING!!
ドドドド
STOMP STOMP STOMP STOMP STOMP STOMP
I WANNA DO IT *TOOO!!*
SHA-MIKO?!
I'M GONNA GO BUY A SMARTPHONE! DON'T FOLLOW *MEEE!!*
......??
MOMO, YOU DON'T HAVE MUCH GIRL POWER.

INFORMATION OVERLOAD

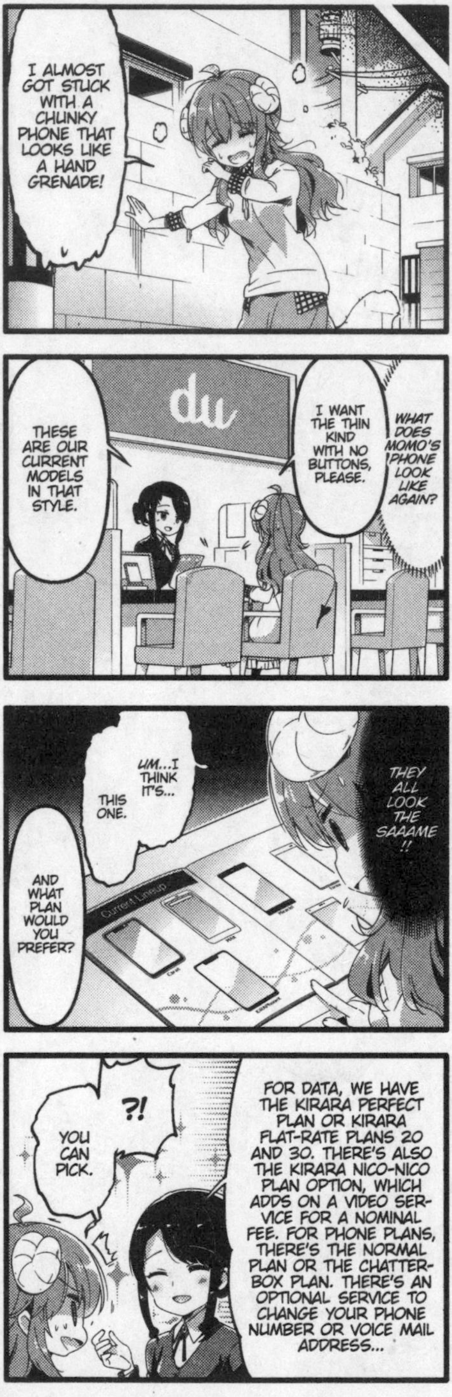
I ALMOST GOT STUCK WITH A CHUNKY PHONE THAT LOOKS LIKE A HAND GRENADE!
du
WHAT DOES MOMO'S PHONE LOOK LIKE AGAIN?
I WANT THE THIN KIND WITH NO BUTTONS, PLEASE.
THESE ARE OUR CURRENT MODELS IN THAT STYLE.
THEY ALL LOOK THE SAAAME!!
UM...I THINK IT'S... THIS ONE.
AND WHAT PLAN WOULD YOU PREFER?
Current Lineup
FOR DATA, WE HAVE THE KIRARA PERFECT PLAN OR KIRARA FLAT-RATE PLANS 20 AND 30. THERE'S ALSO THE KIRARA NICO-NICO PLAN OPTION, WHICH ADDS ON A VIDEO SERVICE FOR A NOMINAL FEE. FOR PHONE PLANS, THERE'S THE NORMAL PLAN OR THE CHATTERBOX PLAN. THERE'S AN OPTIONAL SERVICE TO CHANGE YOUR PHONE NUMBER OR VOICE MAIL ADDRESS...
?!
YOU CAN PICK.

MONTHLY FEE, OVER TEN THOUSAND YEN

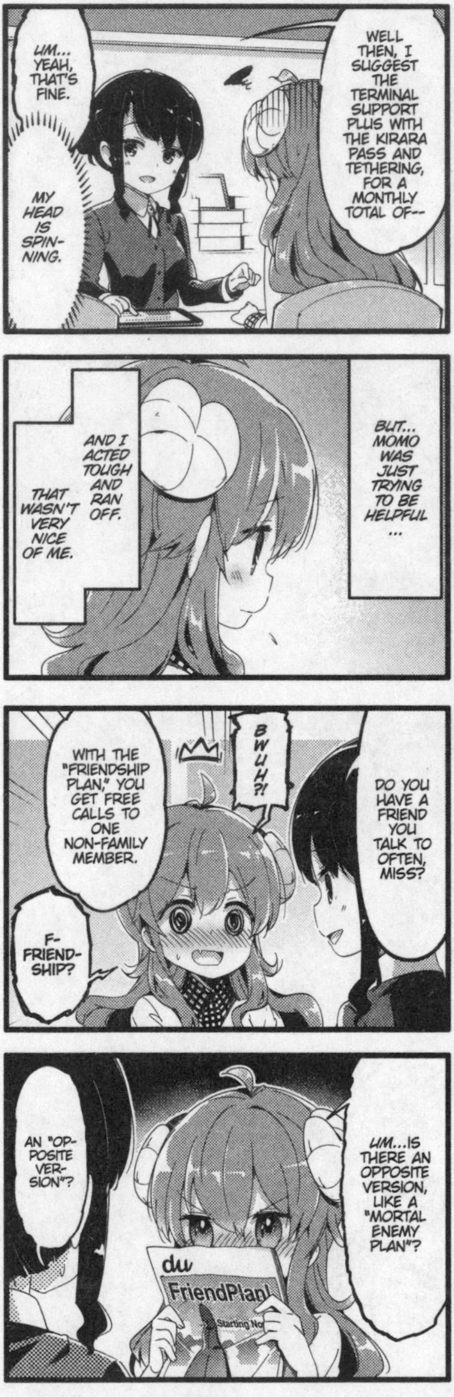
WELL THEN, I SUGGEST THE TERMINAL SUPPORT PLUS WITH THE KIRARA PASS AND TETHERING, FOR A MONTHLY TOTAL OF--
UM... YEAH, THAT'S FINE.
MY HEAD IS SPINNING.
BUT... MOMO WAS JUST TRYING TO BE HELPFUL...
AND I ACTED TOUGH AND RAN OFF.
THAT WASN'T VERY NICE OF ME.
DO YOU HAVE A FRIEND YOU TALK TO OFTEN, MISS?
BWUH?!
WITH THE "FRIENDSHIP PLAN," YOU GET FREE CALLS TO ONE NON-FAMILY MEMBER.
F-FRIENDSHIP?
UM...IS THERE AN OPPOSITE VERSION, LIKE A "MORTAL ENEMY PLAN"?
AN "OPPOSITE VERSION"?
du
FriendPlan!

SMARTPHONES WITHOUT BUTTONS ARE HARD

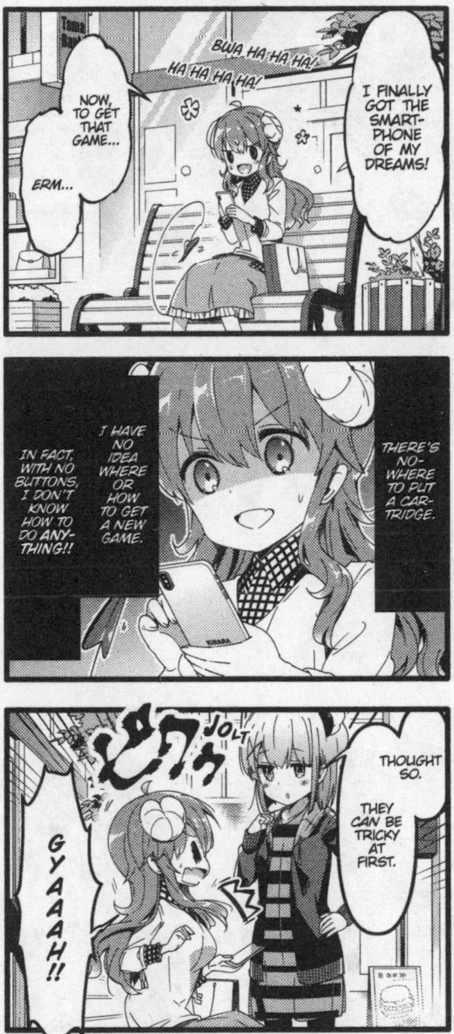

I FINALLY GOT THE SMARTPHONE OF MY DREAMS!
BWA HA HA HA HA!
HA HA HA HA HA!
NOW, TO GET THAT GAME...
ERM...
THERE'S NOWHERE TO PUT A CARTRIDGE.
I HAVE NO IDEA WHERE OR HOW TO GET A NEW GAME.
IN FACT, WITH NO BUTTONS, I DON'T KNOW HOW TO DO ANYTHING!!
THOUGHT SO.
THEY CAN BE TRICKY AT FIRST.
JOLT
GYAAAAH!!
WHAT ARE YOU DOING HERE?!
LET ME SEE THAT.
WH-WHAT ARE YOU UP TO, DARN IIIIT?!
I'M GETTING YOU THAT GAME.

A CONVENIENT APP

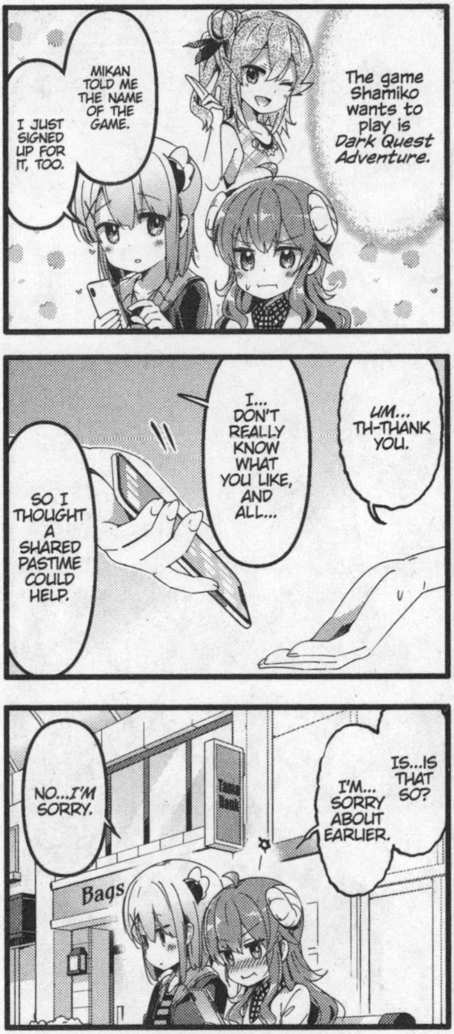

The game Shamiko wants to play is *Dark Quest Adventure.*
MIKAN TOLD ME THE NAME OF THE GAME.
I JUST SIGNED UP FOR IT, TOO.
UM... TH-THANK YOU.
I... DON'T REALLY KNOW WHAT YOU LIKE, AND ALL...
SO I THOUGHT A SHARED PASTIME COULD HELP.
IS...IS THAT SO?
I'M... SORRY ABOUT EARLIER.
NO...I'M SORRY.
Bags
BY THE WAY...WHAT'S THIS "BABYSITTING GPS" APP?
?
DON'T WORRY ABOUT THAT BIT.

BRINGING BACK THE OL' CATCHPHRASE

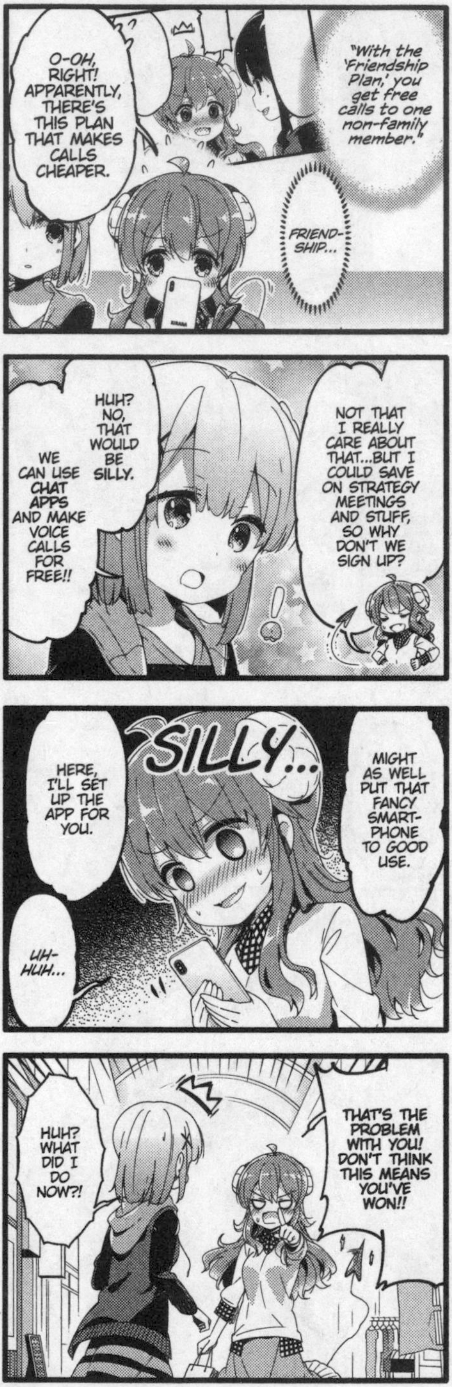
"With the 'Friendship Plan,' you get free calls to one non-family member."
O-OH, RIGHT! APPARENTLY, THERE'S THIS PLAN THAT MAKES CALLS CHEAPER.
FRIEND-SHIP...
NOT THAT I REALLY CARE ABOUT THAT...BUT I COULD SAVE ON STRATEGY MEETINGS AND STUFF, SO WHY DON'T WE SIGN UP?
HUH? NO, THAT WOULD BE SILLY.
WE CAN USE CHAT APPS AND MAKE VOICE CALLS FOR FREE!!
MIGHT AS WELL PUT THAT FANCY SMART-PHONE TO GOOD USE.
SILLY...
HERE, I'LL SET UP THE APP FOR YOU.
UH-HUH...
THAT'S THE PROBLEM WITH YOU! DON'T THINK THIS MEANS YOU'VE WON!!
HUH? WHAT DID I DO NOW?!

LOCAL IS PERMANENTLY FREE

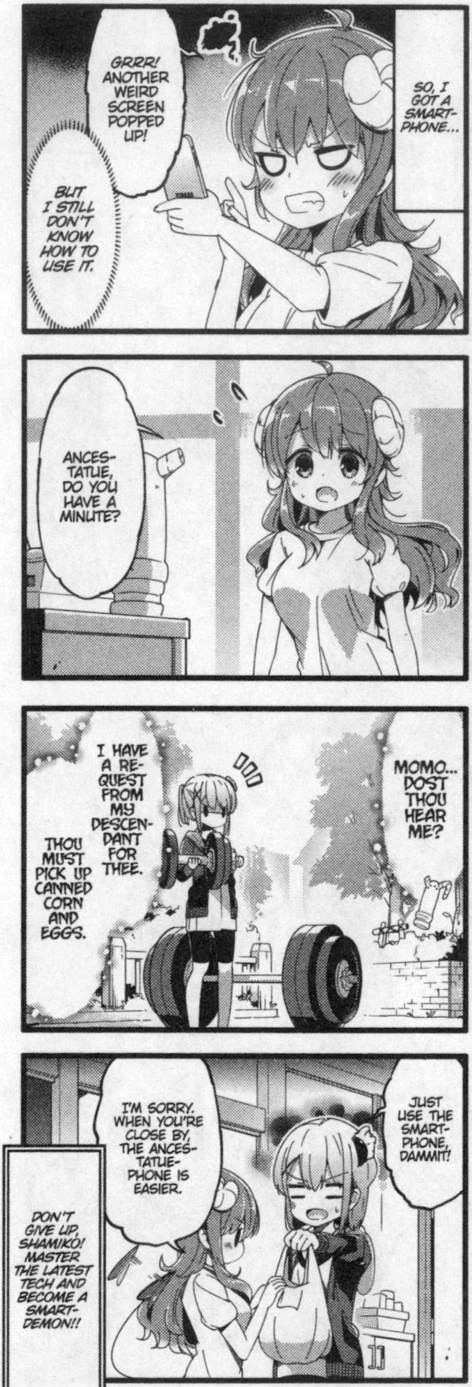
SO, I GOT A SMART-PHONE...
GRRR! ANOTHER WEIRD SCREEN POPPED UP!
BUT I STILL DON'T KNOW HOW TO USE IT.
ANCES-TATUE, DO YOU HAVE A MINUTE?
MOMO... DOST THOU HEAR ME?
I HAVE A RE-QUEST FROM MY DESCEN-DANT FOR THEE.
THOU MUST PICK UP CANNED CORN AND EGGS.
JUST USE THE SMART-PHONE, DAMMIT!
I'M SORRY. WHEN YOU'RE CLOSE BY, THE ANCES-TATUE-PHONE IS EASIER.
DON'T GIVE UP, SHAMIKO! MASTER THE LATEST TECH AND BECOME A SMART-DEMON!!

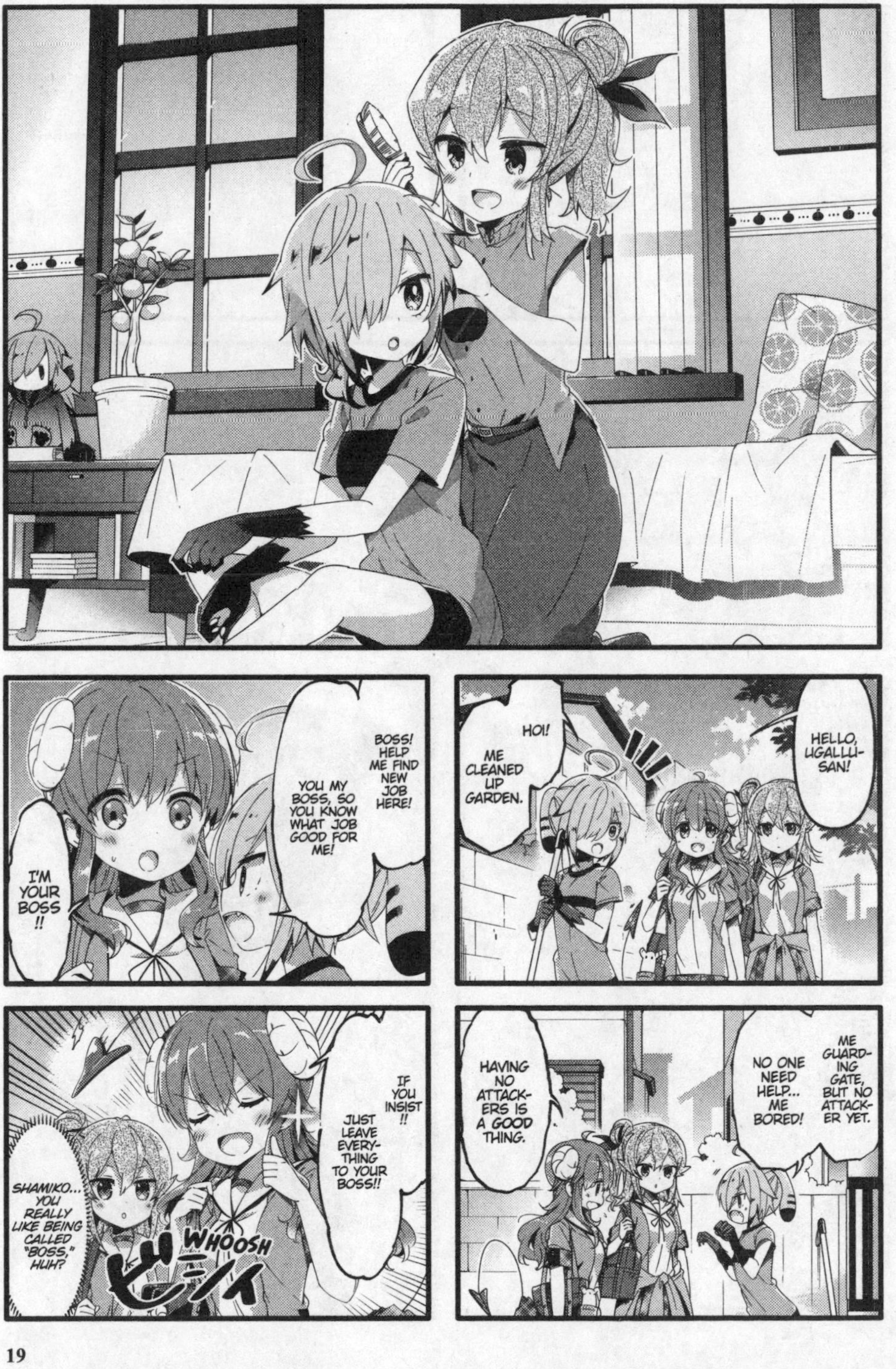
HELLO, UGALLU-SAN!
HOI!
ME CLEANED UP GARDEN.
BOSS! HELP ME FIND NEW JOB HERE!
YOU MY BOSS, SO YOU KNOW WHAT JOB GOOD FOR ME!
I'M YOUR BOSS !!
ME GUARDING GATE, BUT NO ATTACKER YET.
NO ONE NEED HELP... ME BORED!
HAVING NO ATTACKERS IS A GOOD THING.
IF YOU INSIST !!
JUST LEAVE EVERYTHING TO YOUR BOSS!!
SHAMIKO... YOU REALLY LIKE BEING CALLED "BOSS," HUH?
WHOOSH

CLOSE YOUR APPS ONCE IN A WHILE

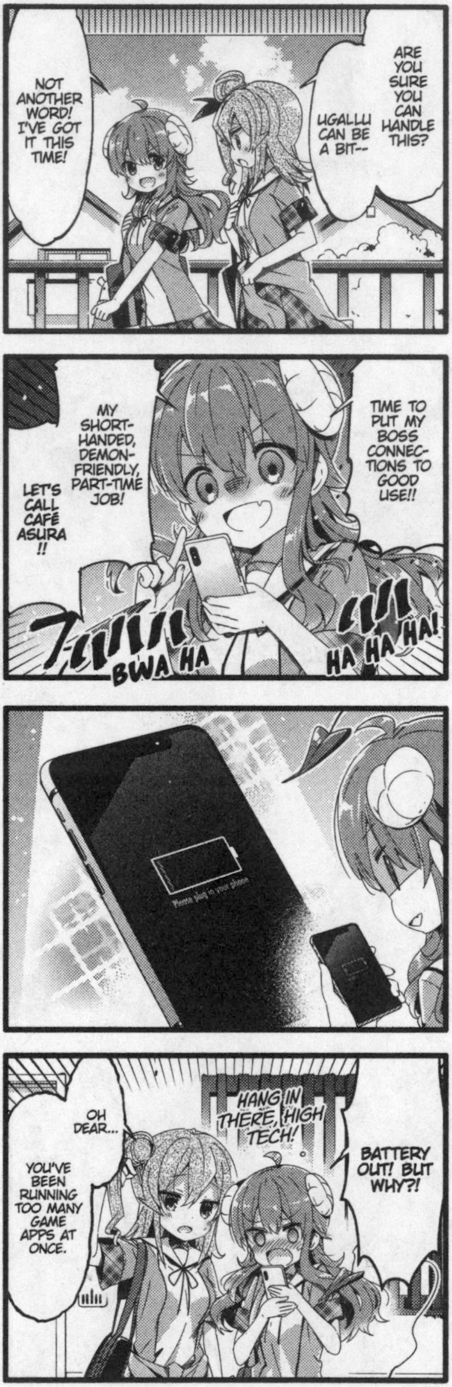
ARE YOU SURE YOU CAN HANDLE THIS?
UGALLU CAN BE A BIT--
NOT ANOTHER WORD! I'VE GOT IT THIS TIME!
TIME TO PUT MY BOSS CONNECTIONS TO GOOD USE!!
MY SHORT-HANDED, DEMON-FRIENDLY, PART-TIME JOB!
LET'S CALL CAFÉ ASURA !!
HA HA HA!
BWA HA
Please plug in your phone
BATTERY OUT! BUT WHY?!
HANG IN THERE, HIGH TECH!
OH DEAR...
YOU'VE BEEN RUNNING TOO MANY GAME APPS AT ONCE.

MAMA MAGICAL GIRL

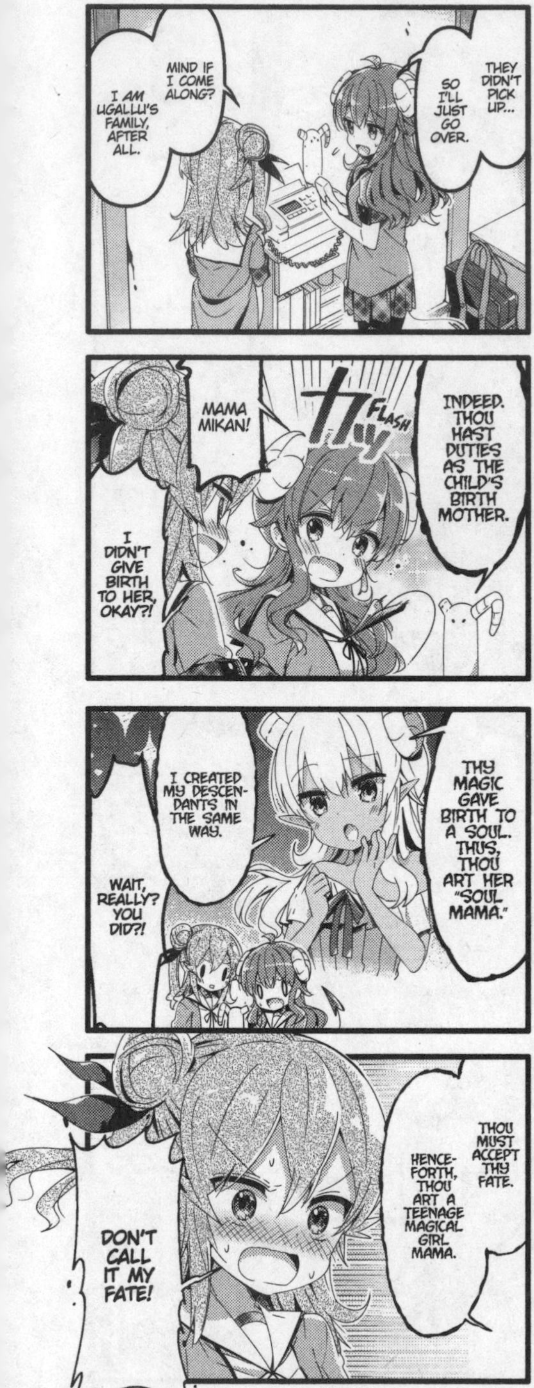
THEY DIDN'T PICK UP...
SO I'LL JUST GO OVER.
MIND IF I COME ALONG?
I AM UGALLU'S FAMILY, AFTER ALL.
INDEED. THOU HAST DUTIES AS THE CHILD'S BIRTH MOTHER.
FLASH
MAMA MIKAN!
I DIDN'T GIVE BIRTH TO HER, OKAY?!
THY MAGIC GAVE BIRTH TO A SOUL. THUS, THOU ART HER "SOUL MAMA."
I CREATED MY DESCENDANTS IN THE SAME WAY.
WAIT, REALLY? YOU DID?!
THOU MUST ACCEPT THY FATE.
HENCEFORTH, THOU ART A TEENAGE MAGICAL GIRL MAMA.
DON'T CALL IT MY FATE!

THIS MIGHT LEAD TO MORE REGULARS

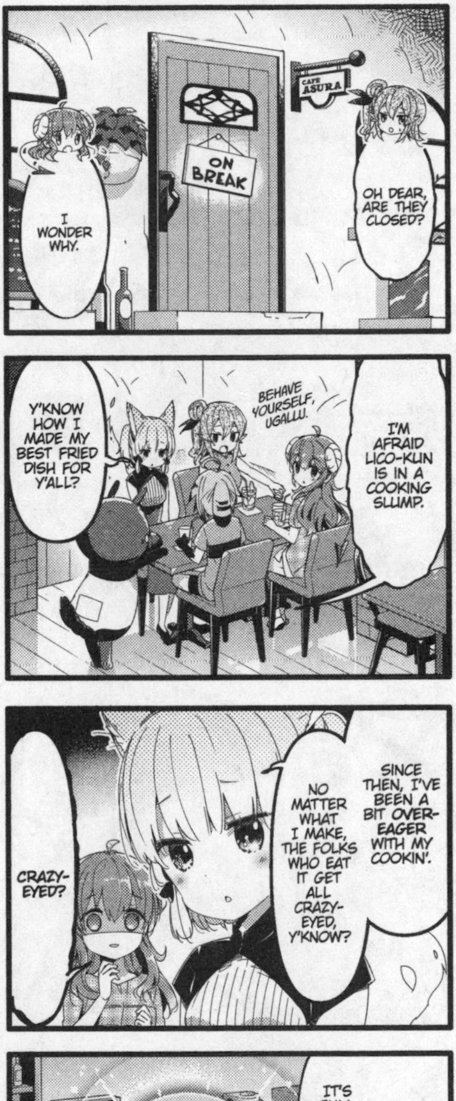
CAFE ASURA
OH DEAR, ARE THEY CLOSED?
ON BREAK
I WONDER WHY.
I'M AFRAID LICO-KUN IS IN A COOKING SLUMP.
BEHAVE YOURSELF, UGALLU.
Y'KNOW HOW I MADE MY BEST FRIED DISH FOR Y'ALL?
SINCE THEN, I'VE BEEN A BIT OVER-EAGER WITH MY COOKIN'.
NO MATTER WHAT I MAKE, THE FOLKS WHO EAT IT GET ALL CRAZY-EYED, Y'KNOW?
CRAZY-EYED?
LOOKIE THERE! THAT FRIDGE IS GLOWIN', AIN'T IT?
IT'S FULL OF MY MESSED-UP MEALS.
THEY'RE GLOWING RIGHT THROUGH THE FRIDGE ...?!

SO MUCH FOR CUSTOMER SERVICE

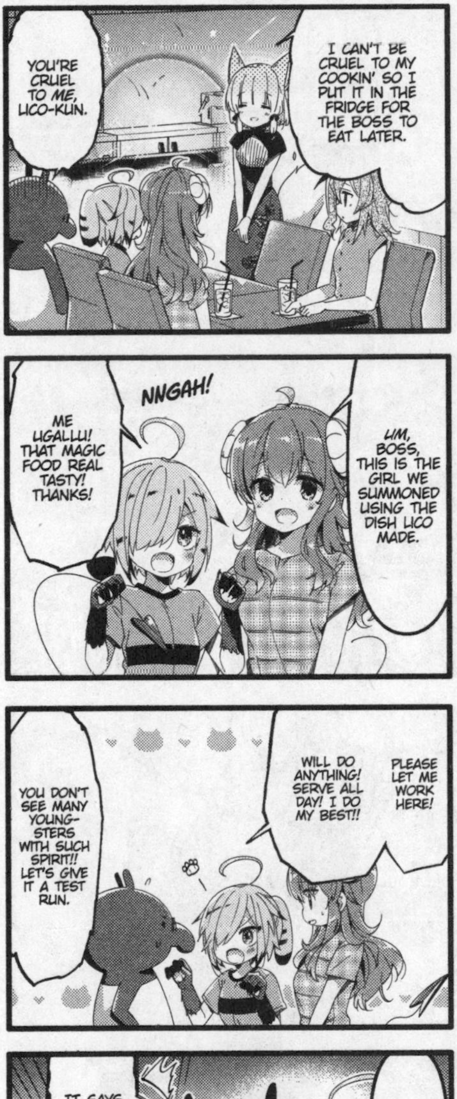
I CAN'T BE CRUEL TO MY COOKIN' SO I PUT IT IN THE FRIDGE FOR THE BOSS TO EAT LATER.
YOU'RE CRUEL TO ME, LICO-KUN.
UM, BOSS, THIS IS THE GIRL WE SUMMONED USING THE DISH LICO MADE.
NNGAH!
ME UGALLU! THAT MAGIC FOOD REAL TASTY! THANKS!
PLEASE LET ME WORK HERE!
WILL DO ANYTHING! SERVE ALL DAY! I DO MY BEST!!
YOU DON'T SEE MANY YOUNGSTERS WITH SUCH SPIRIT!! LET'S GIVE IT A TEST RUN.
SO, WHAT THIS SAY?
IT SAYS L-U-N-C-H.
WAIT, UGALLU-SAN, YOU CAN'T READ?!

BATTLE-ORIENTED DESIGN

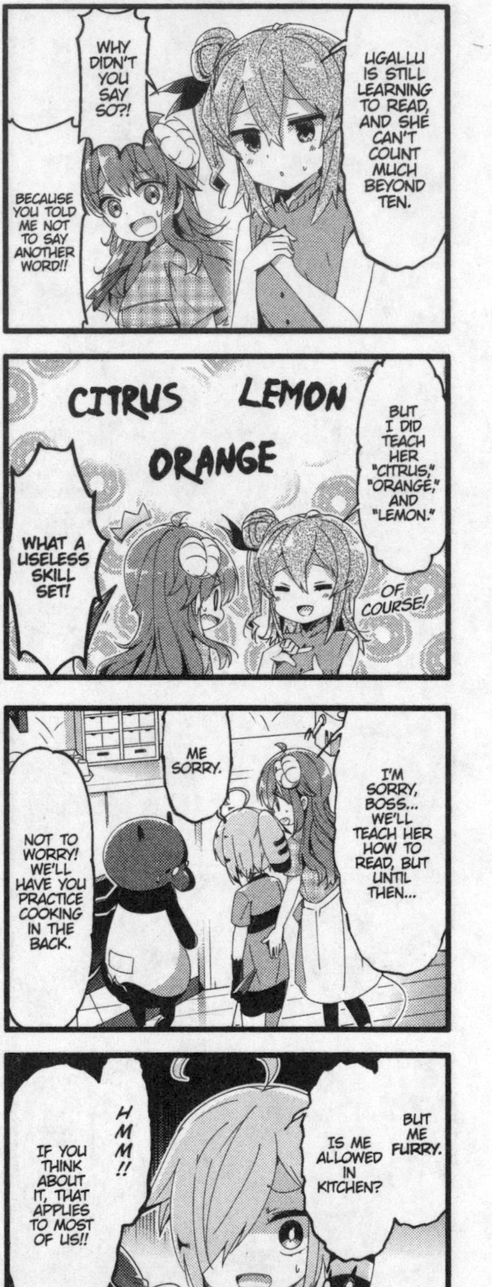
UGALLU IS STILL LEARNING TO READ, AND SHE CAN'T COUNT MUCH BEYOND TEN.
WHY DIDN'T YOU SAY SO?!
BECAUSE YOU TOLD ME NOT TO SAY ANOTHER WORD!!
BUT I DID TEACH HER "CITRUS," "ORANGE," AND "LEMON."
LEMON
CITRUS
ORANGE
OF COURSE!
WHAT A USELESS SKILL SET!
I'M SORRY, BOSS... WE'LL TEACH HER HOW TO READ, BUT UNTIL THEN...
ME SORRY.
NOT TO WORRY! WE'LL HAVE YOU PRACTICE COOKING IN THE BACK.
BUT ME FURRY.
IS ME ALLOWED IN KITCHEN?
HMM!!
IF YOU THINK ABOUT IT, THAT APPLIES TO MOST OF US!!

(IT WAS ONLY THE EAR HAIR)

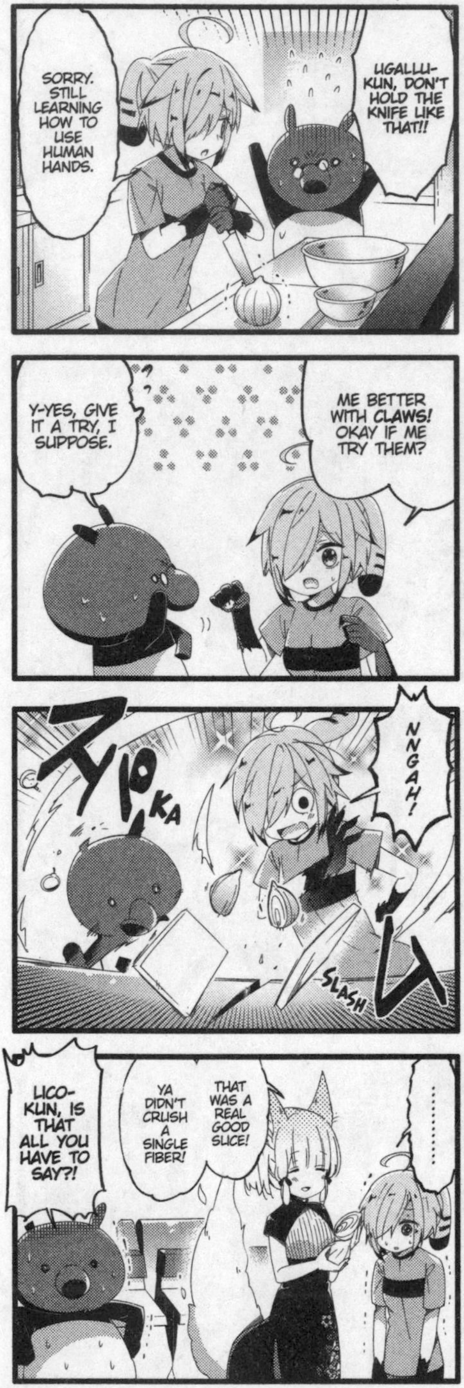
UGALLU-KUN, DON'T HOLD THE KNIFE LIKE THAT!!
SORRY. STILL LEARNING HOW TO USE HUMAN HANDS.
ME BETTER WITH CLAWS! OKAY IF ME TRY THEM?
Y-YES, GIVE IT A TRY, I SUPPOSE.
NNGAH!
KA
SLASH
......
THAT WAS A REAL GOOD SLICE!
YA DIDN'T CRUSH A SINGLE FIBER!
LICO-KUN, IS THAT ALL YOU HAVE TO SAY?!

A RESTAURANT THAT'S BEEN THROUGH HELL

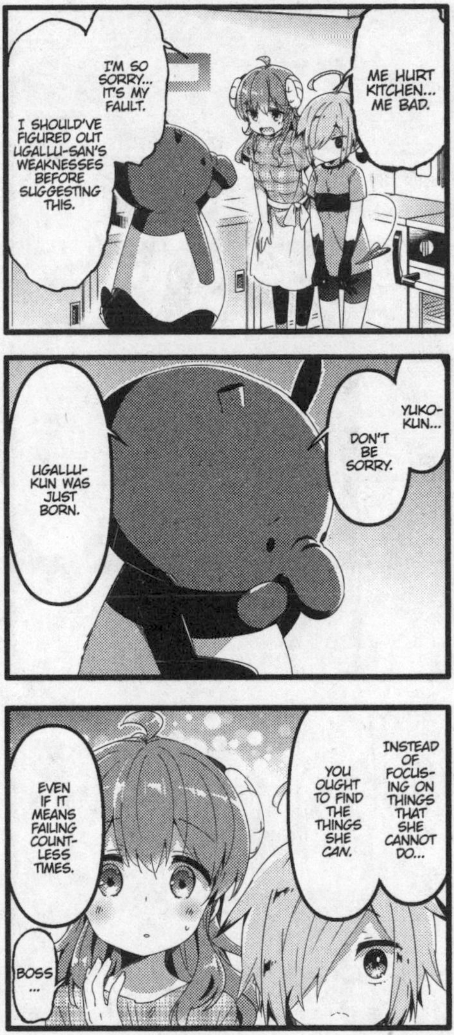
ME HURT KITCHEN... ME BAD.
I'M SO SORRY... IT'S MY FAULT.
I SHOULD'VE FIGURED OUT UGALLU-SAN'S WEAKNESSES BEFORE SUGGESTING THIS.
YUKO-KUN... DON'T BE SORRY.
UGALLU-KUN WAS JUST BORN.
INSTEAD OF FOCUSING ON THINGS THAT SHE CANNOT DO...
YOU OUGHT TO FIND THE THINGS SHE CAN.
EVEN IF IT MEANS FAILING COUNTLESS TIMES.
BOSS...
DON'T WORRY. YOU'RE STILL TEN TIMES BETTER THAN LICO-KUN WAS AT FIRST!
DARN TOOTIN'!! DESTRUCTION'S ALL PART OF THE PLAN!
ONCE YA SET THE PLACE ON FIRE, YOU'RE REALLY COOKIN'!!
UH... HUH...

MAMA MIKAN'S OPINION

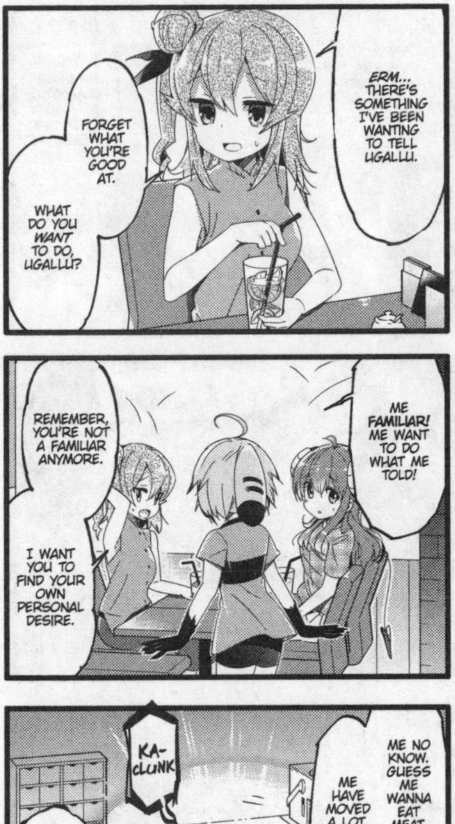
ERM... THERE'S SOMETHING I'VE BEEN WANTING TO TELL UGALLU.
FORGET WHAT YOU'RE GOOD AT.
WHAT DO YOU WANT TO DO, UGALLU?
ME FAMILIAR! ME WANT TO DO WHAT ME TOLD!
REMEMBER, YOU'RE NOT A FAMILIAR ANYMORE.
I WANT YOU TO FIND YOUR OWN PERSONAL DESIRE.
ME NO KNOW. GUESS ME WANNA EAT MEAT, MAYBE.
ME HAVE MOVED A LOT. ME LOW ON ENERGY.
KA-CLUNK
THAT'S MORE OF AN APPETITE THAN A DESIRE.
?!
THUD
KA-
WHAT IS THAT NOISE?!

SORT OF LIKE *GU* POISON*

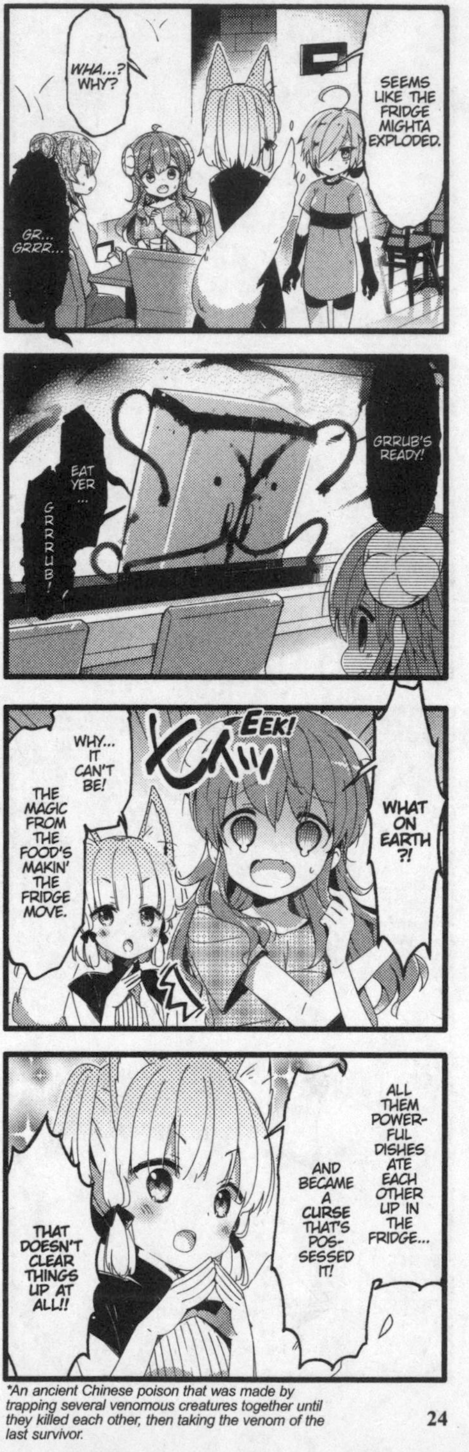
SEEMS LIKE THE FRIDGE MIGHTA EXPLODED.
WHA...? WHY?
GR... GRRR...
GRRRUB'S READY!
EAT YER ...
GRRRUB!
WHAT ON EARTH?!
EEK!
WHY... IT CAN'T BE!
THE MAGIC FROM THE FOOD'S MAKIN' THE FRIDGE MOVE.
ALL THEM POWERFUL DISHES ATE EACH OTHER UP IN THE FRIDGE...
AND BECAME A CURSE THAT'S POSSESSED IT!
THAT DOESN'T CLEAR THINGS UP AT ALL!!

TWO MAMAS ON OFFENSE AND DEFENSE

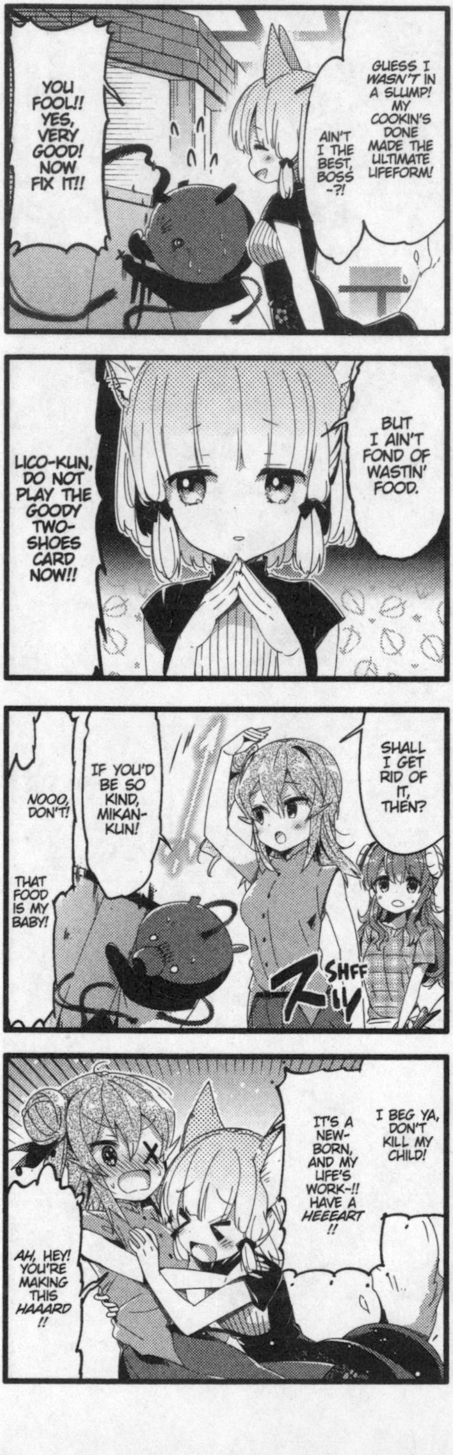
GUESS I *WASN'T* IN A SLUMP! MY COOKIN'S DONE MADE THE ULTIMATE LIFEFORM!
AIN'T I THE BEST, BOSS-?!
YOU FOOL!! YES, VERY GOOD! NOW FIX IT!!
BUT I AIN'T FOND OF WASTIN' FOOD.
LICO-KUN, DO NOT PLAY THE GOODY TWO-SHOES CARD NOW!!
SHALL I GET RID OF IT, THEN?
IF YOU'D BE SO KIND, MIKAN-KUN!
NOOO, DON'T!
THAT FOOD IS MY BABY!
SHFF
I BEG YA, DON'T KILL MY CHILD!
IT'S A NEWBORN, AND MY LIFE'S WORK-!! HAVE A *HEEEART*!!
AH, HEY! YOU'RE MAKING THIS *HAAARD*!!

**An ancient Chinese poison that was made by trapping several venomous creatures together until they killed each other, then taking the venom of the last survivor.*

A TAPIR'S BIG TENTACLE SCENE

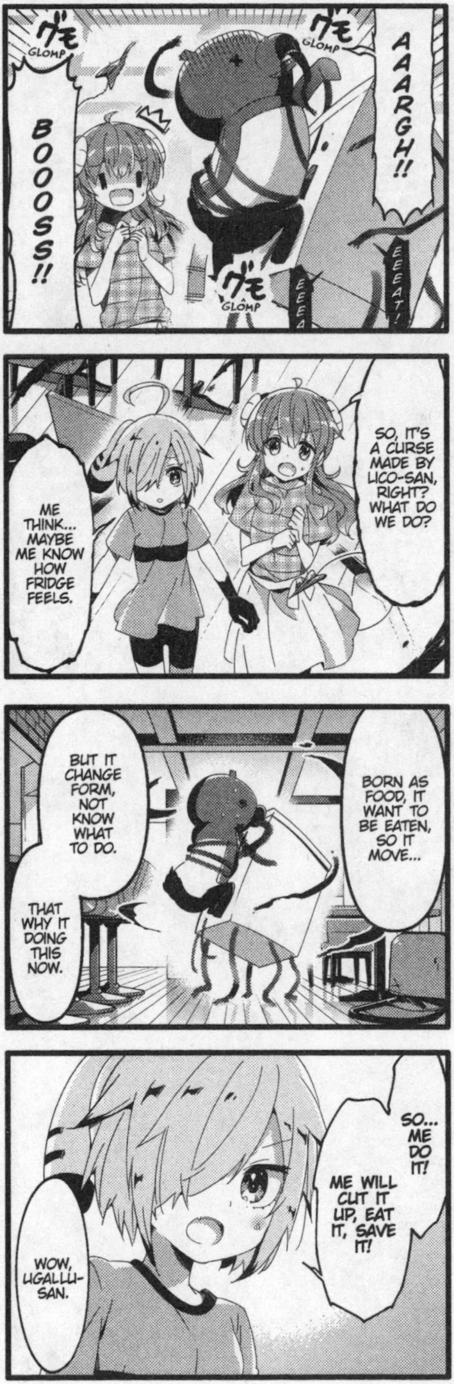
AAAARGH!!
グモ GLOMP
グモ GLOMP
BOOOSS!!
グモ GLOMP
EEEAT!
SO, IT'S A CURSE MADE BY LICO-SAN, RIGHT? WHAT DO WE DO?
ME THINK... MAYBE ME KNOW HOW FRIDGE FEELS.
BORN AS FOOD, IT WANT TO BE EATEN, SO IT MOVE...
BUT IT CHANGE FORM, NOT KNOW WHAT TO DO.
THAT WHY IT DOING THIS NOW.
SO... ME DO IT!
ME WILL CUT IT UP, EAT IT, SAVE IT!
WOW, UGALLU-SAN.

CAN ERASE MOST THINGS THAT WAY

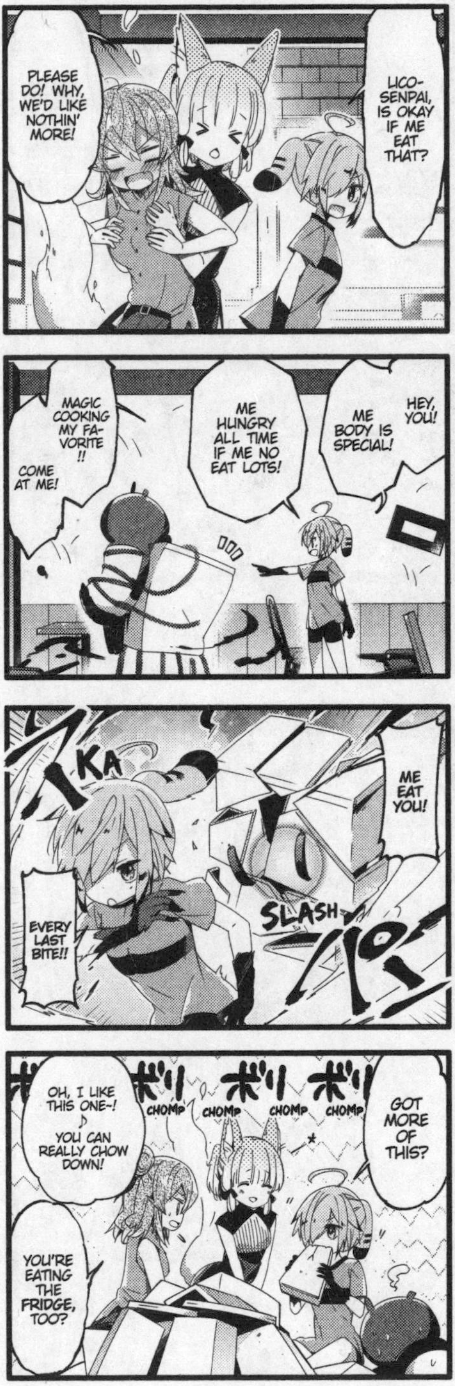
LICO-SENPAI, IS OKAY IF ME EAT THAT?
PLEASE DO! WHY, WE'D LIKE NOTHIN' MORE!
HEY, YOU!
ME BODY IS SPECIAL!
ME HUNGRY ALL TIME IF ME NO EAT LOTS!
MAGIC COOKING MY FA-VORITE!!
COME AT ME!
ME EAT YOU!
KA
SLASH
EVERY LAST BITE!!
GOT MORE OF THIS?
ボリ CHOMP
ボリ CHOMP
ボリ CHOMP
ボリ CHOMP
OH, I LIKE THIS ONE-! ♪ YOU CAN REALLY CHOW DOWN!
YOU'RE EATING THE FRIDGE, TOO?

YUKO'S PRECIOUS WORKPLACE

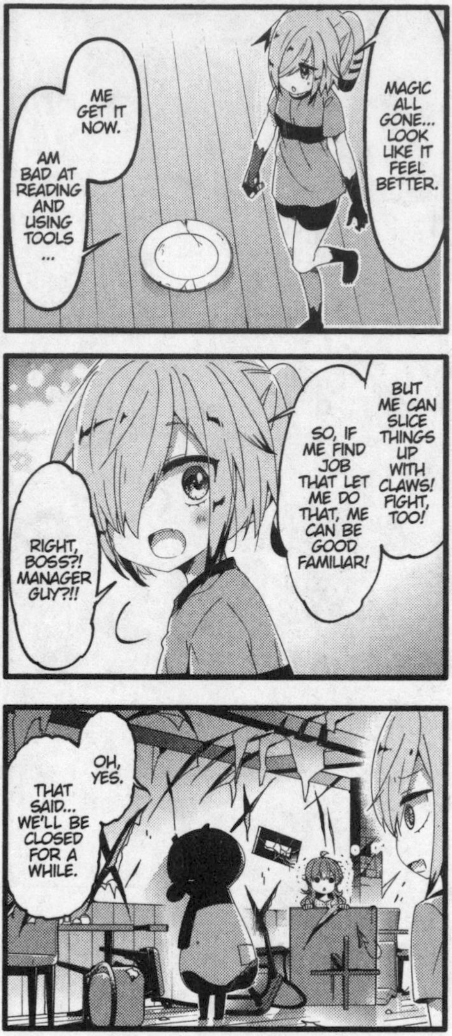
MAGIC ALL GONE... LOOK LIKE IT FEEL BETTER.
ME GET IT NOW.
AM BAD AT READING AND USING TOOLS ...
BUT ME CAN SLICE THINGS UP WITH CLAWS! FIGHT, TOO!
SO, IF ME FIND JOB THAT LET ME DO THAT, ME CAN BE GOOD FAMILIAR!
RIGHT, BOSS?! MANAGER GUY?!!
OH, YES.
THAT SAID... WE'LL BE CLOSED FOR A WHILE.
I'M AFRAID I'LL HAVE TO FIRE UGALLU-KUN FOR NOW.
I'M SORRY, I'M SORRY, I'M SO SORRY!
PLEASE, DON'T APOLOGIZE !!

BEATEN TO THE BOSS

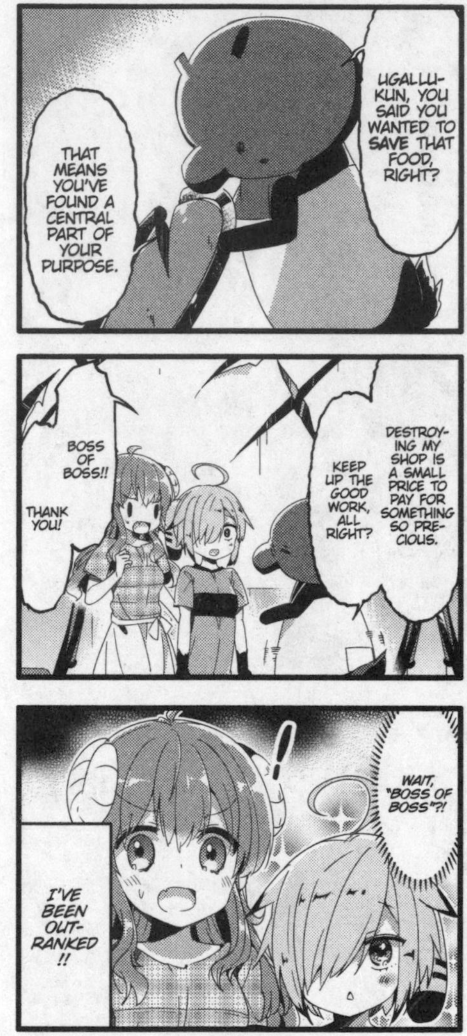
UGALLU-KUN, YOU SAID YOU WANTED TO SAVE THAT FOOD, RIGHT?
THAT MEANS YOU'VE FOUND A CENTRAL PART OF YOUR PURPOSE.
DESTROYING MY SHOP IS A SMALL PRICE TO PAY FOR SOMETHING SO PRECIOUS.
KEEP UP THE GOOD WORK, ALL RIGHT?
BOSS OF BOSS!!
THANK YOU!
!
WAIT, "BOSS OF BOSS"?!
I'VE BEEN OUT-RANKED !!
DON'T THINK THIS--I MEAN...
THANK YOU FOR THE LESSON!!
WH-WHAT DID YOU LEARN?!
DON'T GIVE UP, SHAMIKO!! LEARN HOW TO BE A BOSS FROM YOUR PREDECES-SORS!!

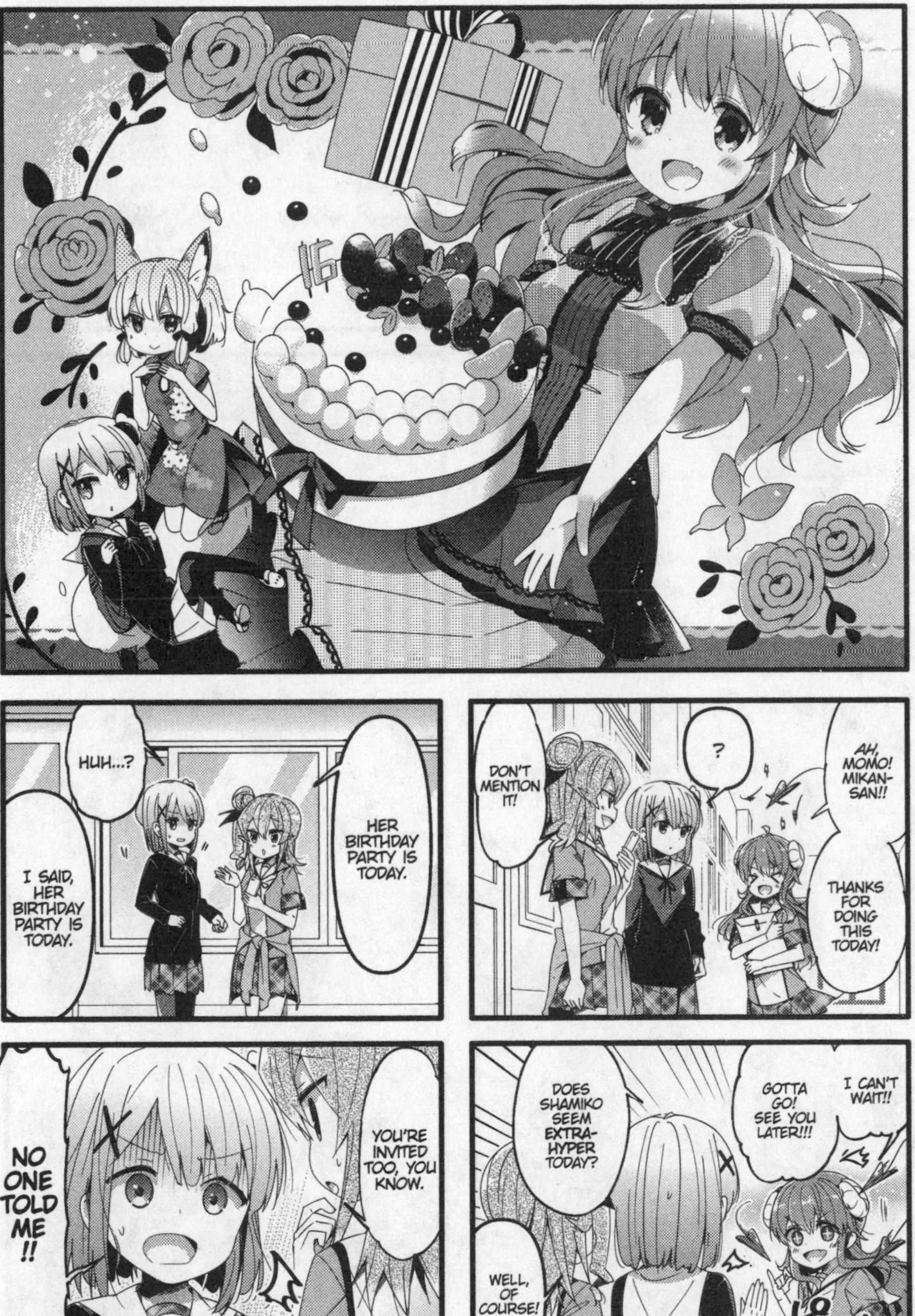
AH, MOMO! MIKAN-SAN!!
THANKS FOR DOING THIS TODAY!
?
DON'T MENTION IT!
HER BIRTHDAY PARTY IS TODAY.
HUH...?
I SAID, HER BIRTHDAY PARTY IS TODAY.
I CAN'T WAIT!!
GOTTA GO! SEE YOU LATER!!!
DOES SHAMIKO SEEM EXTRA-HYPER TODAY?
WELL, OF COURSE!
ピイヤッ
PSHOOOOM
YOU'RE INVITED TOO, YOU KNOW.
NO ONE TOLD ME!!

THE OPINIONS OF THOSE WHO DWELL IN THE LIGHT

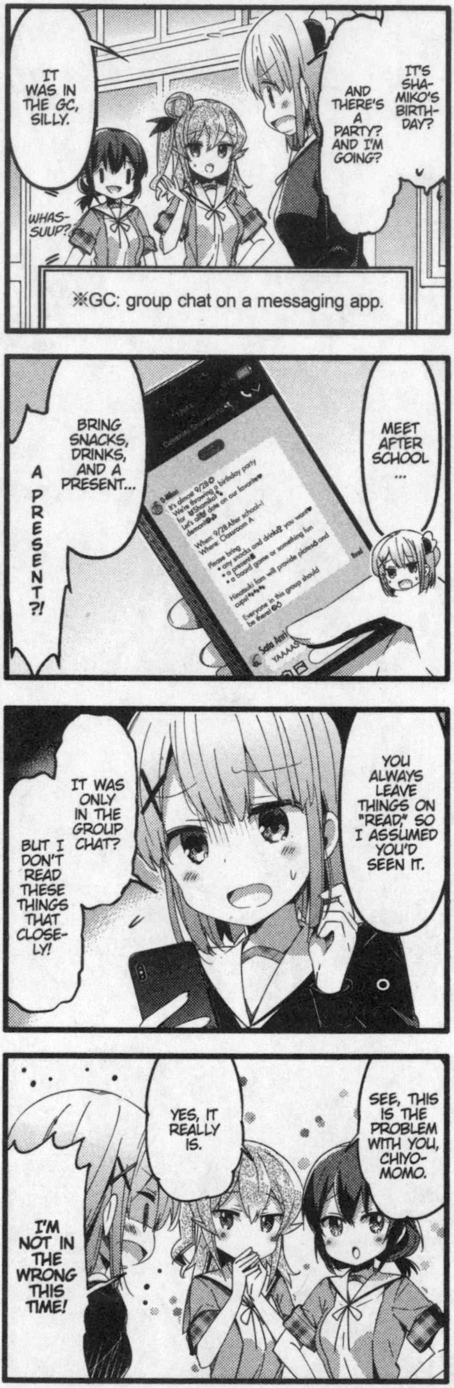
IT'S SHAMIKO'S BIRTHDAY?
AND THERE'S A PARTY? AND I'M GOING?
IT WAS IN THE GC, SILLY.
WHASSUUP?
※GC: group chat on a messaging app.
MEET AFTER SCHOOL ...
BRING SNACKS, DRINKS, AND A PRESENT...
A PRESENT?!
YOU ALWAYS LEAVE THINGS ON "READ," SO I ASSUMED YOU'D SEEN IT.
IT WAS ONLY IN THE GROUP CHAT?
BUT I DON'T READ THESE THINGS THAT CLOSELY!
SEE, THIS IS THE PROBLEM WITH YOU, CHIYOMOMO.
YES, IT REALLY IS.
I'M NOT IN THE WRONG THIS TIME!

ONE PERSON'S OPINION

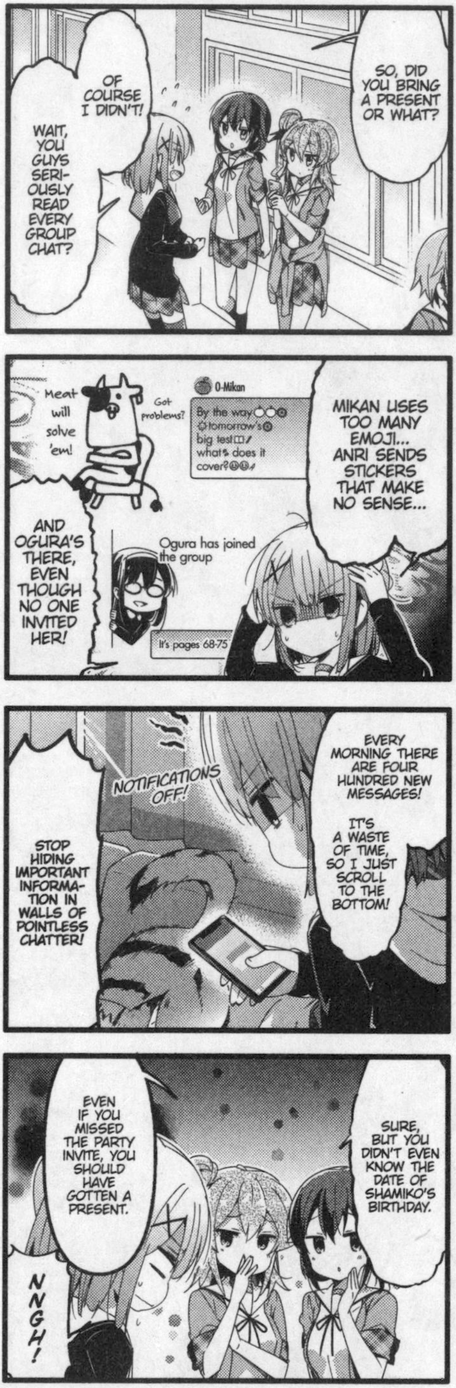
SO, DID YOU BRING A PRESENT OR WHAT?
OF COURSE I DIDN'T!
WAIT, YOU GUYS SERIOUSLY READ EVERY GROUP CHAT?
MIKAN USES TOO MANY EMOJI... ANRI SENDS STICKERS THAT MAKE NO SENSE...
O-Mikan
By the way tomorrow's big test what does it cover?
Got problems?
Meat will solve 'em!
AND OGURA'S THERE, EVEN THOUGH NO ONE INVITED HER!
Ogura has joined the group
It's pages 68-75
EVERY MORNING THERE ARE FOUR HUNDRED NEW MESSAGES!
IT'S A WASTE OF TIME, SO I JUST SCROLL TO THE BOTTOM!
NOTIFICATIONS OFF!
STOP HIDING IMPORTANT INFORMATION IN WALLS OF POINTLESS CHATTER!
SURE, BUT YOU DIDN'T EVEN KNOW THE DATE OF SHAMIKO'S BIRTHDAY.
EVEN IF YOU MISSED THE PARTY INVITE, YOU SHOULD HAVE GOTTEN A PRESENT.
NNGH!

FRESH PEACH SCHOOL ESCAPE

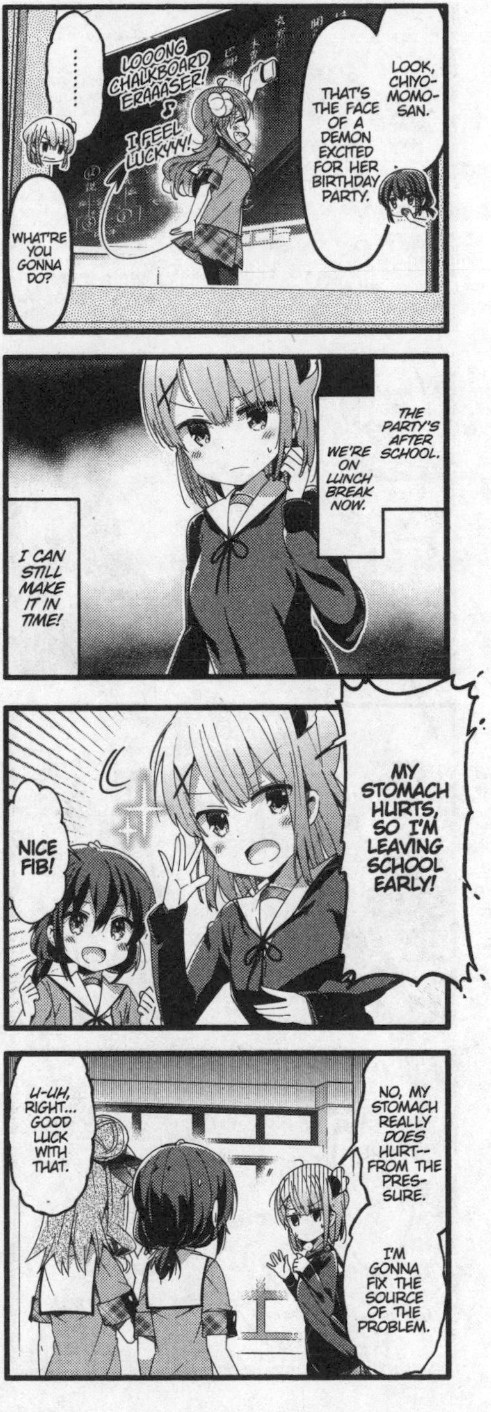
LOOK, CHIYOMOMO-SAN.
THAT'S THE FACE OF A DEMON EXCITED FOR HER BIRTHDAY PARTY.
LOOOONG CHALKBOARD ERAAAASER! & I FEEL LUCKYYY!
……
WHAT'RE YOU GONNA DO?
THE PARTY'S AFTER SCHOOL.
WE'RE ON LUNCH BREAK NOW.
I CAN STILL MAKE IT IN TIME!
MY STOMACH HURTS, SO I'M LEAVING SCHOOL EARLY!
NICE FIB!
NO, MY STOMACH REALLY DOES HURT--FROM THE PRES-SURE.
I'M GONNA FIX THE SOURCE OF THE PROBLEM.
U-UH, RIGHT... GOOD LUCK WITH THAT.

WHAT'S A "CREEPING DOLL"?

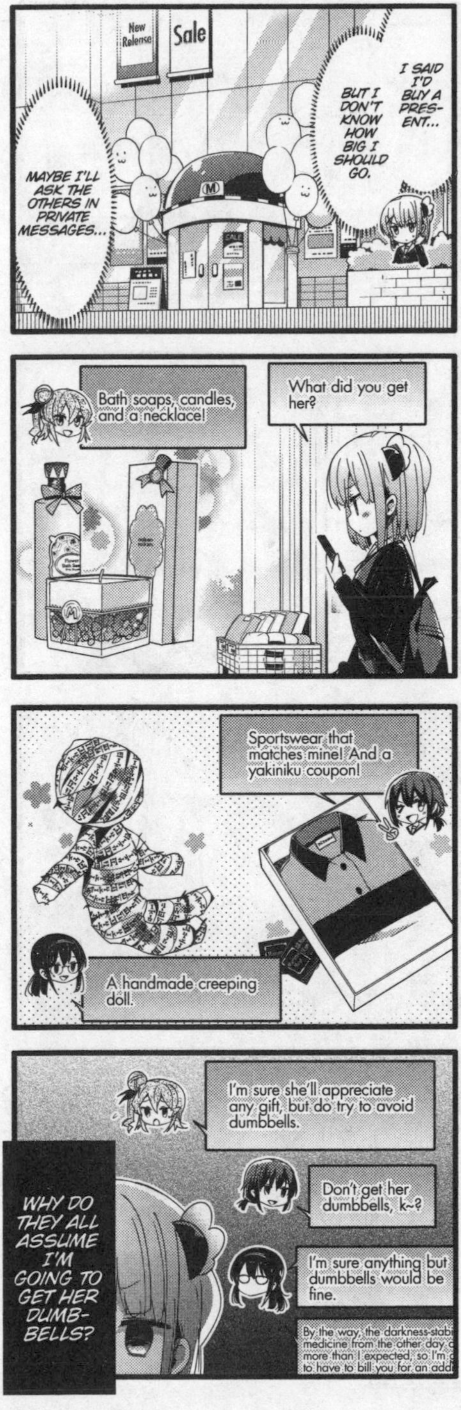
New Release
Sale
I SAID I'D BUY A PRES-ENT...
BUT I DON'T KNOW HOW BIG I SHOULD GO.
MAYBE I'LL ASK THE OTHERS IN PRIVATE MESSAGES...
What did you get her?
Bath soaps, candles, and a necklace!
Sportswear that matches mine! And a yakiniku coupon!
A handmade creeping doll.
I'm sure she'll appreciate any gift, but do try to avoid dumbbells.
Don't get her dumbbells, k~?
I'm sure anything but dumbbells would be fine.
By the way, the darkness-stabi
medicine from the other day c
more than I expected, so I'm g
to have to bill you for an add
WHY DO THEY ALL ASSUME I'M GOING TO GET HER DUMB-BELLS?

IT'S A GARLIC PRESS

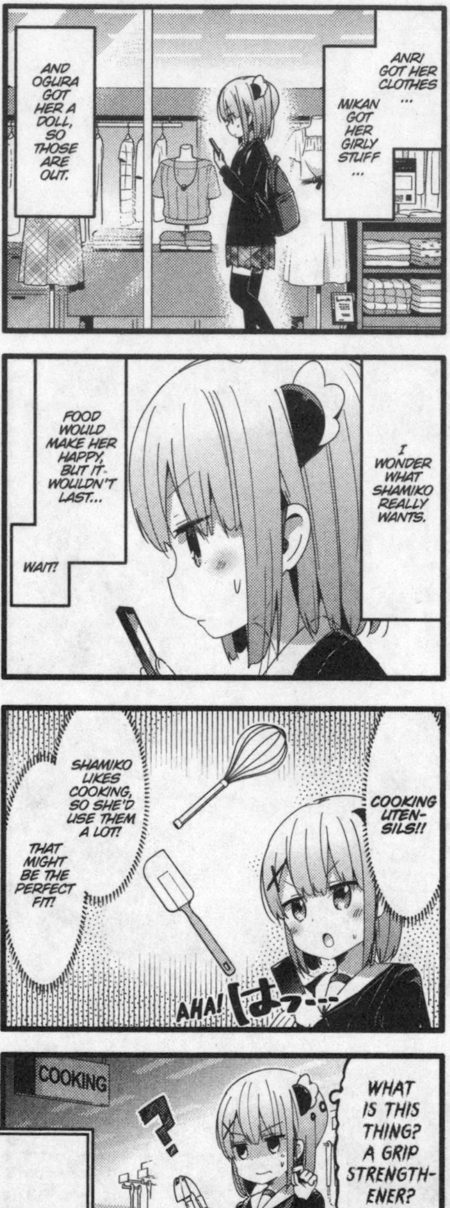
ANRI GOT HER CLOTHES...
MIKAN GOT HER GIRLY STUFF...
AND OGURA GOT HER A DOLL, SO THOSE ARE OUT.
I WONDER WHAT SHAMIKO REALLY WANTS.
FOOD WOULD MAKE HER HAPPY, BUT IT WOULDN'T LAST...
WAIT!
COOKING UTENSILS!!
SHAMIKO LIKES COOKING, SO SHE'D USE THEM A LOT!
THAT MIGHT BE THE PERFECT FIT!
AHA!
COOKING
WHAT IS THIS THING? A GRIP STRENGTHENER? THAT CAN'T BE RIGHT.
TO THOSE WHO CAN'T COOK, THE COOKING AISLE IS A MAZE OF MYSTERIES!!

A WILD LICO-KUN APPEARS!!

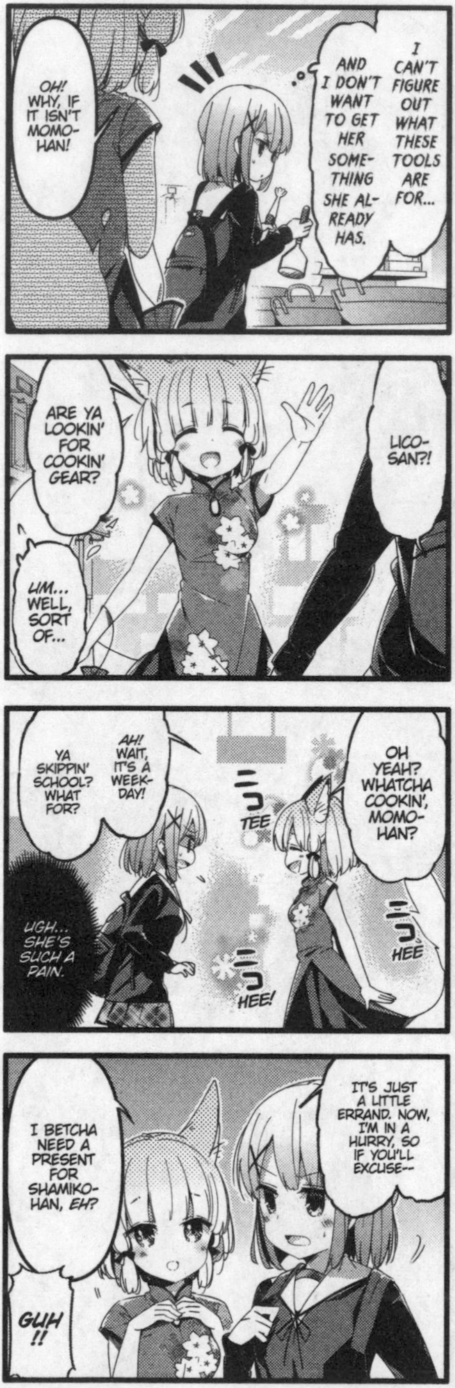
I CAN'T FIGURE OUT WHAT THESE TOOLS ARE FOR...
AND I DON'T WANT TO GET HER SOMETHING SHE ALREADY HAS.
OH! WHY, IF IT ISN'T MOMO-HAN!
LICO-SAN?!
ARE YA LOOKIN' FOR COOKIN' GEAR?
UM... WELL, SORT OF...
OH YEAH? WHATCHA COOKIN', MOMO-HAN?
AH! WAIT, IT'S A WEEKDAY!
YA SKIPPIN' SCHOOL? WHAT FOR?
TEE
HEE
HEE!
UGH... SHE'S SUCH A PAIN.
IT'S JUST A LITTLE ERRAND. NOW, I'M IN A HURRY, SO IF YOU'LL EXCUSE--
I BETCHA NEED A PRESENT FOR SHAMIKO-HAN, EH?
GUH!!

SHE DID USE IT AS A WHISK

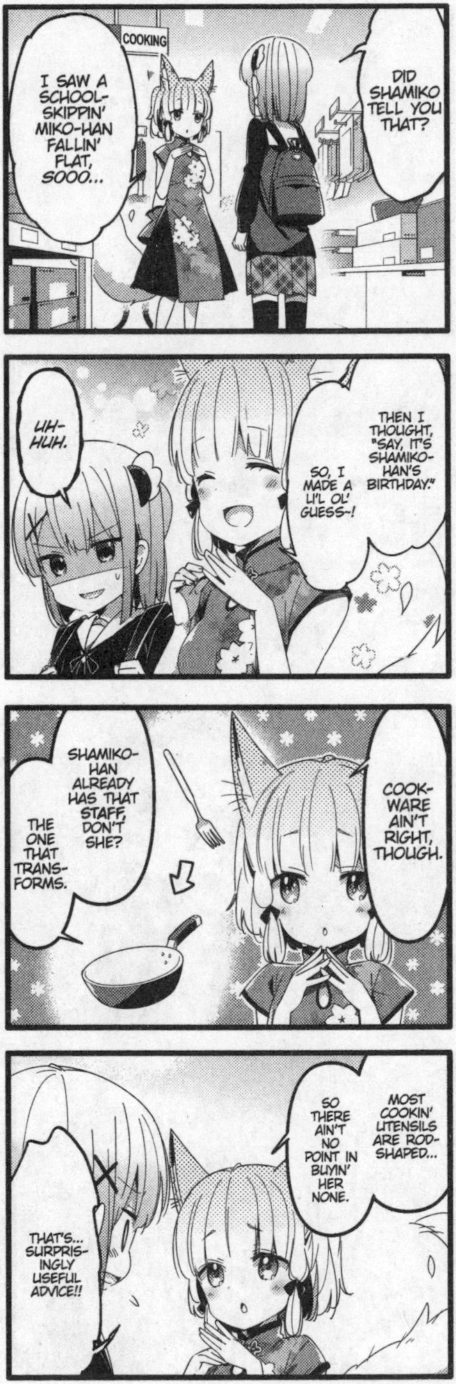
COOKING
DID SHAMIKO TELL YOU THAT?
I SAW A SCHOOL-SKIPPIN' MIKO-HAN FALLIN' FLAT, SOOO...
THEN I THOUGHT, "SAY, IT'S SHAMIKO-HAN'S BIRTHDAY."
SO, I MADE A LI'L OL' GUESS~!
UH-HUH.
COOK-WARE AIN'T RIGHT, THOUGH.
SHAMIKO-HAN ALREADY HAS THAT STAFF, DON'T SHE?
THE ONE THAT TRANS-FORMS.
MOST COOKIN' UTENSILS ARE ROD-SHAPED...
SO THERE AIN'T NO POINT IN BUYIN' HER NONE.
THAT'S... SURPRISINGLY USEFUL ADVICE!!

PRET ↑ ~TY ↓ PLEASE ↑

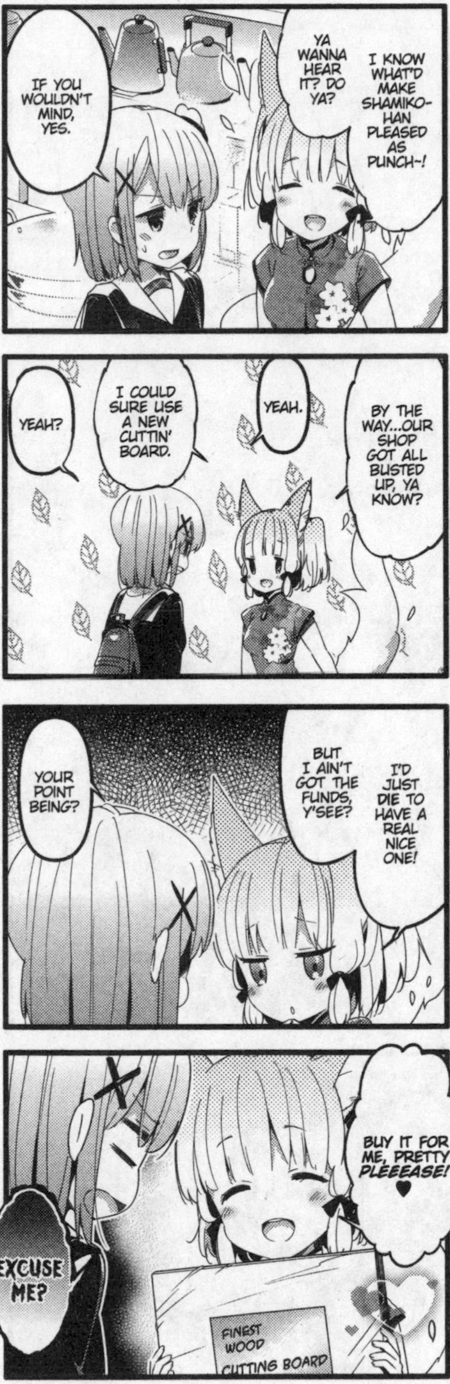
I KNOW WHAT'D MAKE SHAMIKO-HAN PLEASED AS PUNCH~!
YA WANNA HEAR IT? DO YA?
IF YOU WOULDN'T MIND, YES.
BY THE WAY...OUR SHOP GOT ALL BUSTED UP, YA KNOW?
YEAH.
I COULD SURE USE A NEW CUTTIN' BOARD.
YEAH?
I'D JUST DIE TO HAVE A REAL NICE ONE!
BUT I AIN'T GOT THE FUNDS, Y'SEE?
YOUR POINT BEING?
BUY IT FOR ME, PRETTY PLEEEASE! ♥
EXCUSE ME?
FINEST WOOD CUTTING BOARD

LICO-KUN (REALLY DOES MEAN WELL)

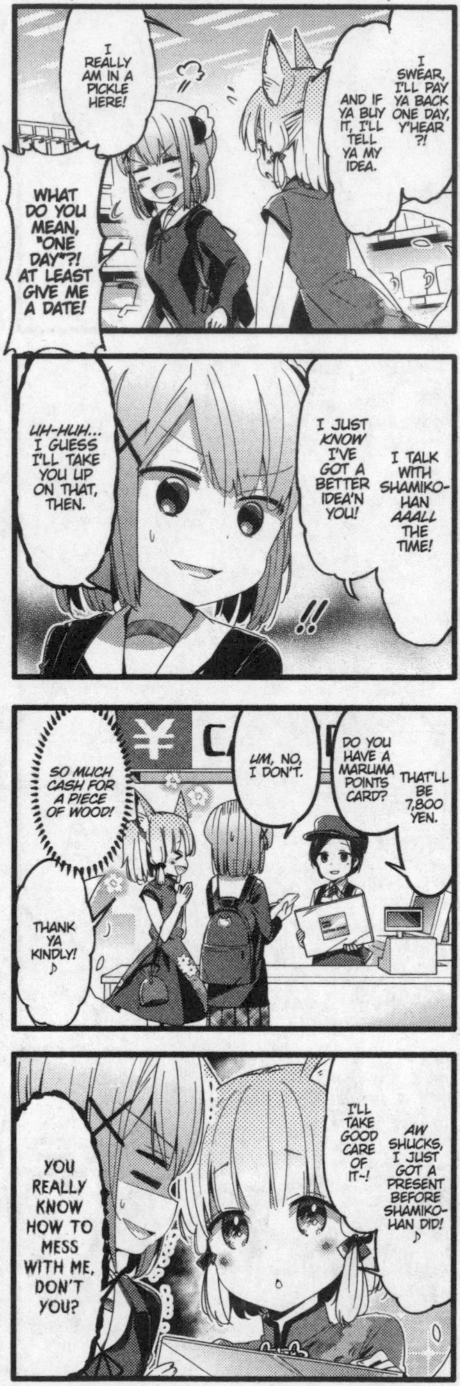
I SWEAR, I'LL PAY YA BACK ONE DAY, Y'HEAR?!
AND IF YA BUY IT, I'LL TELL YA MY IDEA.
I REALLY AM IN A PICKLE HERE!
WHAT DO YOU MEAN, "ONE DAY"?! AT LEAST GIVE ME A DATE!
I TALK WITH SHAMIKO-HAN *AAALL* THE TIME!
I JUST *KNOW* I'VE GOT A BETTER IDEA'N YOU!
UH-HUH... I GUESS I'LL TAKE YOU UP ON THAT, THEN.
!!
THAT'LL BE 7,800 YEN.
DO YOU HAVE A MARUMA POINTS CARD?
UM, NO, I DON'T.
SO MUCH CASH FOR A PIECE OF WOOD!
THANK YA KINDLY! ♪
AW SHUCKS, I JUST GOT A PRESENT BEFORE SHAMIKO-HAN DID! ♪
I'LL TAKE GOOD CARE OF IT~!
YOU REALLY KNOW HOW TO MESS WITH ME, DON'T YOU?

MORE LIKE SCREWBALL

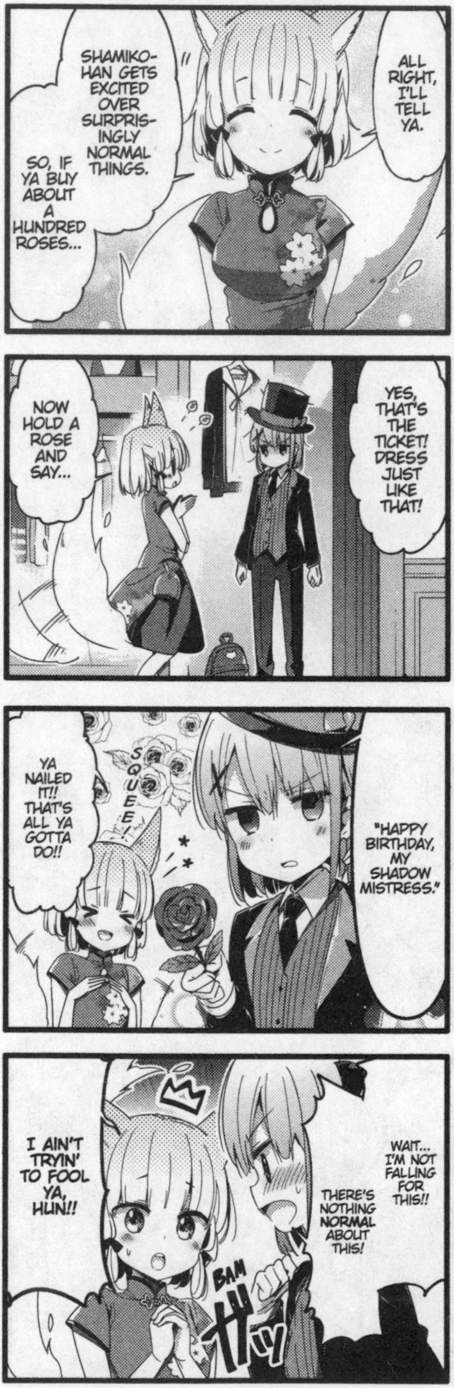
ALL RIGHT, I'LL TELL YA.
SHAMIKO-HAN GETS EXCITED OVER SURPRISINGLY NORMAL THINGS.
SO, IF YA BUY ABOUT A HUNDRED ROSES...
YES, THAT'S THE TICKET! DRESS JUST LIKE THAT!
NOW HOLD A ROSE AND SAY...
"HAPPY BIRTHDAY, MY SHADOW MISTRESS."
SQUEE!
YA NAILED IT!! THAT'S ALL YA GOTTA DO!!
WAIT... I'M NOT FALLING FOR THIS!!
THERE'S NOTHING NORMAL ABOUT THIS!
I AIN'T TRYIN' TO FOOL YA, HUN!!
BAM

A FULL BELLY IS BEST

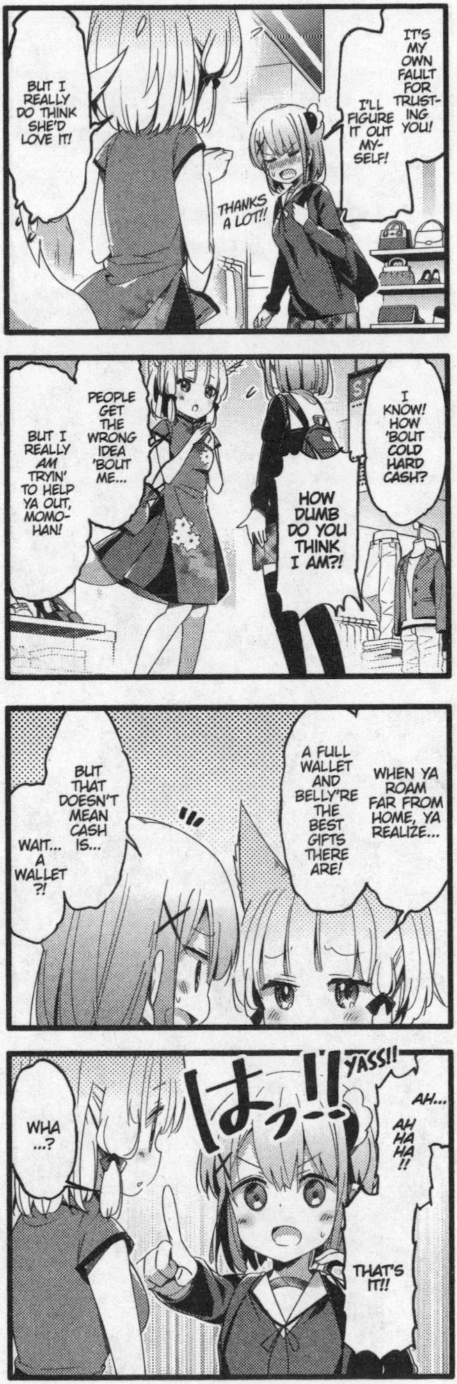
IT'S MY OWN FAULT FOR TRUST-ING YOU!
I'LL FIGURE IT OUT MY-SELF!
THANKS A LOT!!
BUT I REALLY DO THINK SHE'D LOVE IT!
I KNOW! HOW 'BOUT COLD HARD CASH?
HOW DUMB DO YOU THINK I AM?!
PEOPLE GET THE WRONG IDEA 'BOUT ME...
BUT I REALLY AM TRYIN' TO HELP YA OUT, MOMO-HAN!
WHEN YA ROAM FAR FROM HOME, YA REALIZE...
A FULL WALLET AND BELLY'RE THE BEST GIFTS THERE ARE!
BUT THAT DOESN'T MEAN CASH IS...
WAIT... A WALLET?!
YASS!!
AH... AH HA HA!!
はっ!!
THAT'S IT!!
WHA...?

UPGRADING FROM A TRANSPARENT WALLET

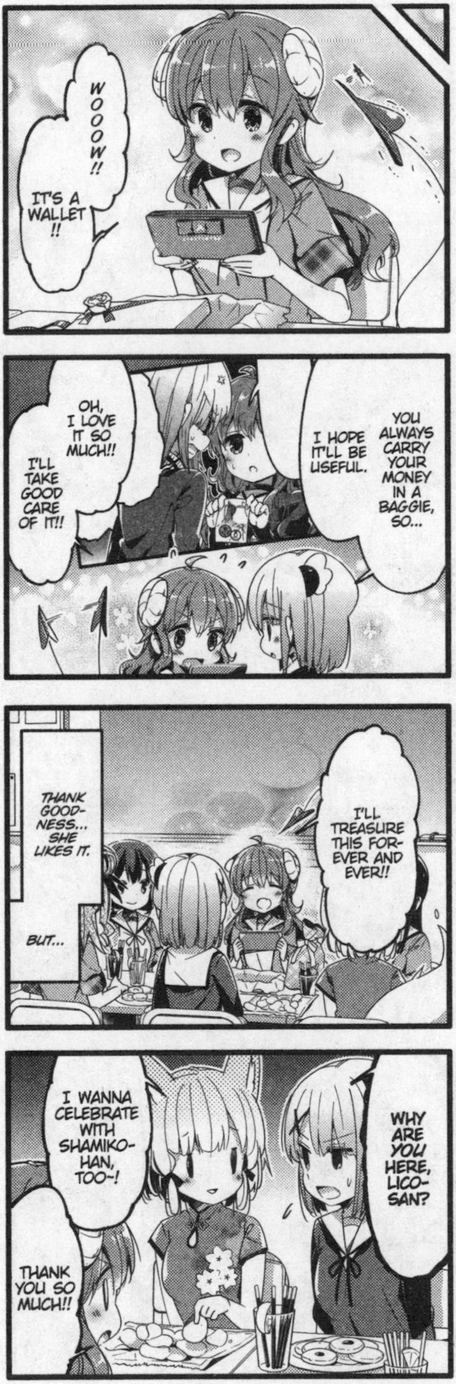
WOOOOW!!
IT'S A WALLET!!
YOU ALWAYS CARRY YOUR MONEY IN A BAGGIE, SO...
I HOPE IT'LL BE USEFUL.
OH, I LOVE IT SO MUCH!!
I'LL TAKE GOOD CARE OF IT!!
I'LL TREASURE THIS FOR-EVER AND EVER!!
THANK GOOD-NESS... SHE LIKES IT.
BUT...
WHY ARE YOU HERE, LICO-SAN?
I WANNA CELEBRATE WITH SHAMIKO-HAN, TOO~!
THANK YOU SO MUCH!!

SHAMIKO ASCENDS

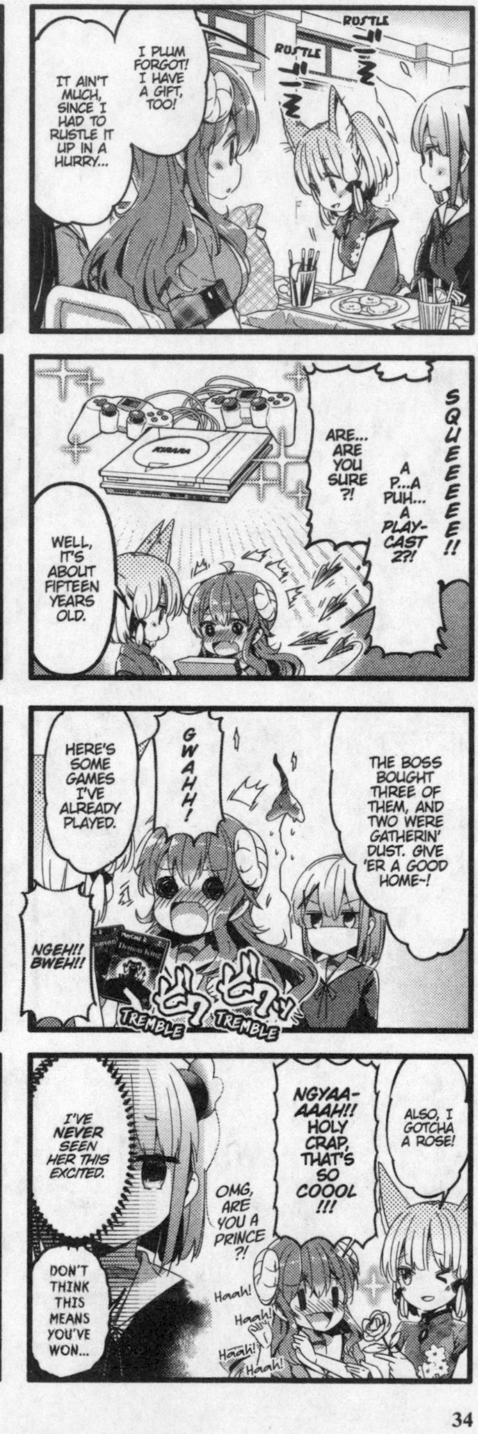
RUSTLE
RUSTLE
I PLUM FORGOT! I HAVE A GIFT, TOO!
IT AIN'T MUCH, SINCE I HAD TO RUSTLE IT UP IN A HURRY...
SQUEEEEEE!!
A P...A PUH... A PLAY-CAST 2?!
ARE... ARE YOU SURE?!
KIRARA
WELL, IT'S ABOUT FIFTEEN YEARS OLD.
THE BOSS BOUGHT THREE OF THEM, AND TWO WERE GATHERIN' DUST. GIVE 'ER A GOOD HOME~!
GWAHH!
HERE'S SOME GAMES I'VE ALREADY PLAYED.
NGEH!! BWEH!!
TREMBLE
TREMBLE
ALSO, I GOTCHA A ROSE!
NGYAA-AAAH!! HOLY CRAP, THAT'S SO COOOL!!!
OMG, ARE YOU A PRINCE?!
I'VE NEVER SEEN HER THIS EXCITED.
DON'T THINK THIS MEANS YOU'VE WON...
Haah!
Haah!
Haah!
Haah!

SHE USES IT EVEN LESS THAN THE DOLL

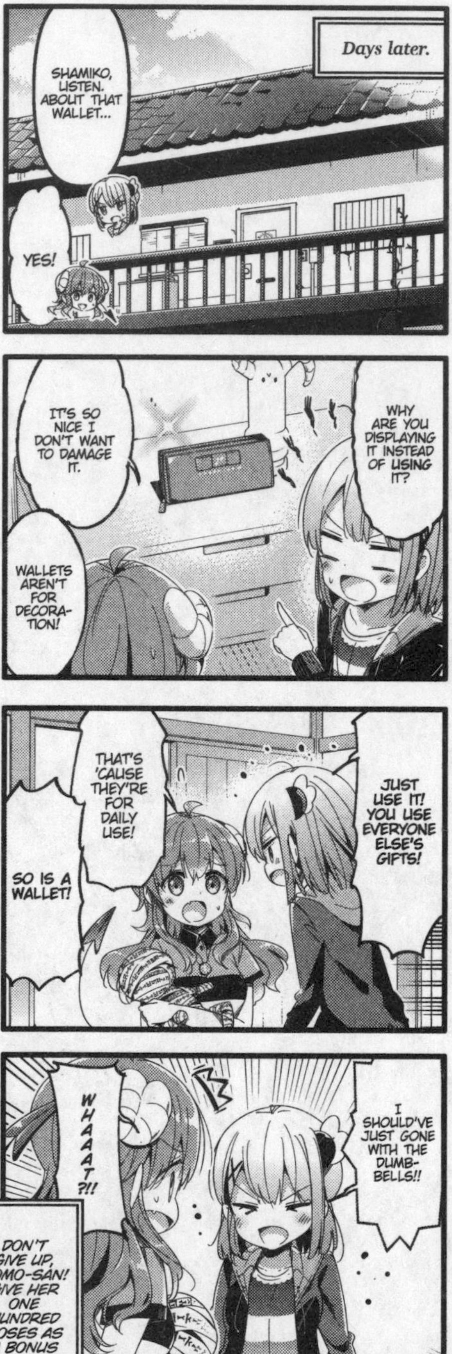
Days later.
SHAMIKO, LISTEN. ABOUT THAT WALLET...
YES!
WHY ARE YOU DISPLAYING IT INSTEAD OF USING IT?
IT'S SO NICE I DON'T WANT TO DAMAGE IT.
WALLETS AREN'T FOR DECORATION!
JUST USE IT! YOU USE EVERYONE ELSE'S GIFTS!
THAT'S 'CAUSE THEY'RE FOR DAILY USE!
SO IS A WALLET!
I SHOULD'VE JUST GONE WITH THE DUMBBELLS!!
WHAAAAT?!!
DON'T GIVE UP, MOMO-SAN! GIVE HER ONE HUNDRED ROSES AS A BONUS GIFT!

The Demon Girl Next Door

The Demon Girl Next Door

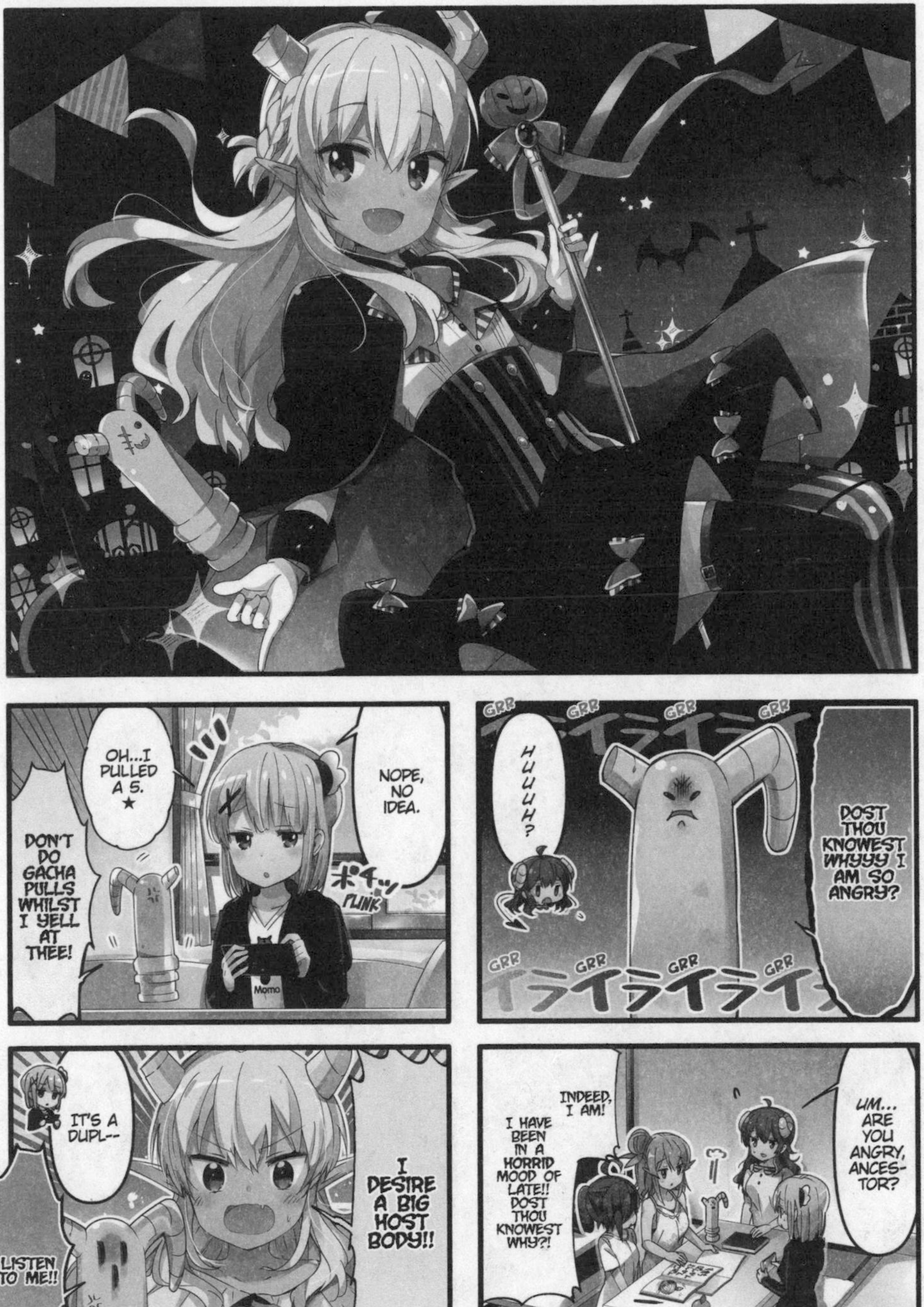
GRR GRR GRR GRR
イライライ
DOST THOU KNOWEST WHYYY I AM SO ANGRY?
HUUUH?
GRR GRR GRR GRR
イライライライ
NOPE, NO IDEA.
OH...I PULLED A 5.★
ポキッ
PLINK
DON'T DO GACHA PULLS WHILST I YELL AT THEE!
UM... ARE YOU ANGRY, ANCES-TOR?
INDEED, I AM!
I HAVE BEEN IN A HORRID MOOD OF LATE!! DOST THOU KNOWEST WHY?!
I DESIRE A BIG HOST BODY!!
IT'S A DUPL--
LISTEN TO ME!!

PEACH FEELINGS

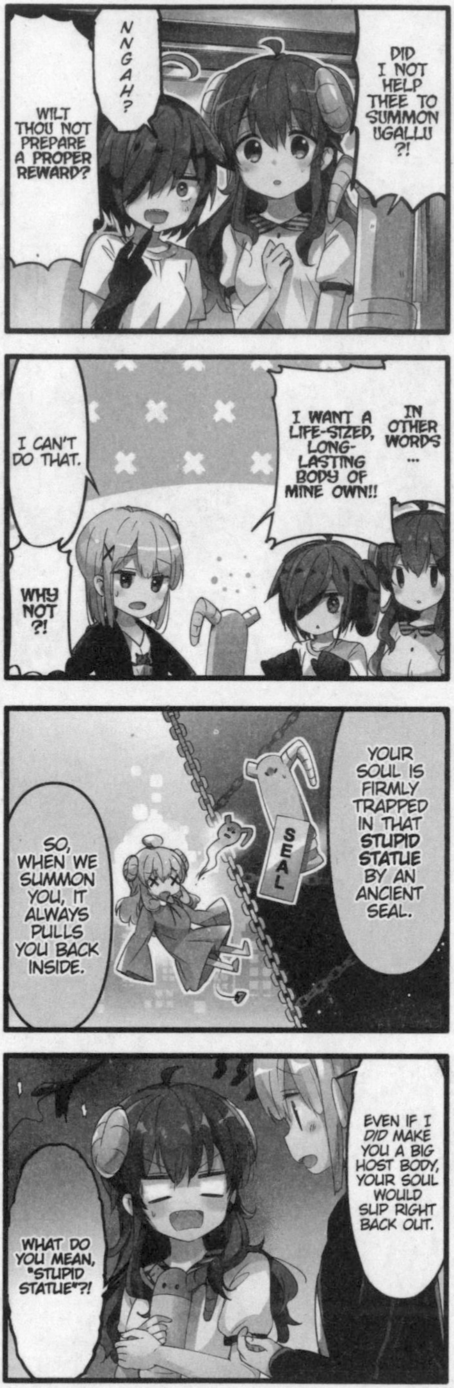
DID I NOT HELP THEE TO SUMMON UGALLU?!
NNGAH?
WILT THOU NOT PREPARE A PROPER REWARD?
IN OTHER WORDS...
I WANT A LIFE-SIZED, LONG-LASTING BODY OF MINE OWN!!
I CAN'T DO THAT.
WHY NOT?!
YOUR SOUL IS FIRMLY TRAPPED IN THAT STUPID STATUE BY AN ANCIENT SEAL.
SEAL
SO, WHEN WE SUMMON YOU, IT ALWAYS PULLS YOU BACK INSIDE.
EVEN IF I DID MAKE YOU A BIG HOST BODY, YOUR SOUL WOULD SLIP RIGHT BACK OUT.
WHAT DO YOU MEAN, "STUPID STATUE"?!

GAZING UPON ANCESTATUE MADE HER TEAR UP

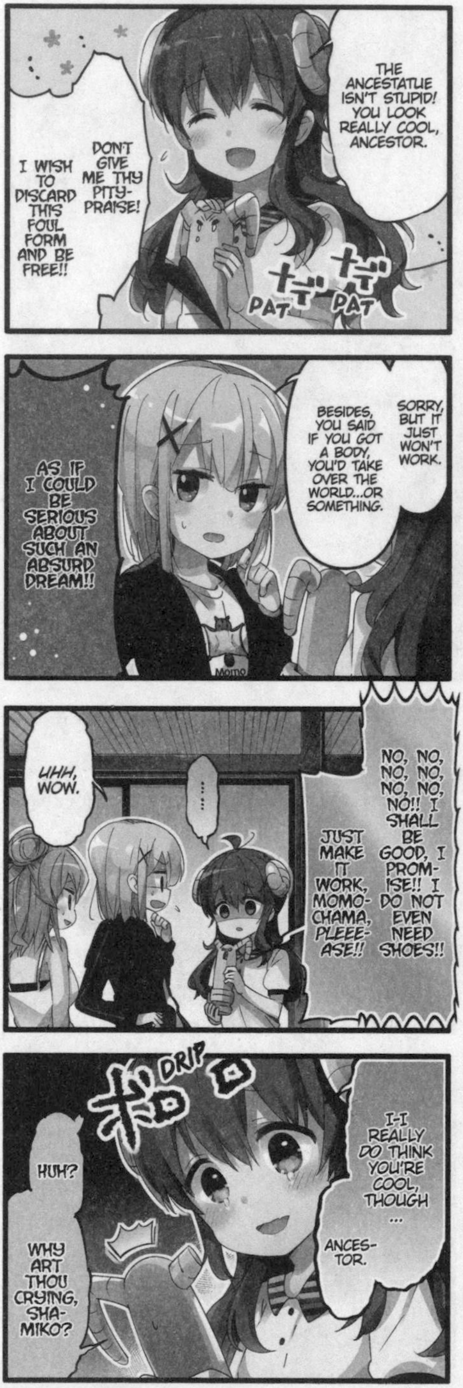
THE ANCESTATUE ISN'T STUPID! YOU LOOK REALLY COOL, ANCESTOR.
DON'T GIVE ME THY PITY-PRAISE!
I WISH TO DISCARD THIS FOUL FORM AND BE FREE!!
PAT PAT
SORRY, BUT IT JUST WON'T WORK.
BESIDES, YOU SAID IF YOU GOT A BODY, YOU'D TAKE OVER THE WORLD...OR SOMETHING.
AS IF I COULD BE SERIOUS ABOUT SUCH AN ABSURD DREAM!!
NO, NO, NO, NO, NO, NO, NO!! I SHALL BE GOOD, I PROMISE!! I DO NOT EVEN NEED SHOES!!
JUST MAKE IT WORK, MOMO-CHAMA, PLEEEASE!!
....
UHH, WOW.
DRIP
I-I REALLY DO THINK YOU'RE COOL, THOUGH... ANCESTOR.
HUH?
WHY ART THOU CRYING, SHAMIKO?

I SMELL A SURPRISE ENTRANCE

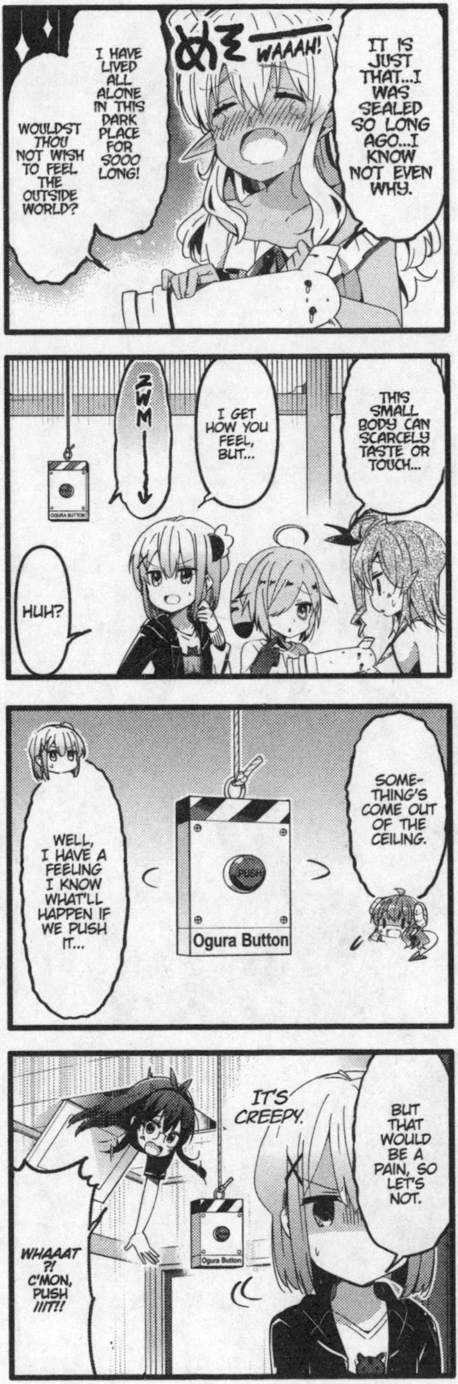
IT IS JUST THAT...I WAS SEALED SO LONG AGO...I KNOW NOT EVEN WHY.
めそ— WAAAH!
I HAVE LIVED ALL ALONE IN THIS DARK PLACE FOR SOOO LONG!
WOULDST THOU NOT WISH TO FEEL THE OUTSIDE WORLD?
THIS SMALL BODY CAN SCARCELY TASTE OR TOUCH...
I GET HOW YOU FEEL, BUT...
ZWM
Ogura Button
HUH?
SOMETHING'S COME OUT OF THE CEILING.
PUSH
Ogura Button
WELL, I HAVE A FEELING I KNOW WHAT'LL HAPPEN IF WE PUSH IT...
BUT THAT WOULD BE A PAIN, SO LET'S NOT.
IT'S CREEPY.
Ogura Button
WHAAAT?! C'MON, PUSH IIIT!!

CAN'T WE JUST CALL YOU ON THE PHONE?

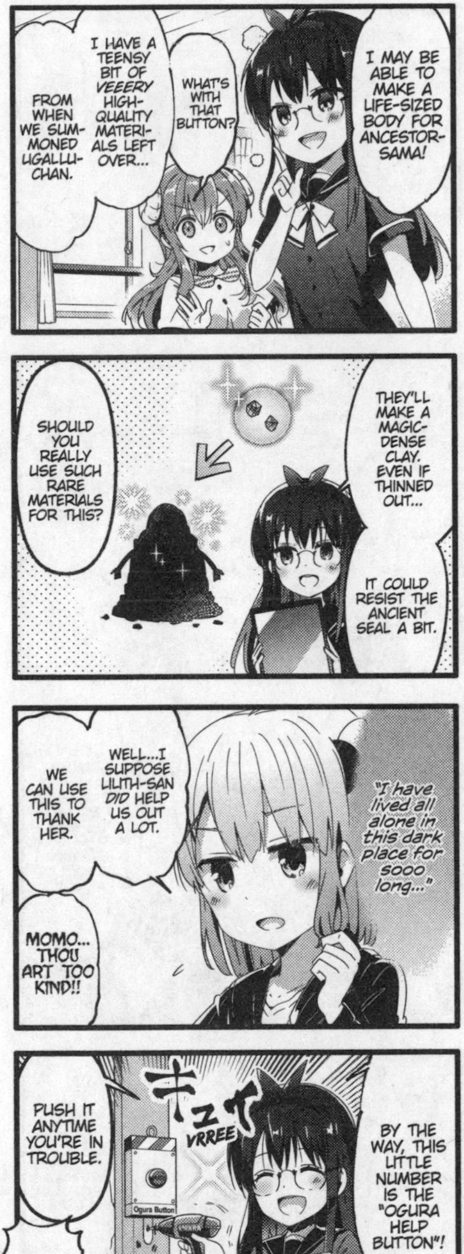
I MAY BE ABLE TO MAKE A LIFE-SIZED BODY FOR ANCESTOR-SAMA!
WHAT'S WITH THAT BUTTON?
I HAVE A TEENSY BIT OF VEEERY HIGH-QUALITY MATERIALS LEFT OVER...
FROM WHEN WE SUMMONED UGALLU-CHAN.
THEY'LL MAKE A MAGIC-DENSE CLAY. EVEN IF THINNED OUT...
SHOULD YOU REALLY USE SUCH RARE MATERIALS FOR THIS?
IT COULD RESIST THE ANCIENT SEAL A BIT.
"I have lived all alone in this dark place for sooo long..."
WELL...I SUPPOSE LILITH-SAN DID HELP US OUT A LOT.
WE CAN USE THIS TO THANK HER.
MOMO... THOU ART TOO KIND!!
BY THE WAY, THIS LITTLE NUMBER IS THE "OGURA HELP BUTTON"!
VRREE
PUSH IT ANYTIME YOU'RE IN TROUBLE.
Ogura Button
A DRILL?!
EEEEE
EEE

ACCIDENTAL PEACH BOMB

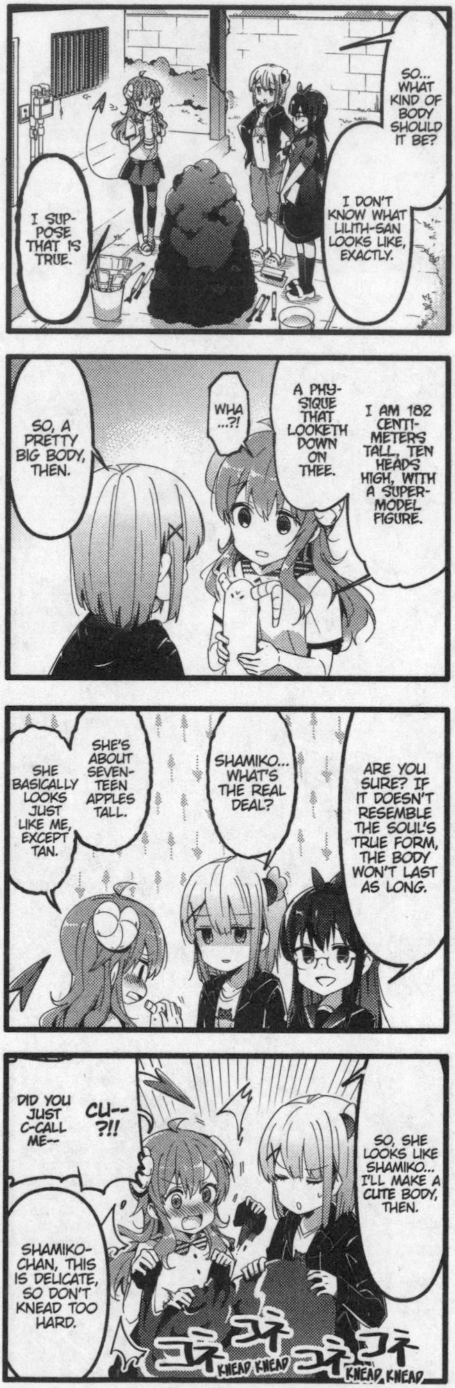
SO... WHAT KIND OF BODY SHOULD IT BE?
I DON'T KNOW WHAT LILITH-SAN LOOKS LIKE, EXACTLY.
I SUPPOSE THAT IS TRUE.
I AM 182 CENTIMETERS TALL, TEN HEADS HIGH, WITH A SUPERMODEL FIGURE.
A PHYSIQUE THAT LOOKETH DOWN ON THEE.
WHA...?!
SO, A PRETTY BIG BODY, THEN.
ARE YOU SURE? IF IT DOESN'T RESEMBLE THE SOUL'S TRUE FORM, THE BODY WON'T LAST AS LONG.
SHAMIKO... WHAT'S THE REAL DEAL?
SHE'S ABOUT SEVENTEEN APPLES TALL.
SHE BASICALLY LOOKS JUST LIKE ME, EXCEPT TAN.
SO, SHE LOOKS LIKE SHAMIKO... I'LL MAKE A CUTE BODY, THEN.
CU--?!!
DID YOU JUST C-CALL ME--
SHAMIKO-CHAN, THIS IS DELICATE, SO DON'T KNEAD TOO HARD.
コネ KNEAD コネ KNEAD コネ KNEAD コネ KNEAD

LILICADA

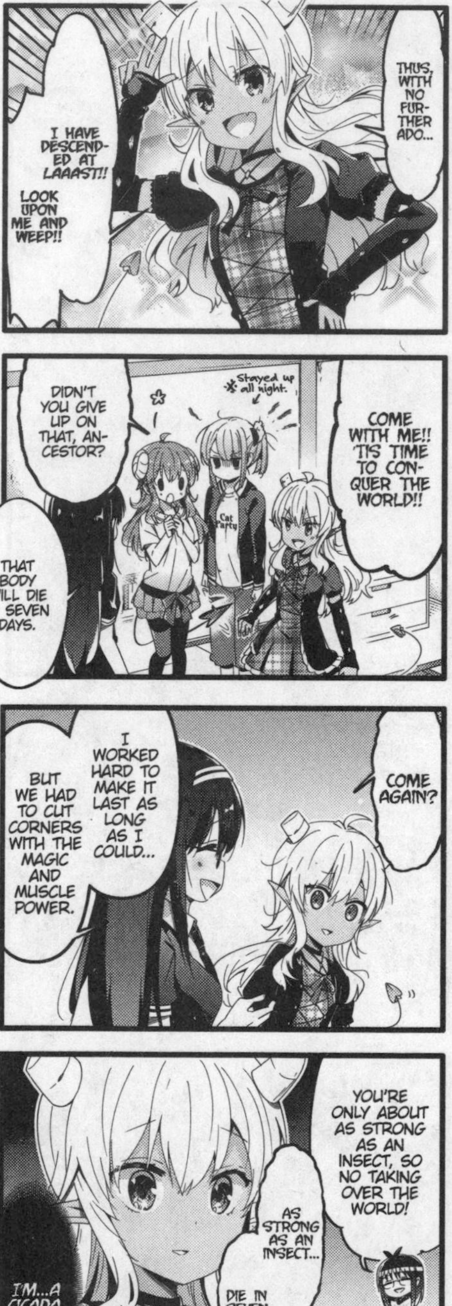
THUS, WITH NO FURTHER ADO...
I HAVE DESCENDED AT LAAAST!!
LOOK UPON ME AND WEEP!!
COME WITH ME!! 'TIS TIME TO CONQUER THE WORLD!!
*Stayed up all night.
DIDN'T YOU GIVE UP ON THAT, ANCESTOR?
THAT BODY WILL DIE IN SEVEN DAYS.
COME AGAIN?
I WORKED HARD TO MAKE IT LAST AS LONG AS I COULD...
BUT WE HAD TO CUT CORNERS WITH THE MAGIC AND MUSCLE POWER.
YOU'RE ONLY ABOUT AS STRONG AS AN INSECT, SO NO TAKING OVER THE WORLD!
AS STRONG AS AN INSECT...
DIE IN SEVEN DAYS...
I'M...A CICADA.

A RARE NO-GO FROM SHAMIKO

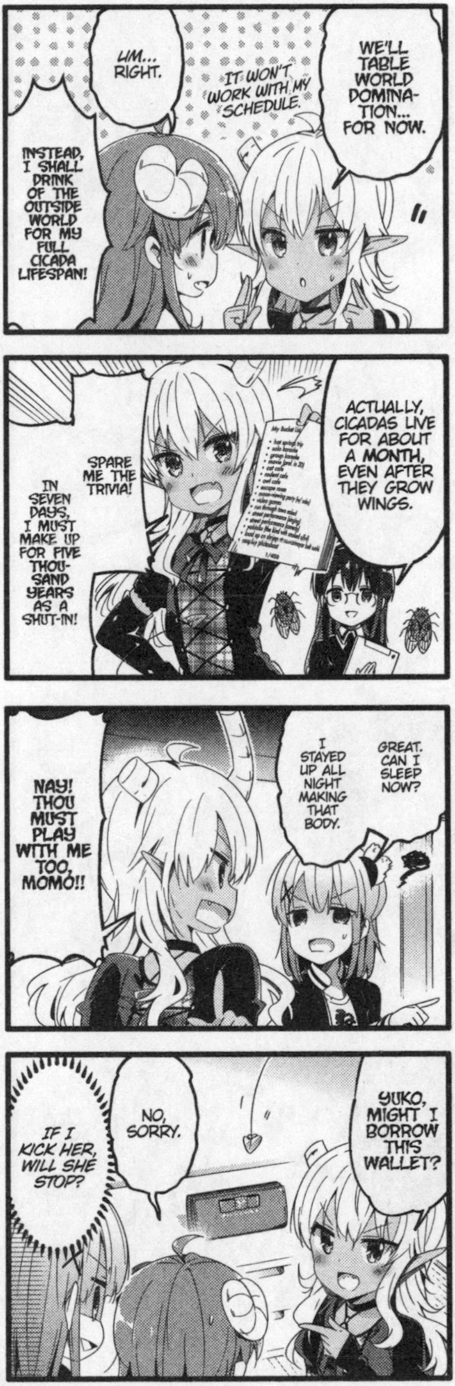
WE'LL TABLE WORLD DOMINATION... FOR NOW.
IT WON'T WORK WITH MY SCHEDULE.
UM... RIGHT.
INSTEAD, I SHALL DRINK OF THE OUTSIDE WORLD FOR MY FULL CICADA LIFESPAN!
ACTUALLY, CICADAS LIVE FOR ABOUT A MONTH, EVEN AFTER THEY GROW WINGS.
SPARE ME THE TRIVIA!
IN SEVEN DAYS, I MUST MAKE UP FOR FIVE THOUSAND YEARS AS A SHUT-IN!
GREAT. CAN I SLEEP NOW?
I STAYED UP ALL NIGHT MAKING THAT BODY.
NAY! THOU MUST PLAY WITH ME TOO, MOMO!!
YUKO, MIGHT I BORROW THIS WALLET?
NO, SORRY.
IF I KICK HER, WILL SHE STOP?

THIS CAN ONLY END IN VOMITING

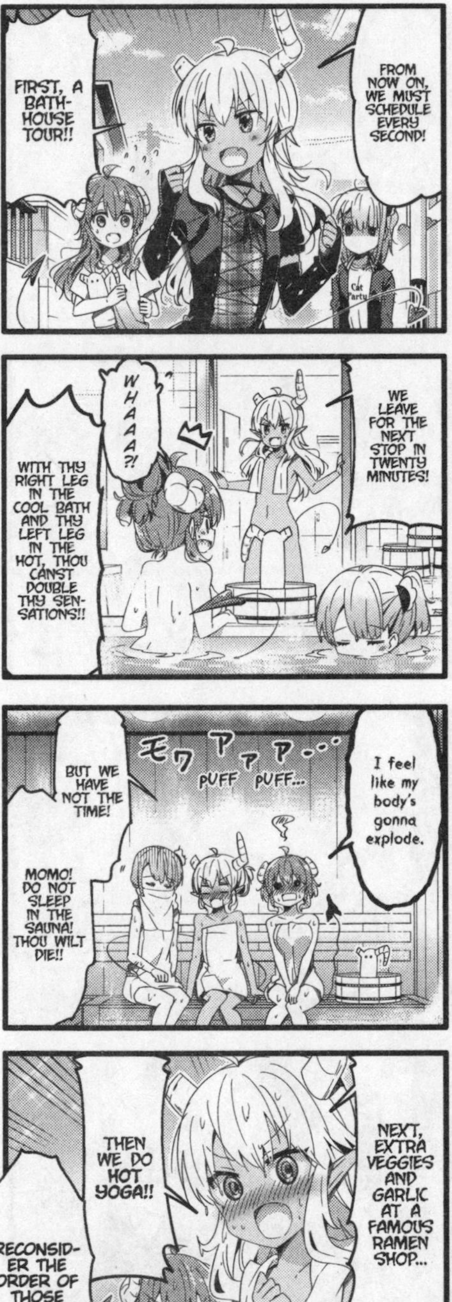
FROM NOW ON, WE MUST SCHEDULE EVERY SECOND!
FIRST, A BATH-HOUSE TOUR!!
Cat Party
WE LEAVE FOR THE NEXT STOP IN TWENTY MINUTES!
WHAAAA?!
WITH THY RIGHT LEG IN THE COOL BATH AND THY LEFT LEG IN THE HOT, THOU CANST DOUBLE THY SENSATIONS!!
I feel like my body's gonna explode.
モワァァァ...
PUFF PUFF...
BUT WE HAVE NOT THE TIME!
MOMO! DO NOT SLEEP IN THE SAUNA! THOU WILT DIE!!
NEXT, EXTRA VEGGIES AND GARLIC AT A FAMOUS RAMEN SHOP...
THEN WE DO HOT YOGA!!
RECONSIDER THE ORDER OF THOSE THINGS!

SCREENTONE-FILLED FACE

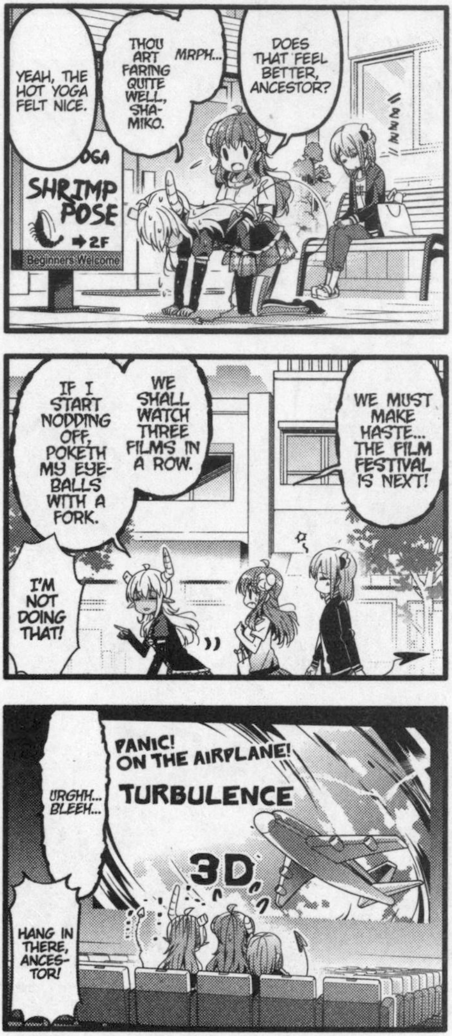
DOES THAT FEEL BETTER, ANCESTOR?
ZZZ
MRPH...
THOU ART FARING QUITE WELL, SHAMIKO.
YEAH, THE HOT YOGA FELT NICE.
OGA
SHRIMP POSE
➔ 2F
Beginners Welcome
WE MUST MAKE HASTE... THE FILM FESTIVAL IS NEXT!
WE SHALL WATCH THREE FILMS IN A ROW.
IF I START NODDING OFF, POKETH MY EYEBALLS WITH A FORK.
I'M NOT DOING THAT!
PANIC! ON THE AIRPLANE!
TURBULENCE
3D
URGHH... BLEEH...
HANG IN THERE, ANCESTOR!
WE MUST TAKE A CUTE SELFIE FOR SOCIAL MEDIA AFTER THE MOVIE.
THAT FACE WILL FREAK PEOPLE OUT!
LET'S JUST UNWIND A BIT!

DEMON AND MAGICAL GIRL SLUMBER PARTY

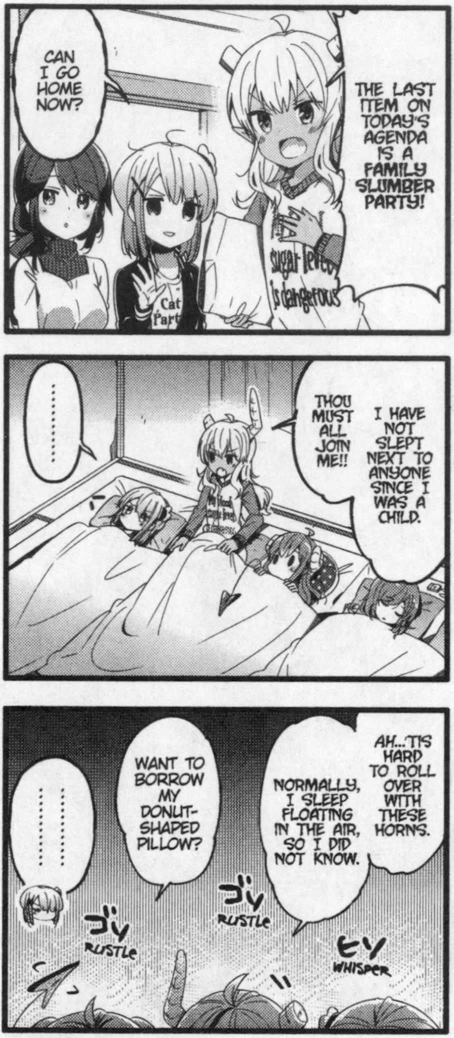
THE LAST ITEM ON TODAY'S AGENDA IS A FAMILY SLUMBER PARTY!
sugar level is dangerous
Cat Party
CAN I GO HOME NOW?
I HAVE NOT SLEPT NEXT TO ANYONE SINCE I WAS A CHILD.
THOU MUST ALL JOIN ME!!
......
AH...TIS HARD TO ROLL OVER WITH THESE HORNS.
NORMALLY, I SLEEP FLOATING IN THE AIR, SO I DID NOT KNOW.
WANT TO BORROW MY DONUT-SHAPED PILLOW?
......
ゴソ RUSTLE
ゴソ RUSTLE
ヒソ WHISPER
NOW, WHAT ARE THOSE THINGS ON THY HEAD, MOMO?
I WANNA PUT HER TO SLEEP WITH A CHOKEHOLD.

RECKLESS USE OF SKILLS

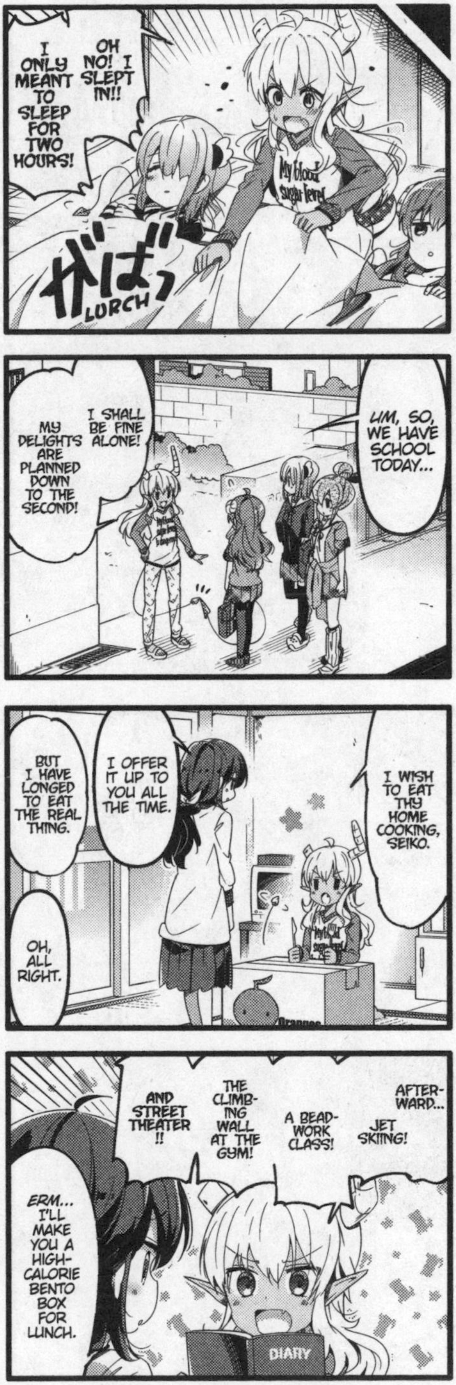
OH NO! I SLEPT IN!!
I ONLY MEANT TO SLEEP FOR TWO HOURS!
がばっ
LURCH
UM, SO, WE HAVE SCHOOL TODAY...
I SHALL BE FINE ALONE!
MY DELIGHTS ARE PLANNED DOWN TO THE SECOND!
I WISH TO EAT THY HOME COOKING, SEIKO.
I OFFER IT UP TO YOU ALL THE TIME.
BUT I HAVE LONGED TO EAT THE REAL THING.
OH, ALL RIGHT.
AFTERWARD... JET SKIING!
A BEADWORK CLASS!
THE CLIMBING WALL AT THE GYM!
AND STREET THEATER!!
ERM... I'LL MAKE YOU A HIGH-CALORIE BENTO BOX FOR LUNCH.
DIARY

ANCESTOR BREAKDOWN

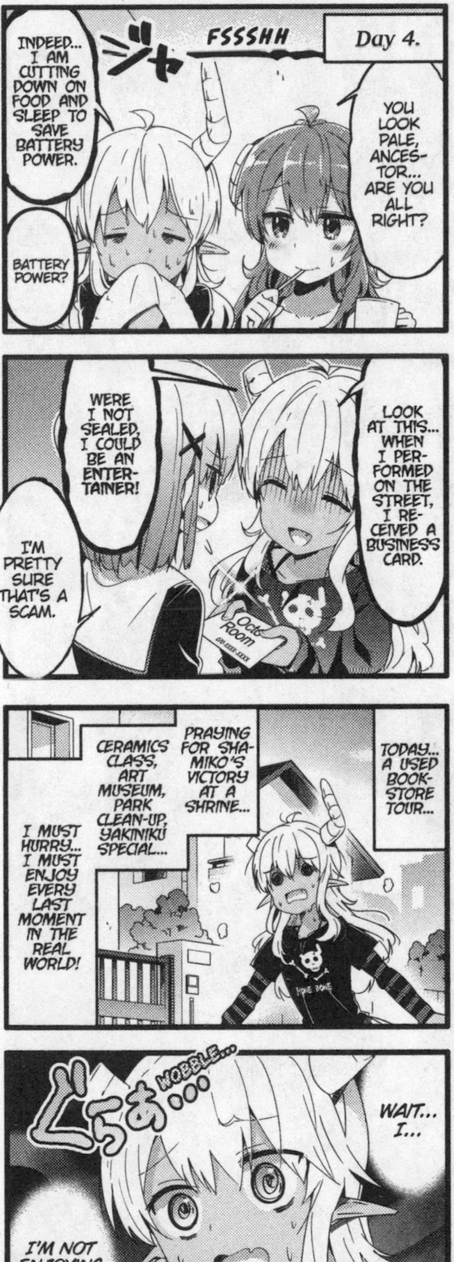
Day 4.
ジャ
FSSSHH
YOU LOOK PALE, ANCESTOR... ARE YOU ALL RIGHT?
INDEED... I AM CUTTING DOWN ON FOOD AND SLEEP TO SAVE BATTERY POWER.
BATTERY POWER?
LOOK AT THIS... WHEN I PERFORMED ON THE STREET, I RECEIVED A BUSINESS CARD.
WERE I NOT SEALED, I COULD BE AN ENTERTAINER!
I'M PRETTY SURE THAT'S A SCAM.
TODAY... A USED BOOKSTORE TOUR...
PRAYING FOR SHAMIKO'S VICTORY AT A SHRINE...
CERAMICS CLASS, ART MUSEUM, PARK CLEAN-UP, YAKINIKU SPECIAL...
I MUST HURRY... I MUST ENJOY EVERY LAST MOMENT IN THE REAL WORLD!
WAIT... I...
ぐらあ
WOBBLE...
I'M NOT ENJOYING THIS AT ALL! BUT WHY?

HER SPIRIT'S IN A BAD STATE

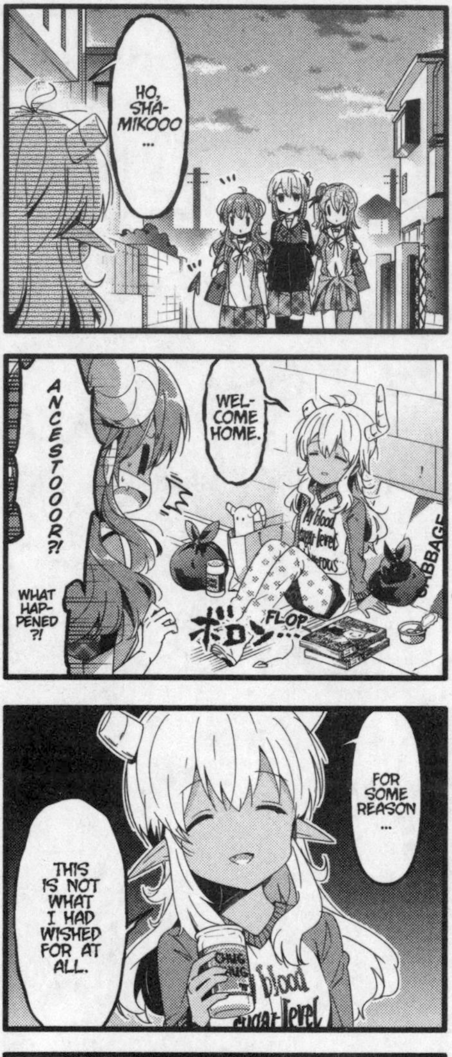
HO, SHAMIKOOO...
WELCOME HOME.
ANCESTOOOOR?!
WHAT HAPPENED?!
FLOP
GARBAGE
FOR SOME REASON...
THIS IS NOT WHAT I HAD WISHED FOR AT ALL.
I HAVE PLAYED AS HARD AS I COULD, BUT MY HEART IS NOT IN IT.
I AM TIRED... I MISS MY SEAL SPACE.
BUT IT'S YOUR FIRST TIME OUT IN FIVE THOUSAND YEARS!
SLUUUMP

ANCESTOR'S FINAL THREE DAYS

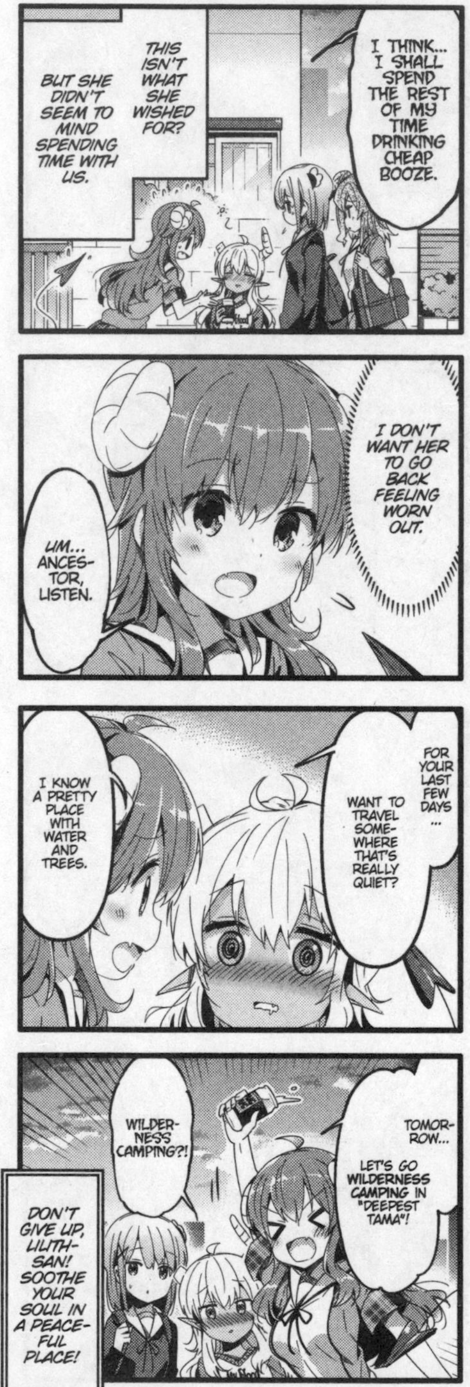
I THINK... I SHALL SPEND THE REST OF MY TIME DRINKING CHEAP BOOZE.
THIS ISN'T WHAT SHE WISHED FOR?
BUT SHE DIDN'T SEEM TO MIND SPENDING TIME WITH US.
I DON'T WANT HER TO GO BACK FEELING WORN OUT.
UM... ANCESTOR, LISTEN.
FOR YOUR LAST FEW DAYS...
WANT TO TRAVEL SOMEWHERE THAT'S REALLY QUIET?
I KNOW A PRETTY PLACE WITH WATER AND TREES.
TOMORROW...
LET'S GO WILDERNESS CAMPING IN "DEEPEST TAMA"!
WILDERNESS CAMPING?!
DON'T GIVE UP, LILITH-SAN! SOOTHE YOUR SOUL IN A PEACEFUL PLACE!

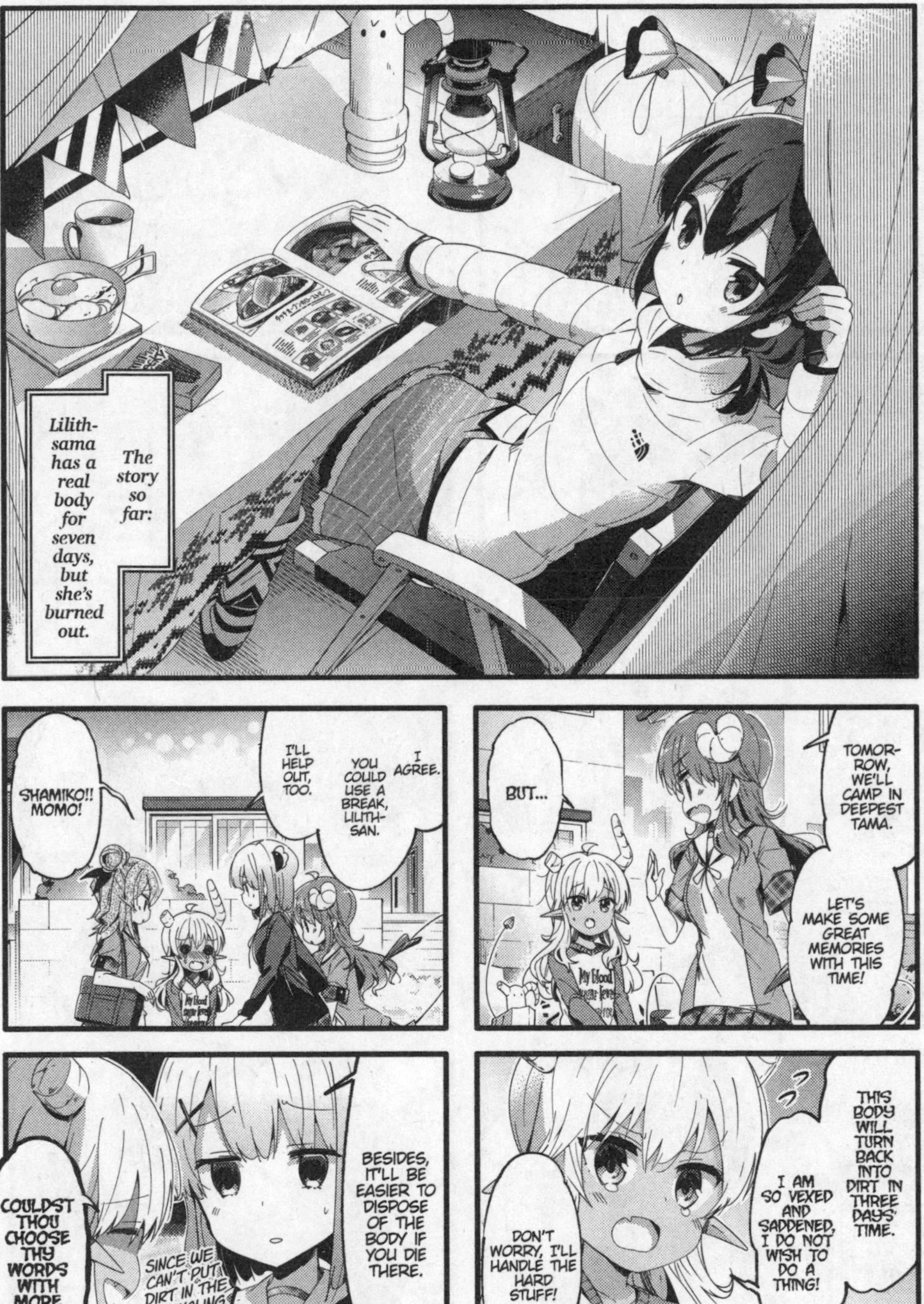
The story so far:
Lilith-sama has a real body for seven days, but she's burned out.
TOMORROW, WE'LL CAMP IN DEEPEST TAMA.
LET'S MAKE SOME GREAT MEMORIES WITH THIS TIME!
BUT...
I AGREE.
YOU COULD USE A BREAK, LILITH-SAN.
I'LL HELP OUT, TOO.
SHAMIKO!! MOMO!
THIS BODY WILL TURN BACK INTO DIRT IN THREE DAYS' TIME.
I AM SO VEXED AND SADDENED, I DO NOT WISH TO DO A THING!
DON'T WORRY, I'LL HANDLE THE HARD STUFF!
BESIDES, IT'LL BE EASIER TO DISPOSE OF THE BODY IF YOU DIE THERE.
SINCE WE CAN'T PUT DIRT IN THE RECYCLING.
COULDST THOU CHOOSE THY WORDS WITH MORE CARE?

BECOME A DEMON WHO DOESN'T UNDERESTIMATE MOUNTAINS

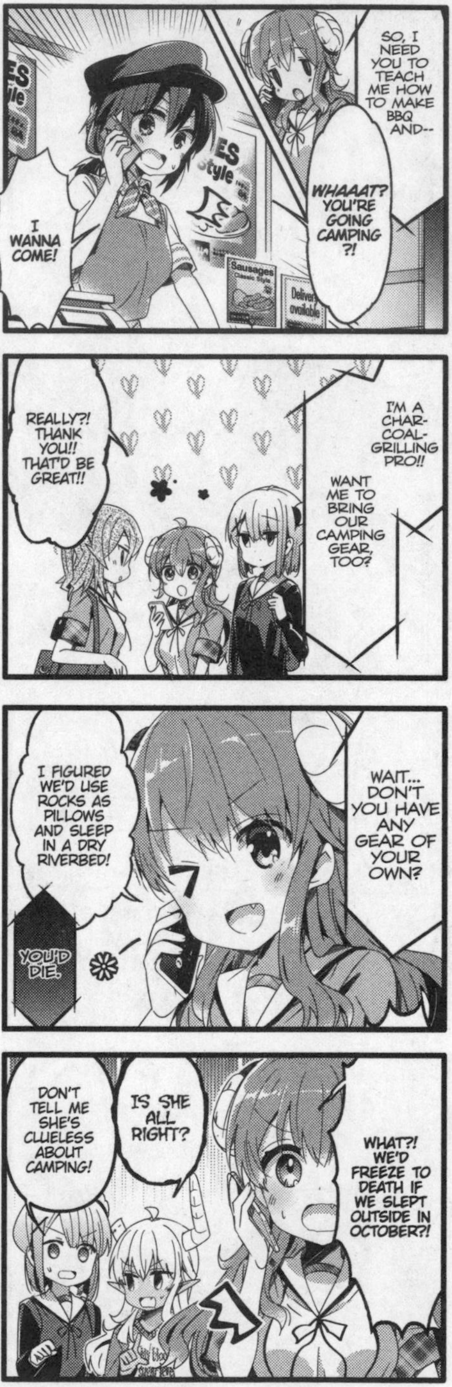
SO, I NEED YOU TO TEACH ME HOW TO MAKE BBQ AND--
WHAAAT? YOU'RE GOING CAMPING?!
I WANNA COME!
Sausages
Delivery available
I'M A CHARCOAL-GRILLING PRO!!
WANT ME TO BRING OUR CAMPING GEAR, TOO?
REALLY?! THANK YOU!! THAT'D BE GREAT!!
WAIT... DON'T YOU HAVE ANY GEAR OF YOUR OWN?
I FIGURED WE'D USE ROCKS AS PILLOWS AND SLEEP IN A DRY RIVERBED!
YOU'D DIE.
WHAT?! WE'D FREEZE TO DEATH IF WE SLEPT OUTSIDE IN OCTOBER?!
IS SHE ALL RIGHT?
DON'T TELL ME SHE'S CLUELESS ABOUT CAMPING!

I'LL COME RUNNING, NO MATTER HOW FAR

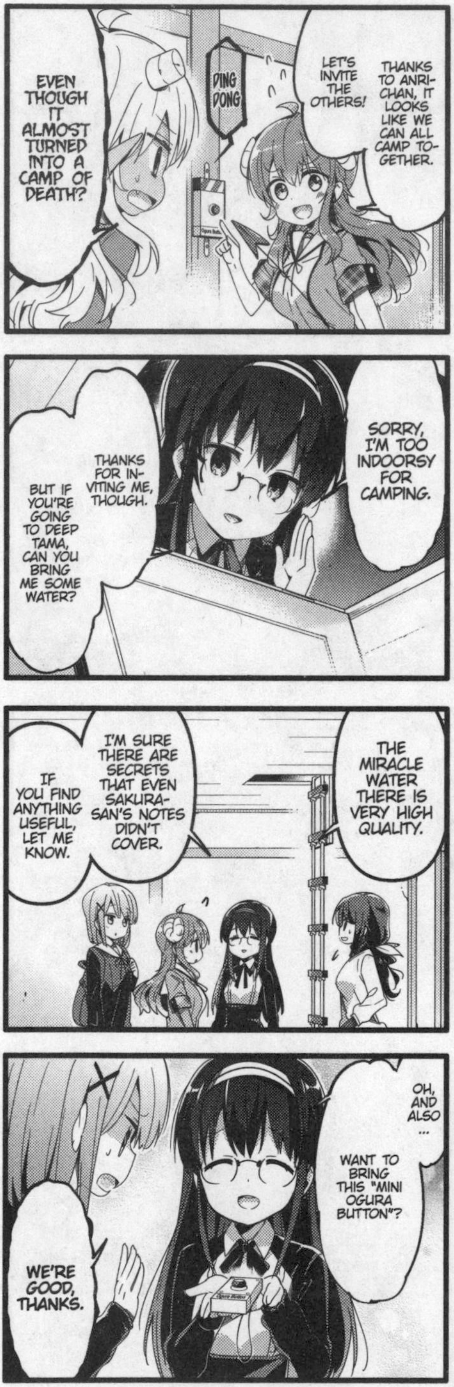
THANKS TO ANRI-CHAN, IT LOOKS LIKE WE CAN ALL CAMP TOGETHER.
LET'S INVITE THE OTHERS!
DING DONG
EVEN THOUGH IT ALMOST TURNED INTO A CAMP OF DEATH?
SORRY, I'M TOO INDOORSY FOR CAMPING.
THANKS FOR INVITING ME, THOUGH.
BUT IF YOU'RE GOING TO DEEP TAMA, CAN YOU BRING ME SOME WATER?
THE MIRACLE WATER THERE IS VERY HIGH QUALITY.
I'M SURE THERE ARE SECRETS THAT EVEN SAKURA-SAN'S NOTES DIDN'T COVER.
IF YOU FIND ANYTHING USEFUL, LET ME KNOW.
OH, AND ALSO...
WANT TO BRING THIS "MINI OGURA BUTTON"?
WE'RE GOOD, THANKS.

ANRI-CHAN ENJOYS THE MOUNTAINS

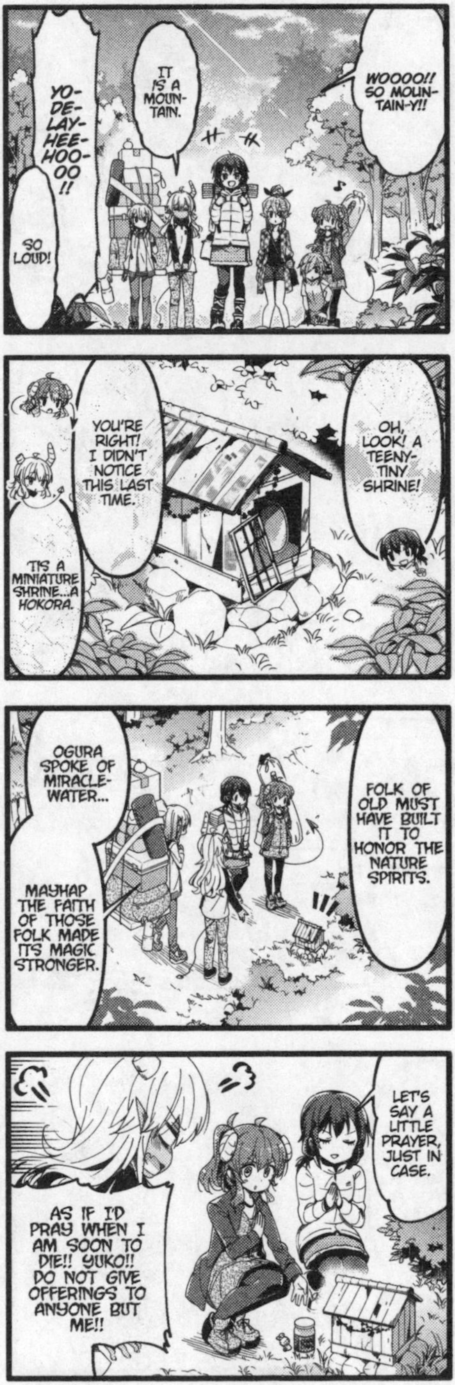
WOOOO!! SO MOUNTAIN-Y!!
IT IS A MOUNTAIN.
YO-DE-LAY-HEE-HOOO!!
SO LOUD!
OH, LOOK! A TEENY-TINY SHRINE!
YOU'RE RIGHT! I DIDN'T NOTICE THIS LAST TIME.
TIS A MINIATURE SHRINE...A HOKORA.
FOLK OF OLD MUST HAVE BUILT IT TO HONOR THE NATURE SPIRITS.
OGURA SPOKE OF MIRACLE-WATER...
MAYHAP THE FAITH OF THOSE FOLK MADE ITS MAGIC STRONGER.
LET'S SAY A LITTLE PRAYER, JUST IN CASE.
AS IF I'D PRAY WHEN I AM SOON TO DIE!! YUKO!! DO NOT GIVE OFFERINGS TO ANYONE BUT ME!!

A SEASONAL CHILL

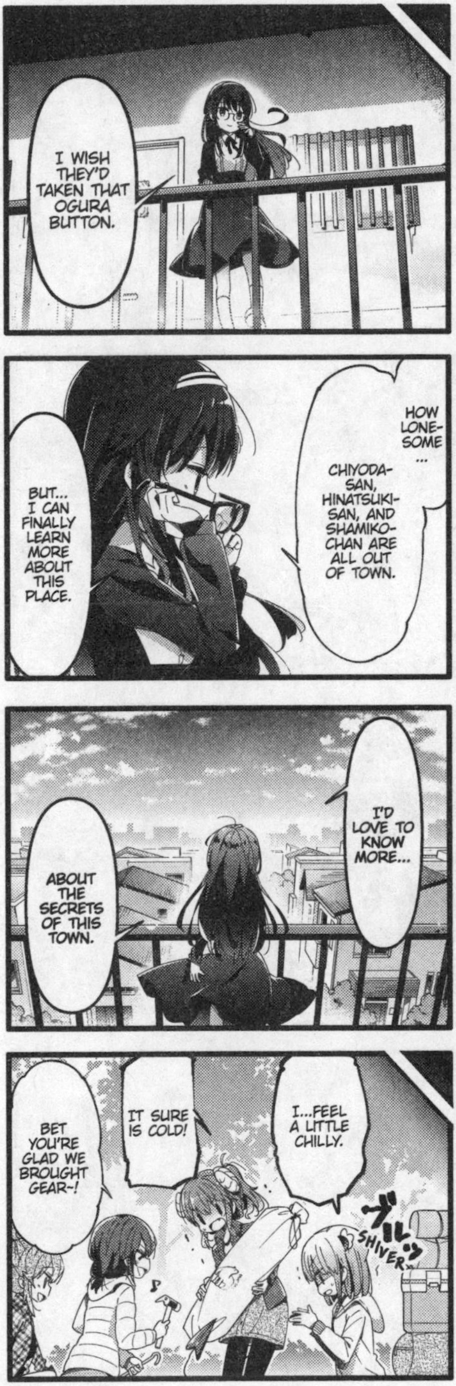
I WISH THEY'D TAKEN THAT OGURA BUTTON.
HOW LONESOME...
CHIYODA-SAN, HINATSUKI-SAN, AND SHAMIKO-CHAN ARE ALL OUT OF TOWN.
BUT... I CAN FINALLY LEARN MORE ABOUT THIS PLACE.
I'D LOVE TO KNOW MORE...
ABOUT THE SECRETS OF THIS TOWN.
I...FEEL A LITTLE CHILLY.
IT SURE IS COLD!
BET YOU'RE GLAD WE BROUGHT GEAR~!
SHIVER

BONFIRE FUN

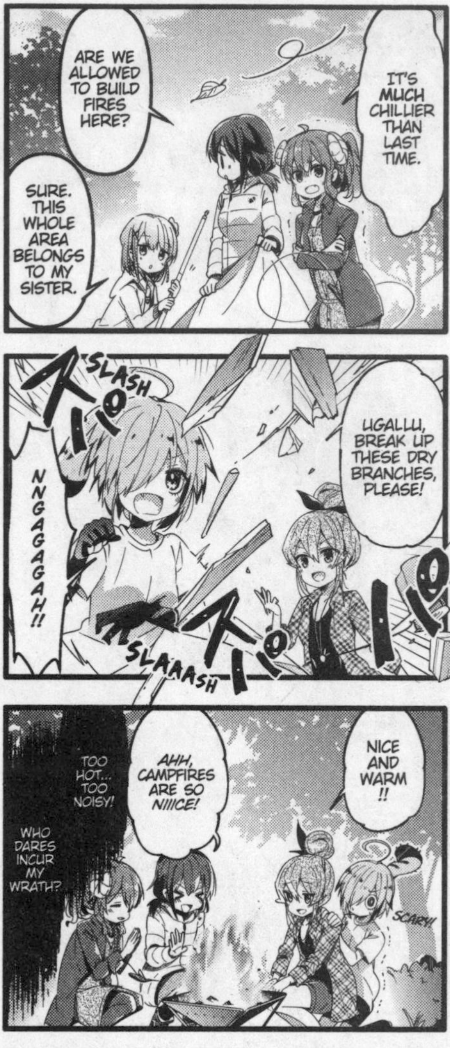
IT'S MUCH CHILLIER THAN LAST TIME.
ARE WE ALLOWED TO BUILD FIRES HERE?
SURE. THIS WHOLE AREA BELONGS TO MY SISTER.
UGALLU, BREAK UP THESE DRY BRANCHES, PLEASE!
SLASH
NNGAGAGAH!!
SLAAAASH
NICE AND WARM!!
AHH, CAMPFIRES ARE SO NIIICE!
TOO HOT... TOO NOISY!
WHO DARES INCUR MY WRATH?
SCARY!
DID YOU SAY SOMETHING?
?
NO, NOT A PEEP.
ANRI, HEAT THIS UP JUST RIGHT FOR ME.
I DON'T KNOW SQUAT ABOUT SAKE! DO IT YOURSELF!

I THINK YOU SHOULD JUST SMILE

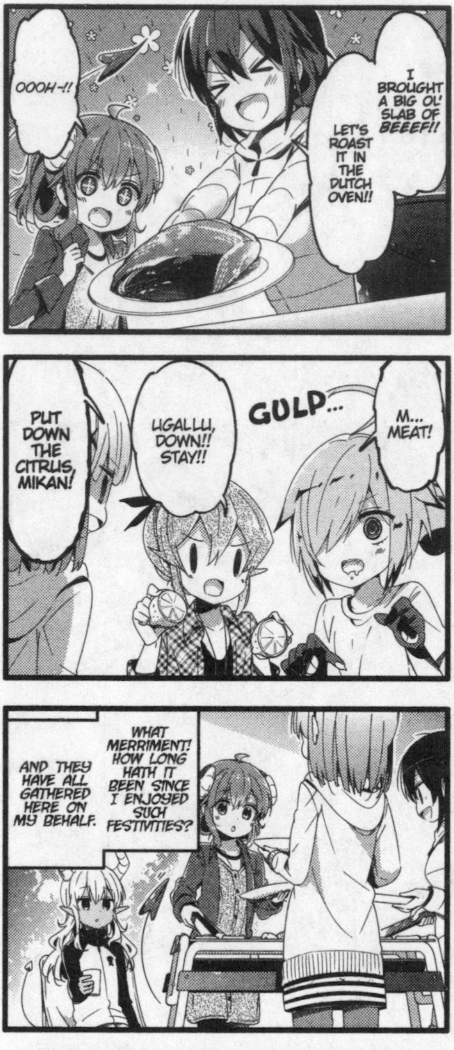
I BROUGHT A BIG OL' SLAB OF BEEEF!!
LET'S ROAST IT IN THE DUTCH OVEN!!
OOOH~!!
M... MEAT!
GULP...
UGALLU, DOWN!! STAY!!
PUT DOWN THE CITRUS, MIKAN!
WHAT MERRIMENT! HOW LONG HATH IT BEEN SINCE I ENJOYED SUCH FESTIVITIES?
AND THEY HAVE ALL GATHERED HERE ON MY BEHALF.
FIRST, LET US HAVE A MOMENT OF SILENCE FOR SHAMISEN'S LAST THREE DAYS.
OKAY, CHEERS!!
HOW AM I TO REACT TO SUCH A TOAST?

SIDE EFFECT OF CITRUS-BASED COCKTAILS

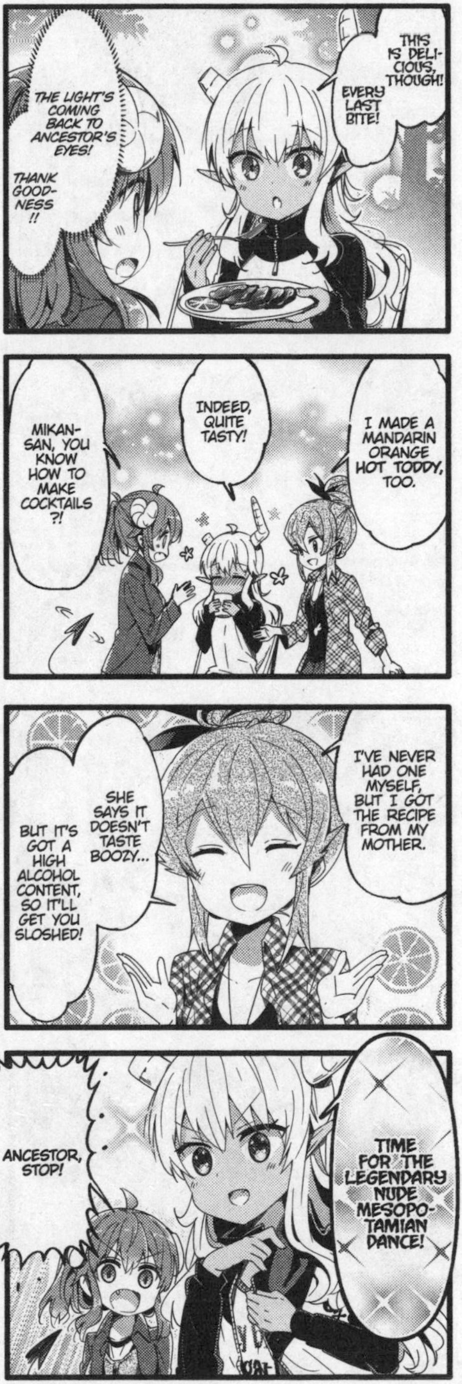

THIS IS DELICIOUS, THOUGH!
EVERY LAST BITE!
THE LIGHT'S COMING BACK TO ANCESTOR'S EYES!
THANK GOODNESS!!
I MADE A MANDARIN ORANGE HOT TODDY, TOO.
INDEED, QUITE TASTY!
MIKAN-SAN, YOU KNOW HOW TO MAKE COCKTAILS?!
I'VE NEVER HAD ONE MYSELF, BUT I GOT THE RECIPE FROM MY MOTHER.
SHE SAYS IT DOESN'T TASTE BOOZY...
BUT IT'S GOT A HIGH ALCOHOL CONTENT, SO IT'LL GET YOU SLOSHED!
TIME FOR THE LEGENDARY NUDE MESOPOTAMIAN DANCE!
ANCESTOR, STOP!

SHE'S SINGING A PUBLIC DOMAIN SONG

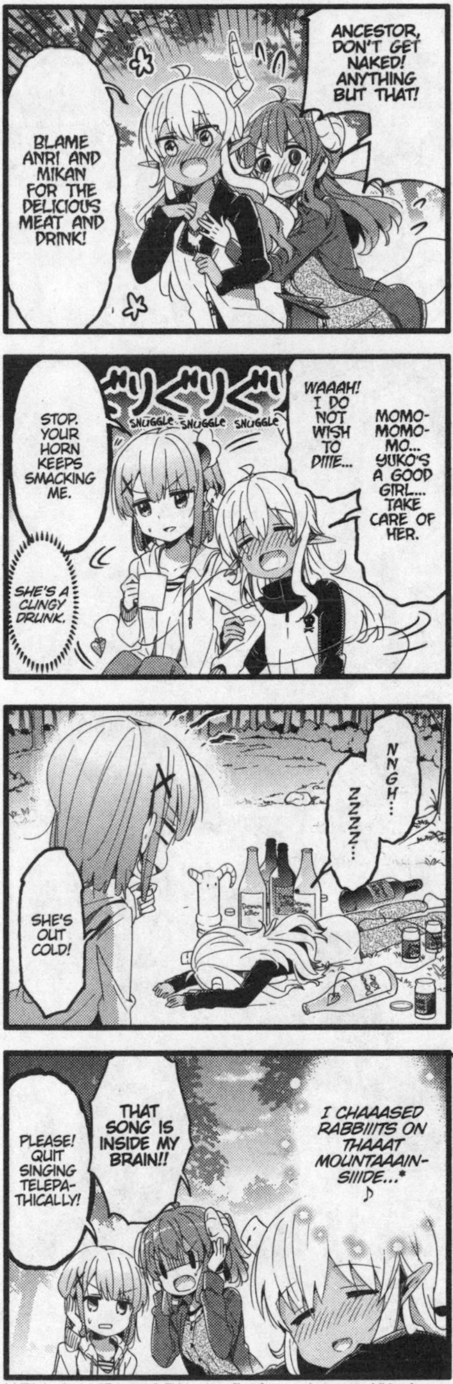

ANCESTOR, DON'T GET NAKED! ANYTHING BUT THAT!
BLAME ANRI AND MIKAN FOR THE DELICIOUS MEAT AND DRINK!
MOMOMOMO... YUKO'S A GOOD GIRL... TAKE CARE OF HER.
WAAAH! I DO NOT WISH TO DIIIE...
SNUGGLE SNUGGLE SNUGGLE
STOP. YOUR HORN KEEPS SMACKING ME.
SHE'S A CLINGY DRUNK.
NNGH...
ZZZZ...
SHE'S OUT COLD!
I CHAAASED RABBIIITS ON THAAAT MOUNTAAAIN-SIIIDE...* ♪
THAT SONG IS INSIDE MY BRAIN!!
PLEASE! QUIT SINGING TELEPATHICALLY!

** Lilith is singing "Furusato" ("Hometown"), a famous Japanese children's song.*

I DREW EVERY STAR WITH GREAT CARE

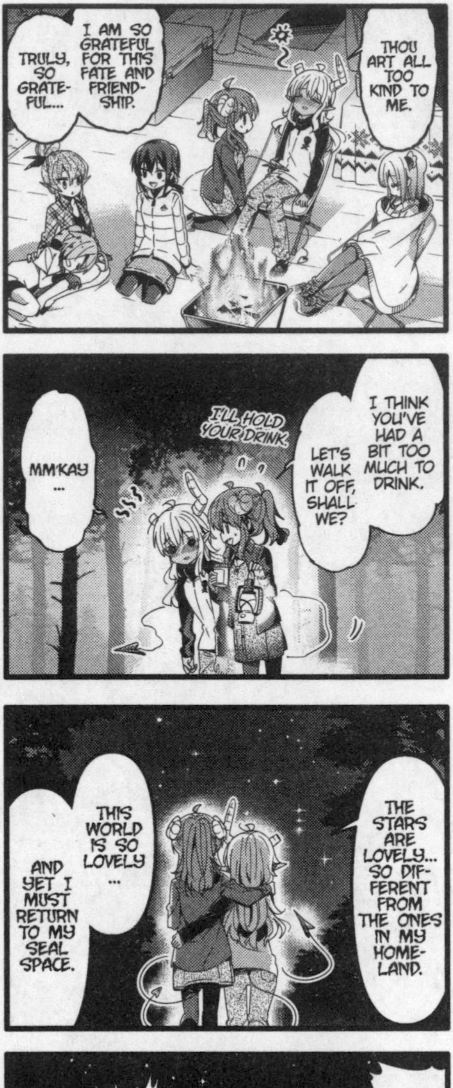
THOU ART ALL TOO KIND TO ME.
I AM SO GRATEFUL FOR THIS FATE AND FRIENDSHIP.
TRULY, SO GRATEFUL...
I THINK YOU'VE HAD A BIT TOO MUCH TO DRINK.
LET'S WALK IT OFF, SHALL WE?
I'LL HOLD YOUR DRINK.
MM'KAY ...
THE STARS ARE LOVELY... SO DIFFERENT FROM THE ONES IN MY HOMELAND.
THIS WORLD IS SO LOVELY ...
AND YET I MUST RETURN TO MY SEAL SPACE.
BLEEEEEEGH!!
ANCESTOOOOR!
PLEASE ENJOY THE NICE STARRY SKY WHILE ANCESTOR IS BARFING.

BEST USE OF THE STAFF YET

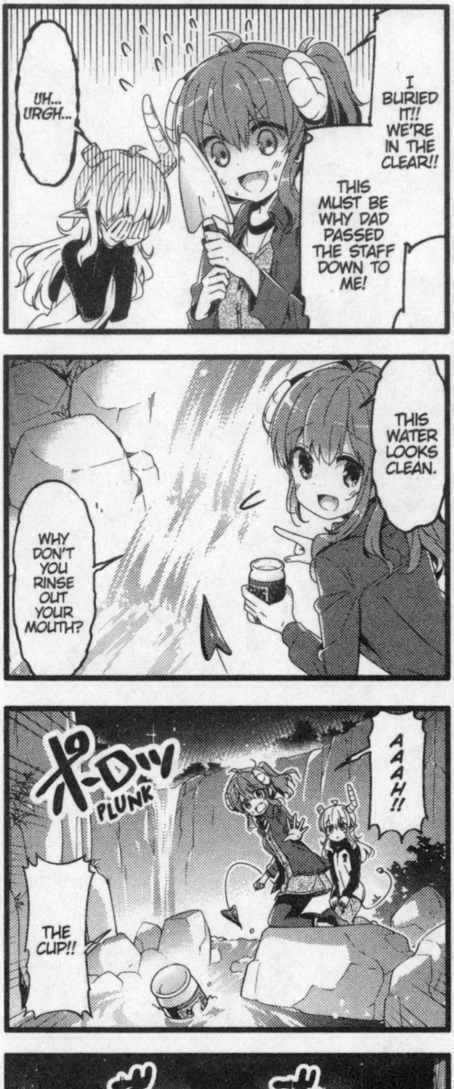
I BURIED IT!! WE'RE IN THE CLEAR!!
THIS MUST BE WHY DAD PASSED THE STAFF DOWN TO ME!
UH... URGH...
THIS WATER LOOKS CLEAN.
WHY DON'T YOU RINSE OUT YOUR MOUTH?
AAAAH!!
PLUNK
THE CUP!!
DO NOT...
DUUN
FLING TRASH...
DUN
INTO THE RIVER!!
?!

A DEMON IN SUDDEN DISTRESS

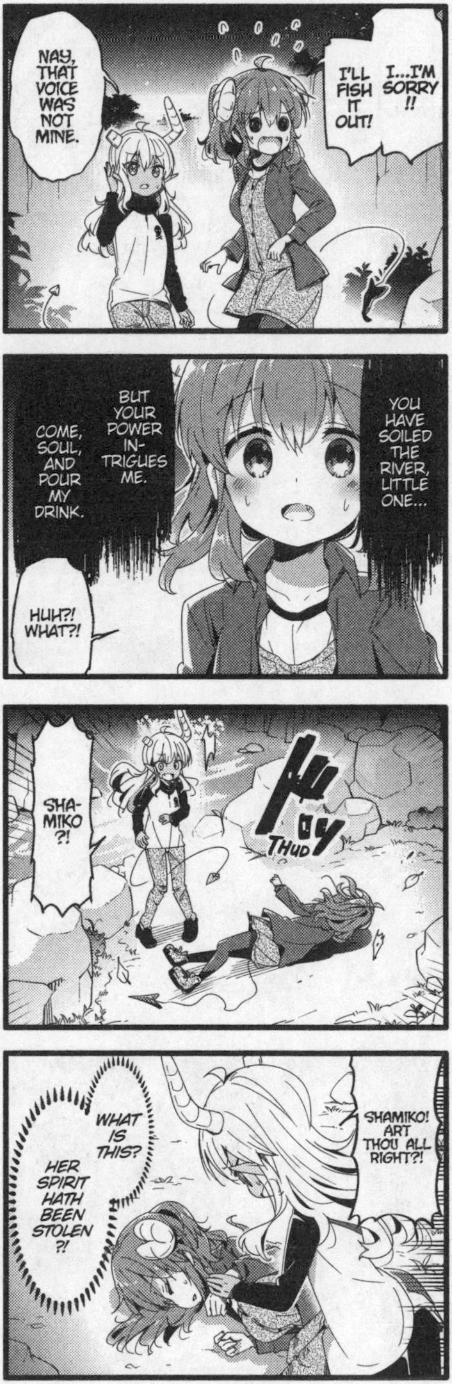
I...I'M SORRY!!
I'LL FISH IT OUT!
NAY, THAT VOICE WAS NOT MINE.
YOU HAVE SOILED THE RIVER, LITTLE ONE...
BUT YOUR POWER INTRIGUES ME.
COME, SOUL, AND POUR MY DRINK.
HUH?! WHAT?!
THUD
SHAMIKO?!
SHAMIKO! ART THOU ALL RIGHT?!
WHAT IS THIS?
HER SPIRIT HATH BEEN STOLEN?!

A DEMON IN A SNAKE

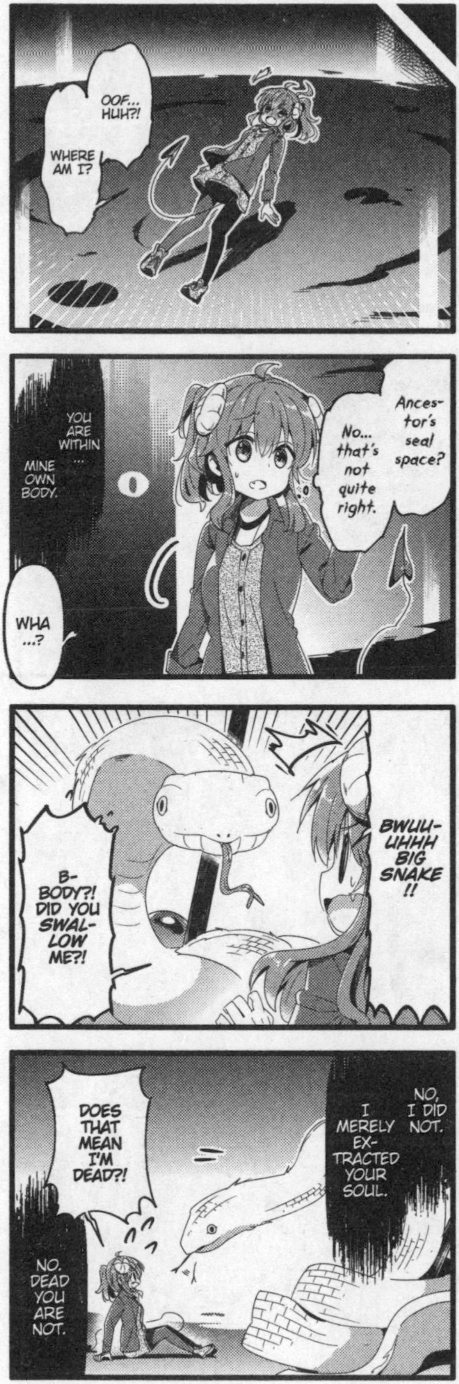
OOF... HUH?!
WHERE AM I?
Ancestor's seal space?
No... that's not quite right.
YOU ARE WITHIN... MINE OWN BODY.
WHA...?
BWUUUHHH BIG SNAKE!!
B-BODY?! DID YOU SWALLOW ME?!
NO, I DID NOT.
I MERELY EXTRACTED YOUR SOUL.
DOES THAT MEAN I'M DEAD?!
NO. DEAD YOU ARE NOT.

SURPRISINGLY KIND-HEARTED

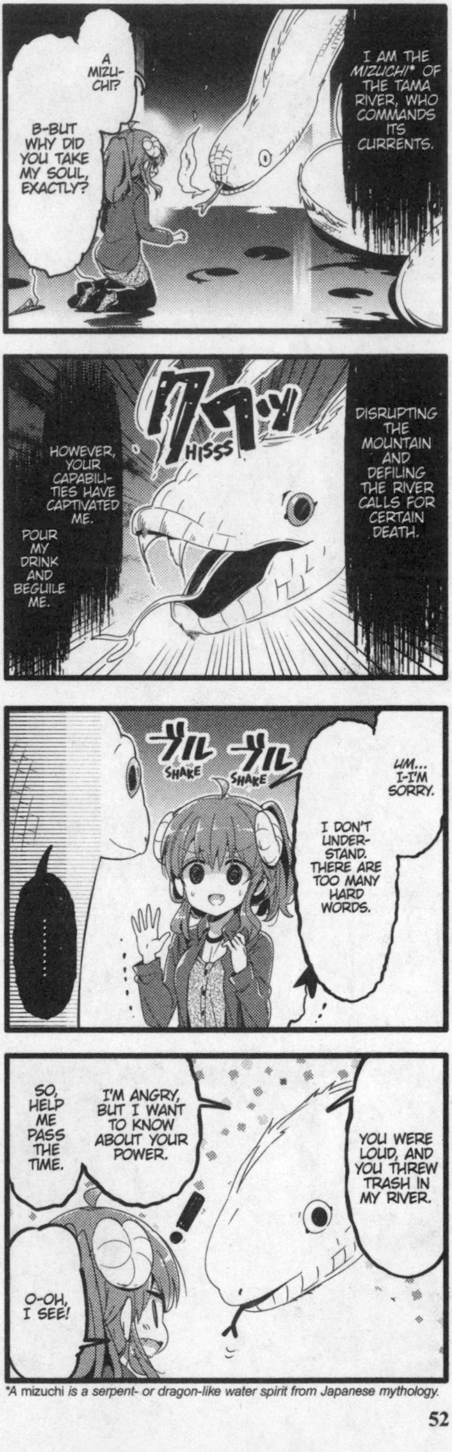
I AM THE MIZUCHI* OF THE TAMA RIVER, WHO COMMANDS ITS CURRENTS.
A MIZUCHI?
B-BUT WHY DID YOU TAKE MY SOUL, EXACTLY?
DISRUPTING THE MOUNTAIN AND DEFILING THE RIVER CALLS FOR CERTAIN DEATH.
HISSS
HOWEVER, YOUR CAPABILITIES HAVE CAPTIVATED ME.
POUR MY DRINK AND BEGUILE ME.
UM... I-I'M SORRY.
I DON'T UNDERSTAND. THERE ARE TOO MANY HARD WORDS.
SHAKE
SHAKE
......
YOU WERE LOUD, AND YOU THREW TRASH IN MY RIVER.
I'M ANGRY, BUT I WANT TO KNOW ABOUT YOUR POWER.
SO, HELP ME PASS THE TIME.
!
O-OH, I SEE!

*A mizuchi is a serpent- or dragon-like water spirit from Japanese mythology.

SMARTPHONES ARE NO GOOD HERE

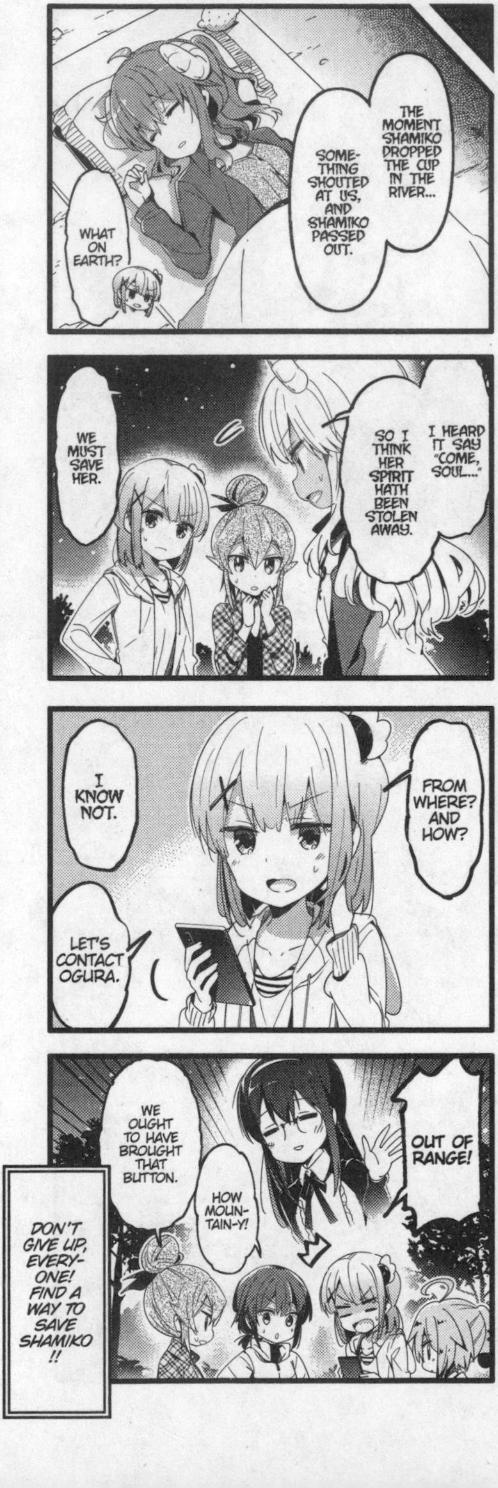
THE MOMENT SHAMIKO DROPPED THE CUP IN THE RIVER...
SOMETHING SHOUTED AT US, AND SHAMIKO PASSED OUT.
WHAT ON EARTH?
I HEARD IT SAY "COME, SOUL..."
SO I THINK HER SPIRIT HATH BEEN STOLEN AWAY.
WE MUST SAVE HER.
FROM WHERE? AND HOW?
I KNOW NOT.
LET'S CONTACT OGURA.
OUT OF RANGE!
WE OUGHT TO HAVE BROUGHT THAT BUTTON.
HOW MOUNTAIN-Y!
DON'T GIVE UP, EVERYONE! FIND A WAY TO SAVE SHAMIKO!!

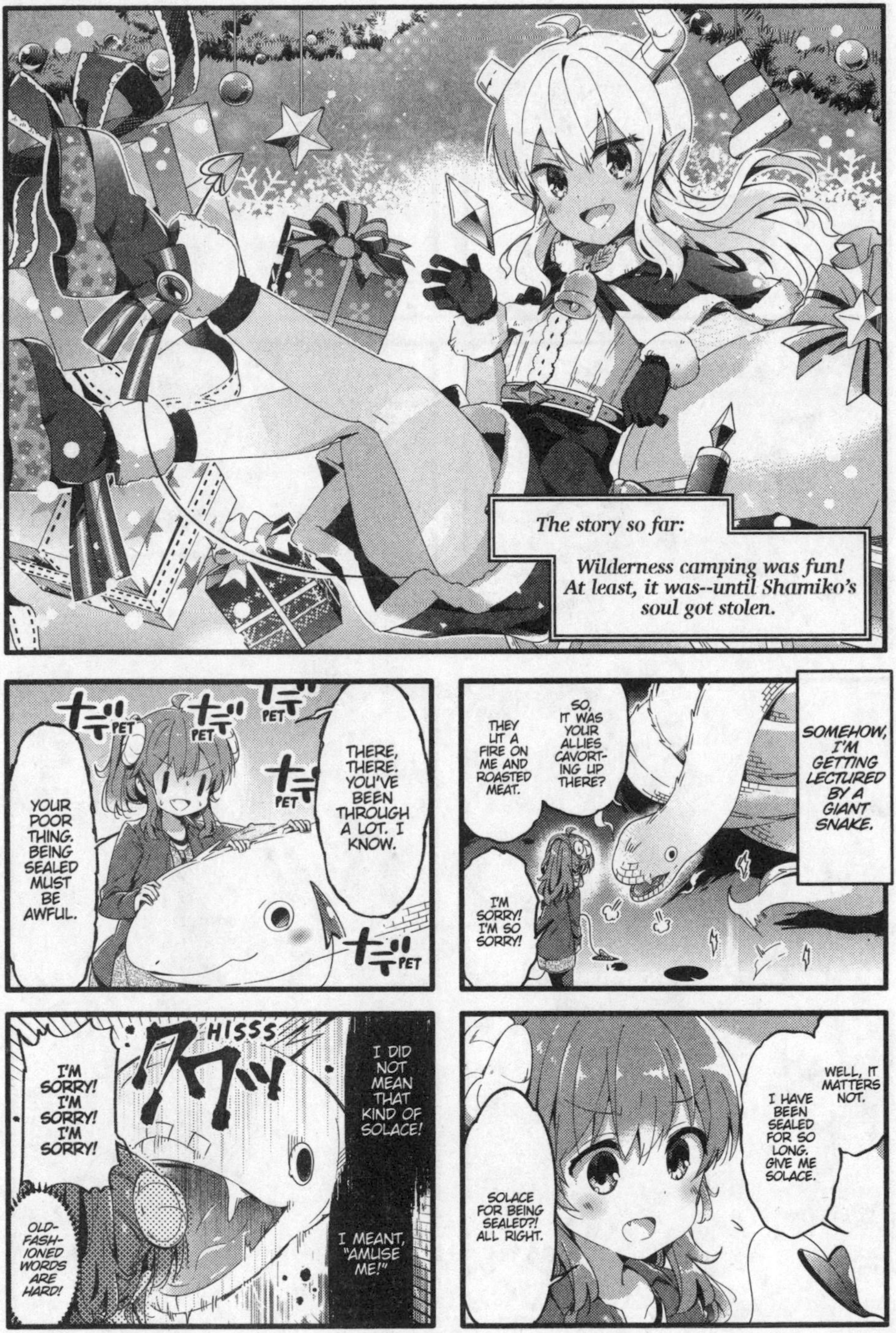
The story so far:
Wilderness camping was fun! At least, it was--until Shamiko's soul got stolen.
SOMEHOW, I'M GETTING LECTURED BY A GIANT SNAKE.
SO, IT WAS YOUR ALLIES CAVORTING UP THERE?
THEY LIT A FIRE ON ME AND ROASTED MEAT.
I'M SORRY! I'M SO SORRY!
PET
PET
PET
PET
THERE, THERE. YOU'VE BEEN THROUGH A LOT. I KNOW.
YOUR POOR THING. BEING SEALED MUST BE AWFUL.
PET
WELL, IT MATTERS NOT.
I HAVE BEEN SEALED FOR SO LONG. GIVE ME SOLACE.
SOLACE FOR BEING SEALED?! ALL RIGHT.
I DID NOT MEAN THAT KIND OF SOLACE!
I MEANT, "AMUSE ME!"
HISSS
I'M SORRY! I'M SORRY! I'M SORRY!
OLD-FASHIONED WORDS ARE HARD!

ANCESTOR CHOOSES HER WORDS

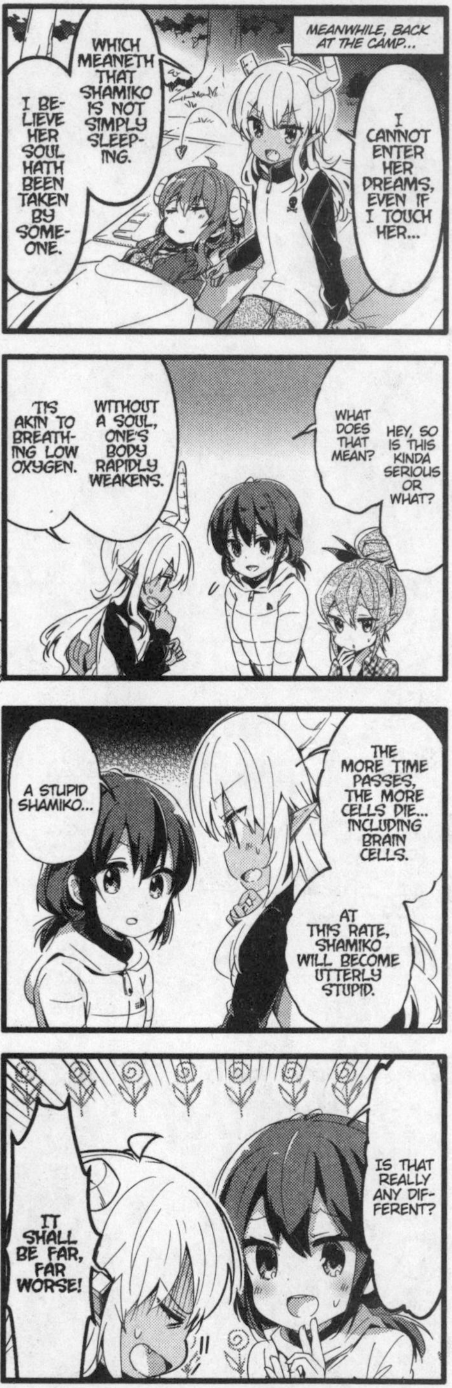
MEANWHILE, BACK AT THE CAMP...
I CANNOT ENTER HER DREAMS, EVEN IF I TOUCH HER...
WHICH MEANETH THAT SHAMIKO IS NOT SIMPLY SLEEPING.
I BELIEVE HER SOUL HATH BEEN TAKEN BY SOMEONE.
HEY, SO IS THIS KINDA SERIOUS OR WHAT?
WHAT DOES THAT MEAN?
WITHOUT A SOUL, ONE'S BODY RAPIDLY WEAKENS.
'TIS AKIN TO BREATHING LOW OXYGEN.
THE MORE TIME PASSES, THE MORE CELLS DIE... INCLUDING BRAIN CELLS.
AT THIS RATE, SHAMIKO WILL BECOME UTTERLY STUPID.
A STUPID SHAMIKO...
IS THAT REALLY ANY DIFFERENT?
IT SHALL BE FAR, FAR WORSE!

FRESH PEACH SIMPLE LOG

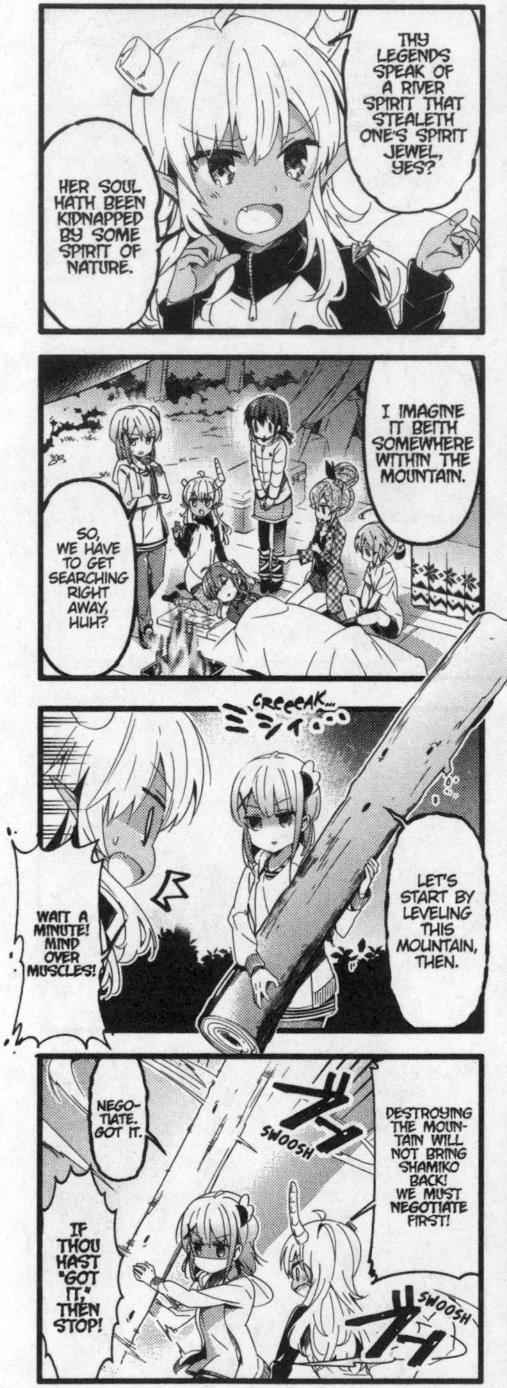
THY LEGENDS SPEAK OF A RIVER SPIRIT THAT STEALETH ONE'S SPIRIT JEWEL, YES?
HER SOUL HATH BEEN KIDNAPPED BY SOME SPIRIT OF NATURE.
I IMAGINE IT BEITH SOMEWHERE WITHIN THE MOUNTAIN.
SO, WE HAVE TO GET SEARCHING RIGHT AWAY, HUH?
CREEEAK...
LET'S START BY LEVELING THIS MOUNTAIN, THEN.
WAIT A MINUTE! MIND OVER MUSCLES!
DESTROYING THE MOUNTAIN WILL NOT BRING SHAMIKO BACK! WE MUST NEGOTIATE FIRST!
SWOOSH
NEGOTIATE. GOT IT.
SWOOSH
IF THOU HAST "GOT IT," THEN STOP!

SUM IT UP A LITTLE SHORTER

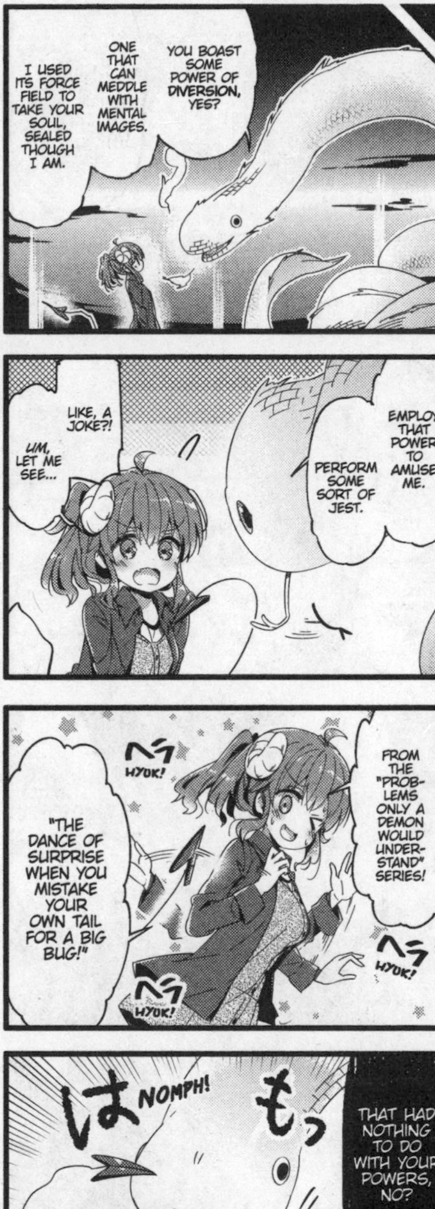
YOU BOAST SOME POWER OF DIVERSION, YES?
ONE THAT CAN MEDDLE WITH MENTAL IMAGES.
I USED ITS FORCE FIELD TO TAKE YOUR SOUL, SEALED THOUGH I AM.
EMPLOY THAT POWER TO AMUSE ME.
PERFORM SOME SORT OF JEST.
LIKE, A JOKE?!
UM, LET ME SEE...
FROM THE "PROBLEMS ONLY A DEMON WOULD UNDERSTAND" SERIES!
ヘラ HYOK!
"THE DANCE OF SURPRISE WHEN YOU MISTAKE YOUR OWN TAIL FOR A BIG BUG!"
ヘラ HYOK!
ヘラ HYOK!
THAT HAD NOTHING TO DO WITH YOUR POWERS, NO?
はもっ NOMPH!
I'M SORRY! PLEASE DON'T EAT ME!

UNNECESSARY INFORMATION

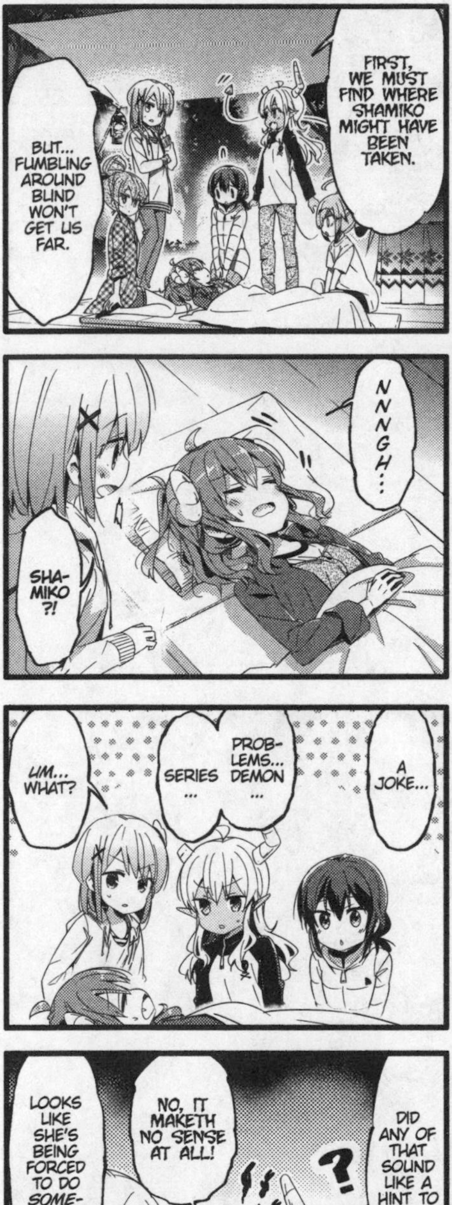
FIRST, WE MUST FIND WHERE SHAMIKO MIGHT HAVE BEEN TAKEN.
BUT... FUMBLING AROUND BLIND WON'T GET US FAR.
NNNGH...
SHA-MIKO?!
A JOKE...
PROB-LEMS... DEMON ...
SERIES ...
UM... WHAT?
DID ANY OF THAT SOUND LIKE A HINT TO YOU?
NO, IT MAKETH NO SENSE AT ALL!
LOOKS LIKE SHE'S BEING FORCED TO DO SOME-THING.

GLOWING DIAMONDS, AN ANCESTRAL TECHNIQUE

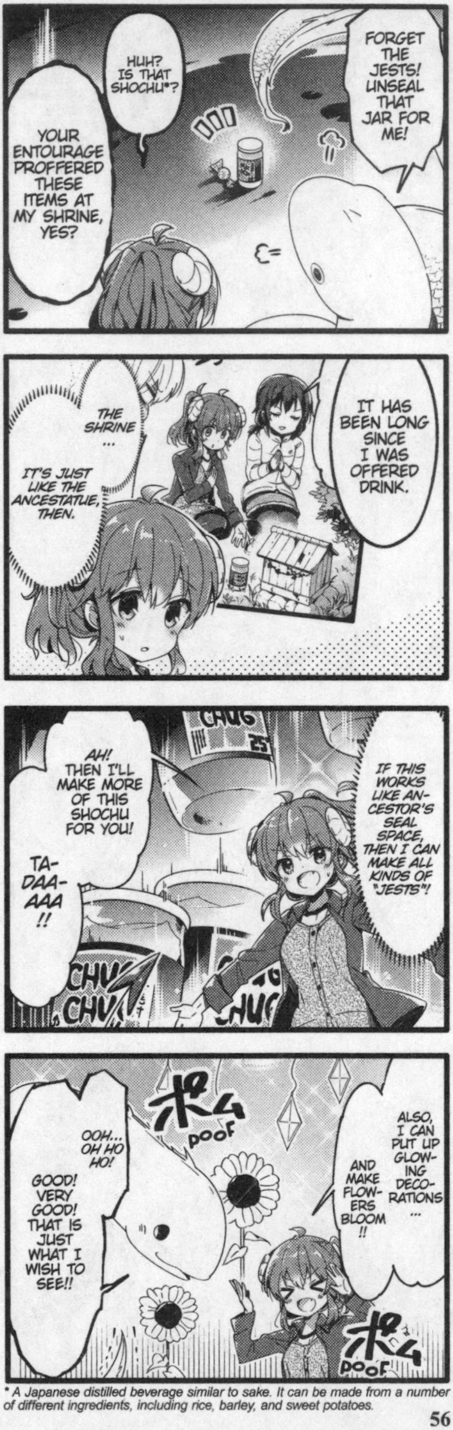
FORGET THE JESTS! UNSEAL THAT JAR FOR ME!
HUH? IS THAT SHOCHU*?
YOUR ENTOURAGE PROFFERED THESE ITEMS AT MY SHRINE, YES?
IT HAS BEEN LONG SINCE I WAS OFFERED DRINK.
THE SHRINE ...
IT'S JUST LIKE THE ANCESTATUE, THEN.
CHUG
IF THIS WORKS LIKE ANCESTOR'S SEAL SPACE, THEN I CAN MAKE ALL KINDS OF "JESTS"!
AH! THEN I'LL MAKE MORE OF THIS SHOCHU FOR YOU!
TA-DAAA-AAA!!
ALSO, I CAN PUT UP GLOWING DECORATIONS ...
AND MAKE FLOWERS BLOOM!!
ポム
POOF
OOH... OH HO HO!
GOOD! VERY GOOD! THAT IS JUST WHAT I WISH TO SEE!!
ポム
POOF

NO ONE CAN EVER KNOW

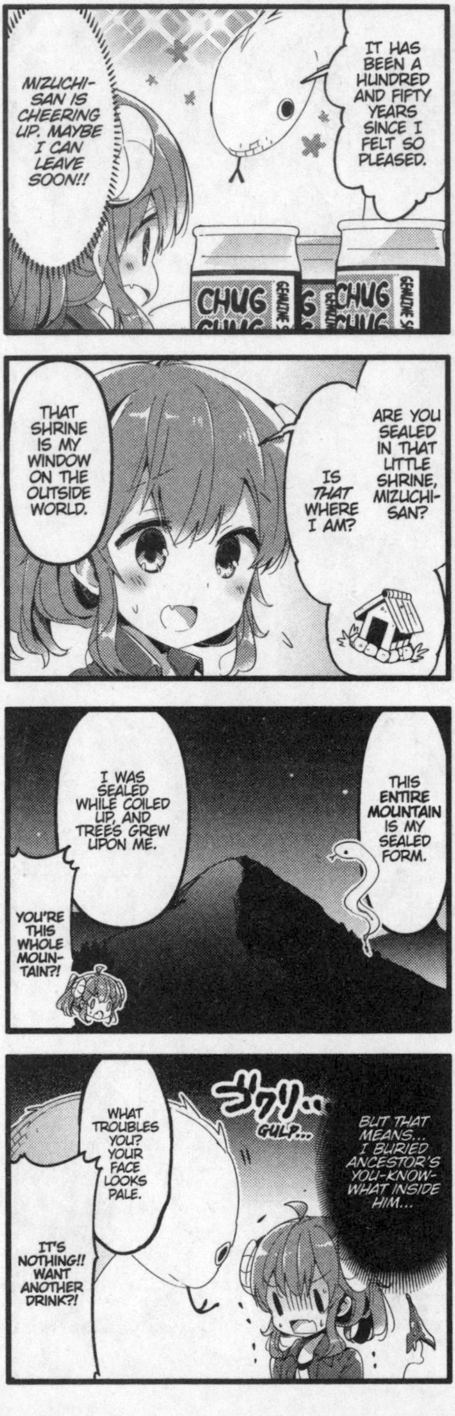
IT HAS BEEN A HUNDRED AND FIFTY YEARS SINCE I FELT SO PLEASED.
MIZUCHI-SAN IS CHEERING UP. MAYBE I CAN LEAVE SOON!!
CHUG
ARE YOU SEALED IN THAT LITTLE SHRINE, MIZUCHI-SAN?
IS THAT WHERE I AM?
THAT SHRINE IS MY WINDOW ON THE OUTSIDE WORLD.
THIS ENTIRE MOUNTAIN IS MY SEALED FORM.
I WAS SEALED WHILE COILED UP, AND TREES GREW UPON ME.
YOU'RE THIS WHOLE MOUNTAIN?!
BUT THAT MEANS... I BURIED ANCESTOR'S YOU-KNOW-WHAT INSIDE HIM...
ゴクリ..
GULP...
WHAT TROUBLES YOU? YOUR FACE LOOKS PALE.
IT'S NOTHING!! WANT ANOTHER DRINK?!

* *A Japanese distilled beverage similar to sake. It can be made from a number of different ingredients, including rice, barley, and sweet potatoes.*

MOMO'S NUMBER ONE FAN

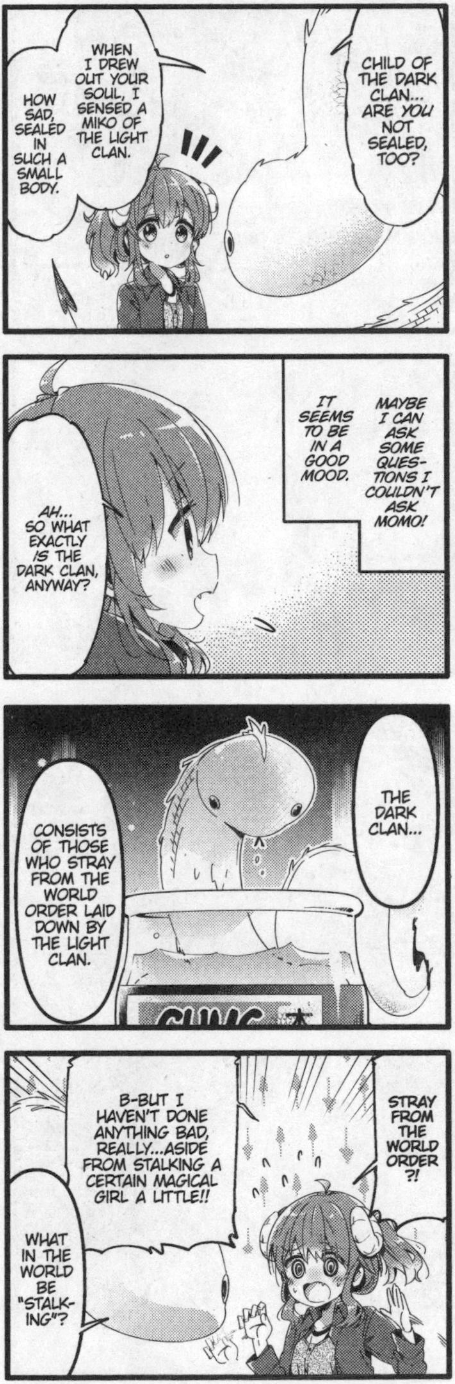
CHILD OF THE DARK CLAN... ARE YOU NOT SEALED, TOO?
WHEN I DREW OUT YOUR SOUL, I SENSED A MIKO OF THE LIGHT CLAN.
HOW SAD, SEALED IN SUCH A SMALL BODY.
MAYBE I CAN ASK SOME QUESTIONS I COULDN'T ASK MOMO!
IT SEEMS TO BE IN A GOOD MOOD.
AH... SO WHAT EXACTLY IS THE DARK CLAN, ANYWAY?
THE DARK CLAN...
CONSISTS OF THOSE WHO STRAY FROM THE WORLD ORDER LAID DOWN BY THE LIGHT CLAN.
STRAY FROM THE WORLD ORDER?!
B-BUT I HAVEN'T DONE ANYTHING BAD, REALLY...ASIDE FROM STALKING A CERTAIN MAGICAL GIRL A LITTLE!!
WHAT IN THE WORLD BE "STALKING"?

THE TRUE NATURE OF THE LIGHT CLAN, REVEALED!

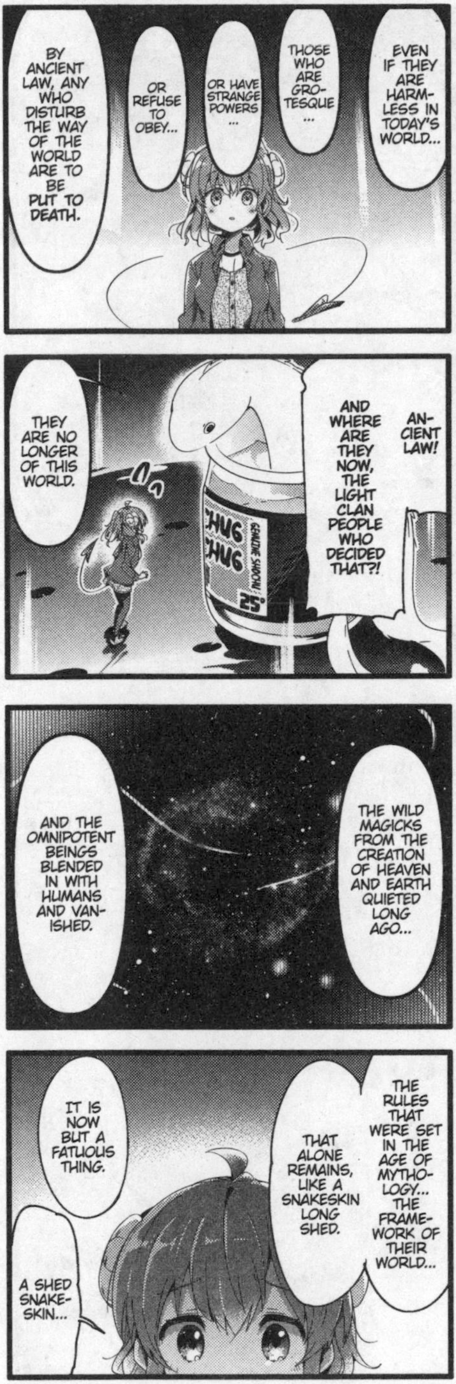
EVEN IF THEY ARE HARMLESS IN TODAY'S WORLD...
THOSE WHO ARE GROTESQUE...
OR HAVE STRANGE POWERS...
OR REFUSE TO OBEY...
BY ANCIENT LAW, ANY WHO DISTURB THE WAY OF THE WORLD ARE TO BE PUT TO DEATH.
ANCIENT LAW!
AND WHERE ARE THEY NOW, THE LIGHT CLAN PEOPLE WHO DECIDED THAT?!
CHUG CHUG
25°
THEY ARE NO LONGER OF THIS WORLD.
THE WILD MAGICKS FROM THE CREATION OF HEAVEN AND EARTH QUIETED LONG AGO...
AND THE OMNIPOTENT BEINGS BLENDED IN WITH HUMANS AND VANISHED.
THE RULES THAT WERE SET IN THE AGE OF MYTHOLOGY... THE FRAMEWORK OF THEIR WORLD...
THAT ALONE REMAINS, LIKE A SNAKESKIN LONG SHED.
IT IS NOW BUT A FATUOUS THING.
A SHED SNAKESKIN...

SUCCEEDED A LITTLE TOO WELL

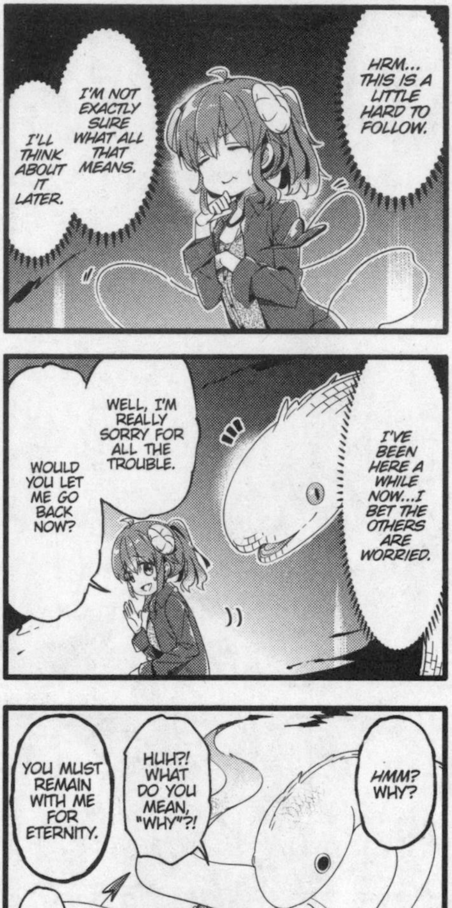
HRM... THIS IS A LITTLE HARD TO FOLLOW.
I'M NOT EXACTLY SURE WHAT ALL THAT MEANS.
I'LL THINK ABOUT IT LATER.
I'VE BEEN HERE A WHILE NOW...I BET THE OTHERS ARE WORRIED.
WELL, I'M REALLY SORRY FOR ALL THE TROUBLE.
WOULD YOU LET ME GO BACK NOW?
HMM? WHY?
HUH?! WHAT DO YOU MEAN, "WHY"?!
YOU MUST REMAIN WITH ME FOR ETERNITY.
......?
I HAVE TAKEN A LIKING TO YOU.
THEREFORE, YOU SHALL GIVE ME SOLACE FOREVER!!
WH... WHAAAAAA?!

WHAT'S THE POINT OF FAKE TREASURE?

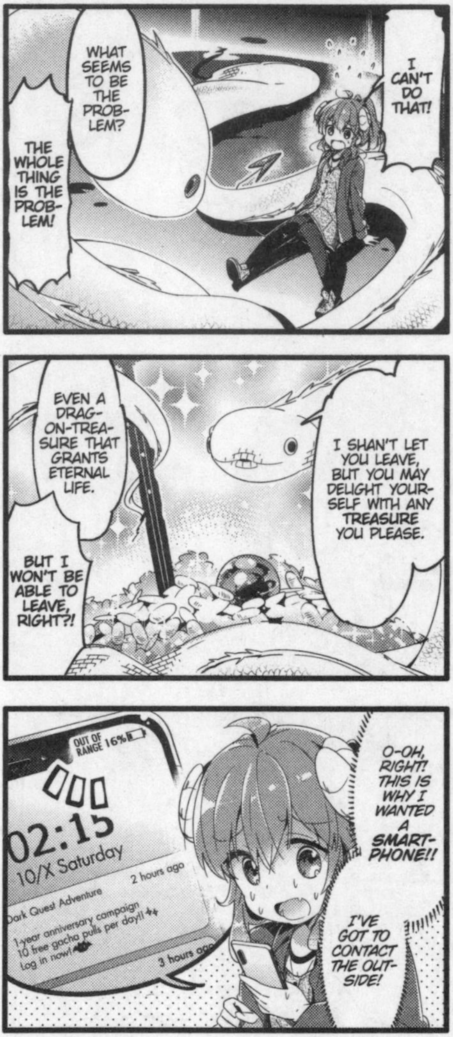
I CAN'T DO THAT!
WHAT SEEMS TO BE THE PROBLEM?
THE WHOLE THING IS THE PROBLEM!
I SHAN'T LET YOU LEAVE, BUT YOU MAY DELIGHT YOURSELF WITH ANY TREASURE YOU PLEASE.
EVEN A DRAGON-TREASURE THAT GRANTS ETERNAL LIFE.
BUT I WON'T BE ABLE TO LEAVE, RIGHT?!
O-OH, RIGHT! THIS IS WHY I WANTED A SMARTPHONE!!
I'VE GOT TO CONTACT THE OUTSIDE!
OUT OF RANGE 16%
02:15
10/X Saturday
2 hours ago
Dark Quest Adventure
1-year anniversary campaign
10 free gacha pulls per day!!
Log in now!
3 hours ago
BUT I'M PAYING OVER TEN THOUSAND YEN A MOOONTH!!
IF IT IS GOLD YOU DESIRE, THERE IS PLENTY TO BE HAD RIGHT HERE.
BUT I WON'T BE ABLE TO LEAVE, RIIIGHT?!

BECOME A DEMON WHO'S GOOD AT MAKING CONTACT

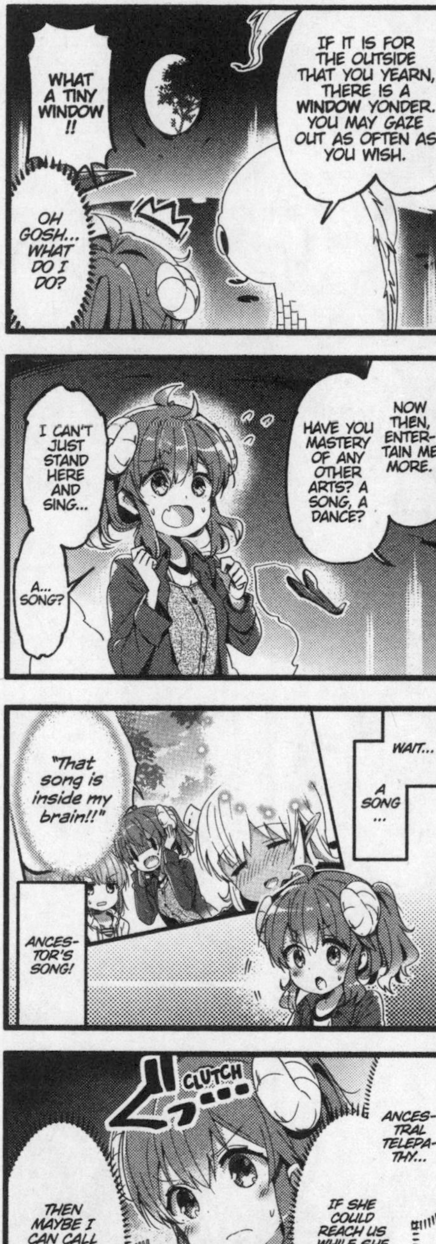
IF IT IS FOR THE OUTSIDE THAT YOU YEARN, THERE IS A WINDOW YONDER. YOU MAY GAZE OUT AS OFTEN AS YOU WISH.
WHAT A TINY WINDOW !!
OH GOSH... WHAT DO I DO?
NOW THEN, ENTERTAIN ME MORE.
HAVE YOU MASTERY OF ANY OTHER ARTS? A SONG, A DANCE?
I CAN'T JUST STAND HERE AND SING...
A... SONG?
WAIT...
A SONG ...
"That song is inside my brain!!"
ANCESTOR'S SONG!
CLUTCH
ANCESTRAL TELEPATHY...
IF SHE COULD REACH US WHILE SHE WAS SO LOW ON ENERGY...
THEN MAYBE I CAN CALL FOR HELP FROM IN HERE, TOO!!

MAX VOLUME FROM THE GET-GO

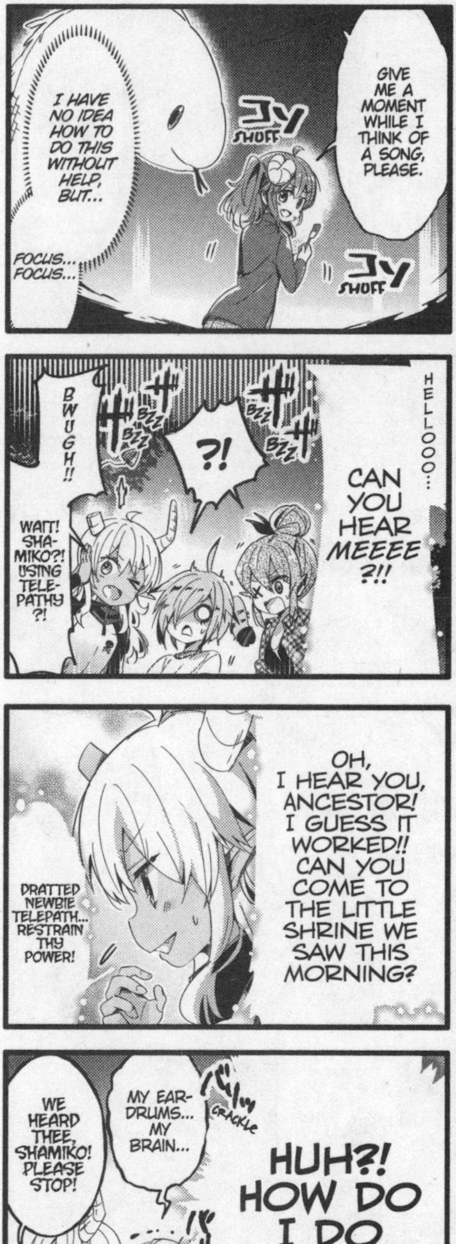
GIVE ME A MOMENT WHILE I THINK OF A SONG, PLEASE.
SHUFF
I HAVE NO IDEA HOW TO DO THIS WITHOUT HELP, BUT...
FOCUS... FOCUS...
SHUFF
HELLOOO...
CAN YOU HEAR MEEEE?!!
BZZ
BZZ
?!
BZZ
BZZ
BWUGH!!
WAIT! SHAMIKO?! USING TELEPATHY?!
OH, I HEAR YOU, ANCESTOR! I GUESS IT WORKED!! CAN YOU COME TO THE LITTLE SHRINE WE SAW THIS MORNING?
DRATTED NEWBIE TELEPATH... RESTRAIN THY POWER!
HUH?! HOW DO I DO THAT?!
CRACKLE
MY EARDRUMS... MY BRAIN...
WE HEARD THEE, SHAMIKO! PLEASE STOP!
CRACKLE
CRACKLE

MIKAN WANTS THE HIGH GROUND

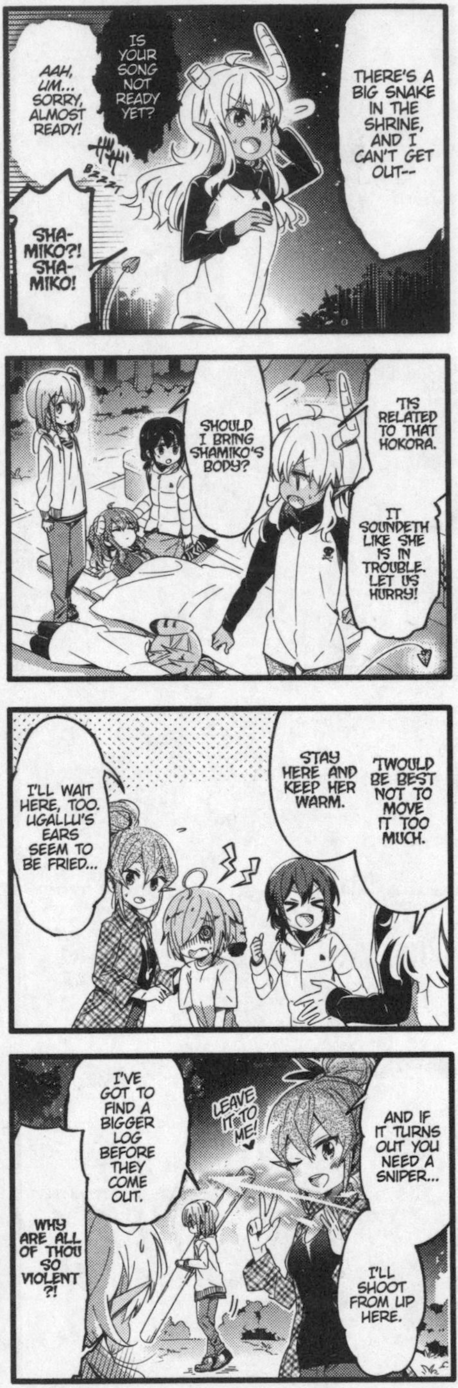
THERE'S A BIG SNAKE IN THE SHRINE, AND I CAN'T GET OUT--
IS YOUR SONG NOT READY YET?
AAH, UM... SORRY, ALMOST READY!
BZZZT
SHAMIKO?! SHAMIKO!
'TIS RELATED TO THAT HOKORA.
IT SOUNDETH LIKE SHE IS IN TROUBLE. LET US HURRY!
SHOULD I BRING SHAMIKO'S BODY?
'TWOULD BE BEST NOT TO MOVE IT TOO MUCH.
STAY HERE AND KEEP HER WARM.
I'LL WAIT HERE, TOO. UGALLU'S EARS SEEM TO BE FRIED...
AND IF IT TURNS OUT YOU NEED A SNIPER...
I'LL SHOOT FROM UP HERE.
LEAVE IT TO ME!
I'VE GOT TO FIND A BIGGER LOG BEFORE THEY COME OUT.
WHY ARE ALL OF THOU SO VIOLENT?!

BECOME A DEMON WHO'S GOOD WITH HER TAIL

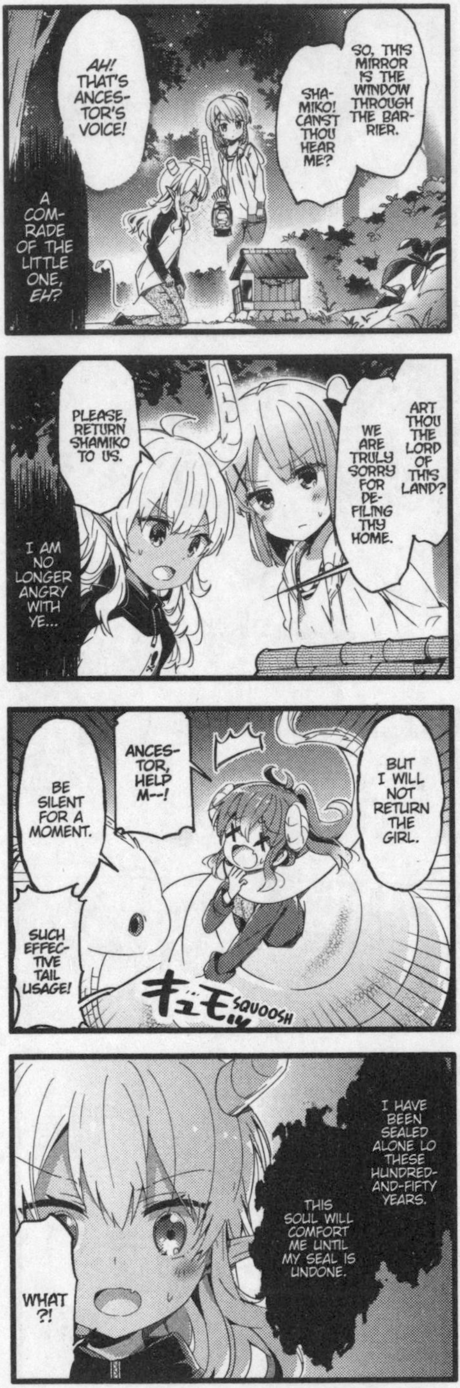
SO, THIS MIRROR IS THE WINDOW THROUGH THE BARRIER.
SHAMIKO! CANST THOU HEAR ME?
AH! THAT'S ANCESTOR'S VOICE!
A COMRADE OF THE LITTLE ONE, EH?
ART THOU THE LORD OF THIS LAND?
WE ARE TRULY SORRY FOR DEFILING THY HOME.
PLEASE, RETURN SHAMIKO TO US.
I AM NO LONGER ANGRY WITH YE...
BUT I WILL NOT RETURN THE GIRL.
ANCESTOR, HELP M--!
BE SILENT FOR A MOMENT.
SUCH EFFECTIVE TAIL USAGE!
キュモッ SQUOOSH
I HAVE BEEN SEALED ALONE LO THESE HUNDRED-AND-FIFTY YEARS.
THIS SOUL WILL COMFORT ME UNTIL MY SEAL IS UNDONE.
WHAT?!

ANCESTOR'S EQUIVALENT SOUL EXCHANGE

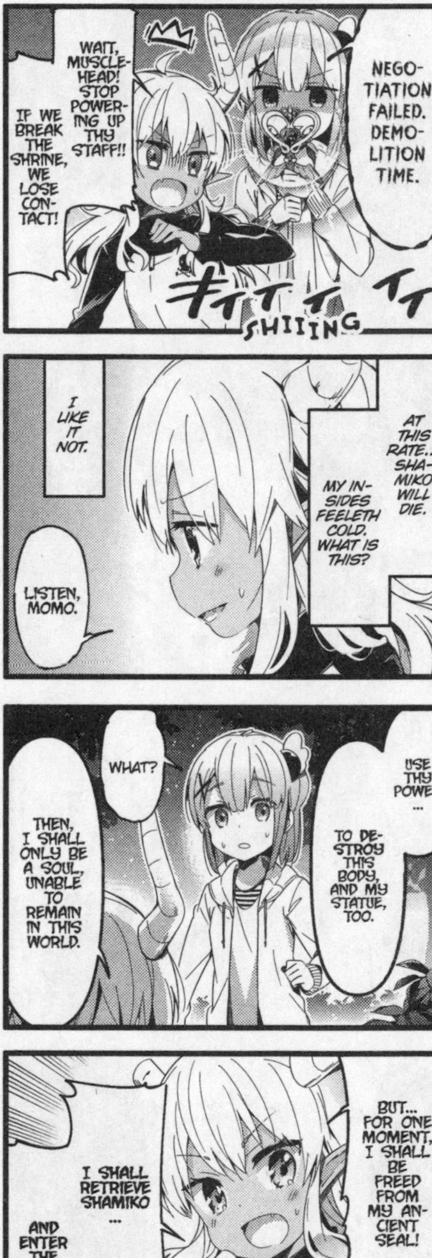
NEGOTIATION FAILED. DEMOLITION TIME.
WAIT, MUSCLEHEAD! STOP POWERING UP THY STAFF!!
IF WE BREAK THE SHRINE, WE LOSE CONTACT!
SHIIING
AT THIS RATE... SHAMIKO WILL DIE.
MY INSIDES FEELETH COLD. WHAT IS THIS?
I LIKE IT NOT.
LISTEN, MOMO.
USE THY POWER...
TO DESTROY THIS BODY, AND MY STATUE, TOO.
WHAT?
THEN, I SHALL ONLY BE A SOUL, UNABLE TO REMAIN IN THIS WORLD.
BUT... FOR ONE MOMENT, I SHALL BE FREED FROM MY ANCIENT SEAL!
I SHALL RETRIEVE SHAMIKO...
AND ENTER THE SHRINE IN HER STEAD!

DON'T BURY THE LEDE

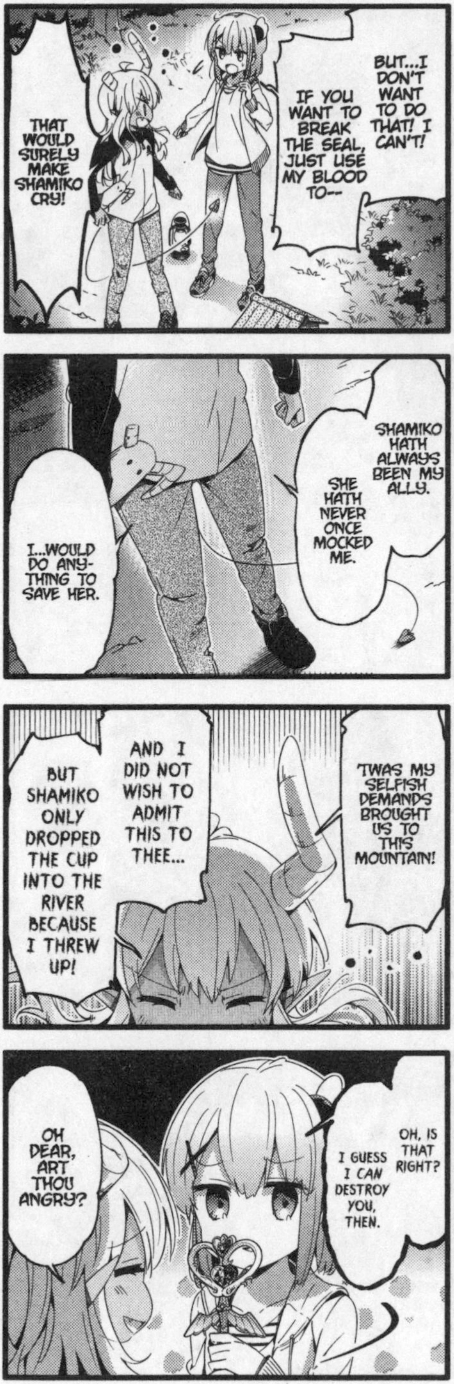
BUT...I DON'T WANT TO DO THAT! I CAN'T!
IF YOU WANT TO BREAK THE SEAL, JUST USE MY BLOOD TO--
THAT WOULD SURELY MAKE SHAMIKO CRY!
SHAMIKO HATH ALWAYS BEEN MY ALLY.
SHE HATH NEVER ONCE MOCKED ME.
I...WOULD DO ANYTHING TO SAVE HER.
'TWAS MY SELFISH DEMANDS BROUGHT US TO THIS MOUNTAIN!
AND I DID NOT WISH TO ADMIT THIS TO THEE...
BUT SHAMIKO ONLY DROPPED THE CUP INTO THE RIVER BECAUSE I THREW UP!
OH, IS THAT RIGHT?
I GUESS I CAN DESTROY YOU, THEN.
OH DEAR, ART THOU ANGRY?

ANCESTRAL BODY BLOW

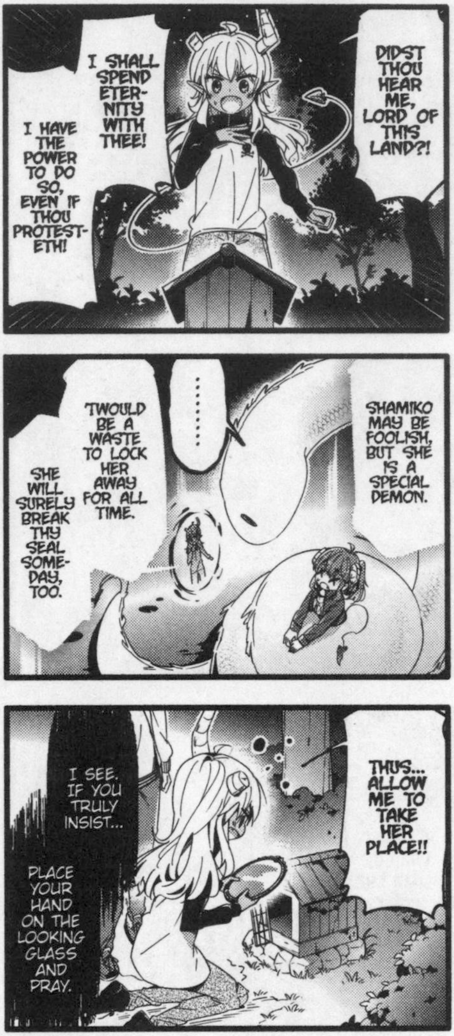
DIDST THOU HEAR ME, LORD OF THIS LAND?!
I SHALL SPEND ETERNITY WITH THEE!
I HAVE THE POWER TO DO SO, EVEN IF THOU PROTESTETH!
SHAMIKO MAY BE FOOLISH, BUT SHE IS A SPECIAL DEMON.
......
'TWOULD BE A WASTE TO LOCK HER AWAY FOR ALL TIME.
SHE WILL SURELY BREAK THY SEAL SOMEDAY, TOO.
THUS... ALLOW ME TO TAKE HER PLACE!!
I SEE. IF YOU TRULY INSIST...
PLACE YOUR HAND ON THE LOOKING GLASS AND PRAY.
FLASH
OOOPH!!!
WH-WHAT IN...?!

REJECTED ROOMMATE REQUEST

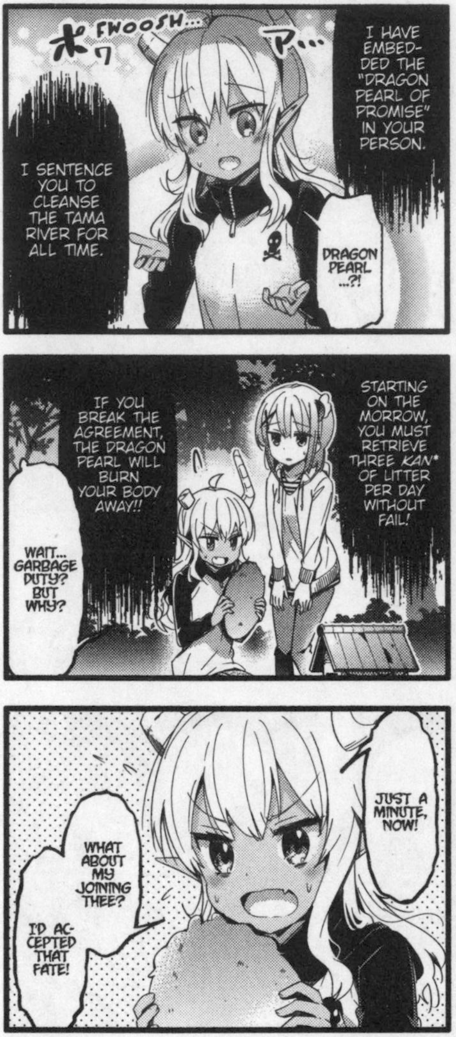
I HAVE EMBEDDED THE "DRAGON PEARL OF PROMISE" IN YOUR PERSON.
ア...
FWOOSH...
DRAGON PEARL ...?!
I SENTENCE YOU TO CLEANSE THE TAMA RIVER FOR ALL TIME.
STARTING ON THE MORROW, YOU MUST RETRIEVE THREE *KAN** OF LITTER PER DAY WITHOUT FAIL!
IF YOU BREAK THE AGREEMENT, THE DRAGON PEARL WILL BURN YOUR BODY AWAY!!
WAIT... GARBAGE DUTY? BUT WHY?
JUST A MINUTE, NOW!
WHAT ABOUT MY JOINING THEE?
I'D ACCEPTED THAT FATE!
I DO NOT WISH TO SPEND ETERNITY WITH YOU.
I DOUBT CONVERSING WITH YOU WOULD AMUSE ME.
MAKES SENSE.
EH?
SO, I HAVE DEVISED AN ALTERNATIVE.

**A kan is an obsolete unit of measurement, weighing approximately 6.6 pounds.*

A HEAVY QUOTA

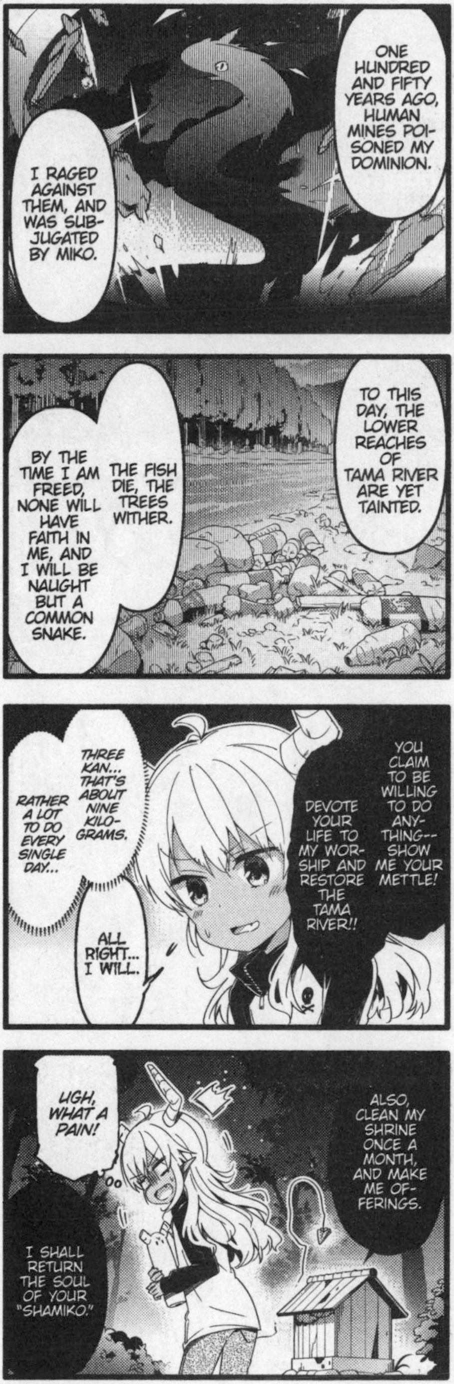
ONE HUNDRED AND FIFTY YEARS AGO, HUMAN MINES POISONED MY DOMINION.
I RAGED AGAINST THEM, AND WAS SUBJUGATED BY MIKO.
TO THIS DAY, THE LOWER REACHES OF TAMA RIVER ARE YET TAINTED.
THE FISH DIE, THE TREES WITHER.
BY THE TIME I AM FREED, NONE WILL HAVE FAITH IN ME, AND I WILL BE NAUGHT BUT A COMMON SNAKE.
YOU CLAIM TO BE WILLING TO DO ANYTHING--SHOW ME YOUR METTLE!
DEVOTE YOUR LIFE TO MY WORSHIP AND RESTORE THE TAMA RIVER!!
THREE KAN... THAT'S ABOUT NINE KILOGRAMS.
RATHER A LOT TO DO EVERY SINGLE DAY...
ALL RIGHT... I WILL.
ALSO, CLEAN MY SHRINE ONCE A MONTH, AND MAKE ME OFFERINGS.
UGH, WHAT A PAIN!
I SHALL RETURN THE SOUL OF YOUR "SHAMIKO."

AN ANCESTOR WITH FAITH IN HER ABILITY TO FLEE

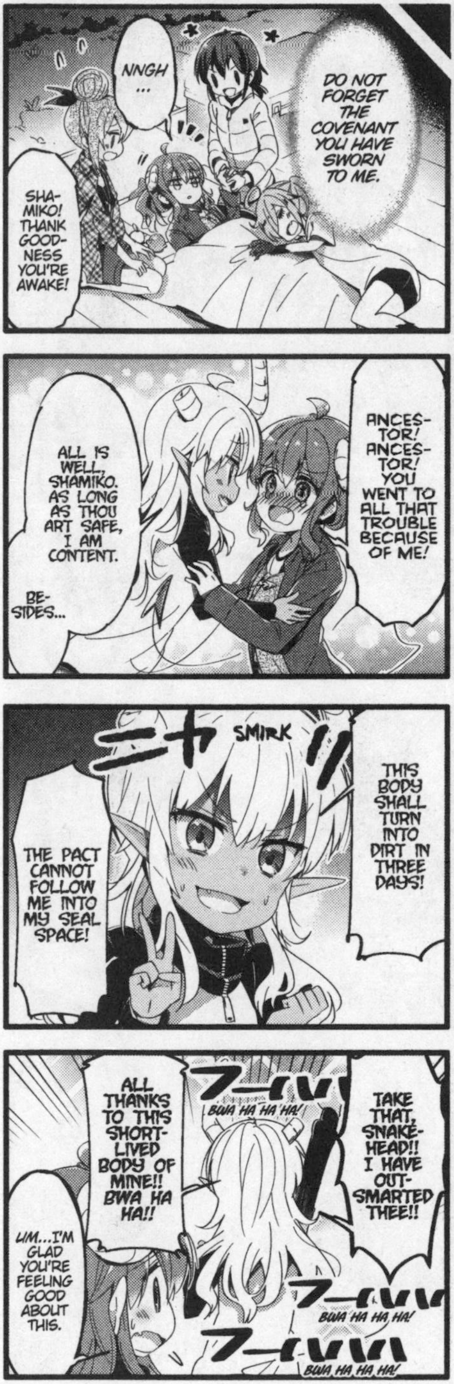
DO NOT FORGET THE COVENANT YOU HAVE SWORN TO ME.
NNGH ...
SHAMIKO! THANK GOODNESS YOU'RE AWAKE!
ANCESTOR! ANCESTOR! YOU WENT TO ALL THAT TROUBLE BECAUSE OF ME!
ALL IS WELL, SHAMIKO. AS LONG AS THOU ART SAFE, I AM CONTENT.
BESIDES...
ニヤ
SMIRK
THIS BODY SHALL TURN INTO DIRT IN THREE DAYS!
THE PACT CANNOT FOLLOW ME INTO MY SEAL SPACE!
TAKE THAT, SNAKEHEAD!! I HAVE OUTSMARTED THEE!!
BWA HA HA HA!
ALL THANKS TO THIS SHORT-LIVED BODY OF MINE!! BWA HA HA!!
BWA HA HA HA!
BWA HA HA HA!
UM...I'M GLAD YOU'RE FEELING GOOD ABOUT THIS.

ANCESTOR CAN'T ESCAPE!!

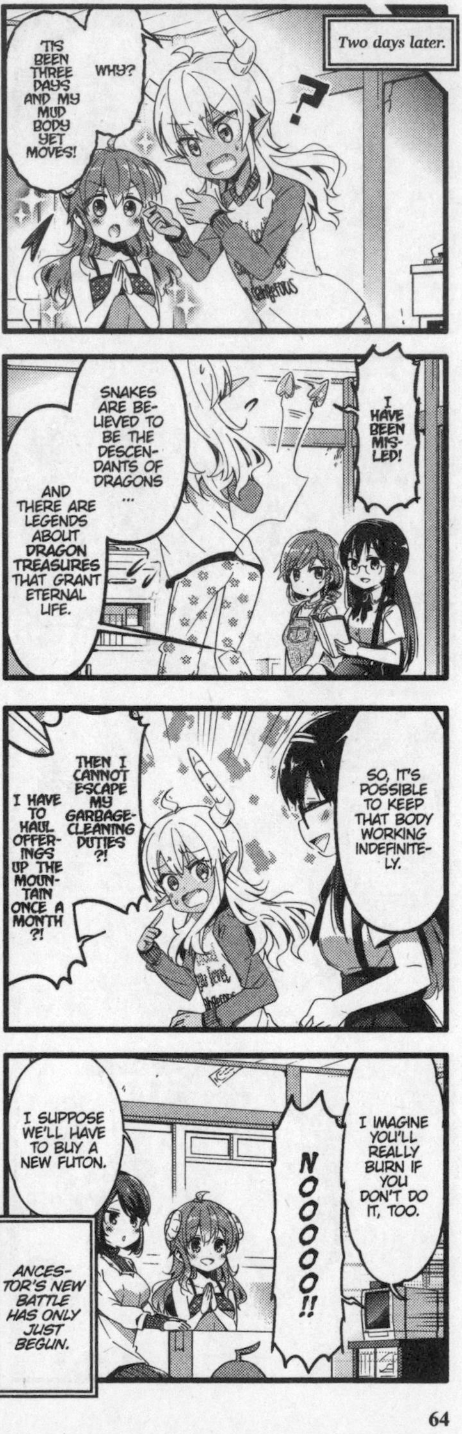
Two days later.
'TIS BEEN THREE DAYS AND MY MUD BODY YET MOVES!
WHY?
?
I HAVE BEEN MISLED!
SNAKES ARE BELIEVED TO BE THE DESCENDANTS OF DRAGONS...
AND THERE ARE LEGENDS ABOUT DRAGON TREASURES THAT GRANT ETERNAL LIFE.
SO, IT'S POSSIBLE TO KEEP THAT BODY WORKING INDEFINITELY.
THEN I CANNOT ESCAPE MY GARBAGE-CLEANING DUTIES?!
I HAVE TO HAUL OFFERINGS UP THE MOUNTAIN ONCE A MONTH?!
I IMAGINE YOU'LL REALLY BURN IF YOU DON'T DO IT, TOO.
NOOOOOO!!
I SUPPOSE WE'LL HAVE TO BUY A NEW FUTON.
ANCESTOR'S NEW BATTLE HAS ONLY JUST BEGUN.

COMMUNITY SERVICE CURSE

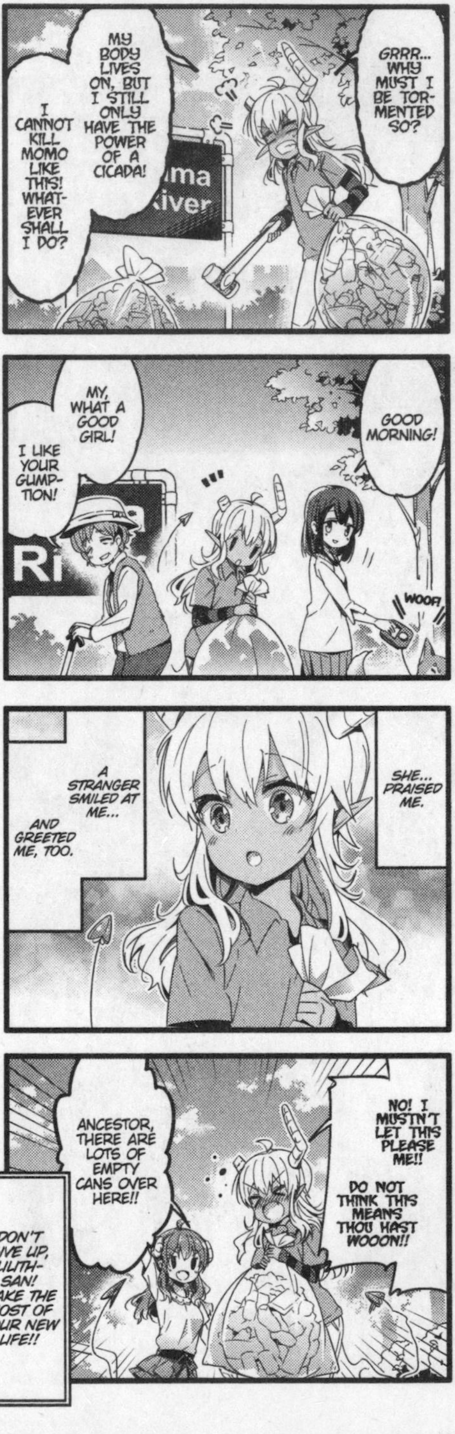
GRRR... WHY MUST I BE TORMENTED SO?
MY BODY LIVES ON, BUT I STILL ONLY HAVE THE POWER OF A CICADA!
I CANNOT KILL MOMO LIKE THIS! WHATEVER SHALL I DO?
GOOD MORNING!
WOOF!
MY, WHAT A GOOD GIRL!
I LIKE YOUR GUMPTION!
SHE... PRAISED ME.
A STRANGER SMILED AT ME...
AND GREETED ME, TOO.
NO! I MUSTN'T LET THIS PLEASE ME!!
DO NOT THINK THIS MEANS THOU HAST WOOON!!
ANCESTOR, THERE ARE LOTS OF EMPTY CANS OVER HERE!!
DON'T GIVE UP, LILITH-SAN! MAKE THE MOST OF YOUR NEW LIFE!!

SECONDS!! DEMON GIRL NEXT DOOR

(CHAPTER 53)

~ THE ACCESSORY OF SHAMIKO'S DREAMS ~

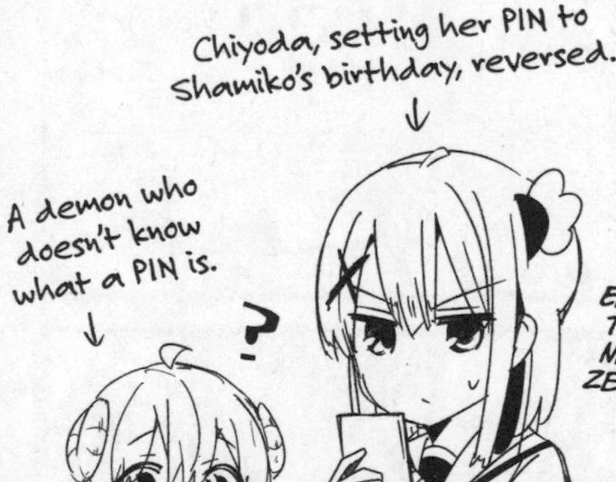
Chiyoda, setting her PIN to Shamiko's birthday, reversed.
EIGHT, TWO, NINE, ZERO...
A demon who doesn't know what a PIN is.
?

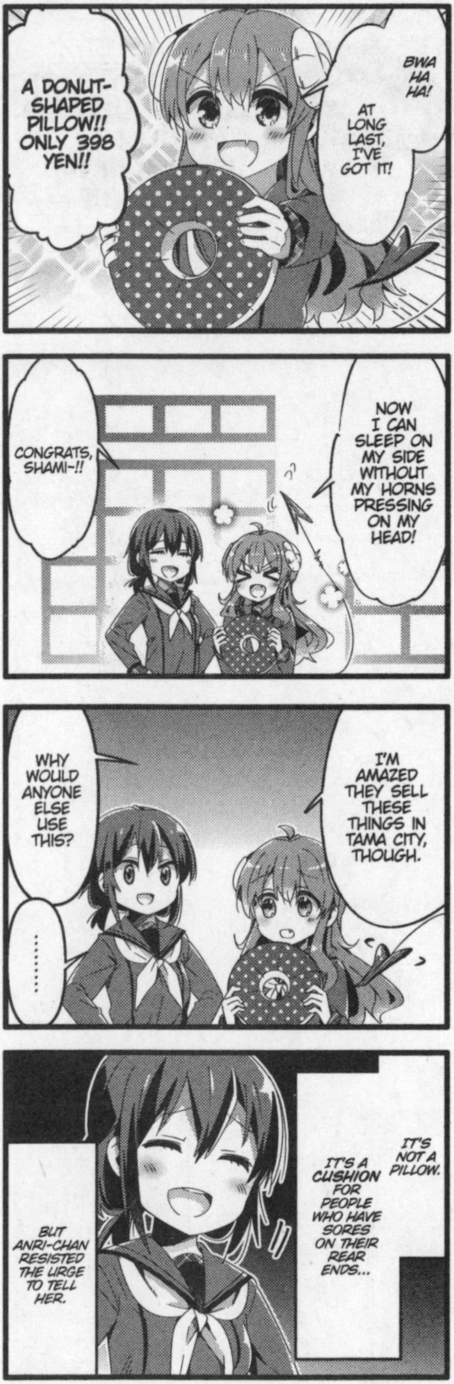
BWA HA HA!
AT LONG LAST, I'VE GOT IT!
A DONUT-SHAPED PILLOW!! ONLY 398 YEN!!
NOW I CAN SLEEP ON MY SIDE WITHOUT MY HORNS PRESSING ON MY HEAD!
CONGRATS, SHAMI~!!
I'M AMAZED THEY SELL THESE THINGS IN TAMA CITY, THOUGH.
WHY WOULD ANYONE ELSE USE THIS?
......
IT'S NOT A PILLOW.
IT'S A CUSHION FOR PEOPLE WHO HAVE SORES ON THEIR REAR ENDS...
BUT ANRI-CHAN RESISTED THE URGE TO TELL HER.

SECONDS!! DEMON GIRL NEXT DOOR

(CHAPTER 58)

~ JOURNEY OF THE CHUG CHUG CUP ~

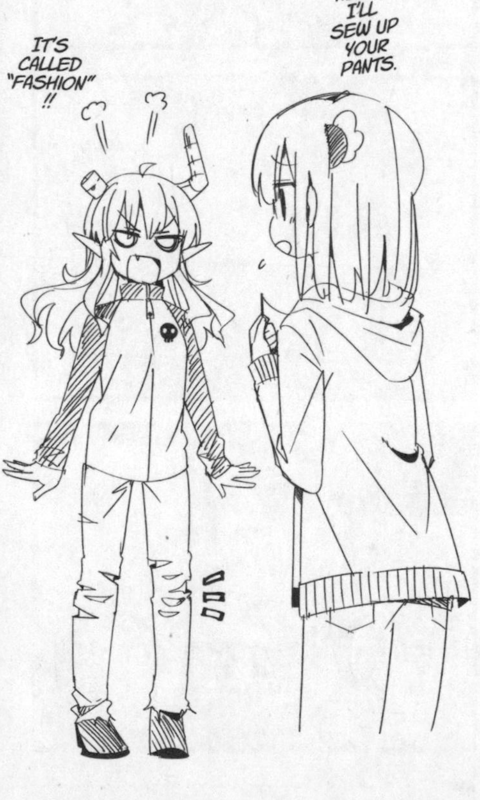
HERE, I'LL SEW UP YOUR PANTS.
IT'S CALLED "FASHION" !!

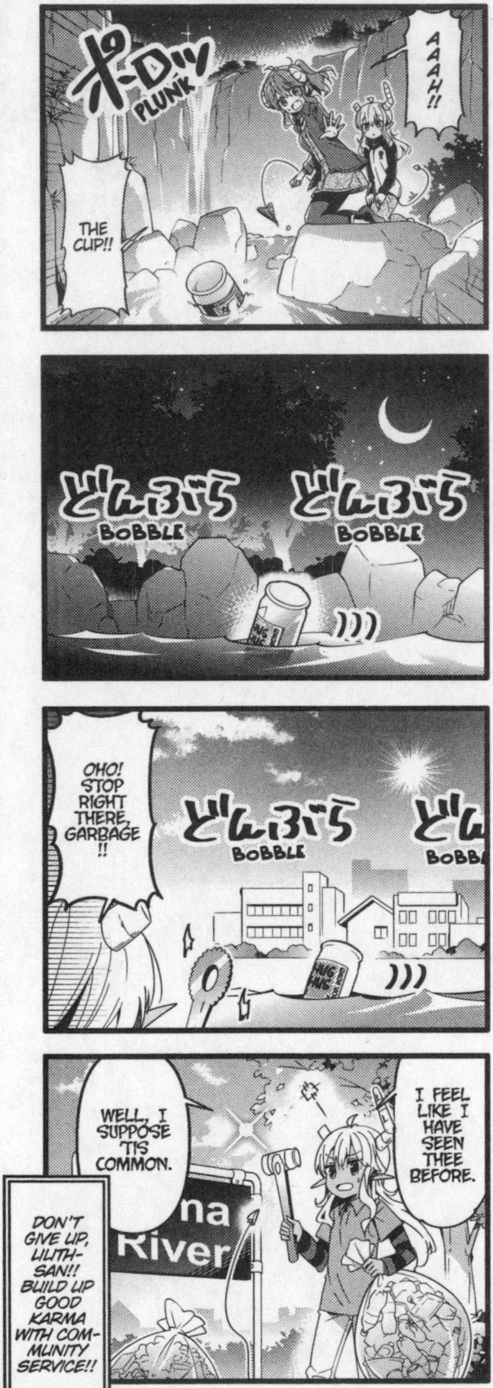
AAAAH!!
ポトッ
PLUNK
THE CUP!!
どんぶら
BOBBLE
どんぶら
BOBBLE
BOBB
どんぶら
BOBBLE
OHO! STOP RIGHT THERE, GARBAGE!!
I FEEL LIKE I HAVE SEEN THEE BEFORE.
WELL, I SUPPOSE TIS COMMON.
na River
DON'T GIVE UP, LILITH-SAN!! BUILD UP GOOD KARMA WITH COMMUNITY SERVICE!!

The Demon Girl Next Door

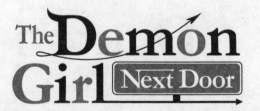

The Demon Girl Next Door

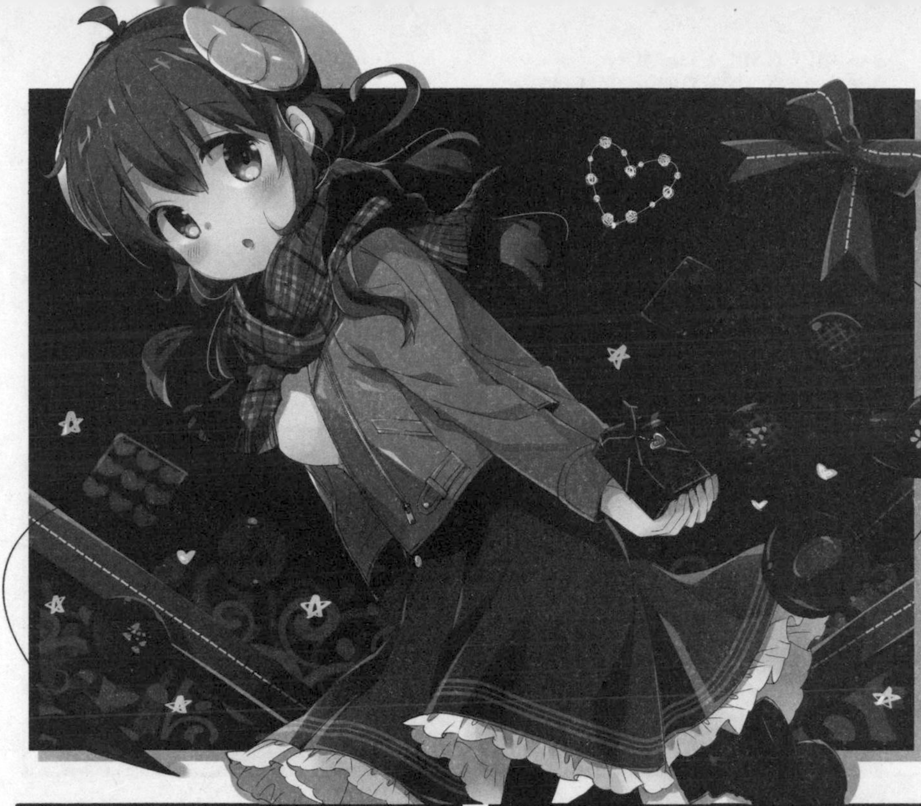

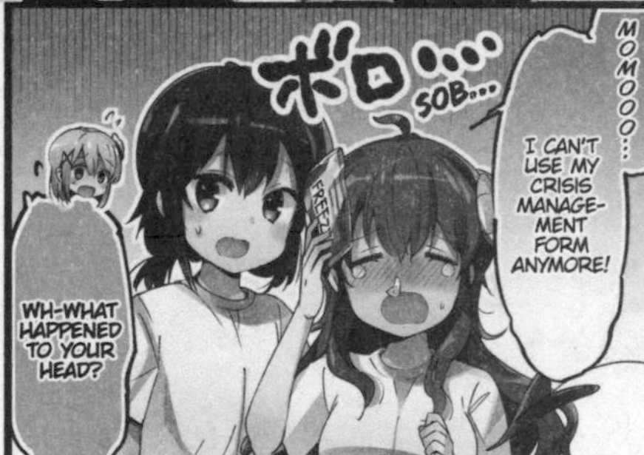
MOMOOOO... I CAN'T USE MY CRISIS MANAGEMENT FORM ANYMORE!
ボロ…
SOB...
WH-WHAT HAPPENED TO YOUR HEAD?

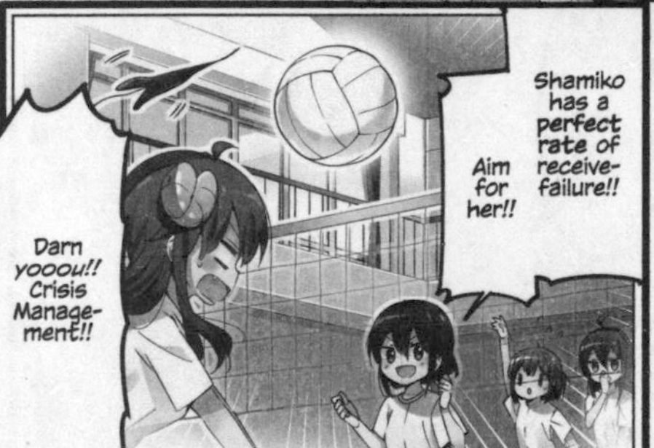
Shamiko has a perfect rate of receive-failure!!
Aim for her!!
Darn yoooou!! Crisis Management!!

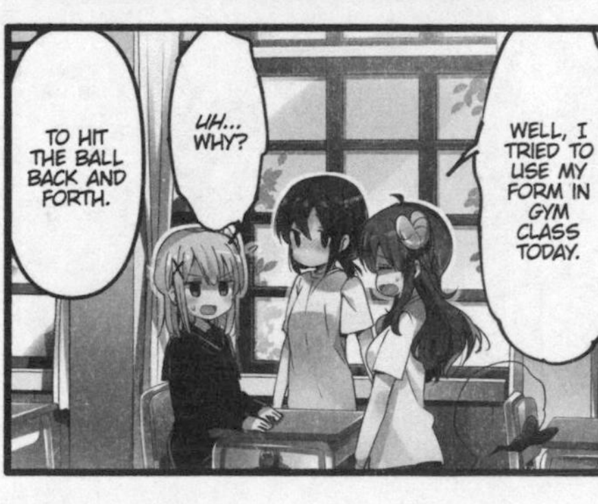
WELL, I TRIED TO USE MY FORM IN GYM CLASS TODAY.
UH... WHY?
TO HIT THE BALL BACK AND FORTH.

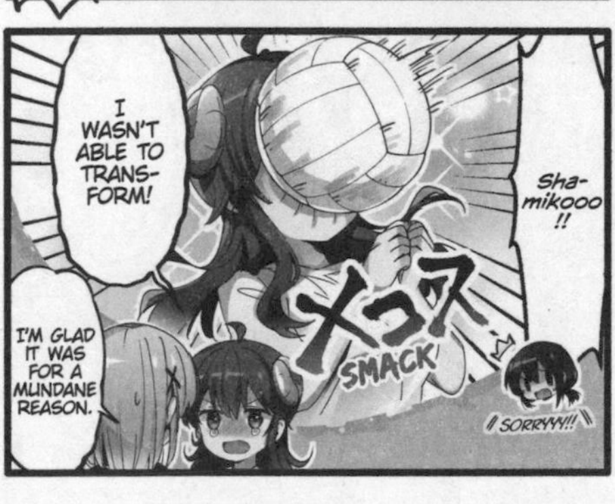
Shamikooo!!
I WASN'T ABLE TO TRANSFORM!
SMACK
SORRYYY!!
I'M GLAD IT WAS FOR A MUNDANE REASON.

PEACHY TOUGH LOVE

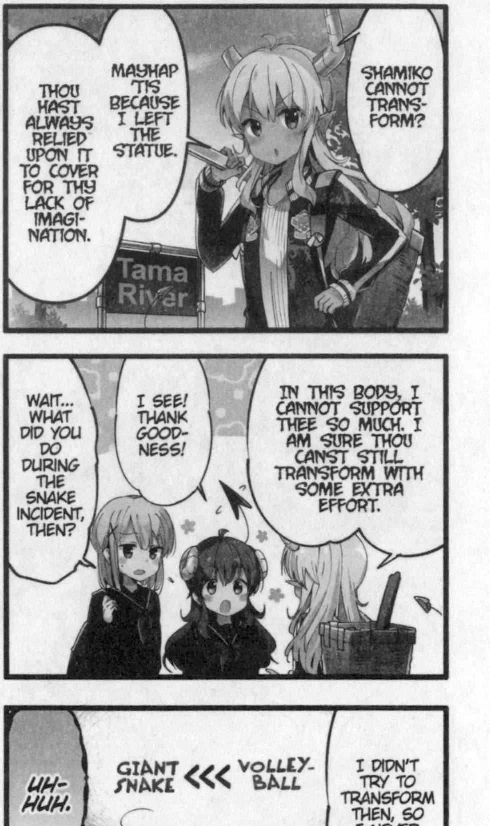
SHAMIKO CANNOT TRANS-FORM?
MAYHAP 'TIS BECAUSE I LEFT THE STATUE.
THOU HAST ALWAYS RELIED UPON IT TO COVER FOR THY LACK OF IMAGI-NATION.
Tama River
IN THIS BODY, I CANNOT SUPPORT THEE SO MUCH. I AM SURE THOU CANST STILL TRANSFORM WITH SOME EXTRA EFFORT.
I SEE! THANK GOOD-NESS!
WAIT... WHAT DID YOU DO DURING THE SNAKE INCIDENT, THEN?
I DIDN'T TRY TO TRANSFORM THEN, SO I NEVER NOTICED!!
GIANT SNAKE <<< VOLLEY-BALL
UH-HUH.
GRIND
GRIND
THIS IS A PROB-LEM.
HERE, GET BACK IN THE STATUE.
WH...?! OUCH! STOP AT ONCE!!
SEE?! THIS IS THE PROB-LEM WITH THEE!!
GRIND
GRIND
GRIND

BECOME A DEMON WHO WON'T GET REPORTED

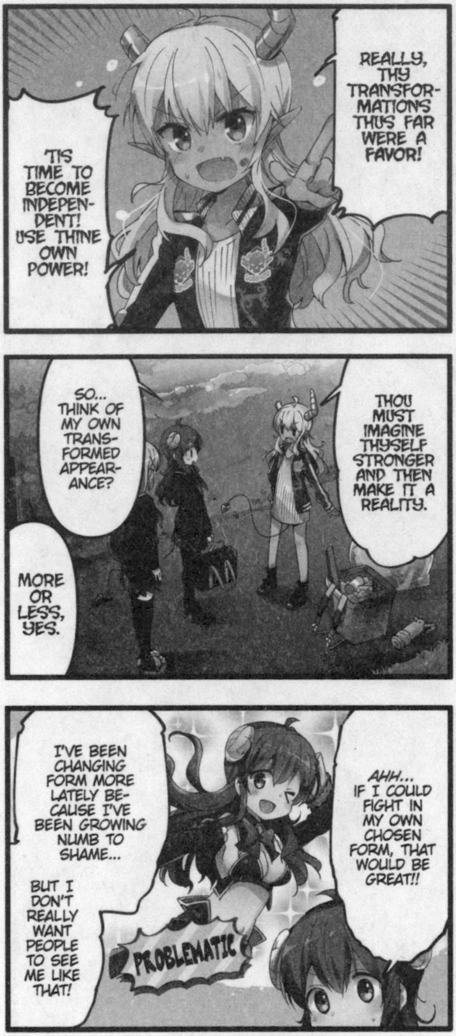
REALLY, THY TRANSFOR-MATIONS THUS FAR WERE A FAVOR!
'TIS TIME TO BECOME INDEPEN-DENT! USE THINE OWN POWER!
THOU MUST IMAGINE THYSELF STRONGER AND THEN MAKE IT A REALITY.
SO... THINK OF MY OWN TRANS-FORMED APPEAR-ANCE?
MORE OR LESS, YES.
AHH... IF I COULD FIGHT IN MY OWN CHOSEN FORM, THAT WOULD BE GREAT!!
I'VE BEEN CHANGING FORM MORE LATELY BE-CAUSE I'VE BEEN GROWING NUMB TO SHAME...
BUT I DON'T REALLY WANT PEOPLE TO SEE ME LIKE THAT!
PROBLEMATIC
I CAN COME UP WITH A BATTLE FORM I CAN SHOW IN PUBLIC!!
NO MORE SCANTILY-CLAD DEMON!!
I DO NOT THINK THERE IS A NEED TO CHANGE THE BASIC GARB--
IT'S TOO COLD FOR BARE SKIN!!

FLEECE LINING IS GREAT, THOUGH

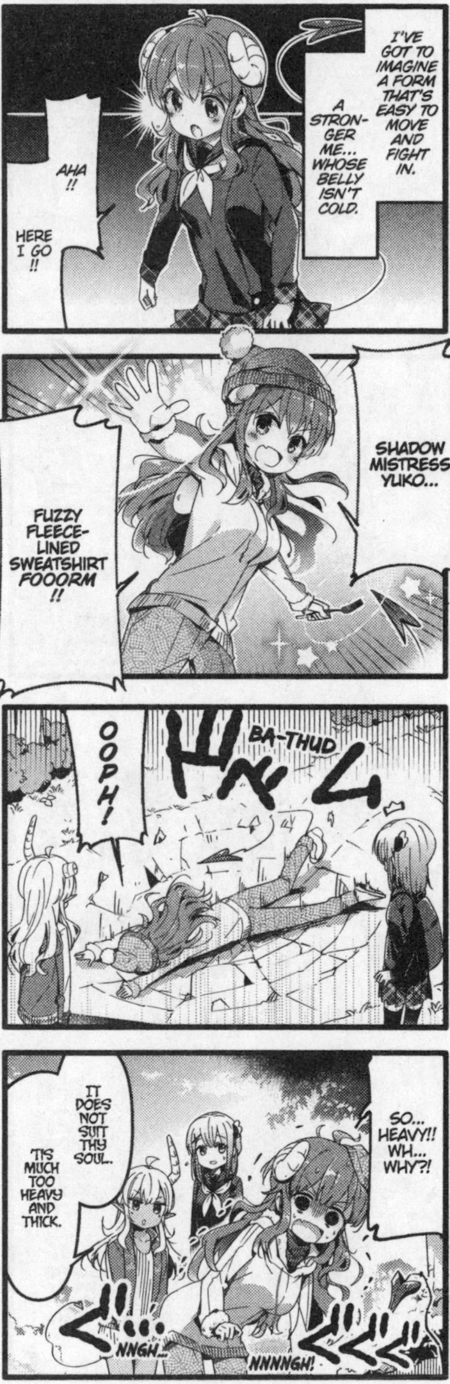
I'VE GOT TO IMAGINE A FORM THAT'S EASY TO MOVE AND FIGHT IN.
A STRONGER ME... WHOSE BELLY ISN'T COLD.
AHA!!
HERE I GO!!
SHADOW MISTRESS YUKO...
FUZZY FLEECE-LINED SWEATSHIRT FOOORM!!
BA-THUD
OOPH!
SO... HEAVY!! WH... WHY?!
IT DOES NOT SUIT THY SOUL.
'TIS MUCH TOO HEAVY AND THICK.
NNNNGH!
NNGH...

IT SUITED HER WHEN SHE WAS THREE

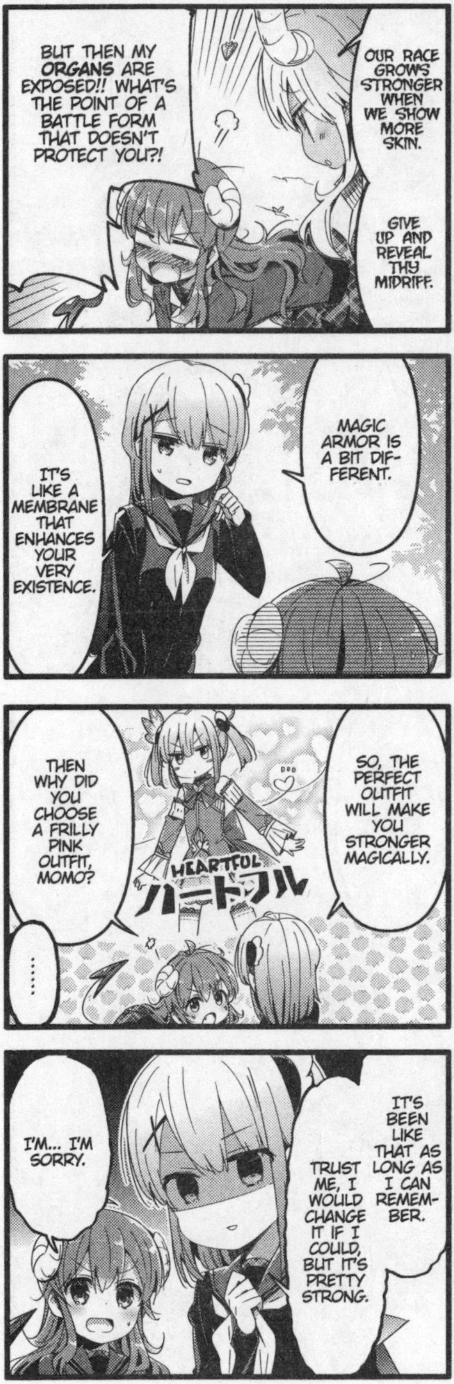
OUR RACE GROWS STRONGER WHEN WE SHOW MORE SKIN.
GIVE UP AND REVEAL THY MIDRIFF.
BUT THEN MY ORGANS ARE EXPOSED!! WHAT'S THE POINT OF A BATTLE FORM THAT DOESN'T PROTECT YOU?!
MAGIC ARMOR IS A BIT DIFFERENT.
IT'S LIKE A MEMBRANE THAT ENHANCES YOUR VERY EXISTENCE.
SO, THE PERFECT OUTFIT WILL MAKE YOU STRONGER MAGICALLY.
HEARTFUL
ハートフル
THEN WHY DID YOU CHOOSE A FRILLY PINK OUTFIT, MOMO?
......
IT'S BEEN LIKE THAT AS LONG AS I CAN REMEMBER.
TRUST ME, I WOULD CHANGE IT IF I COULD, BUT IT'S PRETTY STRONG.
I'M... I'M SORRY.

ANCESTOR'S MYSTERIOUS FONDNESS FOR SKIN

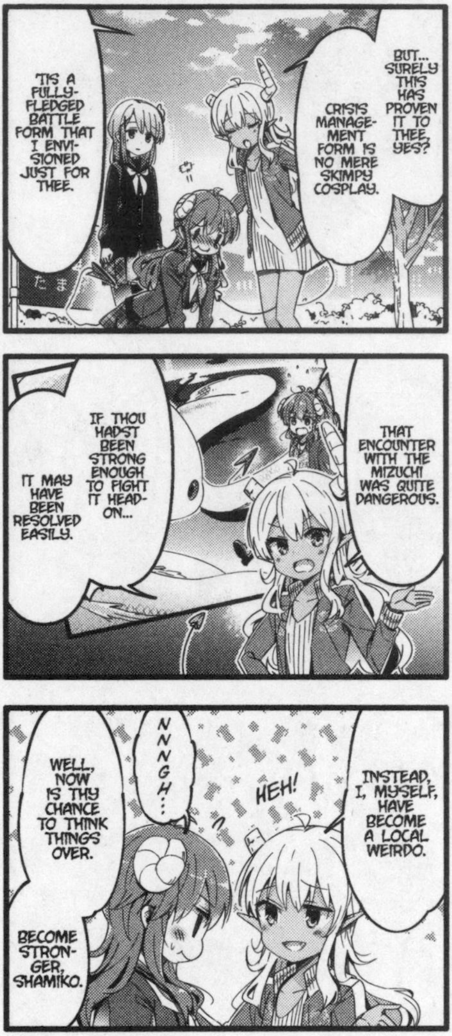
BUT... SURELY THIS HAS PROVEN IT TO THEE, YES?
CRISIS MANAGEMENT FORM IS NO MERE SKIMPY COSPLAY.
'TIS A FULLY-FLEDGED BATTLE FORM THAT I ENVISIONED JUST FOR THEE.
THAT ENCOUNTER WITH THE MIZUCHI WAS QUITE DANGEROUS.
IF THOU HADST BEEN STRONG ENOUGH TO FIGHT IT HEAD-ON...
IT MAY HAVE BEEN RESOLVED EASILY.
INSTEAD, I, MYSELF, HAVE BECOME A LOCAL WEIRDO.
HEH!
NNNGH...
WELL, NOW IS THY CHANCE TO THINK THINGS OVER.
BECOME STRONGER, SHAMIKO.
THOU MUST SHOW MORE SKIN. PERHAPS EVEN ALL OF IT!
LEARN TO LOVE COSPLAY AND EXHIBITIONISM!
SO, IT *IS* COSPLAY AFTER ALL!!

AN EASY BUFFING ABILITY

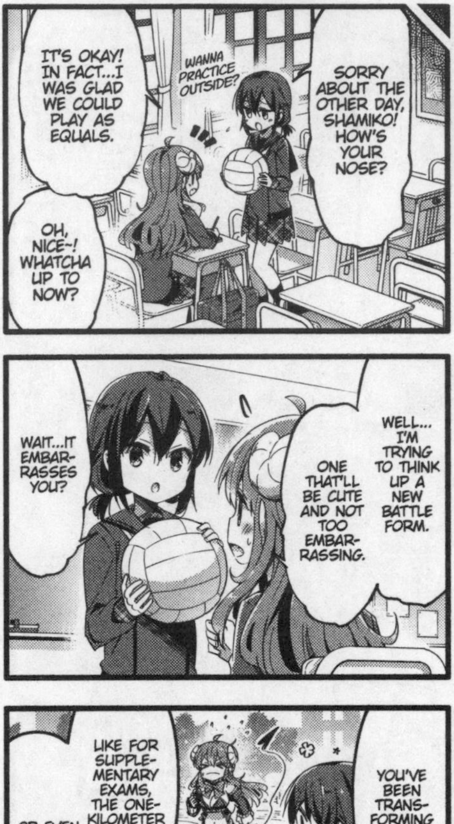
SORRY ABOUT THE OTHER DAY, SHAMIKO! HOW'S YOUR NOSE?
WANNA PRACTICE OUTSIDE?
IT'S OKAY! IN FACT...I WAS GLAD WE COULD PLAY AS EQUALS.
OH, NICE~! WHATCHA UP TO NOW?
WELL... I'M TRYING TO THINK UP A NEW BATTLE FORM.
ONE THAT'LL BE CUTE AND NOT TOO EMBARRASSING.
WAIT...IT EMBARRASSES YOU?
YOU'VE BEEN TRANSFORMING A LOT LATELY.
LIKE FOR SUPPLEMENTARY EXAMS, THE ONE-KILOMETER RUN...
OR EVEN GOING UP MORE THAN TWO FLIGHTS OF STAIRS...
I HATE TO ADMIT IT, BUT...MY WHOLE BODY FEELS BETTER IN THAT OUTFIT.
I DON'T GET SHORT OF BREATH, AND MY BLOOD FLOWS BETTER.
SO, CONVENIENCE WON OUT, HUH?
CLENCH...

ANCESTOR-TURNED-SCHOOLGIRL

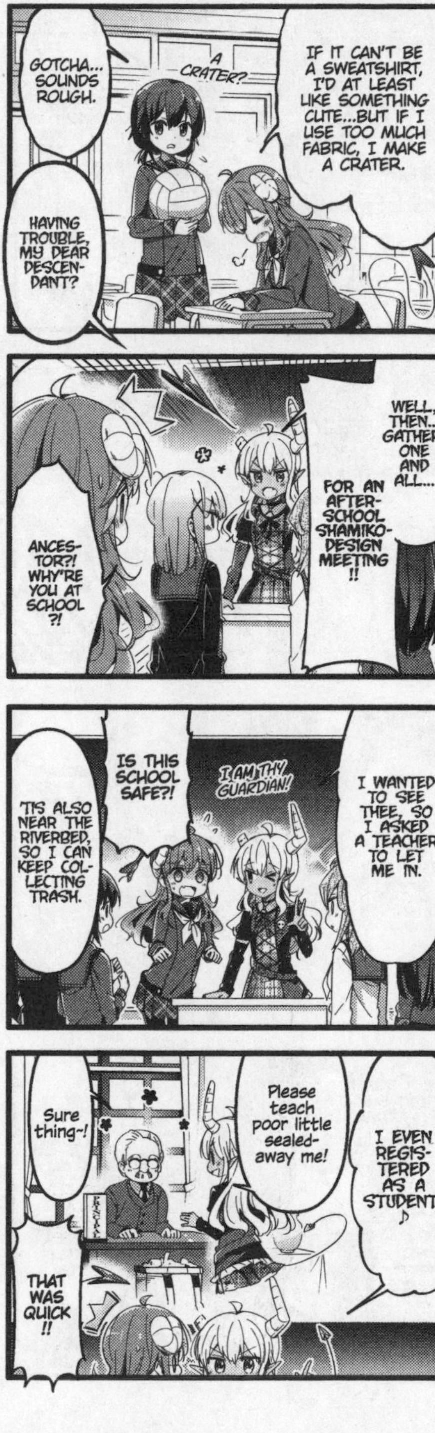
IF IT CAN'T BE A SWEATSHIRT, I'D AT LEAST LIKE SOMETHING CUTE...BUT IF I USE TOO MUCH FABRIC, I MAKE A CRATER.
A CRATER?
GOTCHA... SOUNDS ROUGH.
HAVING TROUBLE, MY DEAR DESCENDANT?
WELL, THEN... GATHER, ONE AND ALL...
FOR AN AFTER-SCHOOL SHAMIKO-DESIGN MEETING!!
ANCESTOR?! WHY'RE YOU AT SCHOOL?!
I WANTED TO SEE THEE, SO I ASKED A TEACHER TO LET ME IN.
I AM THY GUARDIAN!
IS THIS SCHOOL SAFE?!
'TIS ALSO NEAR THE RIVERBED, SO I CAN KEEP COLLECTING TRASH.
I EVEN REGISTERED AS A STUDENT! ♪
Please teach poor little sealed-away me!
Sure thing~!
THAT WAS QUICK!!

NEW-YEAR'S-SASH DEMON

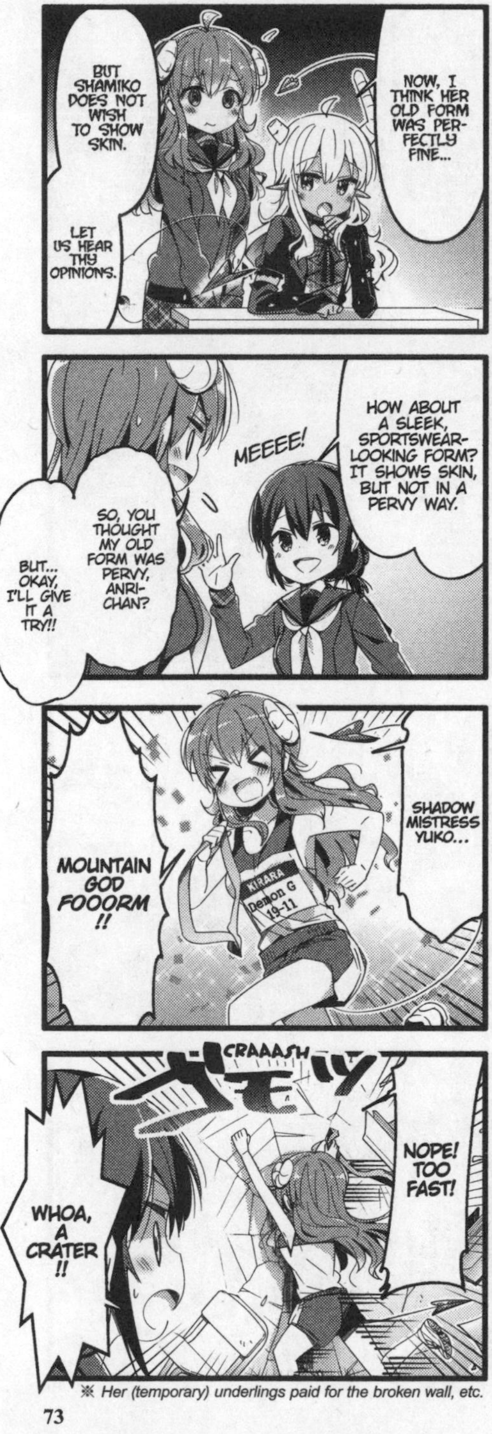
NOW, I THINK HER OLD FORM WAS PERFECTLY FINE...
BUT SHAMIKO DOES NOT WISH TO SHOW SKIN.
LET US HEAR THY OPINIONS.
HOW ABOUT A SLEEK, SPORTSWEAR-LOOKING FORM? IT SHOWS SKIN, BUT NOT IN A PERVY WAY.
MEEEE!
SO, YOU THOUGHT MY OLD FORM WAS PERVY, ANRI-CHAN?
BUT... OKAY, I'LL GIVE IT A TRY!!
SHADOW MISTRESS YUKO...
KIRARA
Demon G
19-11
MOUNTAIN GOD FOOORM!!
CRAAASH
NOPE! TOO FAST!
WHOA, A CRATER!!

※ *Her (temporary) underlings paid for the broken wall, etc.*

SAN CHECK MOMENT

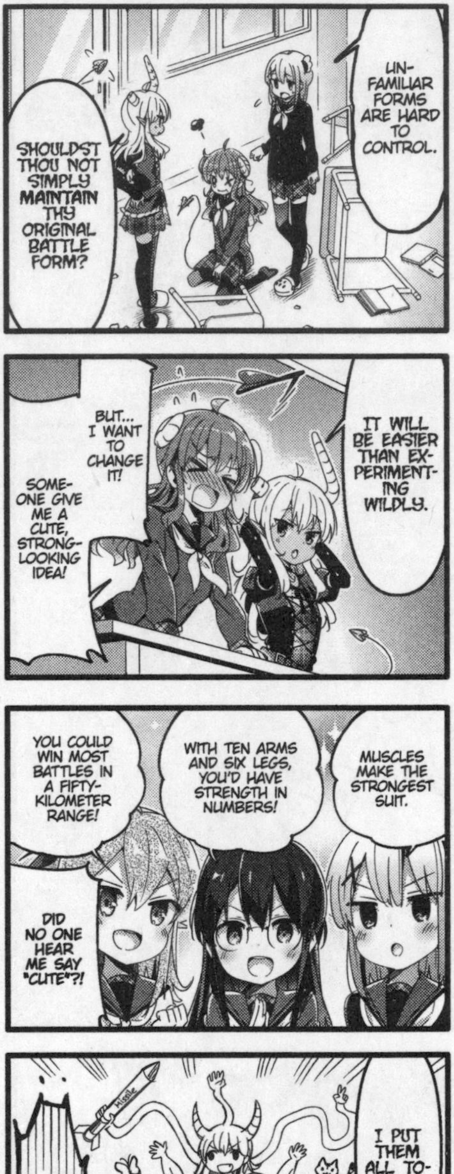
UNFAMILIAR FORMS ARE HARD TO CONTROL.
SHOULDST THOU NOT SIMPLY MAINTAIN THY ORIGINAL BATTLE FORM?
IT WILL BE EASIER THAN EXPERIMENTING WILDLY.
BUT... I WANT TO CHANGE IT!
SOMEONE GIVE ME A CUTE, STRONG-LOOKING IDEA!
MUSCLES MAKE THE STRONGEST SUIT.
WITH TEN ARMS AND SIX LEGS, YOU'D HAVE STRENGTH IN NUMBERS!
YOU COULD WIN MOST BATTLES IN A FIFTY-KILOMETER RANGE!
DID NO ONE HEAR ME SAY "CUTE"?!
I PUT THEM ALL TOGETHER.
I'M GOING CRAZY JUST LOOKING AT THIS!
Missile
About forty km.

MOMO IS ALWAYS SERIOUS

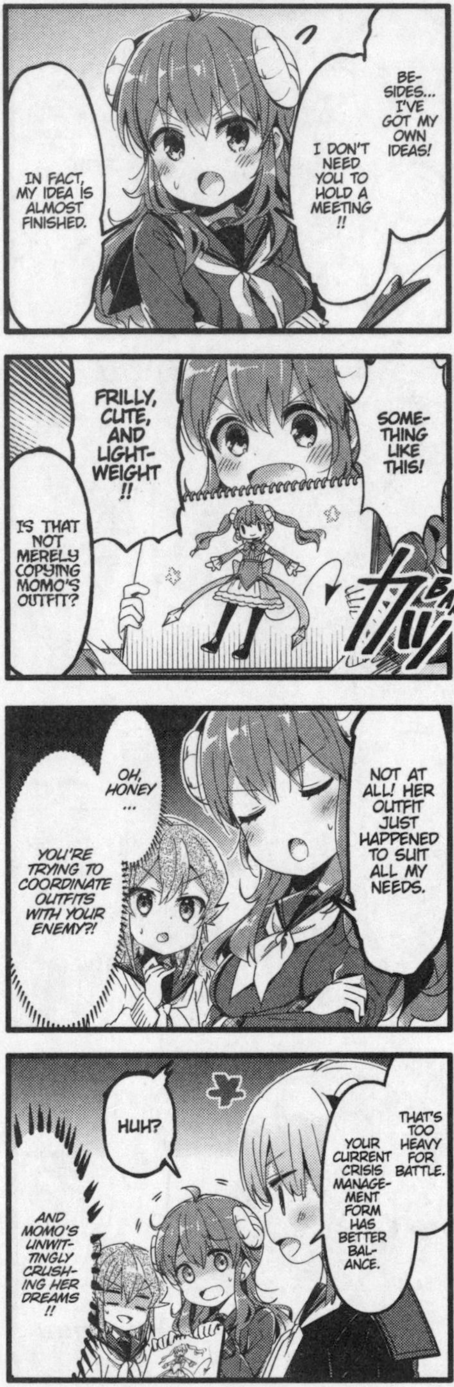
BESIDES... I'VE GOT MY OWN IDEAS!
I DON'T NEED YOU TO HOLD A MEETING!!
IN FACT, MY IDEA IS ALMOST FINISHED.
SOMETHING LIKE THIS!
FRILLY, CUTE, AND LIGHTWEIGHT!!
BAM
IS THAT NOT MERELY COPYING MOMO'S OUTFIT?
NOT AT ALL! HER OUTFIT JUST HAPPENED TO SUIT ALL MY NEEDS.
OH, HONEY...
YOU'RE TRYING TO COORDINATE OUTFITS WITH YOUR ENEMY?!
THAT'S TOO HEAVY FOR BATTLE.
YOUR CURRENT CRISIS MANAGEMENT FORM HAS BETTER BALANCE.
HUH?
AND MOMO'S UNWITTINGLY CRUSHING HER DREAMS!!

A DEMON GOES INTO HER SHELL

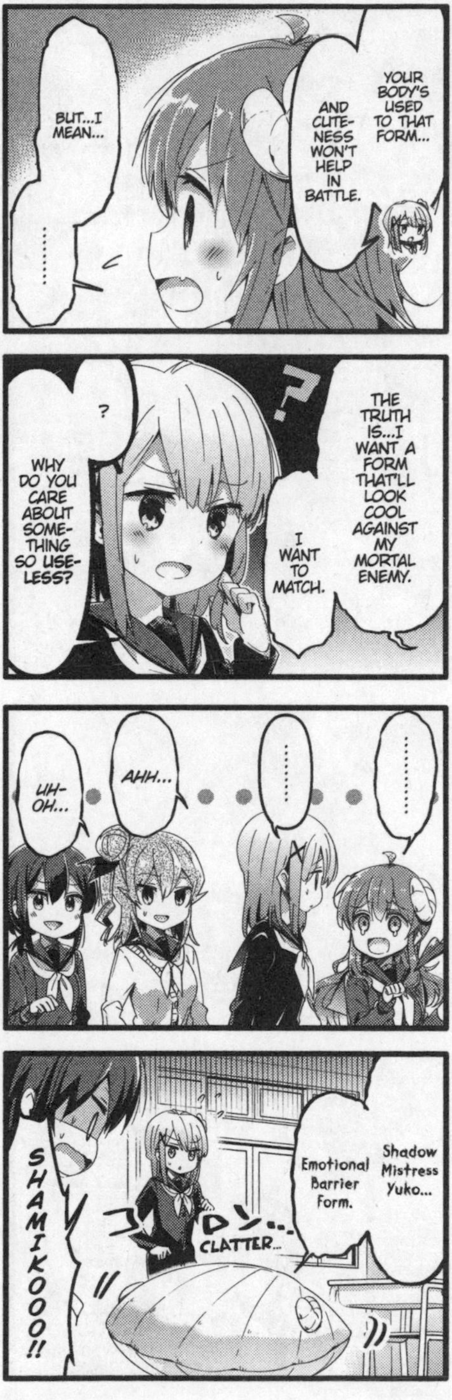
YOUR BODY'S USED TO THAT FORM...
AND CUTENESS WON'T HELP IN BATTLE.
BUT...I MEAN...
......
THE TRUTH IS...I WANT A FORM THAT'LL LOOK COOL AGAINST MY MORTAL ENEMY.
I WANT TO MATCH.
?
?
WHY DO YOU CARE ABOUT SOMETHING SO USELESS?
......
......
AHH...
UH-OH...
Shadow Mistress Yuko...
Emotional Barrier Form.
CLATTER...
SHAMIKOOO!!

SIRATUS ALABASTER FORM

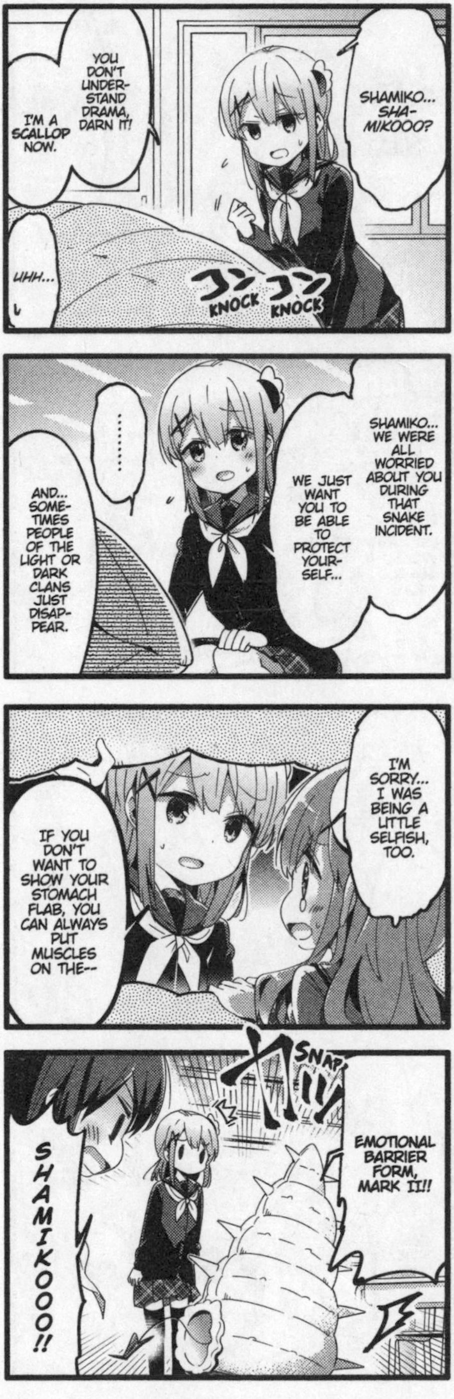
SHAMIKO... SHAMIKOOO?
YOU DON'T UNDERSTAND DRAMA, DARN IT!
I'M A SCALLOP NOW.
KNOCK KNOCK
UHH...
SHAMIKO... WE WERE ALL WORRIED ABOUT YOU DURING THAT SNAKE INCIDENT.
WE JUST WANT YOU TO BE ABLE TO PROTECT YOURSELF...
......
AND... SOMETIMES PEOPLE OF THE LIGHT OR DARK CLANS JUST DISAPPEAR.
I'M SORRY... I WAS BEING A LITTLE SELFISH, TOO.
IF YOU DON'T WANT TO SHOW YOUR STOMACH FLAB, YOU CAN ALWAYS PUT MUSCLES ON THE--
SNAP!
EMOTIONAL BARRIER FORM, MARK II!!
SHAMIKOOOO!!

SHEDDING ARMOR IS DRAMATIC, TOO

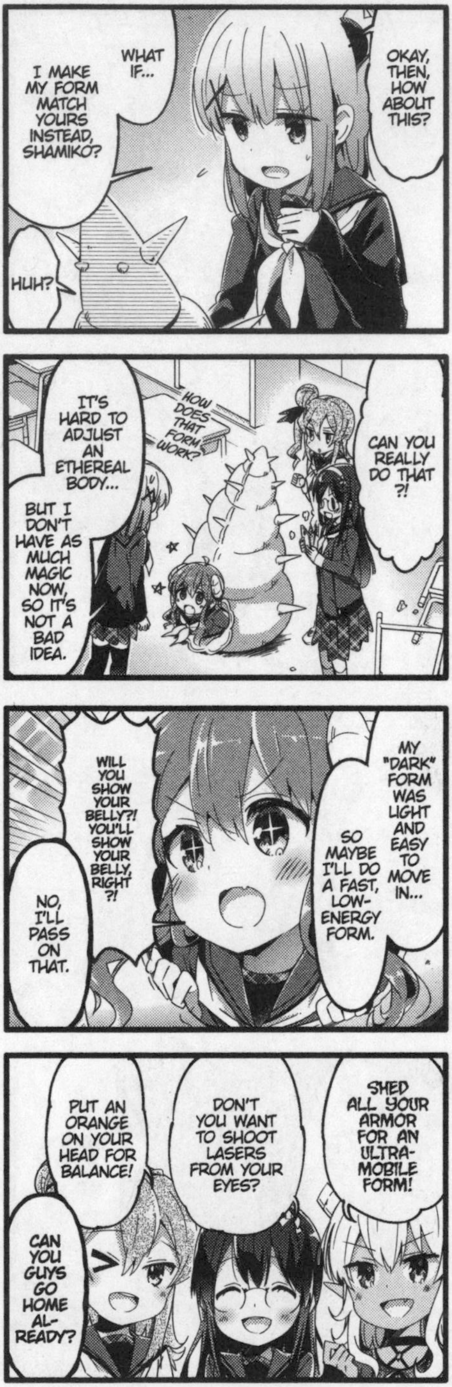
OKAY, THEN, HOW ABOUT THIS?
WHAT IF...
I MAKE MY FORM MATCH YOURS INSTEAD, SHAMIKO?
HUH?
CAN YOU REALLY DO THAT?!
HOW DOES THAT FORM WORK?
IT'S HARD TO ADJUST AN ETHEREAL BODY...
BUT I DON'T HAVE AS MUCH MAGIC NOW, SO IT'S NOT A BAD IDEA.
MY "DARK" FORM WAS LIGHT AND EASY TO MOVE IN...
SO MAYBE I'LL DO A FAST, LOW-ENERGY FORM.
WILL YOU SHOW YOUR BELLY?! YOU'LL SHOW YOUR BELLY, RIGHT?!
NO, I'LL PASS ON THAT.
SHED ALL YOUR ARMOR FOR AN ULTRA-MOBILE FORM!
DON'T YOU WANT TO SHOOT LASERS FROM YOUR EYES?
PUT AN ORANGE ON YOUR HEAD FOR BALANCE!
CAN YOU GUYS GO HOME AL-READY?

DEMON-STILT FORM

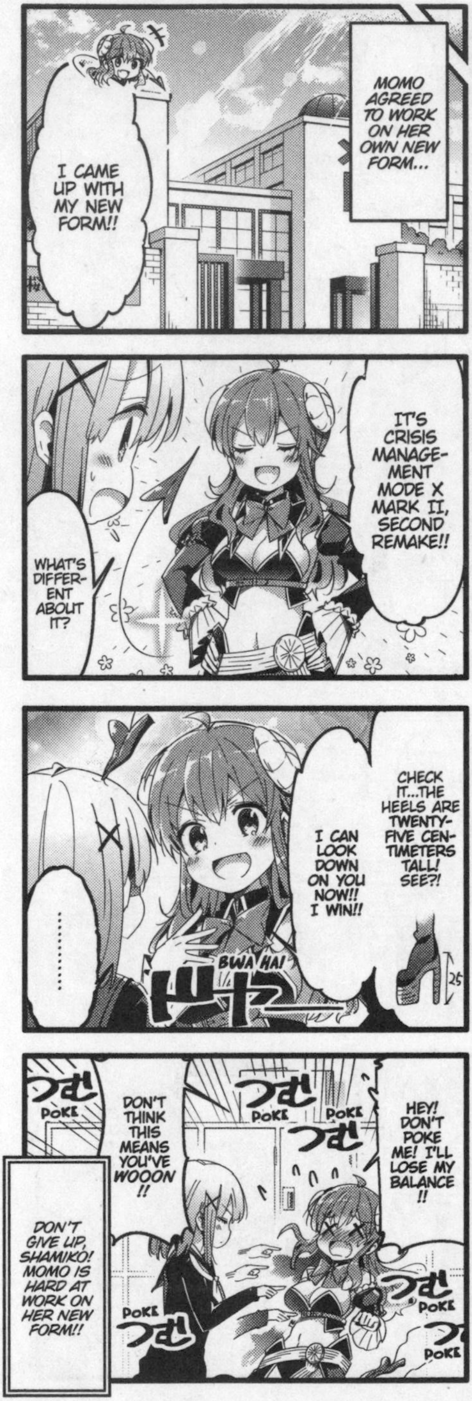
MOMO AGREED TO WORK ON HER OWN NEW FORM...
I CAME UP WITH MY NEW FORM!!
IT'S CRISIS MANAGE-MENT MODE X MARK II, SECOND REMAKE!!
WHAT'S DIFFER-ENT ABOUT IT?
CHECK IT...THE HEELS ARE TWENTY-FIVE CEN-TIMETERS TALL! SEE?!
25
I CAN LOOK DOWN ON YOU NOW!! I WIN!!
BWA HA!
ドヤー
......
HEY! DON'T POKE ME! I'LL LOSE MY BALANCE!!
POKE
つむ
DON'T THINK THIS MEANS YOU'VE WOOON!!
POKE
つむ
POKE
つむ
POKE
つむ
DON'T GIVE UP, SHAMIKO! MOMO IS HARD AT WORK ON HER NEW FORM!!

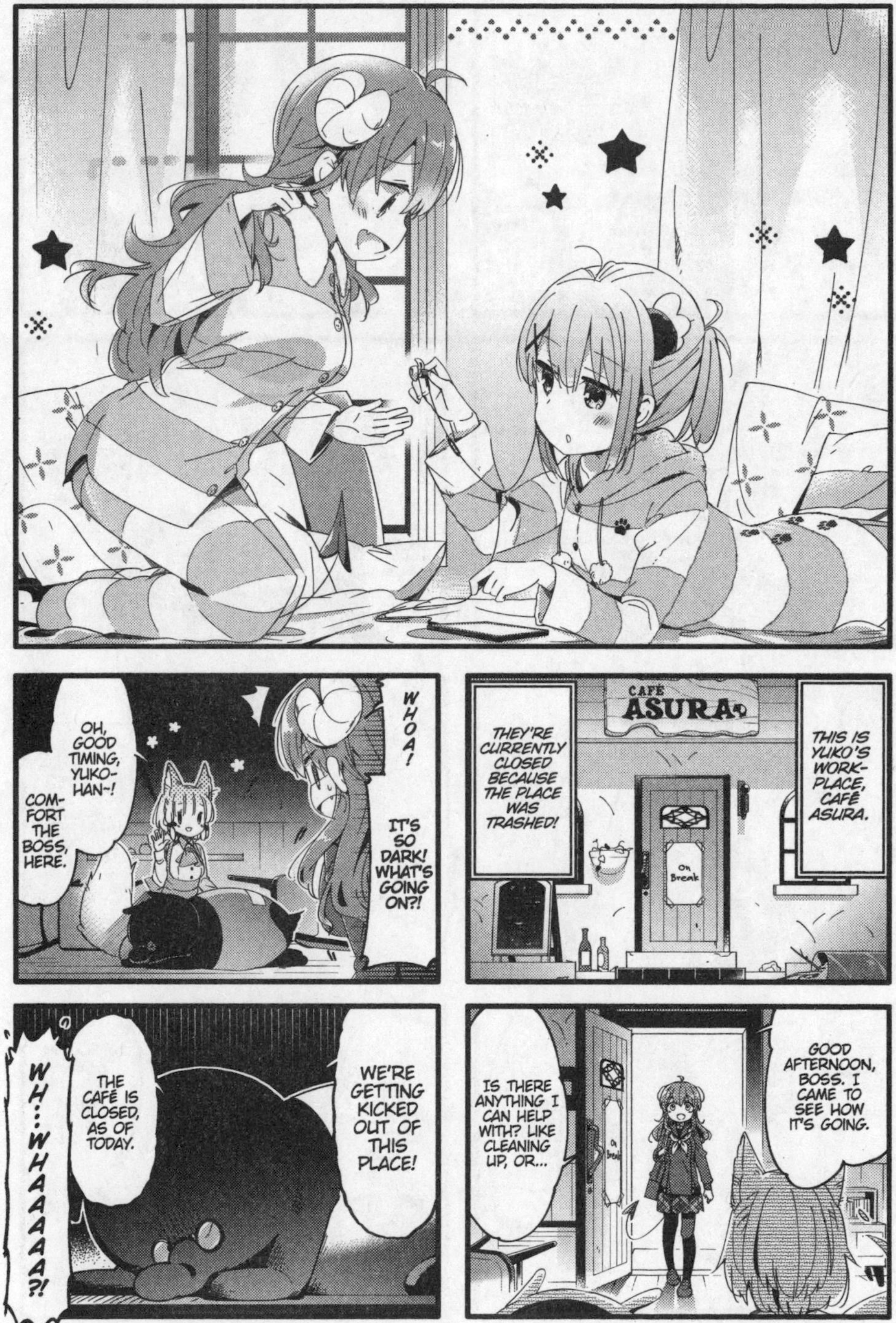
CAFÉ
ASURA
THIS IS YUKO'S WORK-PLACE, CAFÉ ASURA.
THEY'RE CURRENTLY CLOSED BECAUSE THE PLACE WAS TRASHED!
On Break
WHOA!
IT'S SO DARK! WHAT'S GOING ON?!
OH, GOOD TIMING, YUKO-HAN~!
COMFORT THE BOSS, HERE.
GOOD AFTERNOON, BOSS. I CAME TO SEE HOW IT'S GOING.
IS THERE ANYTHING I CAN HELP WITH? LIKE CLEANING UP, OR...
WE'RE GETTING KICKED OUT OF THIS PLACE!
THE CAFÉ IS CLOSED, AS OF TODAY.
WH...WHHAAAAAAA?!

SCORCHED EARTH

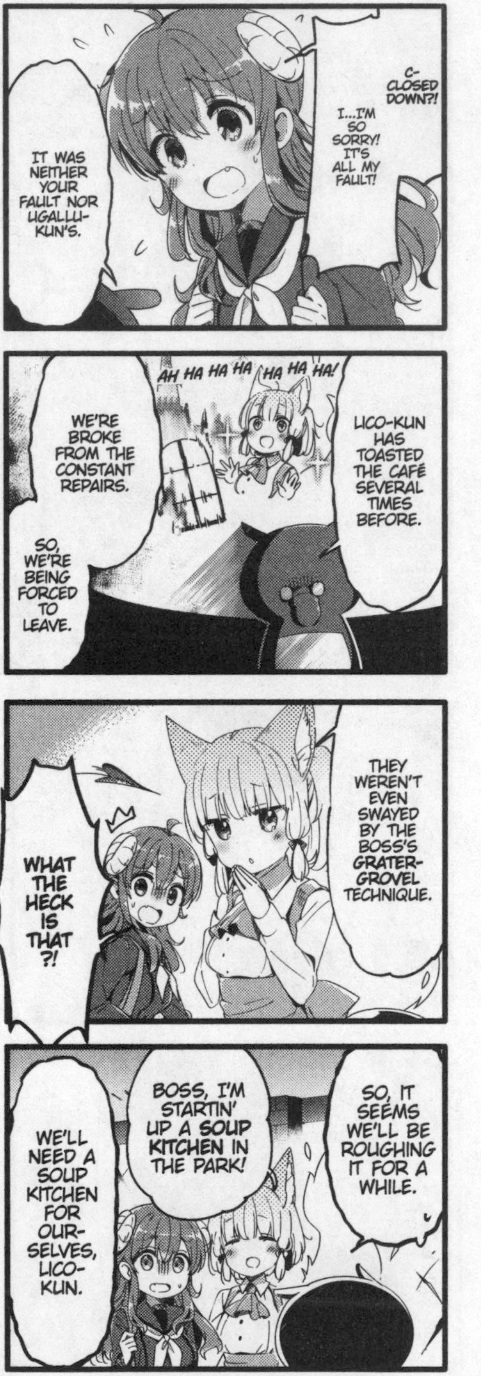
C-CLOSED DOWN?!
I...I'M SO SORRY! IT'S ALL MY FAULT!
IT WAS NEITHER YOUR FAULT NOR UGALLU-KUN'S.
LICO-KUN HAS TOASTED THE CAFÉ SEVERAL TIMES BEFORE.
AH HA HA HA HA HA HA!
WE'RE BROKE FROM THE CONSTANT REPAIRS.
SO, WE'RE BEING FORCED TO LEAVE.
THEY WEREN'T EVEN SWAYED BY THE BOSS'S GRATER-GROVEL TECHNIQUE.
WHAT THE HECK IS THAT?!
SO, IT SEEMS WE'LL BE ROUGHING IT FOR A WHILE.
BOSS, I'M STARTIN' UP A SOUP KITCHEN IN THE PARK!
WE'LL NEED A SOUP KITCHEN FOR OURSELVES, LICO-KUN.

IT'S EASILY CONFUSED WITH A DAFFODIL

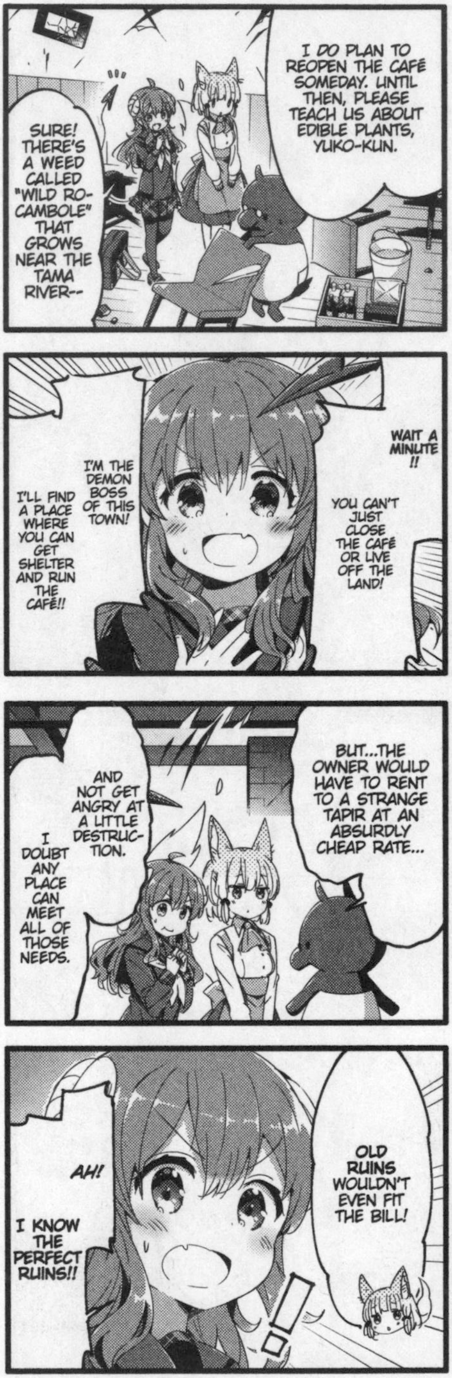
I DO PLAN TO REOPEN THE CAFÉ SOMEDAY. UNTIL THEN, PLEASE TEACH US ABOUT EDIBLE PLANTS, YUKO-KUN.
SURE! THERE'S A WEED CALLED "WILD ROCAMBOLE" THAT GROWS NEAR THE TAMA RIVER--
WAIT A MINUTE!!
YOU CAN'T JUST CLOSE THE CAFÉ OR LIVE OFF THE LAND!
I'M THE DEMON BOSS OF THIS TOWN!
I'LL FIND A PLACE WHERE YOU CAN GET SHELTER AND RUN THE CAFÉ!!
BUT...THE OWNER WOULD HAVE TO RENT TO A STRANGE TAPIR AT AN ABSURDLY CHEAP RATE...
AND NOT GET ANGRY AT A LITTLE DESTRUCTION.
I DOUBT ANY PLACE CAN MEET ALL OF THOSE NEEDS.
OLD RUINS WOULDN'T EVEN FIT THE BILL!
AH!
I KNOW THE PERFECT RUINS!!

GATE-CRASHING DEMON

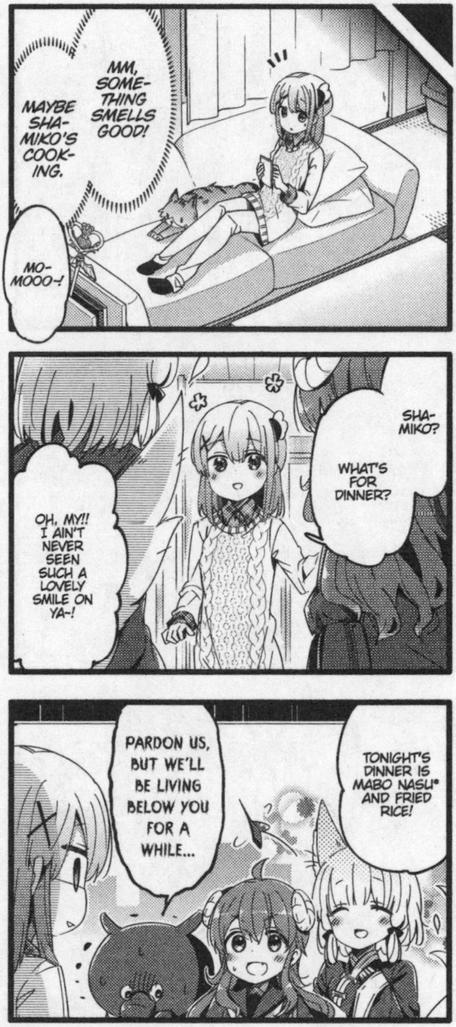
MM, SOMETHING SMELLS GOOD!
MAYBE SHAMIKO'S COOKING.
MO-MOOO~!
SHAMIKO?
WHAT'S FOR DINNER?
OH, MY!! I AIN'T NEVER SEEN SUCH A LOVELY SMILE ON YA~!
TONIGHT'S DINNER IS MABO NASU* AND FRIED RICE!
PARDON US, BUT WE'LL BE LIVING BELOW YOU FOR A WHILE...
EXCUSE ME?
THIS IS THE ONLY PLACE WHERE THEY COULD STAY.

*Mabo nasu is fried eggplant with ground pork in a spicy red sauce.

BRING ON THE STRONG ODORS

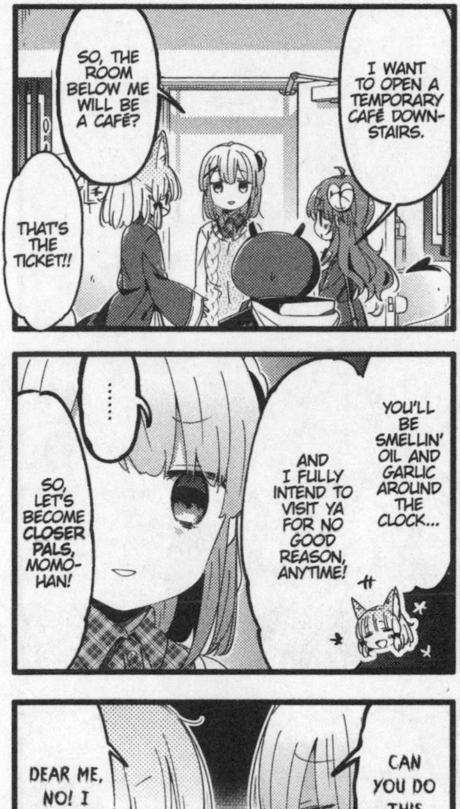
I WANT TO OPEN A TEMPORARY CAFÉ DOWNSTAIRS.
SO, THE ROOM BELOW ME WILL BE A CAFÉ?
THAT'S THE TICKET!!
YOU'LL BE SMELLIN' OIL AND GARLIC AROUND THE CLOCK...
AND I FULLY INTEND TO VISIT YA FOR NO GOOD REASON, ANYTIME!
......
SO, LET'S BECOME CLOSER PALS, MOMO-HAN!
CAN YOU DO THIS SOMEWHERE ELSE? I'LL PAY YOU!
DEAR ME, NO! I COULDN'T GO BORROWIN' MONEY FROM A FRIEND.
DIDN'T YOU MAKE ME BUY YOU A CUTTING BOARD?!
HUH?! WHEN DID THAT HAPPEN?!
WHY, THAT'S EXACTLY WHEN WE BECAME FRIENDS~!

DEMON, BUGGING OUT

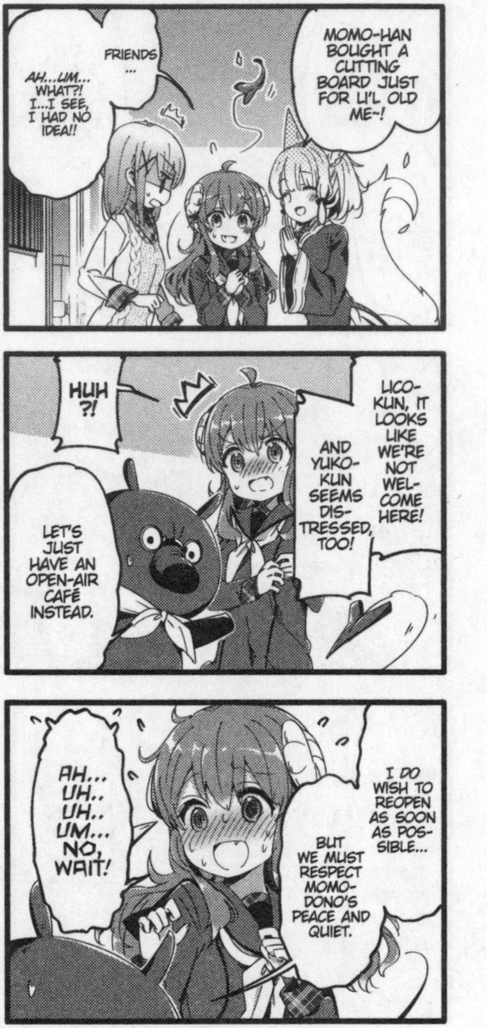
MOMO-HAN BOUGHT A CUTTING BOARD JUST FOR LI'L OLD ME~!
FRIENDS...
AH...UM... WHAT?! I...I SEE, I HAD NO IDEA!!
LICO-KUN, IT LOOKS LIKE WE'RE NOT WEL-COME HERE!
AND YUKO-KUN SEEMS DIS-TRESSED, TOO!
HUH?!
LET'S JUST HAVE AN OPEN-AIR CAFÉ INSTEAD.
I DO WISH TO REOPEN AS SOON AS POS-SIBLE...
BUT WE MUST RESPECT MOMO-DONO'S PEACE AND QUIET.
AH... UH.. UH.. UM... NO, WAIT!
IT'S ALL RIGHT! MOMO HAS ANOTH-ER HOME!
IF IT'S TOO MUCH, SHE CAN GO BACK THERE!!
?!

SUPPORT FROM AN UNEXPECTED ANGLE

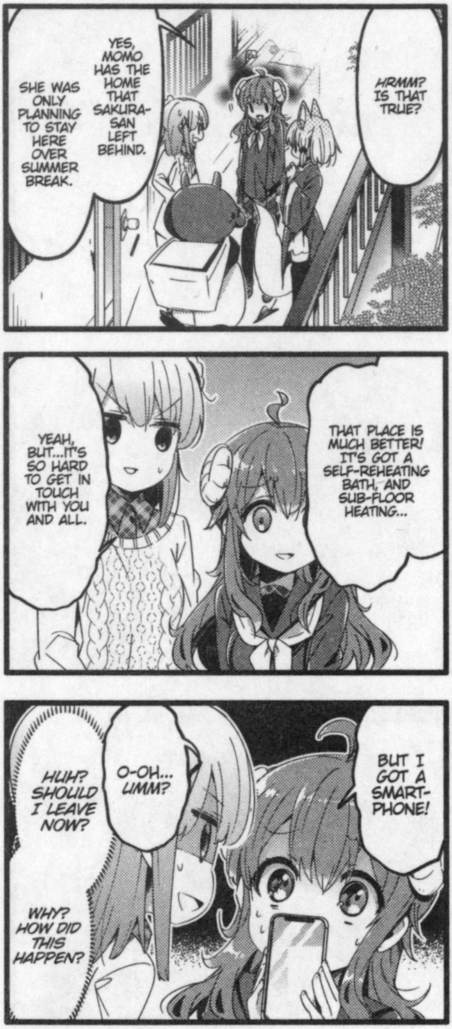
HRMM? IS THAT TRUE?
YES, MOMO HAS THE HOME THAT SAKURA-SAN LEFT BEHIND.
SHE WAS ONLY PLANNING TO STAY HERE OVER SUMMER BREAK.
THAT PLACE IS MUCH BETTER! IT'S GOT A SELF-REHEATING BATH, AND SUB-FLOOR HEATING...
YEAH, BUT...IT'S SO HARD TO GET IN TOUCH WITH YOU AND ALL.
BUT I GOT A SMART-PHONE!
O-OH... UMM?
HUH? SHOULD I LEAVE NOW?
WHY? HOW DID THIS HAPPEN?
IT'S PROBABLY BETTER IF CHIYODA-SAN LIVES NEAR SHAMIKO-CHAN, HMM?
FOR HER DIET.
SOME-ONE'S ON THE ROOF?!
ヌルリ
FWOP
NICE SAVE, OGURA!

BRING ON THE HANG-OUT SPOT

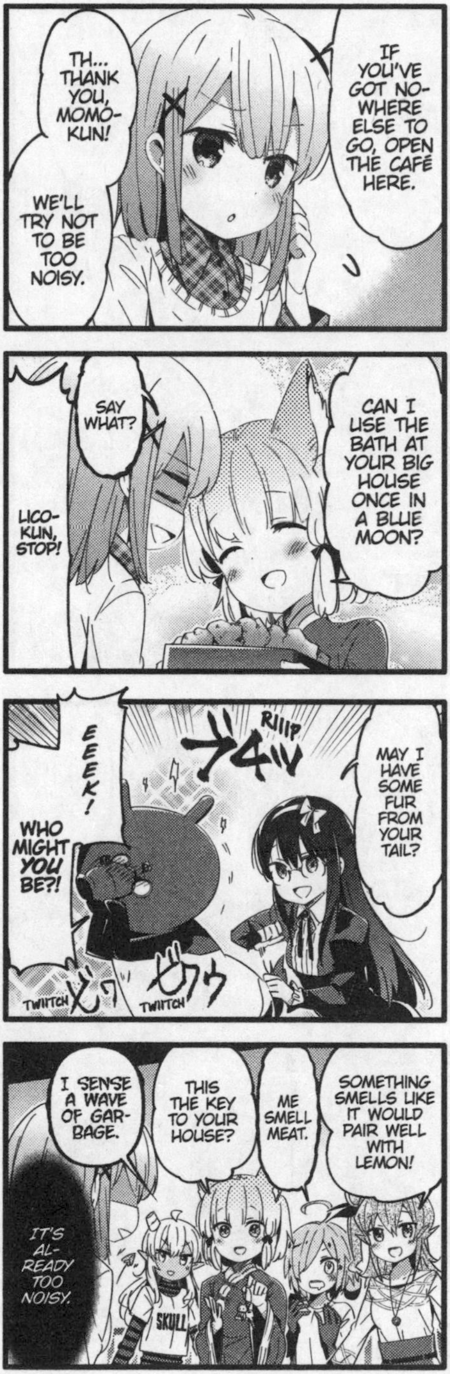
IF YOU'VE GOT NO-WHERE ELSE TO GO, OPEN THE CAFÉ HERE.
TH... THANK YOU, MOMO-KUN!
WE'LL TRY NOT TO BE TOO NOISY.
CAN I USE THE BATH AT YOUR BIG HOUSE ONCE IN A BLUE MOON?
SAY WHAT?
LICO-KUN, STOP!
MAY I HAVE SOME FUR FROM YOUR TAIL?
RIIIP
EEEK!
WHO MIGHT YOU BE?!
TWITCH
TWITCH
SOMETHING SMELLS LIKE IT WOULD PAIR WELL WITH LEMON!
ME SMELL MEAT.
THIS THE KEY TO YOUR HOUSE?
I SENSE A WAVE OF GAR-BAGE.
IT'S AL-READY TOO NOISY.

SAKURA'S TALISMAN

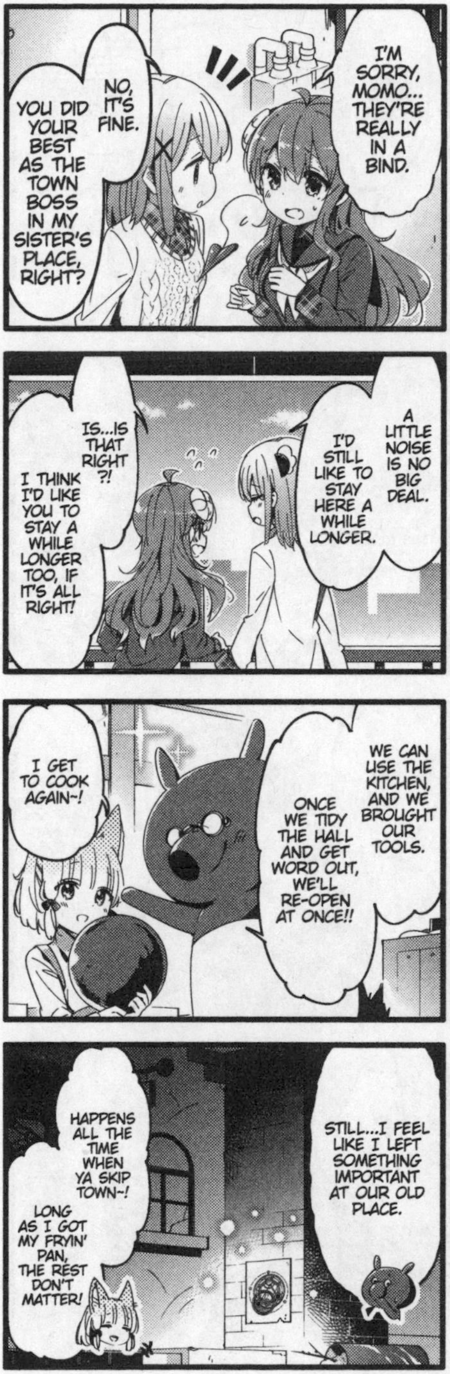
I'M SORRY, MOMO... THEY'RE REALLY IN A BIND.
NO, IT'S FINE.
YOU DID YOUR BEST AS THE TOWN BOSS IN MY SISTER'S PLACE, RIGHT?
A LITTLE NOISE IS NO BIG DEAL.
I'D STILL LIKE TO STAY HERE A WHILE LONGER.
IS...IS THAT RIGHT ?!
I THINK I'D LIKE YOU TO STAY A WHILE LONGER TOO, IF IT'S ALL RIGHT!
WE CAN USE THE KITCHEN, AND WE BROUGHT OUR TOOLS.
ONCE WE TIDY THE HALL AND GET WORD OUT, WE'LL RE-OPEN AT ONCE!!
I GET TO COOK AGAIN~!
STILL...I FEEL LIKE I LEFT SOMETHING IMPORTANT AT OUR OLD PLACE.
HAPPENS ALL THE TIME WHEN YA SKIP TOWN~!
LONG AS I GOT MY FRYIN' PAN, THE REST DON'T MATTER!

YEAR-ROUND FREE-MEAL TICKETS MAKE IT FINE

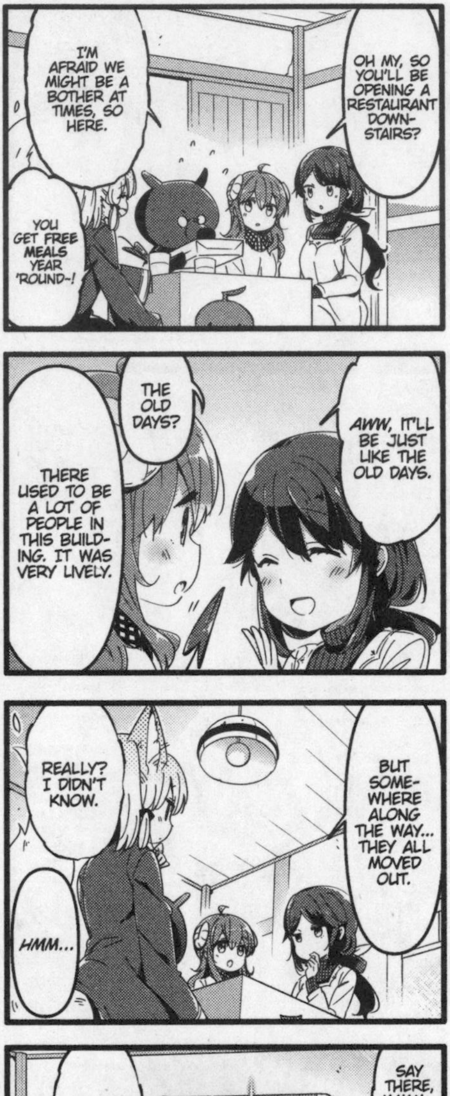
OH MY, SO YOU'LL BE OPENING A RESTAURANT DOWN-STAIRS?
I'M AFRAID WE MIGHT BE A BOTHER AT TIMES, SO HERE.
YOU GET FREE MEALS YEAR 'ROUND~!
AWW, IT'LL BE JUST LIKE THE OLD DAYS.
THE OLD DAYS?
THERE USED TO BE A LOT OF PEOPLE IN THIS BUILD-ING. IT WAS VERY LIVELY.
BUT SOME-WHERE ALONG THE WAY... THEY ALL MOVED OUT.
REALLY? I DIDN'T KNOW.
HMM...
SAY THERE, MA'AM...
MAY I KEEP PREPPED FOOD IN THIS HERE FRIDGE?
AS LONG AS I CAN SHARE IT.
LICO-KUN, DON'T USE OTHER PEOPLE'S REFRIGER-ATORS!

IT'S ALL ABOUT HOW YOU SAY IT

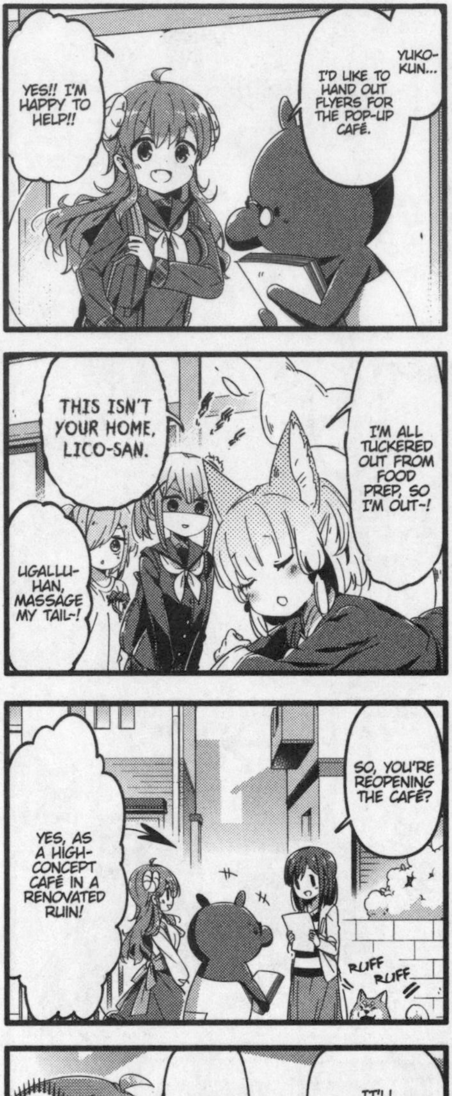
YUKO-KUN...
I'D LIKE TO HAND OUT FLYERS FOR THE POP-UP CAFÉ.
YES!! I'M HAPPY TO HELP!!
I'M ALL TUCKERED OUT FROM FOOD PREP, SO I'M OUT~!
THIS ISN'T YOUR HOME, LICO-SAN.
UGALLU-HAN, MASSAGE MY TAIL~!
SO, YOU'RE REOPENING THE CAFÉ?
YES, AS A HIGH-CONCEPT CAFÉ IN A RENOVATED RUIN!
RUFF RUFF
IT'LL BE VERY GRAMMABLE, SO PLEASE COME!!
OOH~! I CAN'T WAIT~!
MY HOUSE... IS GONNA BE... GRAM-MABLE...

EVEN A HARDCORE FOODIE WOULD BE SCARED OFF

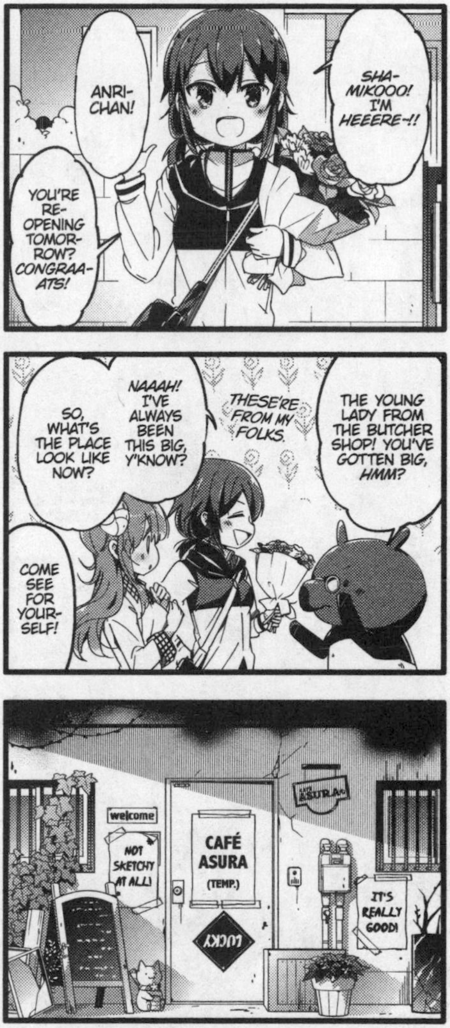
SHA-MIKOOO! I'M HEEERE-!!
ANRI-CHAN!
YOU'RE RE-OPENING TOMORROW? CONGRAAATS!
THE YOUNG LADY FROM THE BUTCHER SHOP! YOU'VE GOTTEN BIG, HMM?
THESE'RE FROM MY FOLKS.
NAAAH! I'VE ALWAYS BEEN THIS BIG, Y'KNOW?
SO, WHAT'S THE PLACE LOOK LIKE NOW?
COME SEE FOR YOURSELF!
welcome
NOT SKETCHY AT ALL!
CAFÉ ASURA (TEMP.)
LUCKY
IT'S REALLY GOOD!
......
YEP, THAT'S PRETTY OFF-PUTTING!!
WHA...?! NO IT'S NOT! IT'S LIKE A FUN HIDEOUT!!

YOU HAVE TO TRY IT TO UNDERSTAND

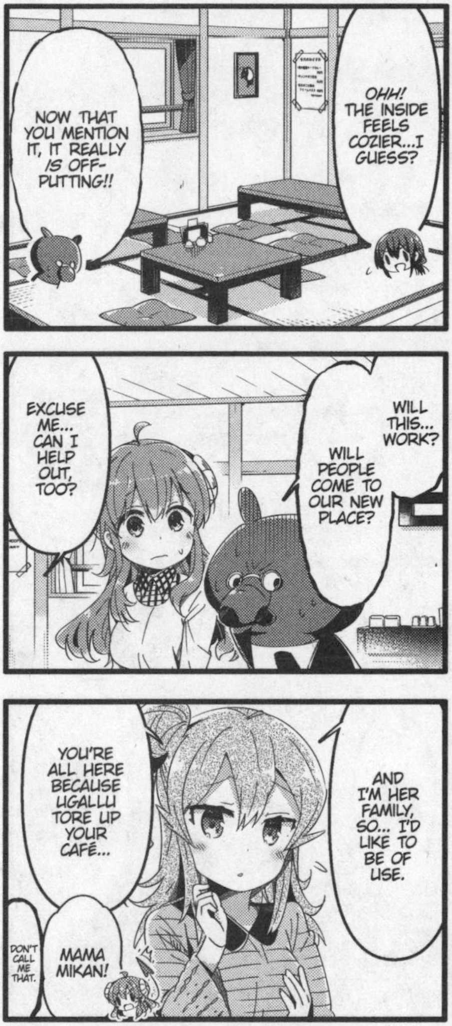
OHH! THE INSIDE FEELS COZIER...I GUESS?
NOW THAT YOU MENTION IT, IT REALLY IS OFF-PUTTING!!
WILL THIS... WORK?
WILL PEOPLE COME TO OUR NEW PLACE?
EXCUSE ME... CAN I HELP OUT, TOO?
YOU'RE ALL HERE BECAUSE UGALLU TORE UP YOUR CAFÉ...
AND I'M HER FAMILY, SO... I'D LIKE TO BE OF USE.
MAMA MIKAN!
DON'T CALL ME THAT.
I BROUGHT SAMPLES, TOO!
ALSO, HERE ARE THE CATALOGS FOR MY FAMILY'S PRODUCTS!!
IF YOU ORDER OUR NEW SALAD DRESSING TODAY, SHIPPING IS FREE!!
MIKAN-SAN, ARE YOU JUST HERE TO MAKE SALES?

I'LL SHOW YA WHAT I'M MADE OF

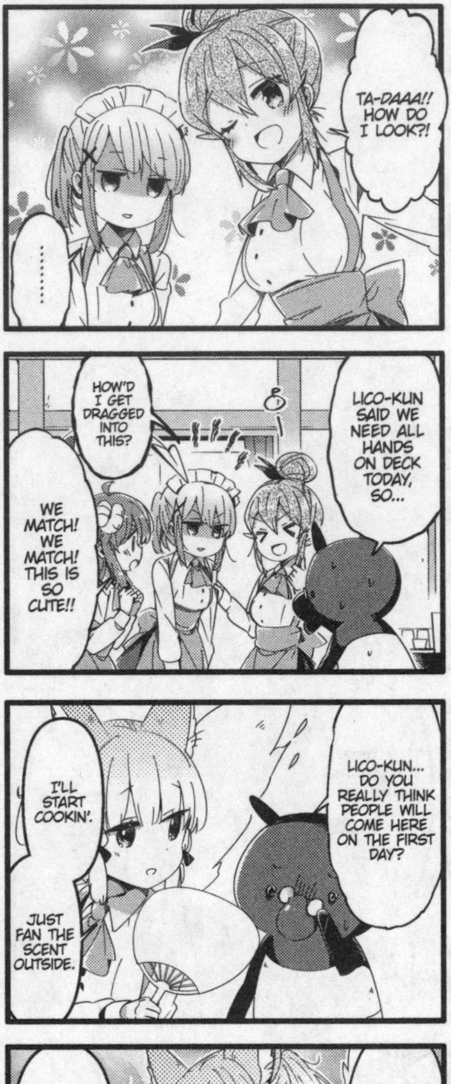
TA-DAAA!! HOW DO I LOOK?!
......
LICO-KUN SAID WE NEED ALL HANDS ON DECK TODAY, SO...
HOW'D I GET DRAGGED INTO THIS?
WE MATCH! WE MATCH! THIS IS SO CUTE!!
LICO-KUN... DO YOU REALLY THINK PEOPLE WILL COME HERE ON THE FIRST DAY?
I'LL START COOKIN'.
JUST FAN THE SCENT OUTSIDE.
I'VE BEEN WIELDING THIS PAN SO LONG...
LIKE I WAS WAITING FOR THIS DAY.
MY HARD WORK AND TASTY FOOD WON'T LET US DOWN!

IT'S JUST PLAIN TASTY THIS TIME

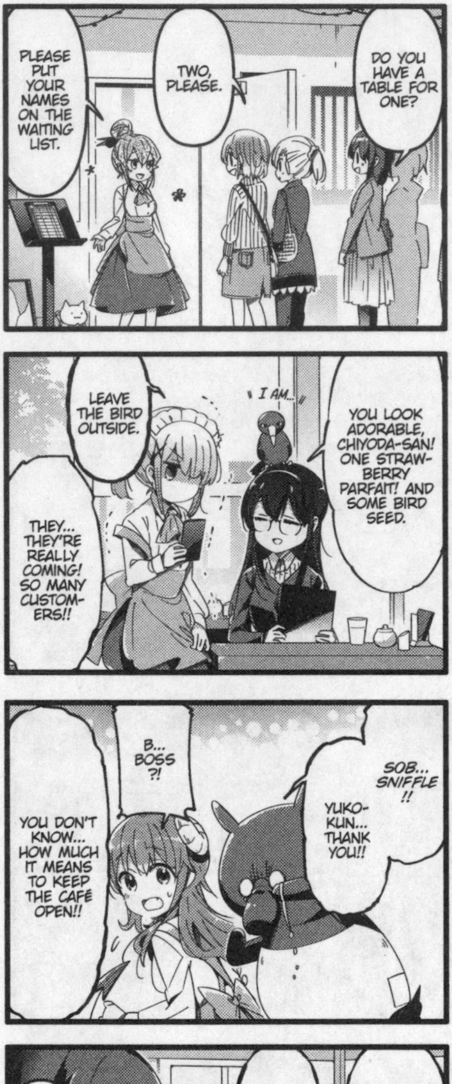
DO YOU HAVE A TABLE FOR ONE?
TWO, PLEASE.
PLEASE PUT YOUR NAMES ON THE WAITING LIST.
YOU LOOK ADORABLE, CHIYODA-SAN! ONE STRAWBERRY PARFAIT! AND SOME BIRD SEED.
I AM...
LEAVE THE BIRD OUTSIDE.
THEY... THEY'RE REALLY COMING! SO MANY CUSTOMERS!!
SOB... SNIFFLE!!
YUKO-KUN... THANK YOU!!
B... BOSS?!
YOU DON'T KNOW... HOW MUCH IT MEANS TO KEEP THE CAFÉ OPEN!!
CURRY... CURRY... ASURA CURRY... AT LAST!
PARFAIT, PARFAIT, PARFAIT, PARFAIT!
WHY ARE THEY REACTING LIKE THAT?

TAPIR EYE JUICE

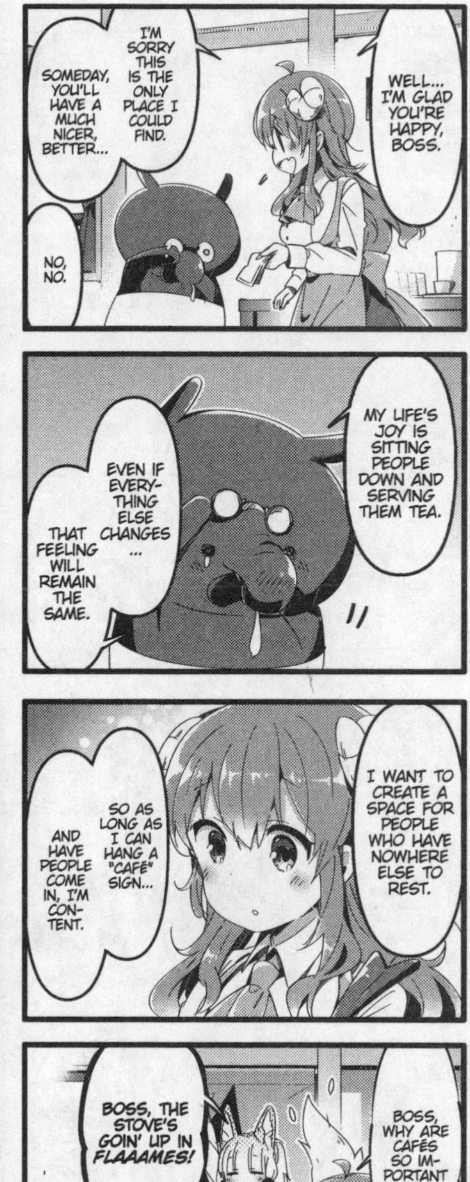
WELL... I'M GLAD YOU'RE HAPPY, BOSS.
I'M SORRY THIS IS THE ONLY PLACE I COULD FIND.
SOMEDAY, YOU'LL HAVE A MUCH NICER, BETTER...
NO, NO.
MY LIFE'S JOY IS SITTING PEOPLE DOWN AND SERVING THEM TEA.
EVEN IF EVERYTHING ELSE CHANGES...
THAT FEELING WILL REMAIN THE SAME.
I WANT TO CREATE A SPACE FOR PEOPLE WHO HAVE NOWHERE ELSE TO REST.
SO AS LONG AS I CAN HANG A "CAFÉ" SIGN...
AND HAVE PEOPLE COME IN, I'M CONTENT.
BOSS, WHY ARE CAFÉS SO IMPORTANT TO--
BOSS, THE STOVE'S GOIN' UP IN *FLAAAMES!*
GOODNESS, LICO-KUN, YOU WORK FAST!!

BECOME A DEMON WHO REMEMBERS IMPORTANT DETAILS

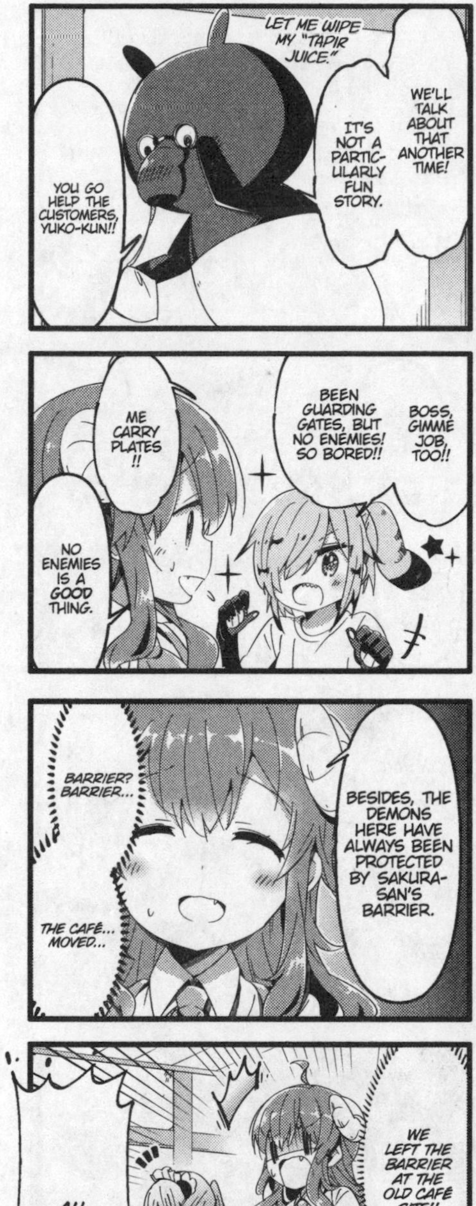
LET ME WIPE MY "TAPIR JUICE."
WE'LL TALK ABOUT THAT ANOTHER TIME!
IT'S NOT A PARTICULARLY FUN STORY.
YOU GO HELP THE CUSTOMERS, YUKO-KUN!!
BOSS, GIMME JOB, TOO!!
BEEN GUARDING GATES, BUT NO ENEMIES! SO BORED!!
ME CARRY PLATES!!
NO ENEMIES IS A GOOD THING.
BESIDES, THE DEMONS HERE HAVE ALWAYS BEEN PROTECTED BY SAKURA-SAN'S BARRIER.
BARRIER? BARRIER...
THE CAFÉ... MOVED...
WE LEFT THE BARRIER AT THE OLD CAFÉ SITE!!
AH... AAAAAH!! MOMO-OOOO!!

THERE AIN'T NOBODY LIKE THAT

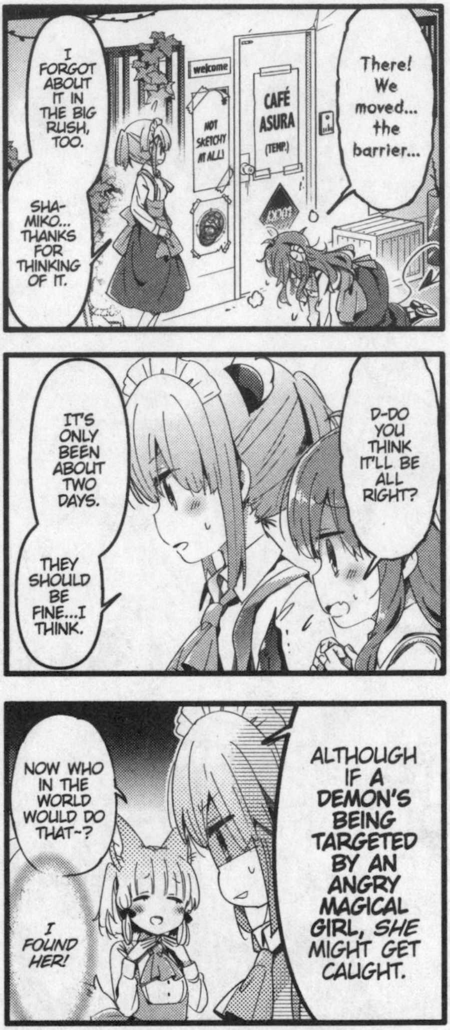
There! We moved... the barrier...
I FORGOT ABOUT IT IN THE BIG RUSH, TOO.
welcome
CAFÉ ASURA (TEMP.)
NOT SKETCHY AT ALL!
SHA-MIKO... THANKS FOR THINKING OF IT.
D-DO YOU THINK IT'LL BE ALL RIGHT?
IT'S ONLY BEEN ABOUT TWO DAYS.
THEY SHOULD BE FINE...I THINK.
ALTHOUGH IF A DEMON'S BEING TARGETED BY AN ANGRY MAGICAL GIRL, SHE MIGHT GET CAUGHT.
NOW WHO IN THE WORLD WOULD DO THAT~?
I FOUND HER!
AFTER TEN LONG YEARS...
I'VE FINALLY SPOTTED HER.

HATH THE TIME COME?

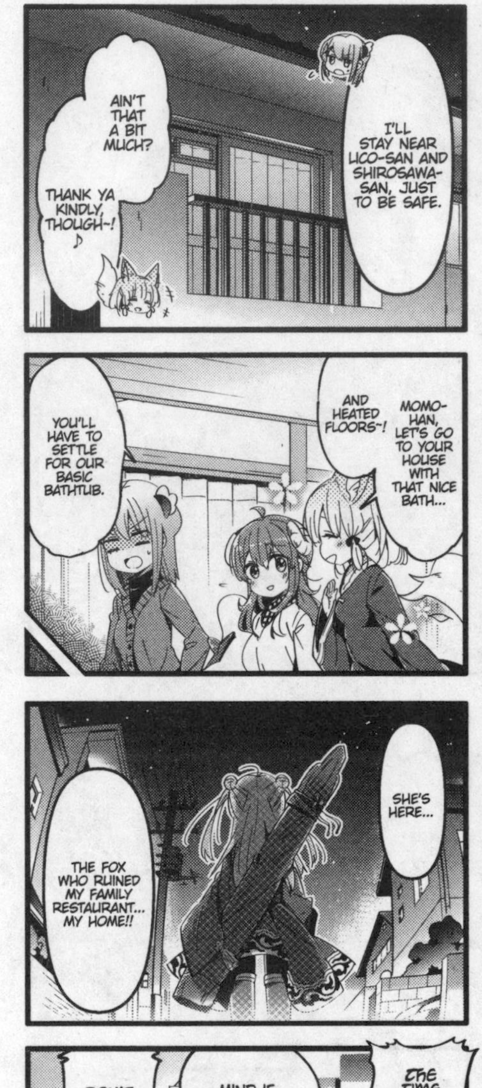
I'LL STAY NEAR LICO-SAN AND SHIROSAWA-SAN, JUST TO BE SAFE.
AIN'T THAT A BIT MUCH?
THANK YA KINDLY, THOUGH~! ♪
MOMO-HAN, LET'S GO TO YOUR HOUSE WITH THAT NICE BATH...
AND HEATED FLOORS~!
YOU'LL HAVE TO SETTLE FOR OUR BASIC BATHTUB.
SHE'S HERE...
THE FOX WHO RUINED MY FAMILY RESTAURANT... MY HOME!!
The time hath come!! Come hath the time!!
MIND IF LI'L LICO BORROWS THIS BED?
DON'T STEAL THE CAT'S SPOT!
DON'T GIVE UP, SHAMIKO!! LOOKS LIKE YOU'VE GOT COMPANY!!

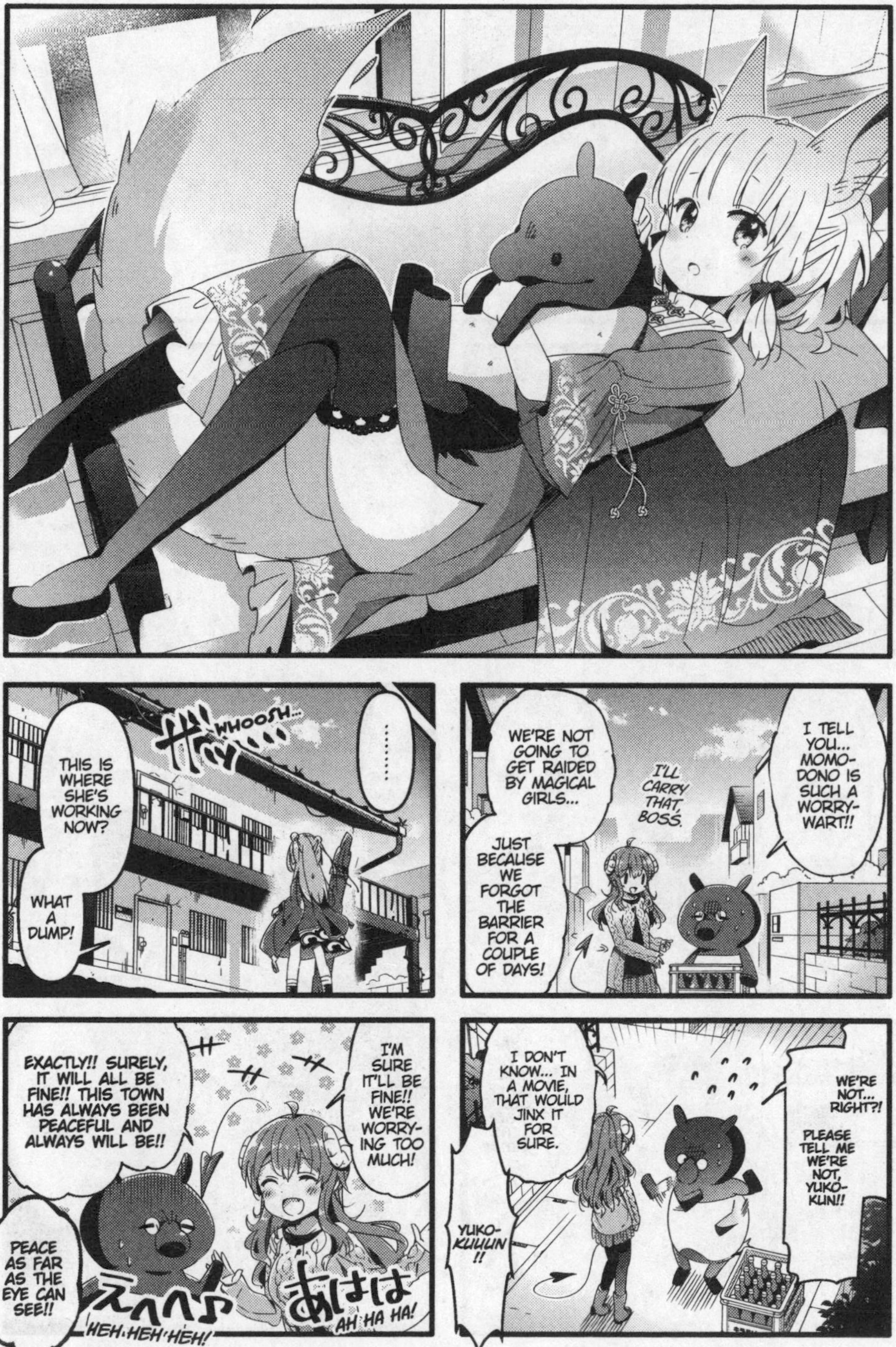
I TELL YOU... MOMO-DONO IS SUCH A WORRY-WART!!
WE'RE NOT GOING TO GET RAIDED BY MAGICAL GIRLS...
I'LL CARRY THAT, BOSS.
JUST BECAUSE WE FORGOT THE BARRIER FOR A COUPLE OF DAYS!
......
WHOOSH...
THIS IS WHERE SHE'S WORKING NOW?
WHAT A DUMP!
WE'RE NOT... RIGHT?!
PLEASE TELL ME WE'RE NOT, YUKO-KUN!!
I DON'T KNOW... IN A MOVIE, THAT WOULD JINX IT FOR SURE.
YUKO-KUUUN!!
I'M SURE IT'LL BE FINE!! WE'RE WORRYING TOO MUCH!
EXACTLY!! SURELY, IT WILL ALL BE FINE!! THIS TOWN HAS ALWAYS BEEN PEACEFUL AND ALWAYS WILL BE!!
あはは
AH HA HA!
えへへ♪
HEH HEH HEH!
PEACE AS FAR AS THE EYE CAN SEE!!

SERVICE WITH A SMILE, Y'HEAR?

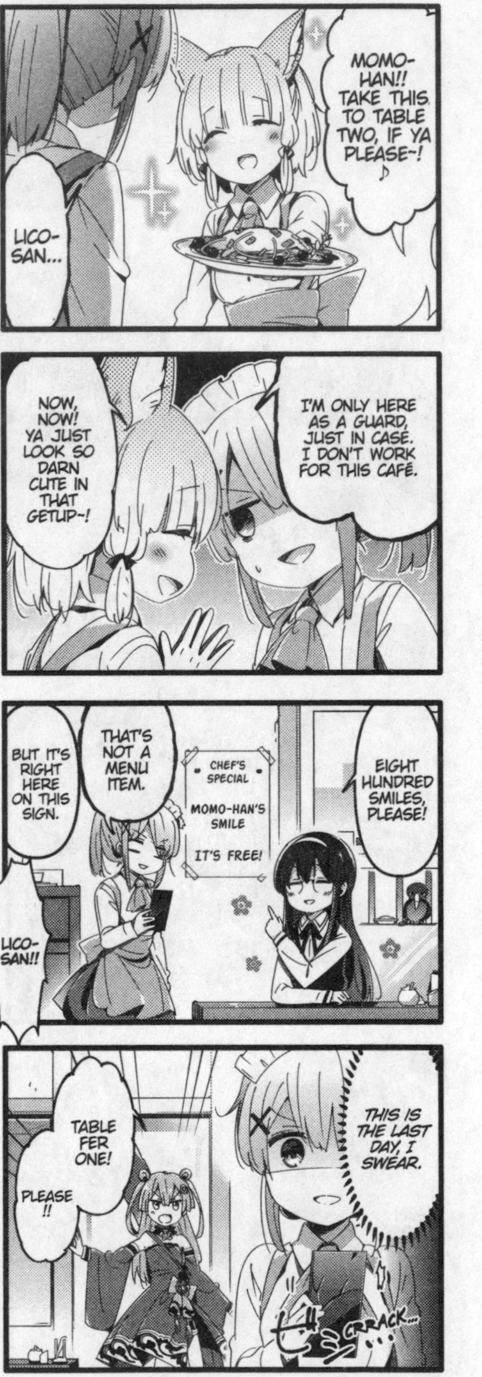
MOMO-HAN!! TAKE THIS TO TABLE TWO, IF YA PLEASE~! ♪
LICO-SAN...
I'M ONLY HERE AS A GUARD, JUST IN CASE. I DON'T WORK FOR THIS CAFÉ.
NOW, NOW! YA JUST LOOK SO DARN CUTE IN THAT GETUP~!
EIGHT HUNDRED SMILES, PLEASE!
CHEF'S SPECIAL
MOMO-HAN'S SMILE
IT'S FREE!
THAT'S NOT A MENU ITEM.
BUT IT'S RIGHT HERE ON THIS SIGN.
LICO-SAN!!
THIS IS THE LAST DAY, I SWEAR.
TABLE FER ONE!
PLEASE!!
CRRACK...

DOING BUSINESS WITH DEADLY DEPLOYMENT

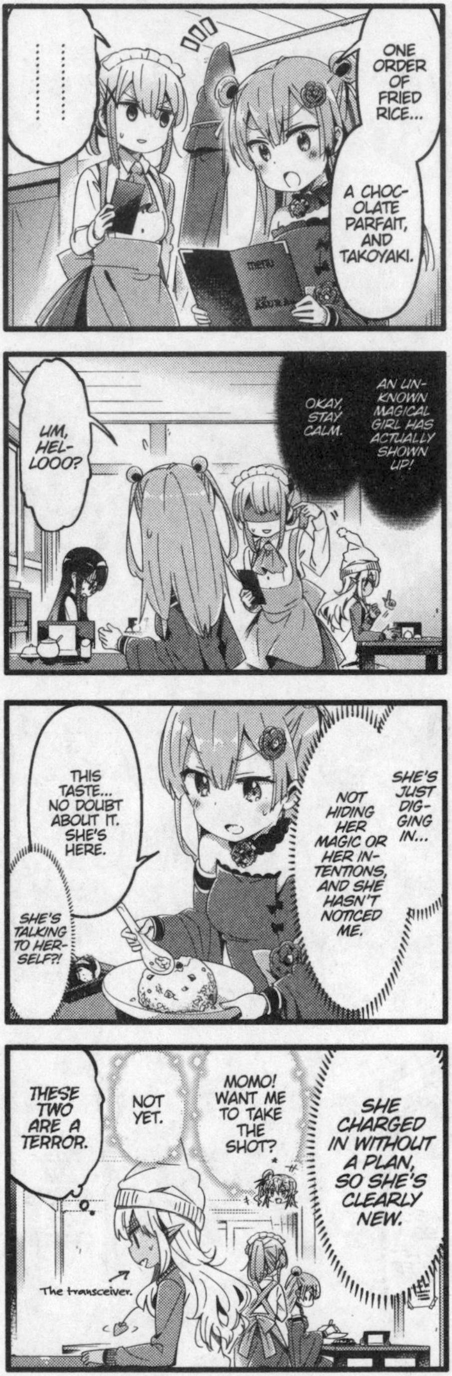
ONE ORDER OF FRIED RICE...
A CHOCOLATE PARFAIT, AND TAKOYAKI.
......
AN UNKNOWN MAGICAL GIRL HAS ACTUALLY SHOWN UP!
OKAY, STAY CALM.
UM, HELLOOO?
SHE'S JUST DIGGING IN...
NOT HIDING HER MAGIC OR HER INTENTIONS, AND SHE HASN'T NOTICED ME.
THIS TASTE... NO DOUBT ABOUT IT. SHE'S HERE.
SHE'S TALKING TO HERSELF?!
SHE CHARGED IN WITHOUT A PLAN, SO SHE'S CLEARLY NEW.
MOMO! WANT ME TO TAKE THE SHOT?
NOT YET.
THESE TWO ARE A TERROR.
The transceiver.

NO KIDDIN'

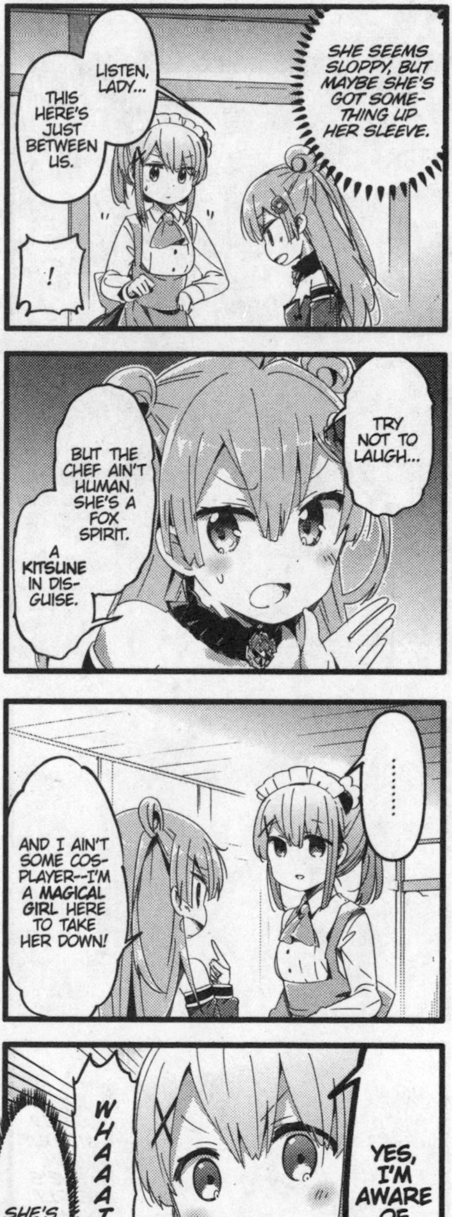
SHE SEEMS SLOPPY, BUT MAYBE SHE'S GOT SOMETHING UP HER SLEEVE.
LISTEN, LADY...
THIS HERE'S JUST BETWEEN US.
!
TRY NOT TO LAUGH...
BUT THE CHEF AIN'T HUMAN. SHE'S A FOX SPIRIT.
A KITSUNE IN DISGUISE.
......
AND I AIN'T SOME COSPLAYER--I'M A MAGICAL GIRL HERE TO TAKE HER DOWN!
YES, I'M AWARE OF THAT!!
WHAAAAT?!
SHE'S SO SIMPLE-MINDED!!

LICO-KUN'S TRUE NATURE, ALREADY REVEALED!!

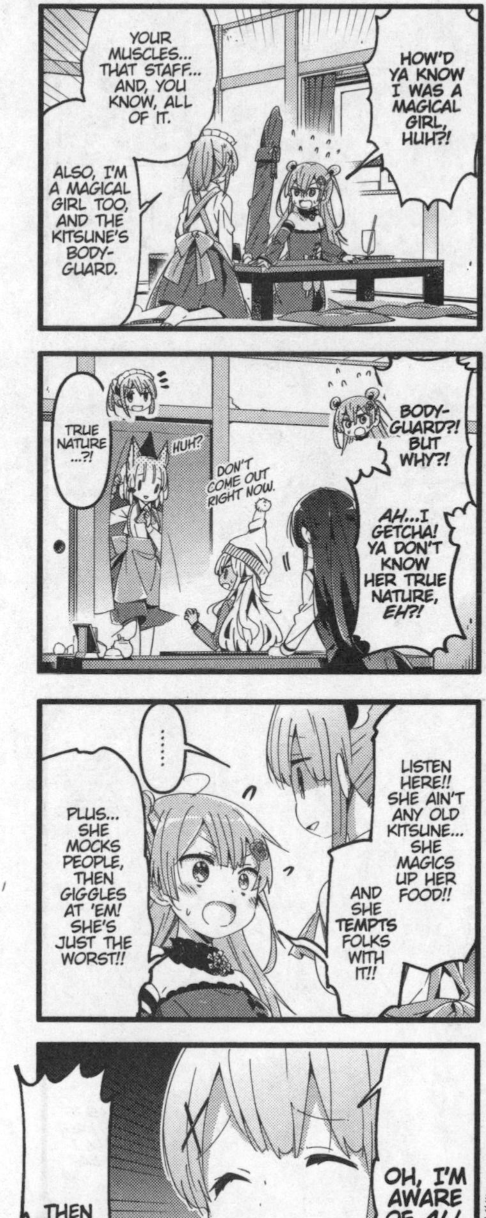
HOW'D YA KNOW I WAS A MAGICAL GIRL, HUH?!
YOUR MUSCLES... THAT STAFF... AND, YOU KNOW, ALL OF IT.
ALSO, I'M A MAGICAL GIRL TOO, AND THE KITSUNE'S BODYGUARD.
BODYGUARD?! BUT WHY?!
AH...I GETCHA! YA DON'T KNOW HER TRUE NATURE, EH?!
DON'T COME OUT RIGHT NOW.
HUH?
TRUE NATURE ...?!
LISTEN HERE!! SHE AIN'T ANY OLD KITSUNE... SHE MAGICS UP HER FOOD!!
AND SHE TEMPTS FOLKS WITH IT!!
......
PLUS... SHE MOCKS PEOPLE, THEN GIGGLES AT 'EM! SHE'S JUST THE WORST!!
OH, I'M AWARE OF ALL THAT!!
THEN WHYYY?!!

RETORTING ONE STEP AT A TIME

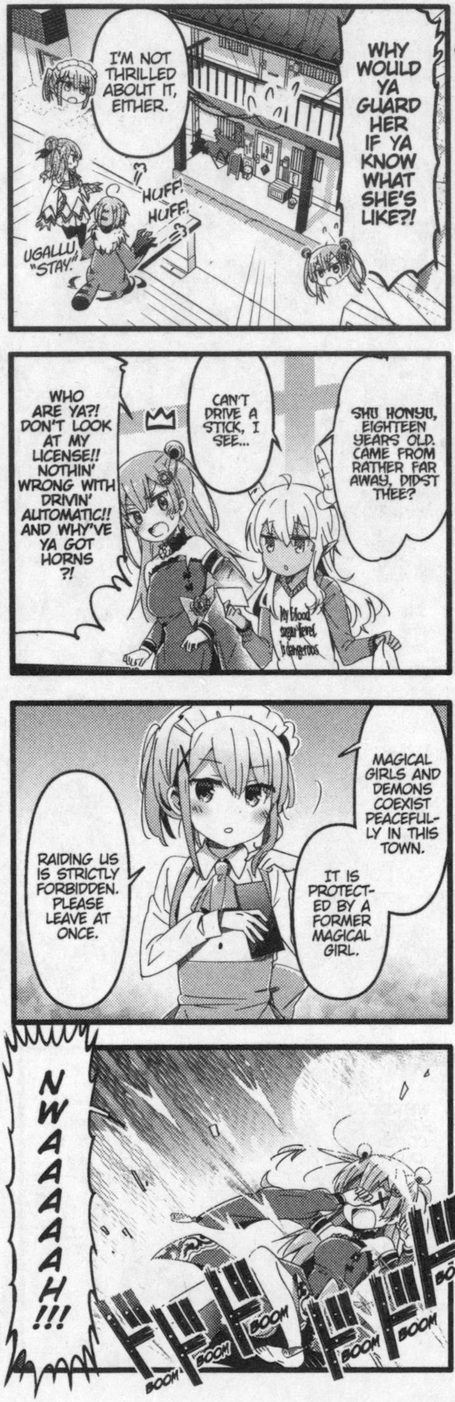
WHY WOULD YA GUARD HER IF YA KNOW WHAT SHE'S LIKE?!
I'M NOT THRILLED ABOUT IT, EITHER.
HUFF! HUFF!
UGALLU, "STAY."
SHU HONYU, EIGHTEEN YEARS OLD. CAME FROM RATHER FAR AWAY, DIDST THEE?
CAN'T DRIVE A STICK, I SEE...
WHO ARE YA?! DON'T LOOK AT MY LICENSE!! NOTHIN' WRONG WITH DRIVIN' AUTOMATIC!! AND WHY'VE YA GOT HORNS?!
MAGICAL GIRLS AND DEMONS COEXIST PEACEFULLY IN THIS TOWN.
IT IS PROTECTED BY A FORMER MAGICAL GIRL.
RAIDING US IS STRICTLY FORBIDDEN. PLEASE LEAVE AT ONCE.
NWAAAAAAH!!!

A CONVENIENT STOPPING-CORD

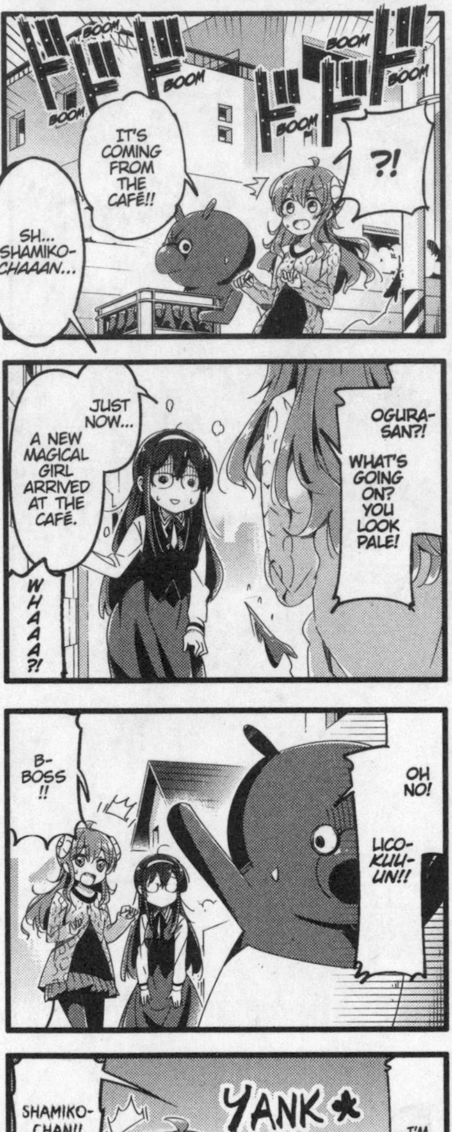
?!
IT'S COMING FROM THE CAFÉ!!
SH... SHAMIKO-CHAAAN...
OGURA-SAN?! WHAT'S GOING ON? YOU LOOK PALE!
JUST NOW... A NEW MAGICAL GIRL ARRIVED AT THE CAFÉ.
WHAAAA?!
OH NO! LICO-KUUUN!!
B-BOSS!!
I'M GOING, TOO!
YANK
SHAMIKO-CHAN!! STOP RIGHT THERE!!
BWEHH!

THE SECRET OF THE BARRIER, REVEALED!

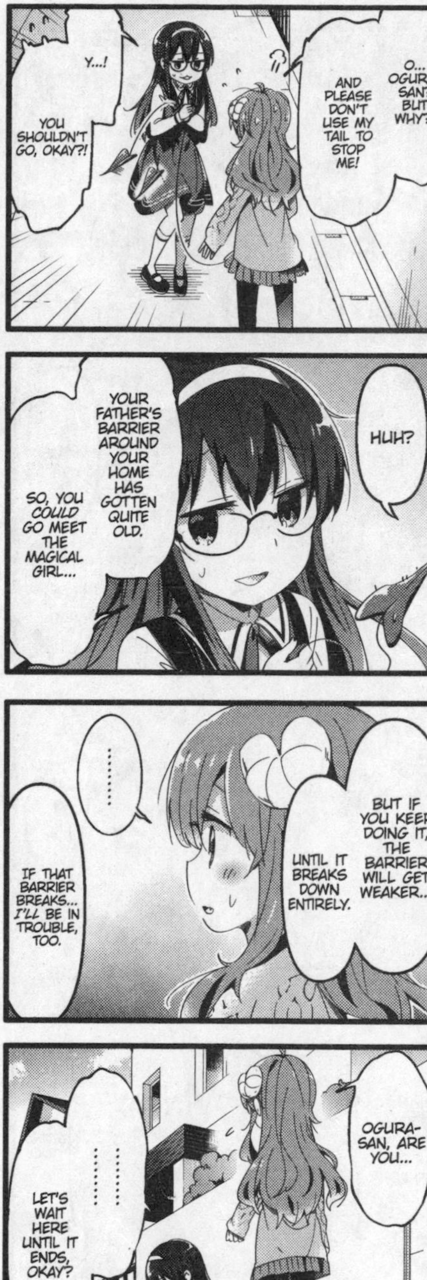
O... OGURA-SAN? BUT WHY?!
AND PLEASE DON'T USE MY TAIL TO STOP ME!
Y...!
YOU SHOULDN'T GO, OKAY?!
HUH?
YOUR FATHER'S BARRIER AROUND YOUR HOME HAS GOTTEN QUITE OLD.
SO, YOU COULD GO MEET THE MAGICAL GIRL...
BUT IF YOU KEEP DOING IT, THE BARRIER WILL GET WEAKER...
UNTIL IT BREAKS DOWN ENTIRELY.
......
IF THAT BARRIER BREAKS... I'LL BE IN TROUBLE, TOO.
OGURA-SAN, ARE YOU...
......
LET'S WAIT HERE UNTIL IT ENDS, OKAY?

A DEMON WHO'S GOTTEN A LITTLE MORE MUSCULAR

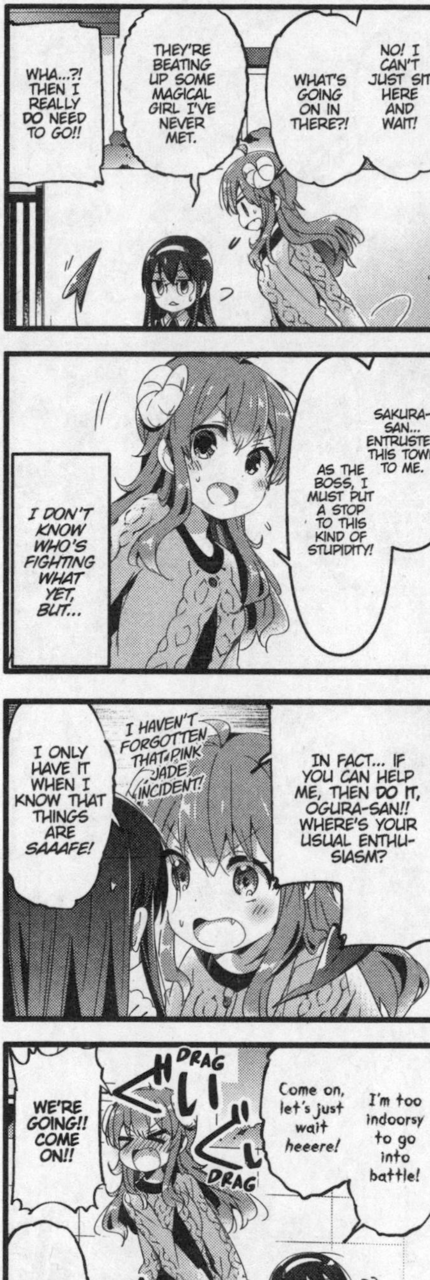
NO! I CAN'T JUST SIT HERE AND WAIT!
WHAT'S GOING ON IN THERE?!
THEY'RE BEATING UP SOME MAGICAL GIRL I'VE NEVER MET.
WHA...?! THEN I REALLY DO NEED TO GO!!
SAKURA-SAN... ENTRUSTED THIS TOWN TO ME.
AS THE BOSS, I MUST PUT A STOP TO THIS KIND OF STUPIDITY!
I DON'T KNOW WHO'S FIGHTING WHAT YET, BUT...
IN FACT... IF YOU CAN HELP ME, THEN DO IT, OGURA-SAN!! WHERE'S YOUR USUAL ENTHUSIASM?
I HAVEN'T FORGOTTEN THAT PINK JADE INCIDENT!
I ONLY HAVE IT WHEN I KNOW THAT THINGS ARE SAAAFE!
I'm too indoorsy to go into battle!
Come on, let's just wait heeere!
DRAG
WE'RE GOING!! COME ON!!
DRAG
I DON'T WAAANNA!
DRAG

MAKE-OR-BREAK MOVE

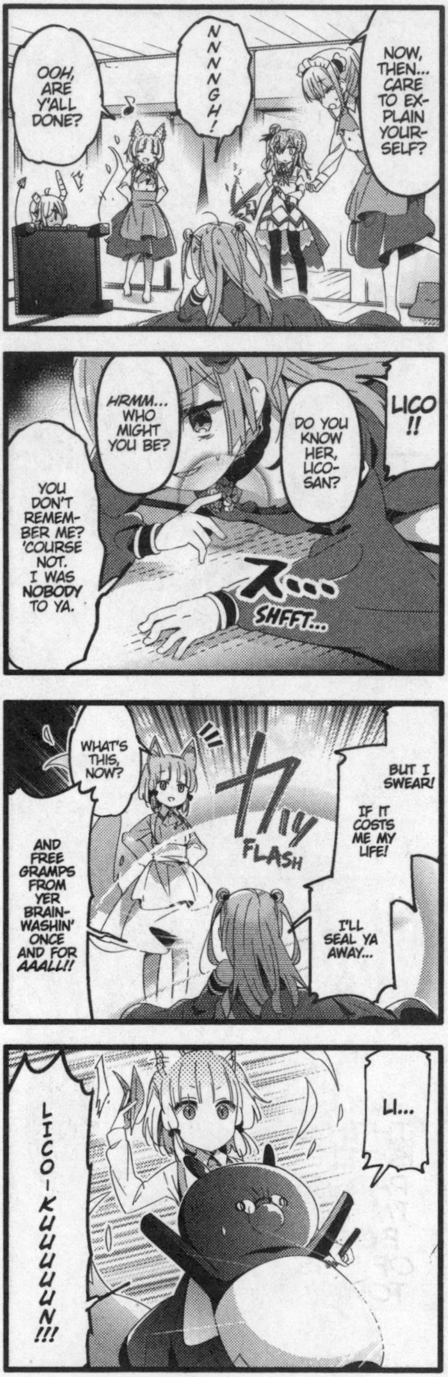
NOW, THEN... CARE TO EXPLAIN YOURSELF?
NNNNGH!
OOH, ARE Y'ALL DONE?
LICO!!
DO YOU KNOW HER, LICO-SAN?
HRMM... WHO MIGHT YOU BE?
YOU DON'T REMEMBER ME? 'COURSE NOT. I WAS NOBODY TO YA.
ス…
SHFFT...
BUT I SWEAR!
IF IT COSTS ME MY LIFE!
I'LL SEAL YA AWAY...
カッ
FLASH
WHAT'S THIS, NOW?
AND FREE GRAMPS FROM YER BRAINWASHIN' ONCE AND FOR AAALL!!
LI...
LICO-KUUUUUN!!!

BECOME A DEMON WHO GETS TO THE BATTLEFIELD ON TIME

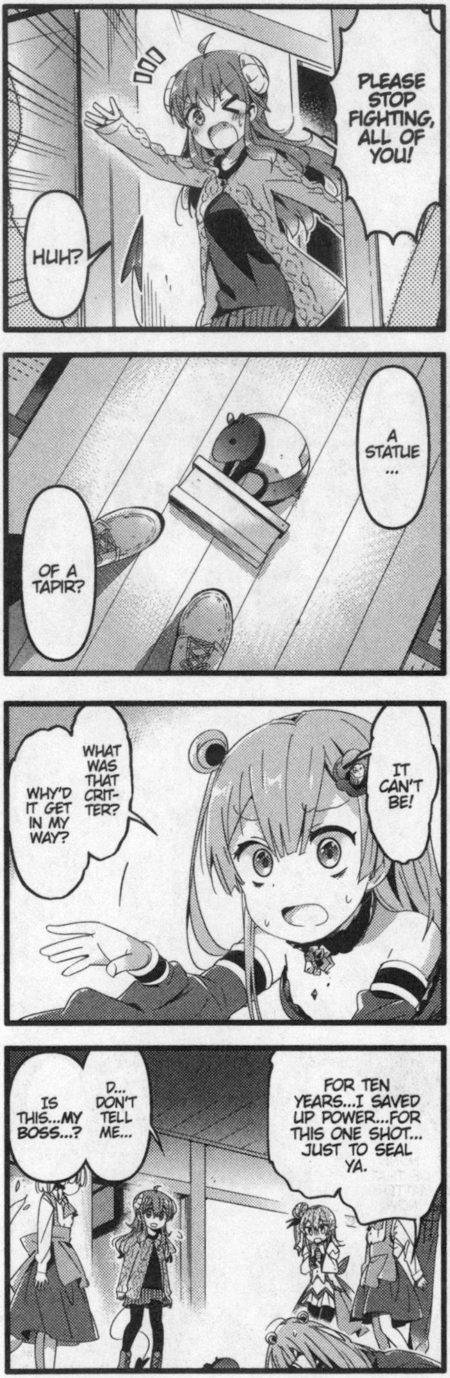
PLEASE STOP FIGHTING, ALL OF YOU!
HUH?
A STATUE...
OF A TAPIR?
IT CAN'T BE!
WHAT WAS THAT CRITTER?
WHY'D IT GET IN MY WAY?
FOR TEN YEARS...I SAVED UP POWER...FOR THIS ONE SHOT... JUST TO SEAL YA.
D... DON'T TELL ME...
IS THIS...MY BOSS...?

FORGET IT

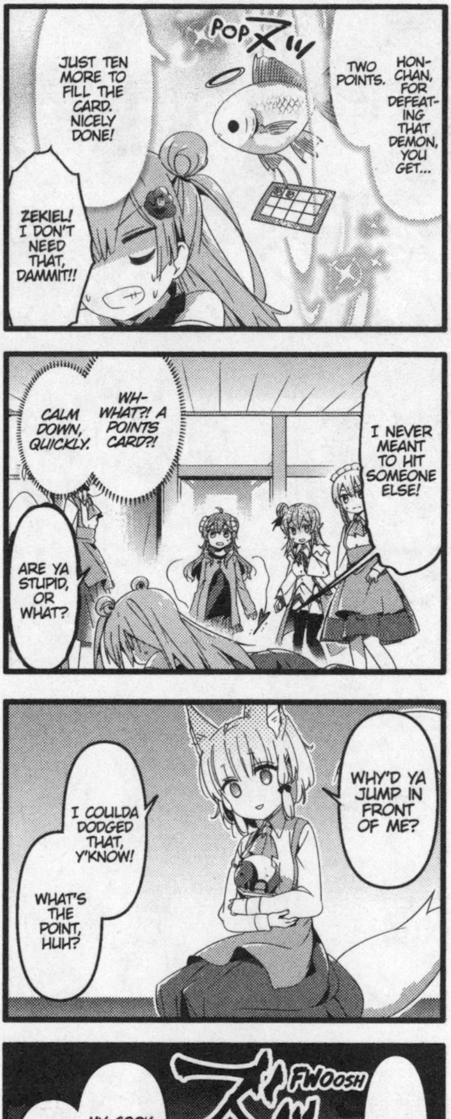
HON-CHAN, FOR DEFEATING THAT DEMON, YOU GET...
TWO POINTS.
POP
JUST TEN MORE TO FILL THE CARD. NICELY DONE!
ZEKIEL! I DON'T NEED THAT, DAMMIT!!
I NEVER MEANT TO HIT SOMEONE ELSE!
WH-WHAT?! A POINTS CARD?!
CALM DOWN, QUICKLY.
ARE YA STUPID, OR WHAT?
WHY'D YA JUMP IN FRONT OF ME?
I COULDA DODGED THAT, Y'KNOW!
WHAT'S THE POINT, HUH?
OH... FORGET IT.
FWOOSH
MY COOK-ING...THE CAFÉ...
NONE OF THAT MATTERS NOW.
?!

DIRECTLY TO THE BRAIN!!

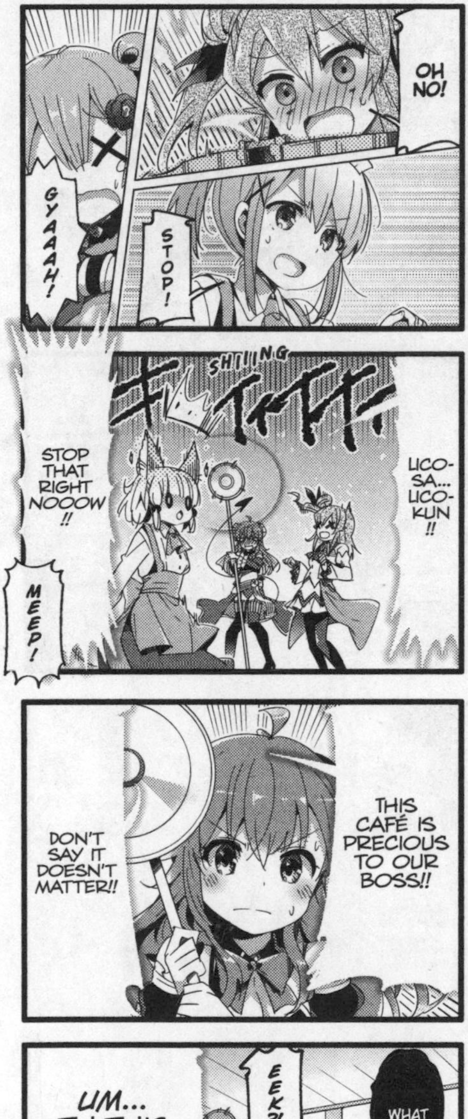
OH NO!
STOP!
GYAAAH!
SHIIING
LICO-SA... LICO-KUN!!
STOP THAT RIGHT NOOOW!!
MEEP!
THIS CAFÉ IS PRECIOUS TO OUR BOSS!!
DON'T SAY IT DOESN'T MATTER!!
WHAT THE...?!
EEK?!
UM... TH-THIS IS TELE-PATHY!! I'M THE BOSS OF THIS TOWN!!

A "SMARTDEMON" WHO ISN'T THAT SMART

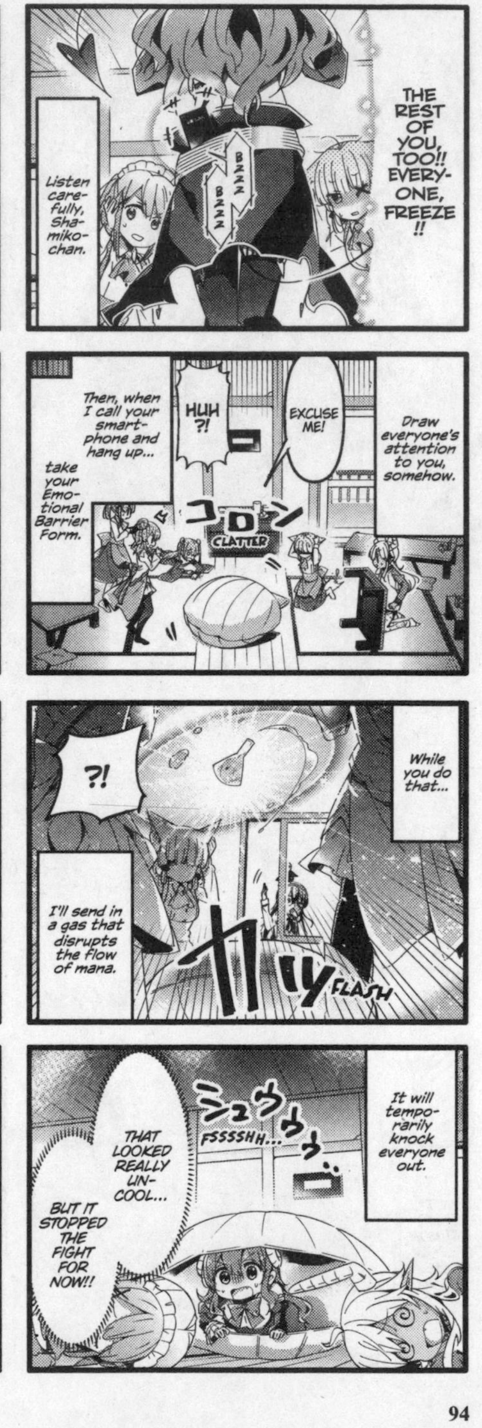
THE REST OF YOU, TOO!! EVERYONE, FREEZE!!
BZZZ BZZZ
Listen carefully, Shamiko-chan.
Draw everyone's attention to you, somehow.
EXCUSE ME!
HUH ?!
Then, when I call your smartphone and hang up...
take your Emotional Barrier Form.
CLATTER
While you do that...
?!
I'll send in a gas that disrupts the flow of mana.
FLASH
It will temporarily knock everyone out.
FSSSSHH...
THAT LOOKED REALLY UNCOOL...
BUT IT STOPPED THE FIGHT FOR NOW!!

MADE WITH PERFECTLY LEGAL COMPONENTS

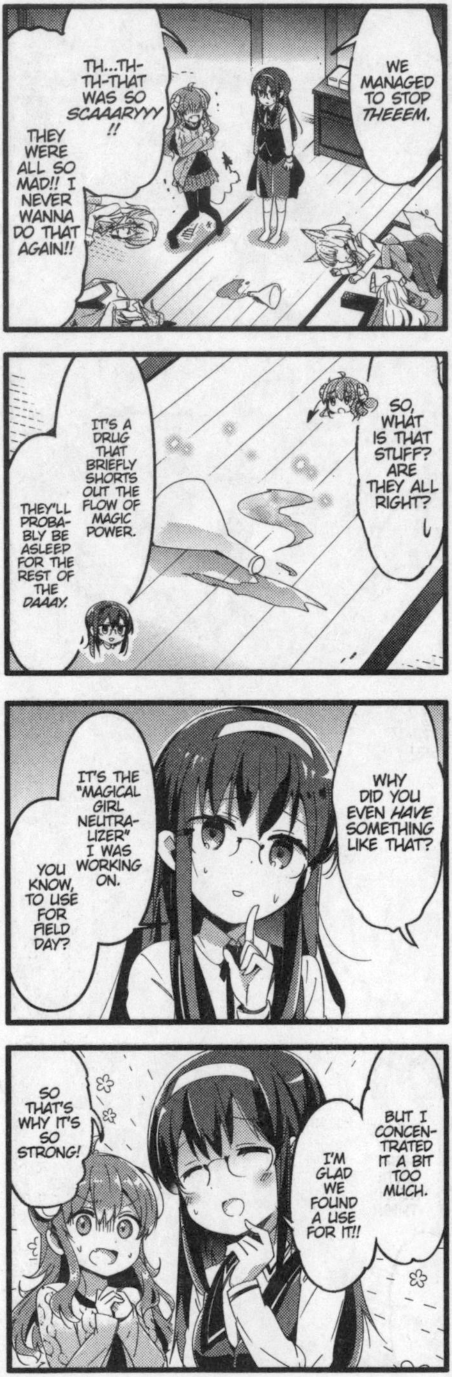
WE MANAGED TO STOP THEEEM.
TH...TH-TH-THAT WAS SO SCAAARYYY!!
THEY WERE ALL SO MAD!! I NEVER WANNA DO THAT AGAIN!!
SO, WHAT IS THAT STUFF? ARE THEY ALL RIGHT?
IT'S A DRUG THAT BRIEFLY SHORTS OUT THE FLOW OF MAGIC POWER.
THEY'LL PROBABLY BE ASLEEP FOR THE REST OF THE DAAAY.
WHY DID YOU EVEN HAVE SOMETHING LIKE THAT?
IT'S THE "MAGICAL GIRL NEUTRALIZER" I WAS WORKING ON.
YOU KNOW, TO USE FOR FIELD DAY?
BUT I CONCENTRATED IT A BIT TOO MUCH.
I'M GLAD WE FOUND A USE FOR IT!!
SO THAT'S WHY IT'S SO STRONG!

A DEMON DEMANDS OVERTIME

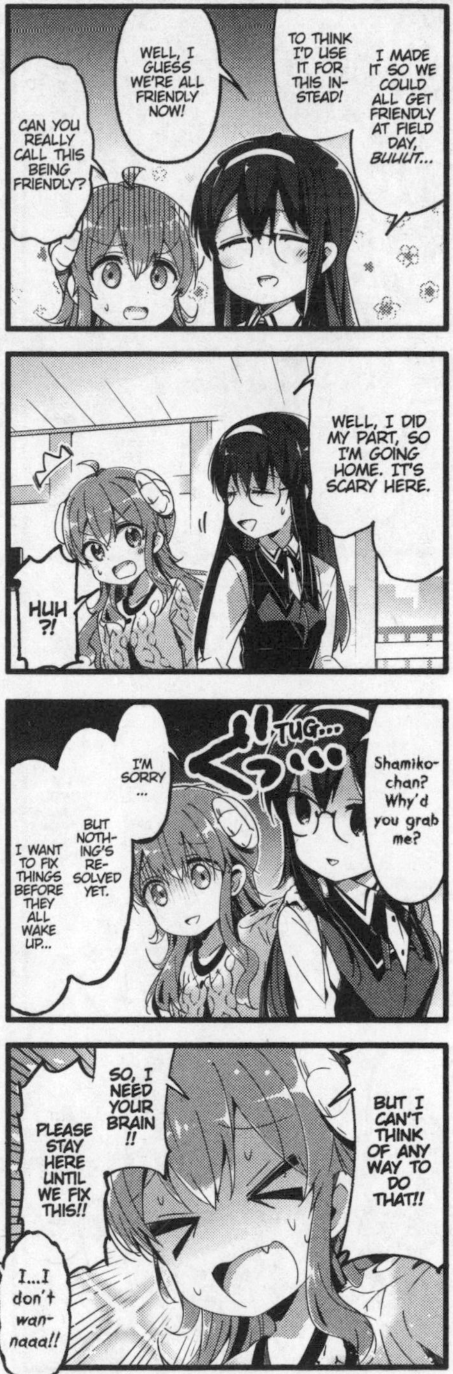
I MADE IT SO WE COULD ALL GET FRIENDLY AT FIELD DAY, BUUUT...
TO THINK I'D USE IT FOR THIS INSTEAD!
WELL, I GUESS WE'RE ALL FRIENDLY NOW!
CAN YOU REALLY CALL THIS BEING FRIENDLY?
WELL, I DID MY PART, SO I'M GOING HOME. IT'S SCARY HERE.
HUH ?!
Shamiko-chan? Why'd you grab me?
TUG...
I'M SORRY ...
BUT NOTHING'S RESOLVED YET.
I WANT TO FIX THINGS BEFORE THEY ALL WAKE UP...
BUT I CAN'T THINK OF ANY WAY TO DO THAT!!
SO, I NEED YOUR BRAIN !!
PLEASE STAY HERE UNTIL WE FIX THIS!!
I...I don't wan-naaa!!

A DEMON TACKLES A DIFFICULT CHALLENGE

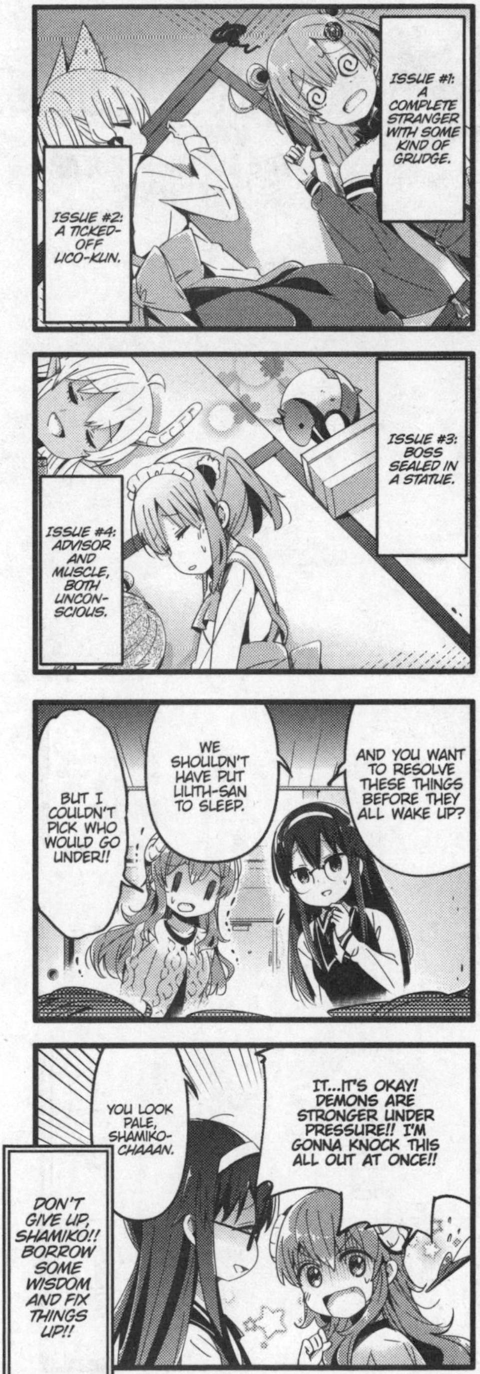
ISSUE #1: A COMPLETE STRANGER WITH SOME KIND OF GRUDGE.
ISSUE #2: A TICKED-OFF LICO-KUN.
ISSUE #3: BOSS SEALED IN A STATUE.
ISSUE #4: ADVISOR AND MUSCLE, BOTH UNCONSCIOUS.
AND YOU WANT TO RESOLVE THESE THINGS BEFORE THEY ALL WAKE UP?
WE SHOULDN'T HAVE PUT LILITH-SAN TO SLEEP.
BUT I COULDN'T PICK WHO WOULD GO UNDER!!
IT...IT'S OKAY! DEMONS ARE STRONGER UNDER PRESSURE!! I'M GONNA KNOCK THIS ALL OUT AT ONCE!!
YOU LOOK PALE, SHAMIKO-CHAAAN.
DON'T GIVE UP, SHAMIKO!! BORROW SOME WISDOM AND FIX THINGS UP!!

SECONDS!! DEMON GIRL NEXT DOOR

(CHAPTER 60)

~ THE SUPER-POPULAR SECRET MENU! ~

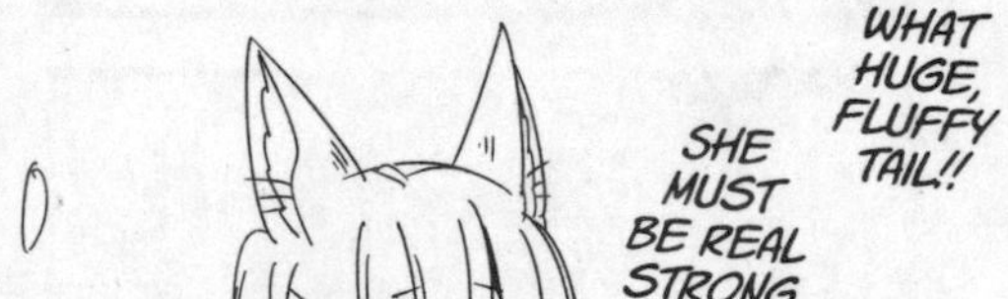
WHAT HUGE, FLUFFY TAIL!!
SHE MUST BE REAL STRONG.
UGALLU'S TAIL STATUS.

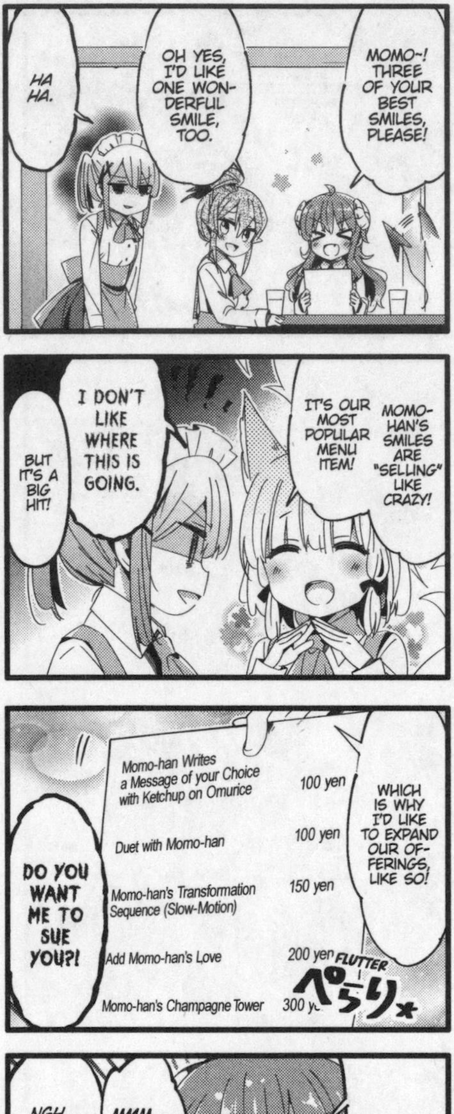
MOMO~! THREE OF YOUR BEST SMILES, PLEASE!
OH YES, I'D LIKE ONE WONDERFUL SMILE, TOO.
HA HA.
MOMO-HAN'S SMILES ARE "SELLING" LIKE CRAZY!
IT'S OUR MOST POPULAR MENU ITEM!
I DON'T LIKE WHERE THIS IS GOING.
BUT IT'S A BIG HIT!
WHICH IS WHY I'D LIKE TO EXPAND OUR OFFERINGS, LIKE SO!
Momo-han Writes a Message of your Choice with Ketchup on Omurice 100 yen
Duet with Momo-han 100 yen
Momo-han's Transformation Sequence (Slow-Motion) 150 yen
Add Momo-han's Love 200 yen
Momo-han's Champagne Tower 300 y
FLUTTER
ぺらり
DO YOU WANT ME TO SUE YOU?!
COULD I REQUEST ADDING "MOMO ACTS SWEET IN DARKNESS COSPLAY"?
MMM... THAT'LL BE TWELVE HUNDRED YEN~!
NGH... TAKE IT OUT OF MY PAYCHECK, PLEASE.
カッ
FLASH
SHAMIKO?

The Demon Girl Next Door

The Demon Girl Next Door

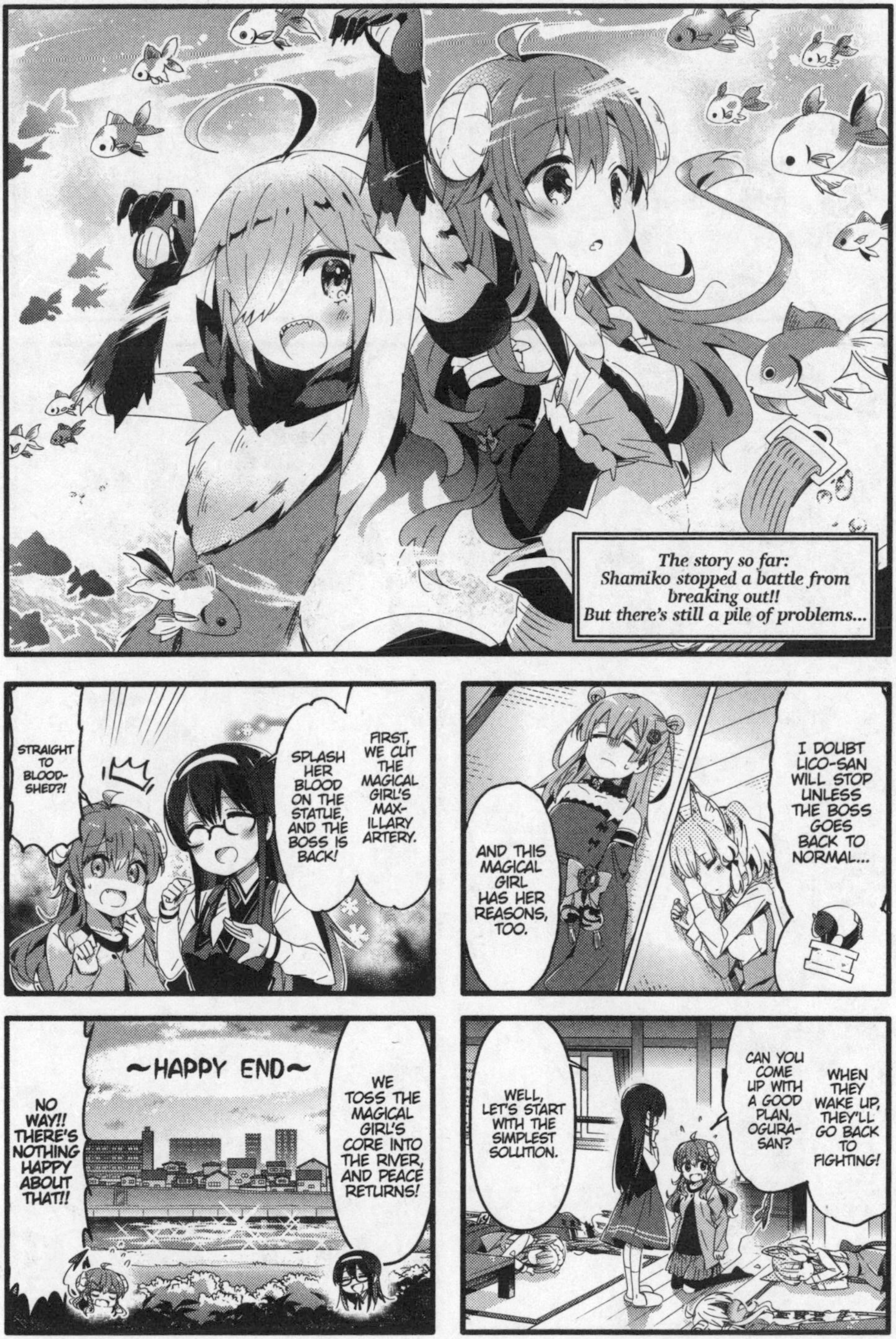
The story so far:
Shamiko stopped a battle from breaking out!!
But there's still a pile of problems...
I DOUBT LICO-SAN WILL STOP UNLESS THE BOSS GOES BACK TO NORMAL...
AND THIS MAGICAL GIRL HAS HER REASONS, TOO.
WHEN THEY WAKE UP, THEY'LL GO BACK TO FIGHTING!
CAN YOU COME UP WITH A GOOD PLAN, OGURA-SAN?
WELL, LET'S START WITH THE SIMPLEST SOLUTION.
FIRST, WE CUT THE MAGICAL GIRL'S MAX-ILLARY ARTERY.
SPLASH HER BLOOD ON THE STATUE, AND THE BOSS IS BACK!
STRAIGHT TO BLOOD-SHED?!
WE TOSS THE MAGICAL GIRL'S CORE INTO THE RIVER, AND PEACE RETURNS!
~HAPPY END~
NO WAY!! THERE'S NOTHING HAPPY ABOUT THAT!!

SHE REMOVED IT ALL LATER

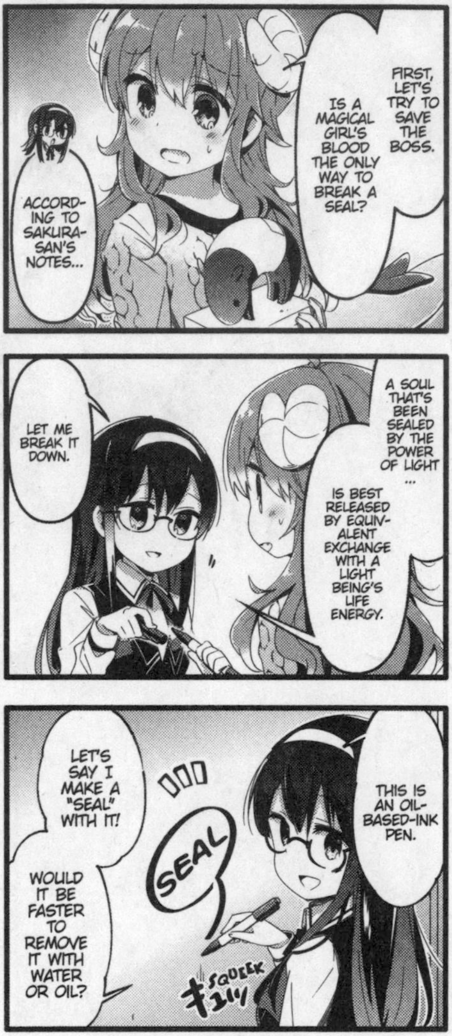
FIRST, LET'S TRY TO SAVE THE BOSS.
IS A MAGICAL GIRL'S BLOOD THE ONLY WAY TO BREAK A SEAL?
ACCORDING TO SAKURA-SAN'S NOTES...
A SOUL THAT'S BEEN SEALED BY THE POWER OF LIGHT ...
IS BEST RELEASED BY EQUIVALENT EXCHANGE WITH A LIGHT BEING'S LIFE ENERGY.
LET ME BREAK IT DOWN.
THIS IS AN OIL-BASED-INK PEN.
LET'S SAY I MAKE A "SEAL" WITH IT!
SEAL
WOULD IT BE FASTER TO REMOVE IT WITH WATER OR OIL?
SQUEEK
WHY, WITH OIL, OF COURSE!
DARKNESS AND LIGHT ARE JUST LIKE OIL AND WATER, YOU SEE?!!
SQUEEK
SQUEEK
SQUEEK
SEAL
SEAL
AAAH... THE CAFÉ WALL!!
SEAL
SEAL
SEAL
SQUEEK
SQUEEK
SQUEEK
SQUEEK

TO YOU, TWO THOUSAND YEARS FROM NOW

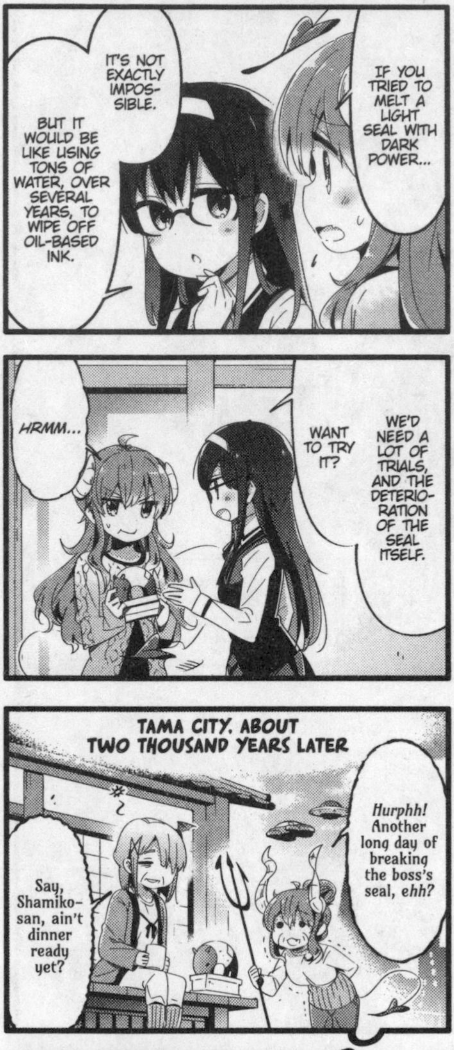
IF YOU TRIED TO MELT A LIGHT SEAL WITH DARK POWER...
IT'S NOT EXACTLY IMPOS-SIBLE.
BUT IT WOULD BE LIKE USING TONS OF WATER, OVER SEVERAL YEARS, TO WIPE OFF OIL-BASED INK.
WE'D NEED A LOT OF TRIALS, AND THE DETERIORATION OF THE SEAL ITSELF.
WANT TO TRY IT?
HRMM...
TAMA CITY, ABOUT TWO THOUSAND YEARS LATER
Hurphh! Another long day of breaking the boss's seal, ehh?
Say, Shamiko-san, ain't dinner ready yet?
That doesn't seem good.
Let's find another way.
YOU'RE SURPRISINGLY IMPATIENT, HMM, SHAMIKO-CHAAAN?

PROBLEM-SOLVING ON THE SPOT

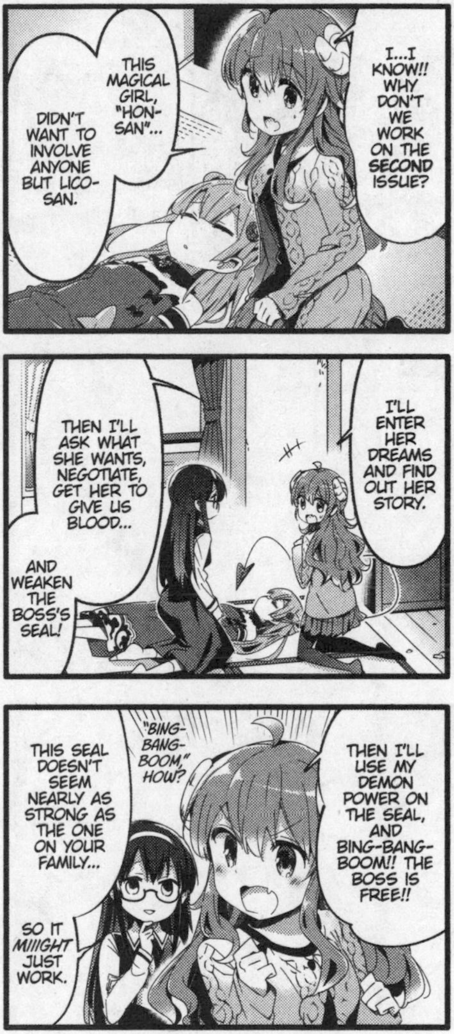
I...I KNOW!! WHY DON'T WE WORK ON THE SECOND ISSUE?
THIS MAGICAL GIRL, "HON-SAN"...
DIDN'T WANT TO INVOLVE ANYONE BUT LICO-SAN.
I'LL ENTER HER DREAMS AND FIND OUT HER STORY.
THEN I'LL ASK WHAT SHE WANTS, NEGOTIATE, GET HER TO GIVE US BLOOD...
AND WEAKEN THE BOSS'S SEAL!
THEN I'LL USE MY DEMON POWER ON THE SEAL, AND BING-BANG-BOOM!! THE BOSS IS FREE!!
"BING-BANG-BOOM," HOW?
THIS SEAL DOESN'T SEEM NEARLY AS STRONG AS THE ONE ON YOUR FAMILY...
SO IT MIIIGHT JUST WORK.
BUT...YOU'LL BE IN A MYSTERY MAGICAL GIRL'S DREAM. WILL YOU BE OKAAAY?
DEMONS ARE INVINCIBLE IN DREAMS!!
I'LL DO IT!! I'LL MANAGE SOMEHOW!! GOOD NIIIGHT!!

WHAT HAPPENED TO "INVINCIBLE"?

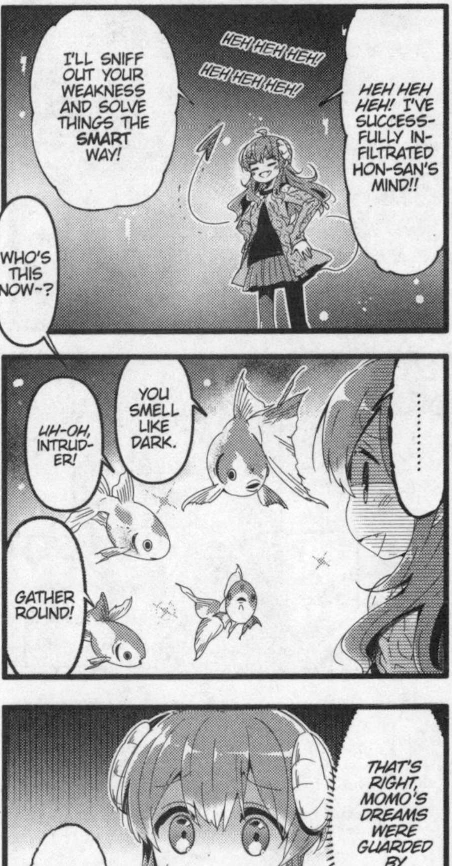
HEH HEH HEH! I'VE SUCCESSFULLY INFILTRATED HON-SAN'S MIND!!
HEH HEH HEH!
HEH HEH HEH!
I'LL SNIFF OUT YOUR WEAKNESS AND SOLVE THINGS THE SMART WAY!
WHO'S THIS NOW~?
......
YOU SMELL LIKE DARK.
UH-OH, INTRUDER!
GATHER ROUND!
THAT'S RIGHT, MOMO'S DREAMS WERE GUARDED BY METAKO, TOO!!
AH... HELLO, THERE...
AAAAAAAAAAH!!
ドドドドドドド
THUD THUD THUD THUD THUD THUD
I CAN'T DO IIIIIIIT!

SNACK TIME STAFF, MISFIRED

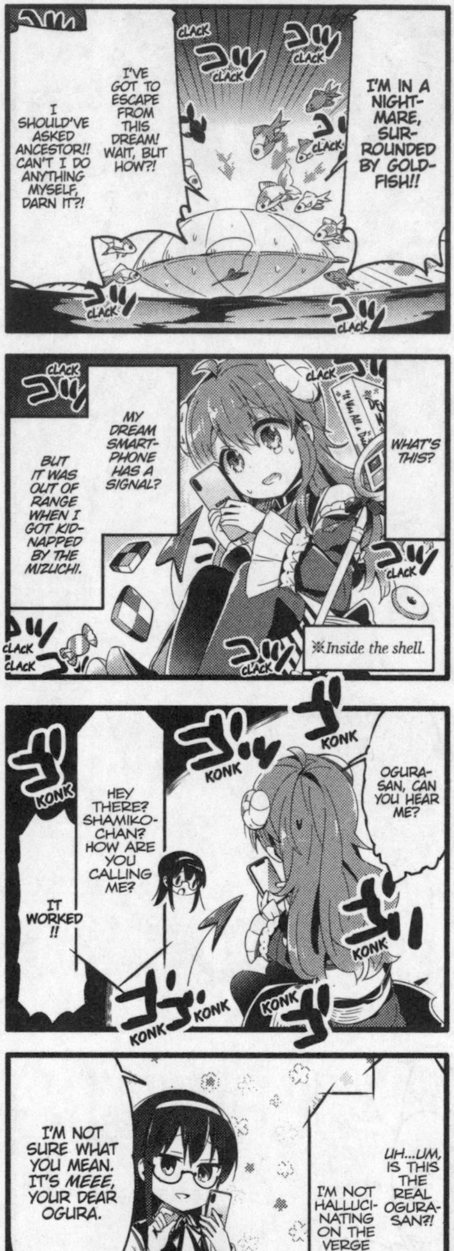

CLACK
I'M IN A NIGHTMARE, SURROUNDED BY GOLDFISH!!
I'VE GOT TO ESCAPE FROM THIS DREAM! WAIT, BUT HOW?!
I SHOULD'VE ASKED ANCESTOR!! CAN'T I DO ANYTHING MYSELF, DARN IT?!
CLACK
WHAT'S THIS?
MY DREAM SMARTPHONE HAS A SIGNAL?
BUT IT WAS OUT OF RANGE WHEN I GOT KIDNAPPED BY THE MIZUCHI.
※Inside the shell.
KONK
OGURA-SAN, CAN YOU HEAR ME?
HEY THERE? SHAMIKO-CHAN? HOW ARE YOU CALLING ME?
IT WORKED!!
UH...UM, IS THIS THE REAL OGURA-SAN?!
I'M NOT HALLUCINATING ON THE VERGE OF DEATH?!
I'M NOT SURE WHAT YOU MEAN. IT'S MEEE, YOUR DEAR OGURA.

ON THE JOB!!

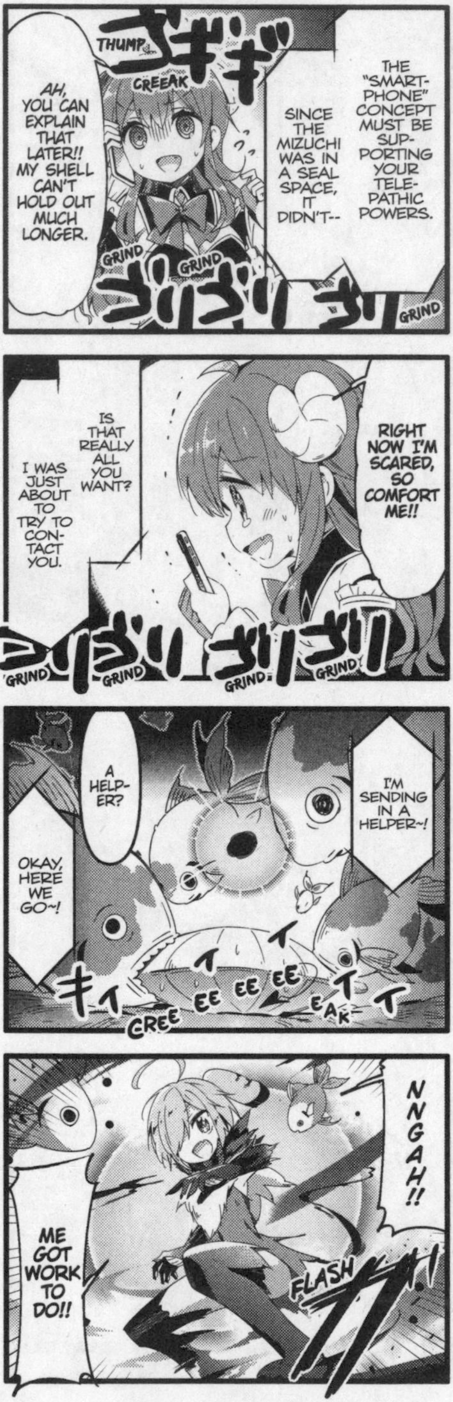

THUMP
CREEAK
THE "SMARTPHONE" CONCEPT MUST BE SUPPORTING YOUR TELEPATHIC POWERS.
SINCE THE MIZUCHI WAS IN A SEAL SPACE, IT DIDN'T--
AH, YOU CAN EXPLAIN THAT LATER!! MY SHELL CAN'T HOLD OUT MUCH LONGER.
GRIND GRIND GRIND
RIGHT NOW I'M SCARED, SO COMFORT ME!!
IS THAT REALLY ALL YOU WANT?
I WAS JUST ABOUT TO TRY TO CONTACT YOU.
GRIND GRIND GRIND GRIND
I'M SENDING IN A HELPER~!
A HELPER?
OKAY, HERE WE GO~!
CREEEEEEEEAK
NNGAH!!
ME GOT WORK TO DO!!
FLASH

GOLDFISH AREN'T VERY TASTY

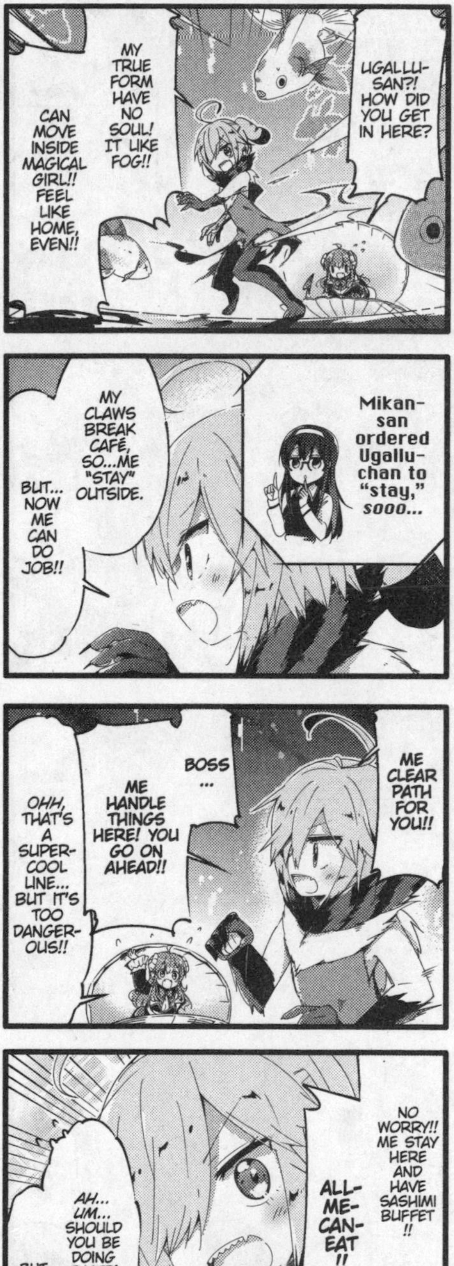
UGALLU-SAN?! HOW DID YOU GET IN HERE?
MY TRUE FORM HAVE NO SOUL! IT LIKE FOG!!
CAN MOVE INSIDE MAGICAL GIRL!! FEEL LIKE HOME, EVEN!!
Mikan-san ordered Ugallu-chan to "stay," sooo...
MY CLAWS BREAK CAFÉ, SO...ME "STAY" OUTSIDE.
BUT... NOW ME CAN DO JOB!!
ME CLEAR PATH FOR YOU!!
BOSS ...
ME HANDLE THINGS HERE! YOU GO ON AHEAD!!
OHH, THAT'S A SUPER-COOL LINE... BUT IT'S TOO DANGEROUS!!
NO WORRY!! ME STAY HERE AND HAVE SASHIMI BUFFET!!
ALL-ME-CAN-EAT!!
AH... UM... SHOULD YOU BE DOING THAT?!
BUT, OKAY THEN!!

HON-CHAN'S PAST, REVEALED!

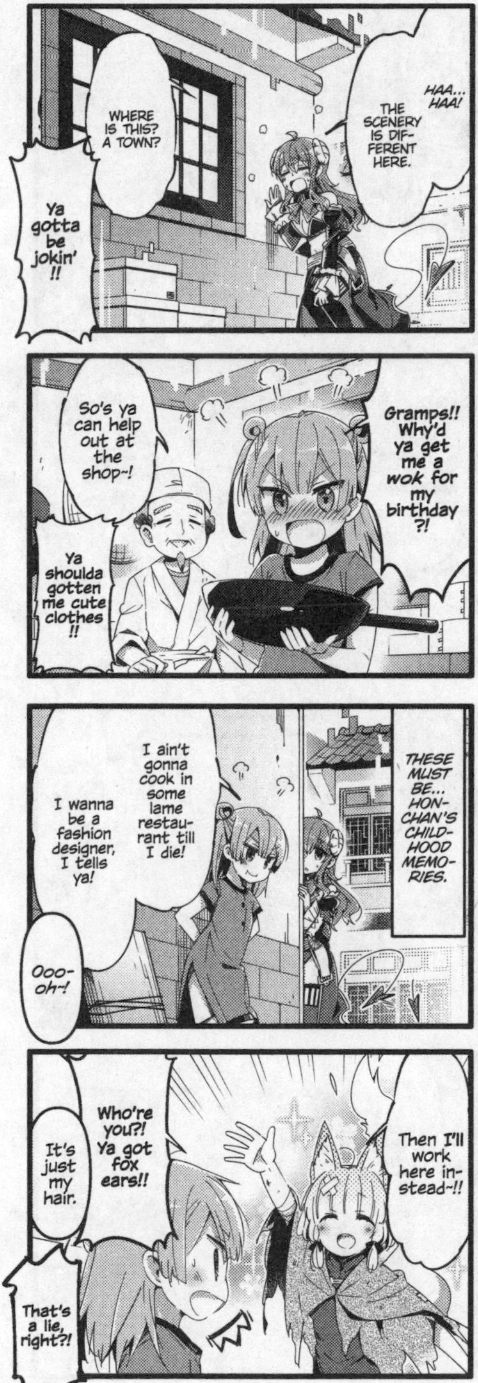
HAA... HAA!
THE SCENERY IS DIFFERENT HERE.
WHERE IS THIS? A TOWN?
Ya gotta be jokin'!!
Gramps!! Why'd ya get me a wok for my birthday?!
So's ya can help out at the shop~!
Ya shoulda gotten me cute clothes!!
THESE MUST BE... HON-CHAN'S CHILDHOOD MEMORIES.
I ain't gonna cook in some lame restaurant till I die!
I wanna be a fashion designer, I tells ya!
Ooo-oh~!
Then I'll work here instead~!!
Who're you?! Ya got fox ears!!
It's just my hair.
That's a lie, right?!

THEY'RE JUST FORGETTIN' THE BAD STUFF

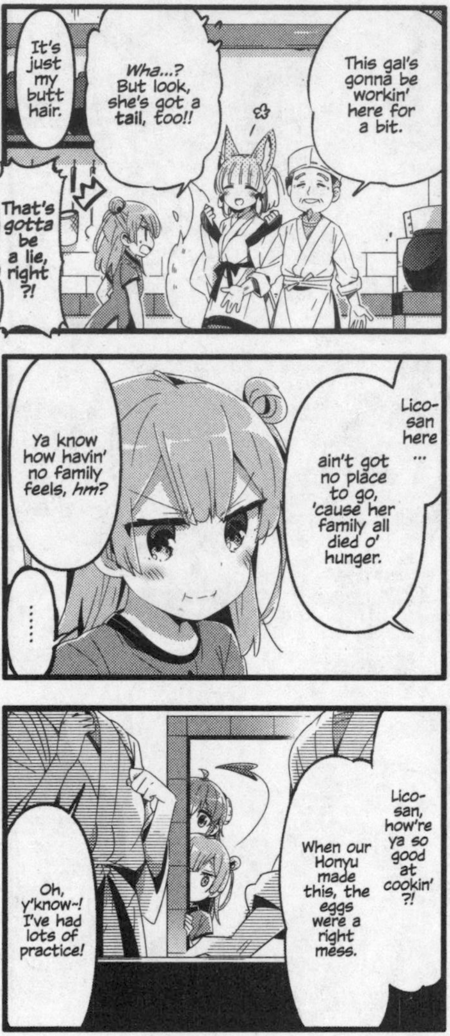
This gal's gonna be workin' here for a bit.
Wha...? But look, she's got a tail, too!!
It's just my butt hair.
That's gotta be a lie, right?!
Lico-san here ... ain't got no place to go, 'cause her family all died o' hunger.
Ya know how havin' no family feels, hm?
......
Lico-san, how're ya so good at cookin'?!
When our Honyu made this, the eggs were a right mess.
Oh, y'know~! I've had lots of practice!
Gramps, this ain't right!! The folks who eat her food are passin' out!!
But they wake up with more energy than ever.
It's still scary!!

A LICO-LIKE CREATURE

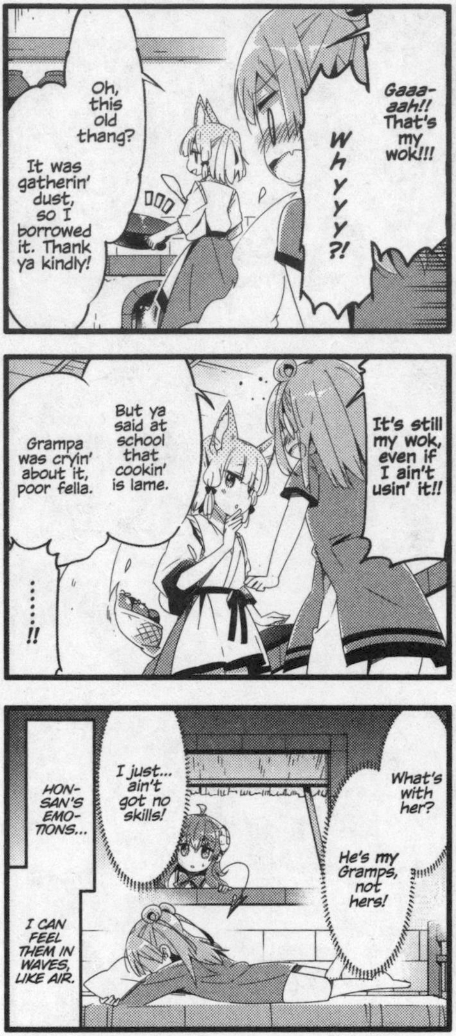
Gaaa-aah!! That's my wok!!!
Whyyyy?!
Oh, this old thang?
It was gatherin' dust, so I borrowed it. Thank ya kindly!
It's still my wok, even if I ain't usin' it!!
But ya said at school that cookin' is lame.
Grampa was cryin' about it, poor fella.
......!!
What's with her?
He's my Gramps, not hers!
I just... ain't got no skills!
HON-SAN'S EMOTIONS...
I CAN FEEL THEM IN WAVES, LIKE AIR.
Say! Ya wanna practice makin' fried rice with me?
Go ahead and call me "Big Sis"~!
Oh, go away!!

HON-CHAN'S DEBUT BATTLE

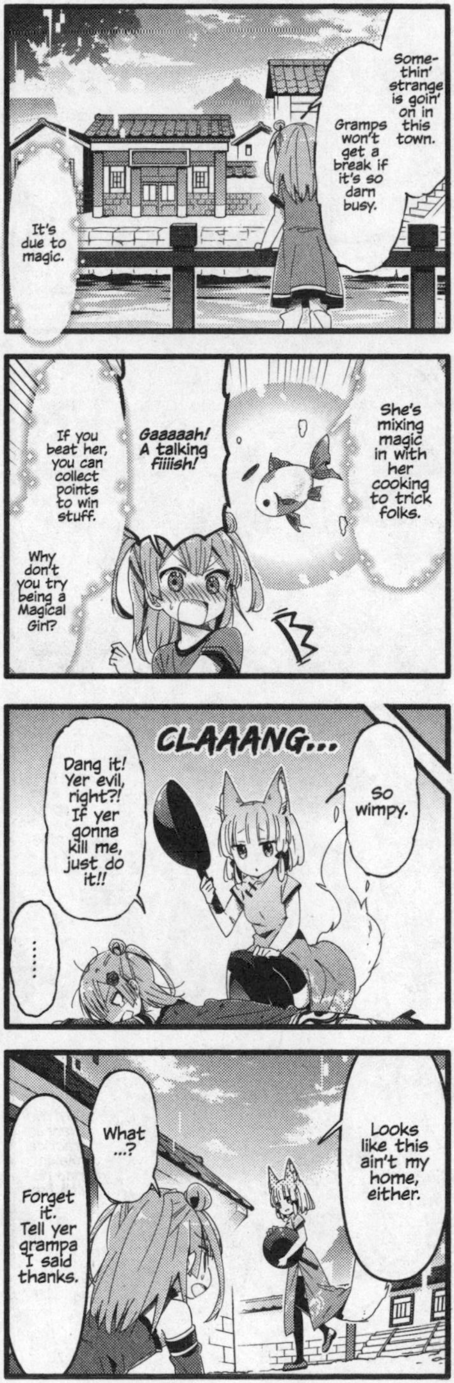
Some-thin' strange is goin' on in this town.
Gramps won't get a break if it's so darn busy.
It's due to magic.
She's mixing magic in with her cooking to trick folks.
Gaaaaah! A talking fiiiish!
If you beat her, you can collect points to win stuff.
Why don't you try being a Magical Girl?
CLAAANG...
So wimpy.
Dang it! Yer evil, right?! If yer gonna kill me, just do it!!
......
Looks like this ain't my home, either.
What ...?
Forget it. Tell yer grampa I said thanks.

LICO STOLE THE PRECIOUS THING

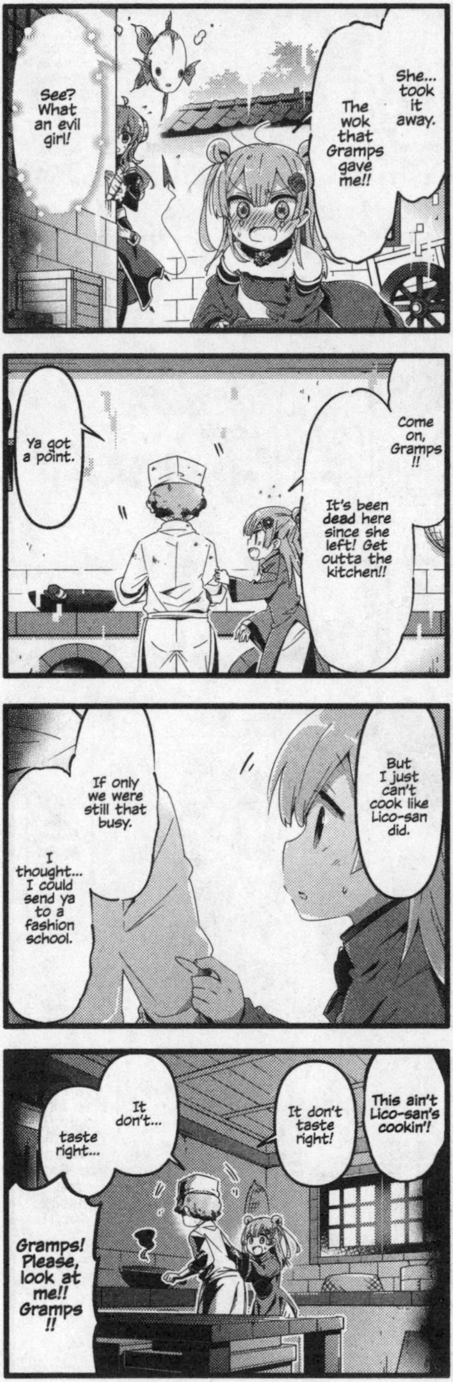
She... took it away.
The wok that Gramps gave me!!
See? What an evil girl!
Come on, Gramps!!
It's been dead here since she left! Get outta the kitchen!!
Ya got a point.
But I just can't cook like Lico-san did.
If only we were still that busy.
I thought... I could send ya to a fashion school.
This ain't Lico-san's cookin'!
It don't taste right!
It don't... taste right...
Gramps! Please, look at me!! Gramps!!

NU-DEMON

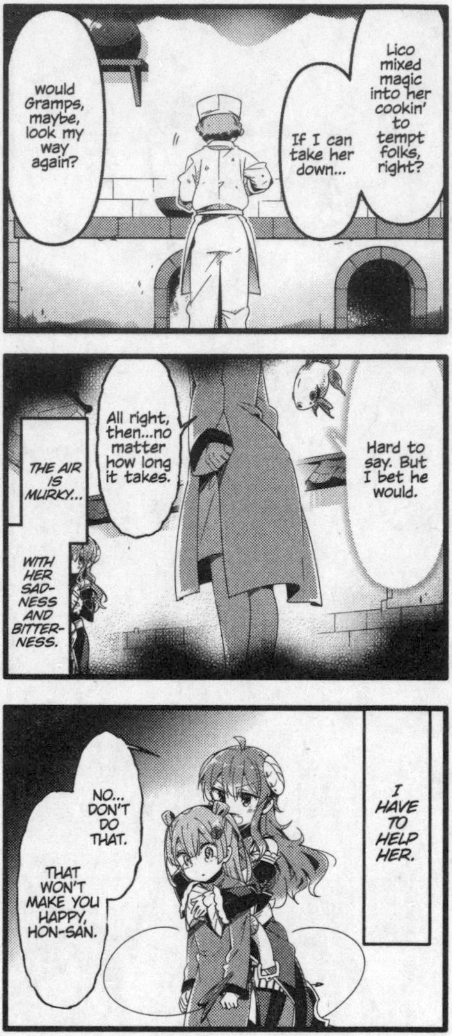
Lico mixed magic into her cookin' to tempt folks, right?
If I can take her down...
would Gramps, maybe, look my way again?
Hard to say. But I bet he would.
All right, then...no matter how long it takes.
THE AIR IS MURKY...
WITH HER SADNESS AND BITTERNESS.
I HAVE TO HELP HER.
NO... DON'T DO THAT.
THAT WON'T MAKE YOU HAPPY, HON-SAN.
WHO... WHO ARE YA?
YER HALF-NEKKID!!
AH, SORRY ABOUT THAT...
I'M JUST YOUR FRIENDLY NEIGHBORHOOD MISTRESS OF DARKNESS!

HOW TO USE DEMON POWERS

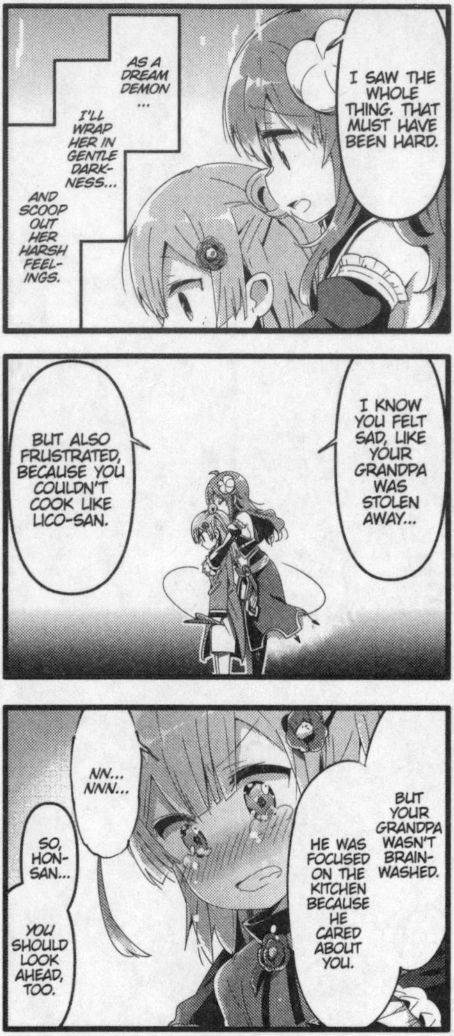
I SAW THE WHOLE THING. THAT MUST HAVE BEEN HARD.
AS A DREAM DEMON...
I'LL WRAP HER IN GENTLE DARKNESS...
AND SCOOP OUT HER HARSH FEELINGS.
I KNOW YOU FELT SAD, LIKE YOUR GRANDPA WAS STOLEN AWAY...
BUT ALSO FRUSTRATED, BECAUSE YOU COULDN'T COOK LIKE LICO-SAN.
BUT YOUR GRANDPA WASN'T BRAINWASHED.
HE WAS FOCUSED ON THE KITCHEN BECAUSE HE CARED ABOUT YOU.
NN... NNN...
SO, HON-SAN...
YOU SHOULD LOOK AHEAD, TOO.
LET'S CLEAN UP...
YOUR MEMORIES TOGETHER.

HALF-NAKED (AGAIN)

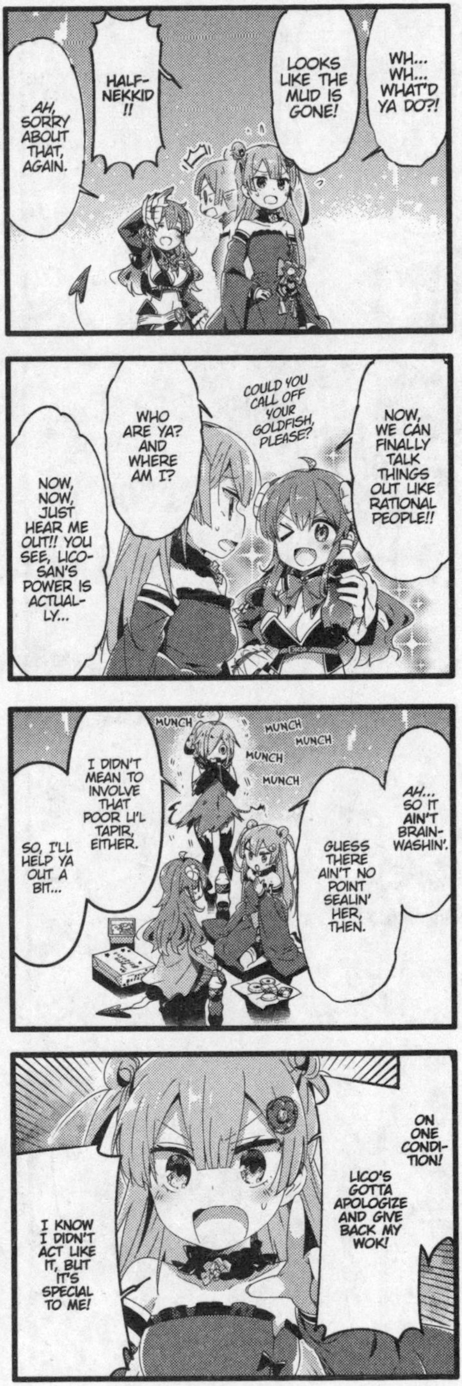
WH... WH... WHAT'D YA DO?!
LOOKS LIKE THE MUD IS GONE!
HALF-NEKKID !!
AH, SORRY ABOUT THAT, AGAIN.
NOW, WE CAN FINALLY TALK THINGS OUT LIKE RATIONAL PEOPLE!!
COULD YOU CALL OFF YOUR GOLDFISH, PLEASE?
WHO ARE YA? AND WHERE AM I?
NOW, NOW, JUST HEAR ME OUT!! YOU SEE, LICO-SAN'S POWER IS ACTUAL-LY...
MUNCH
MUNCH
MUNCH
MUNCH
MUNCH
AH... SO IT AIN'T BRAIN-WASHIN'.
GUESS THERE AIN'T NO POINT SEALIN' HER, THEN.
I DIDN'T MEAN TO INVOLVE THAT POOR LI'L TAPIR, EITHER.
SO, I'LL HELP YA OUT A BIT...
ON ONE CONDITION!
LICO'S GOTTA APOLOGIZE AND GIVE BACK MY WOK!
I KNOW I DIDN'T ACT LIKE IT, BUT IT'S SPECIAL TO ME!

A DEMON WHO MAKES PROMISES TOO READILY

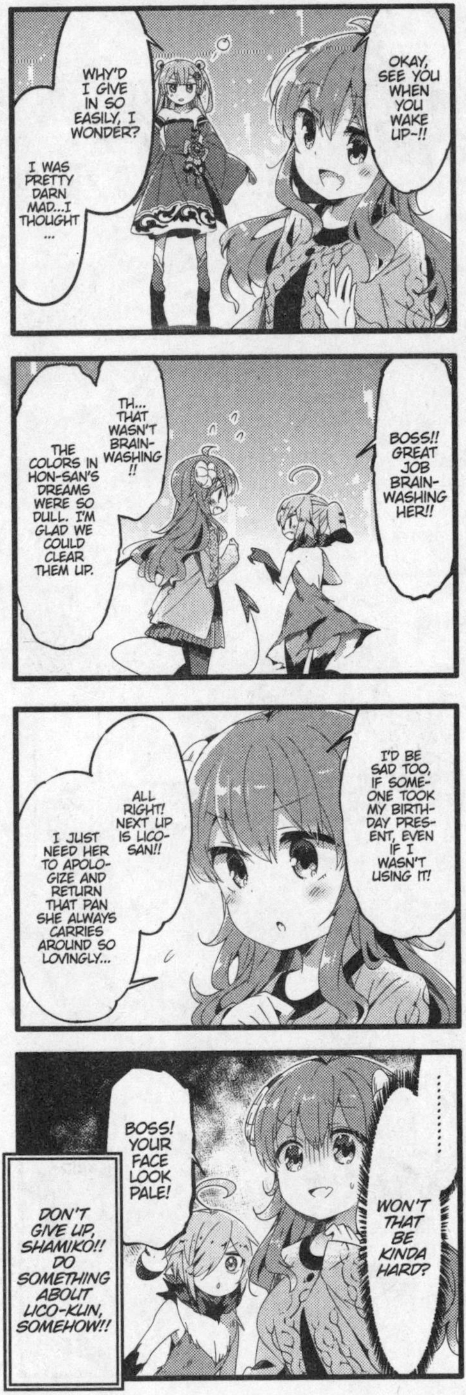
OKAY, SEE YOU WHEN YOU WAKE UP~!!
WHY'D I GIVE IN SO EASILY, I WONDER?
I WAS PRETTY DARN MAD...I THOUGHT ...
BOSS!! GREAT JOB BRAIN-WASHING HER!!
TH... THAT WASN'T BRAIN-WASHING !!
THE COLORS IN HON-SAN'S DREAMS WERE SO DULL. I'M GLAD WE COULD CLEAR THEM UP.
I'D BE SAD TOO, IF SOME-ONE TOOK MY BIRTH-DAY PRES-ENT, EVEN IF I WASN'T USING IT!
ALL RIGHT! NEXT UP IS LICO-SAN!!
I JUST NEED HER TO APOLO-GIZE AND RETURN THAT PAN SHE ALWAYS CARRIES AROUND SO LOVINGLY...
......
WON'T THAT BE KINDA HARD?
BOSS! YOUR FACE LOOK PALE!
DON'T GIVE UP, SHAMIKO!! DO SOMETHING ABOUT LICO-KUN, SOMEHOW!!

SECONDS!! DEMON GIRL NEXT DOOR

(CHAPTER 62)

~ UGALLU-CHAN ON STANDBY ~

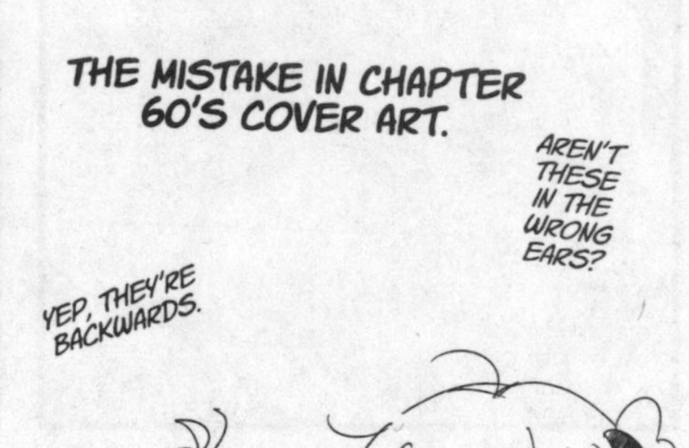
THE MISTAKE IN CHAPTER 60'S COVER ART.
AREN'T THESE IN THE WRONG EARS?
YEP, THEY'RE BACKWARDS.

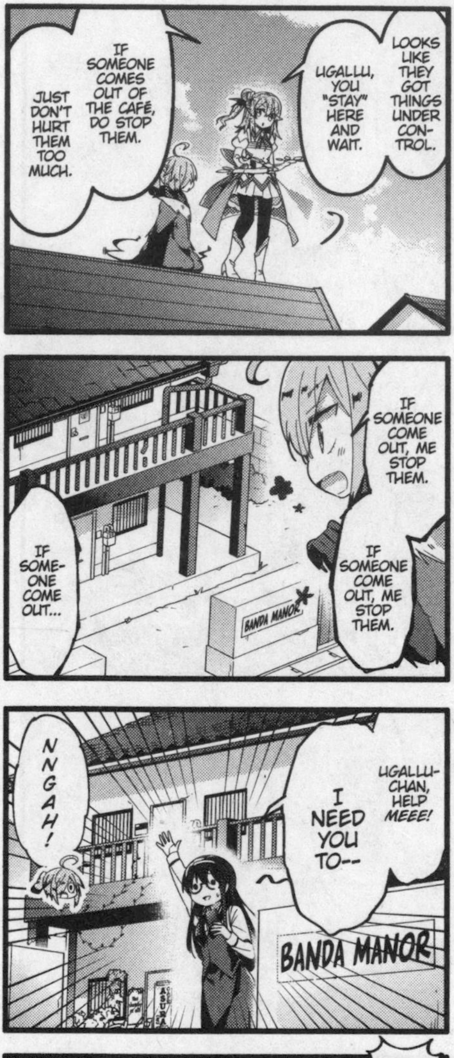
LOOKS LIKE THEY GOT THINGS UNDER CON-TROL.
UGALLU, YOU "STAY" HERE AND WAIT.
IF SOMEONE COMES OUT OF THE CAFÉ, DO STOP THEM.
JUST DON'T HURT THEM TOO MUCH.
IF SOMEONE COME OUT, ME STOP THEM.
IF SOMEONE COME OUT, ME STOP THEM.
BANDA MANOR
IF SOME-ONE COME OUT...
UGALLU-CHAN, HELP MEEE!
I NEED YOU TO--
NNGAH!
BANDA MANOR
STOP THEM!!!
GYAAAAH!!
GRAB
DON'T GIVE UP, UGALLU-CHAN!! TAKE A CLOSE LOOK AT THE PERSON'S FACE AND ADAPT!!

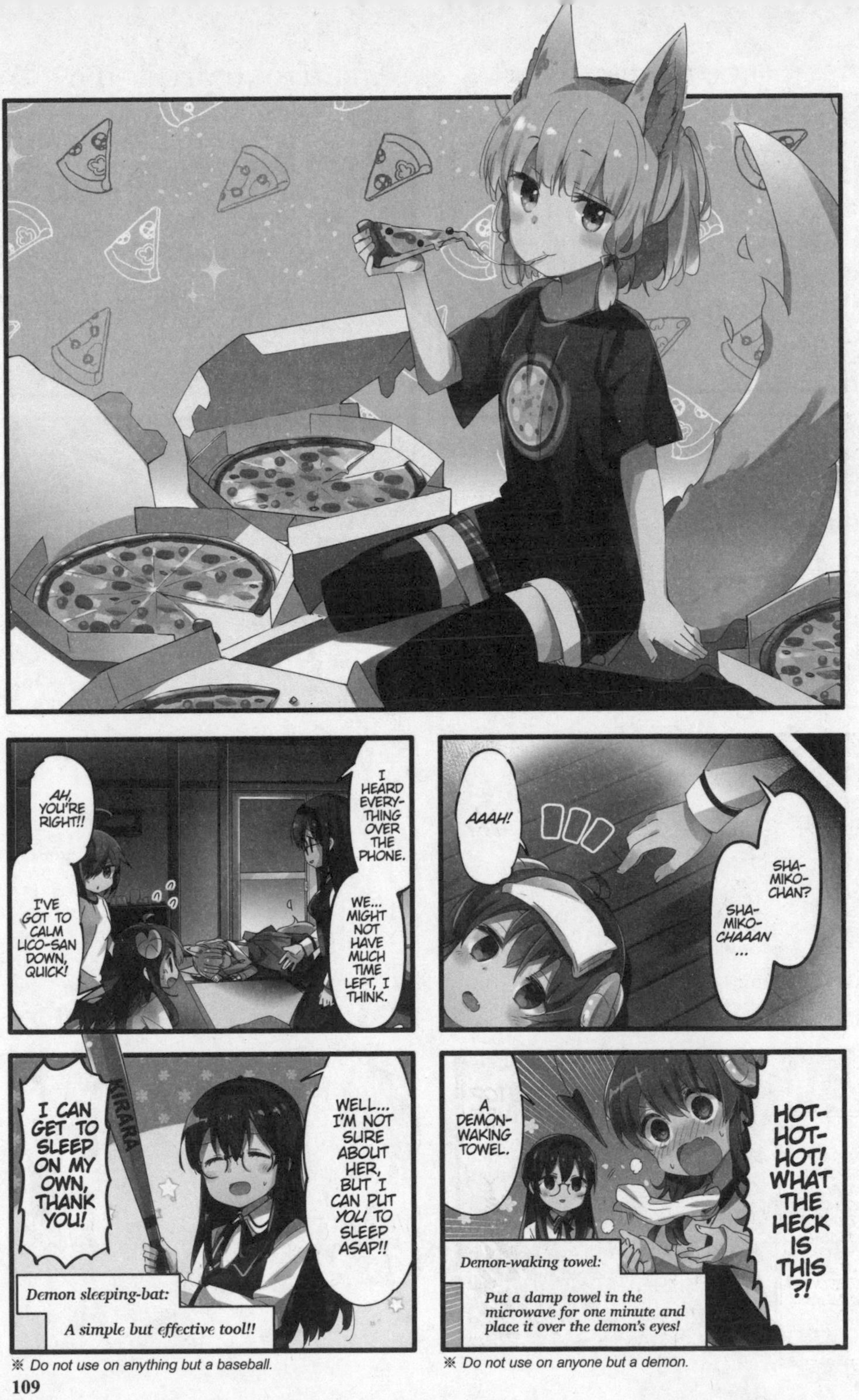
SHA-MIKO-CHAN?
SHA-MIKO-CHAAAN ...
AAAH!
I HEARD EVERY-THING OVER THE PHONE.
WE... MIGHT NOT HAVE MUCH TIME LEFT, I THINK.
AH, YOU'RE RIGHT!!
I'VE GOT TO CALM LICO-SAN DOWN, QUICK!
HOT-HOT-HOT! WHAT THE HECK IS THIS?!
A DEMON-WAKING TOWEL.
Demon-waking towel:
Put a damp towel in the microwave for one minute and place it over the demon's eyes!
WELL... I'M NOT SURE ABOUT HER, BUT I CAN PUT *YOU* TO SLEEP ASAP!!
I CAN GET TO SLEEP ON MY OWN, THANK YOU!
KIRARA
Demon sleeping-bat:
A simple but effective tool!!

※ Do not use on anyone but a demon.

※ Do not use on anything but a baseball.

THE LIMITS OF TECHNOLOGY

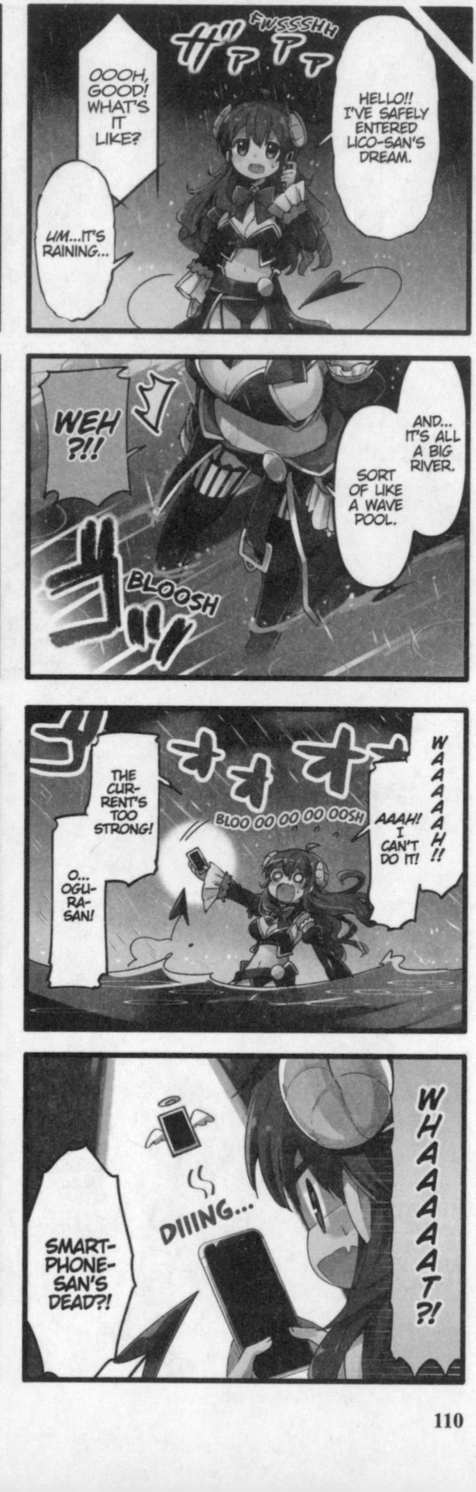
FWSSSHH
HELLO!! I'VE SAFELY ENTERED LICO-SAN'S DREAM.
OOOH, GOOD! WHAT'S IT LIKE?
UM...IT'S RAINING...
AND... IT'S ALL A BIG RIVER.
SORT OF LIKE A WAVE POOL.
WEH ?!!
BLOOSH
WAAAAAAH!!
AAAH! I CAN'T DO IT!
BLOO OO OO OO OOSH
THE CUR-RENT'S TOO STRONG!
O... OGU-RA-SAN!
WHAAAAAAT?!
DIIING...
SMART-PHONE-SAN'S DEAD?!

A DEMON'S FORCED EXIT

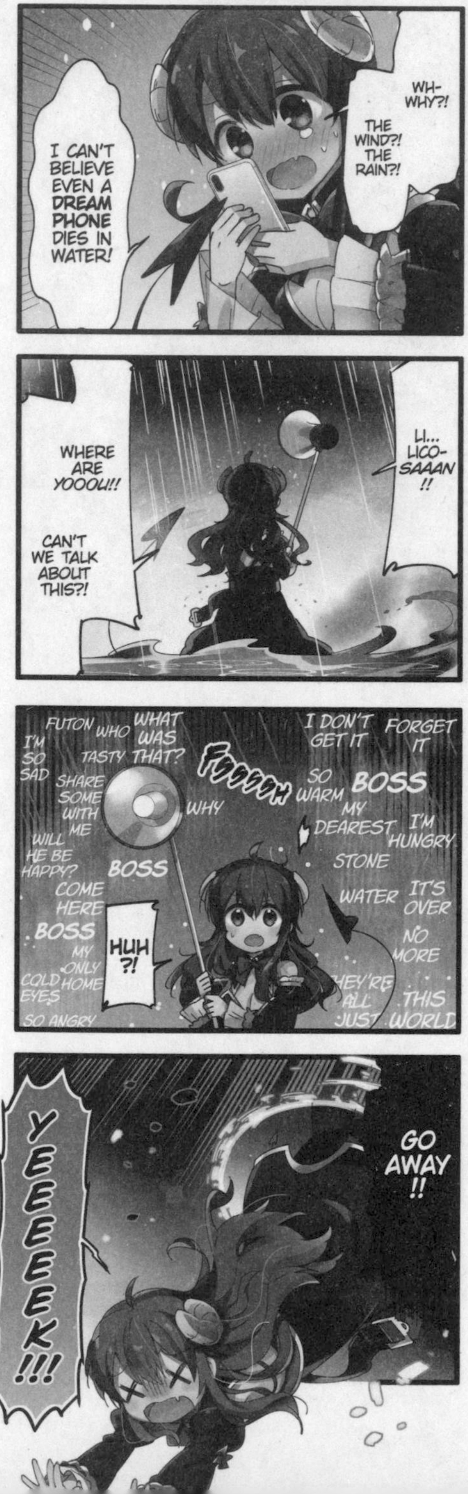
WH-WHY?!
THE WIND?! THE RAIN?!
I CAN'T BELIEVE EVEN A DREAM PHONE DIES IN WATER!
LI... LICO-SAAAN!!
WHERE ARE YOOOU!!
CAN'T WE TALK ABOUT THIS?!
FORGET IT
I DON'T GET IT
WHAT WAS THAT?
WHO
FUTON
I'M SO SAD
TASTY
SHARE SOME WITH ME
FSSSSH
SO WARM
BOSS
MY DEAREST
I'M HUNGRY
WHY
STONE
WILL HE BE HAPPY?
BOSS
COME HERE
WATER
IT'S OVER
BOSS
NO MORE
MY ONLY HOME
THEY'RE ALL JUST
THIS WORLD
COLD EYES
SO ANGRY
HUH ?!
GO AWAY !!
YEEEEEEK!!!

FASTER THAN CHANGING HER MINDSET

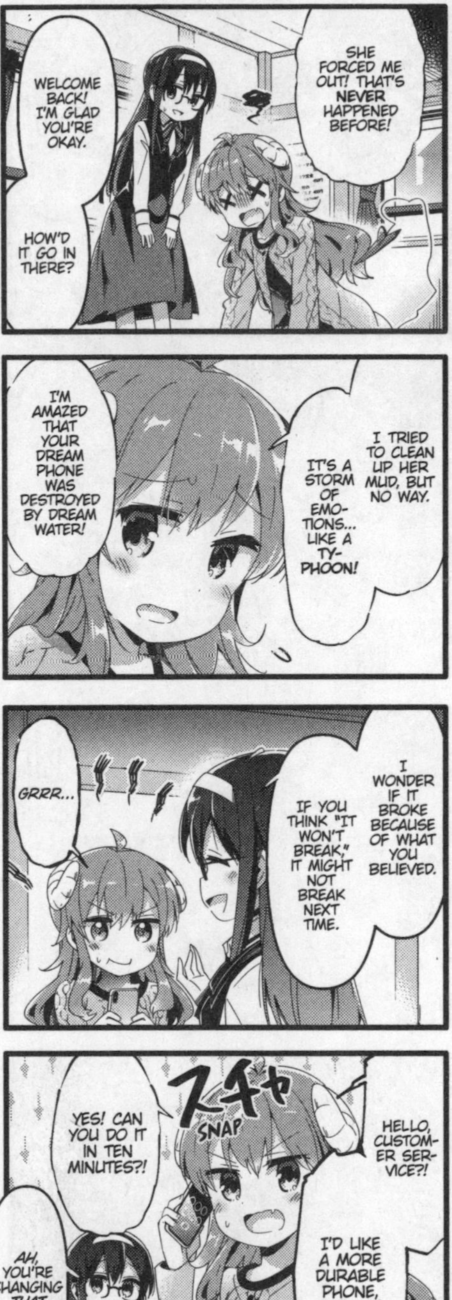
SHE FORCED ME OUT! THAT'S NEVER HAPPENED BEFORE!
WELCOME BACK! I'M GLAD YOU'RE OKAY.
HOW'D IT GO IN THERE?
I TRIED TO CLEAN UP HER MUD, BUT NO WAY.
IT'S A STORM OF EMO-TIONS... LIKE A TY-PHOON!
I'M AMAZED THAT YOUR DREAM PHONE WAS DESTROYED BY DREAM WATER!
I WONDER IF IT BROKE BECAUSE OF WHAT YOU BELIEVED.
IF YOU THINK "IT WON'T BREAK," IT MIGHT NOT BREAK NEXT TIME.
GRRR...
HELLO, CUSTOM-ER SER-VICE?!
スチャ
SNAP
YES! CAN YOU DO IT IN TEN MINUTES?!
I'D LIKE A MORE DURABLE PHONE, PLEASE!
AH, YOU'RE CHANGING *THAT* INSTEAD?

OGURA-SAN IN OVERDRIVE

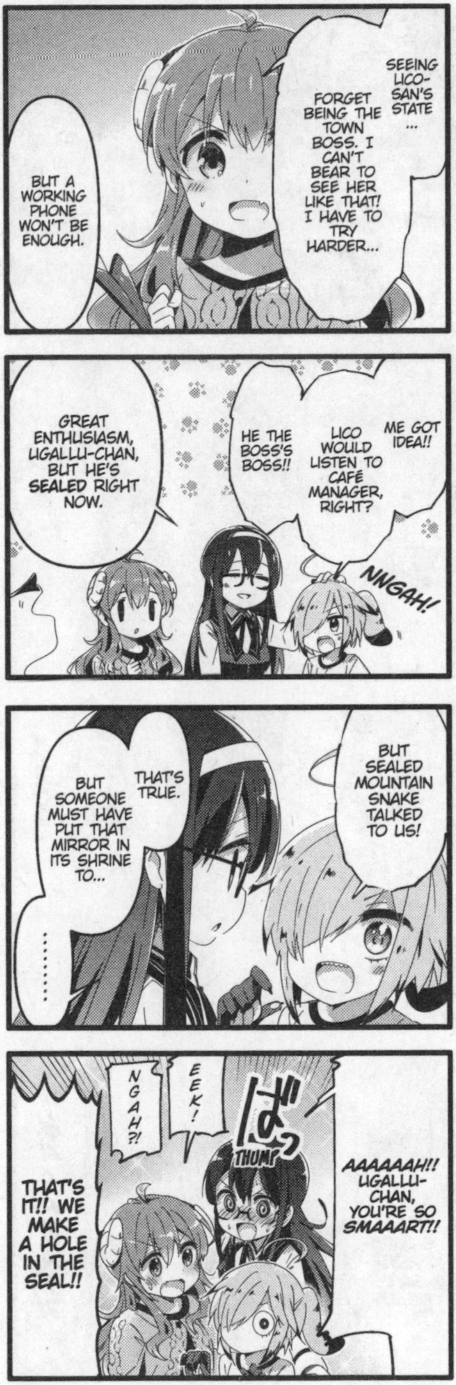
SEEING LICO-SAN'S STATE ...
FORGET BEING THE TOWN BOSS. I CAN'T BEAR TO SEE HER LIKE THAT! I HAVE TO TRY HARDER...
BUT A WORKING PHONE WON'T BE ENOUGH.
ME GOT IDEA!!
LICO WOULD LISTEN TO CAFÉ MANAGER, RIGHT?
HE THE BOSS'S BOSS!!
GREAT ENTHUSIASM, UGALLU-CHAN, BUT HE'S SEALED RIGHT NOW.
NNGAH!
BUT SEALED MOUNTAIN SNAKE TALKED TO US!
THAT'S TRUE.
BUT SOMEONE MUST HAVE PUT THAT MIRROR IN ITS SHRINE TO...
......
AAAAAAH!! UGALLU-CHAN, YOU'RE SO SMAAART!!
ばっ
THUMP
EEK!
NGAH?!
THAT'S IT!! WE MAKE A HOLE IN THE SEAL!!

FROM MANAGER TO GOD

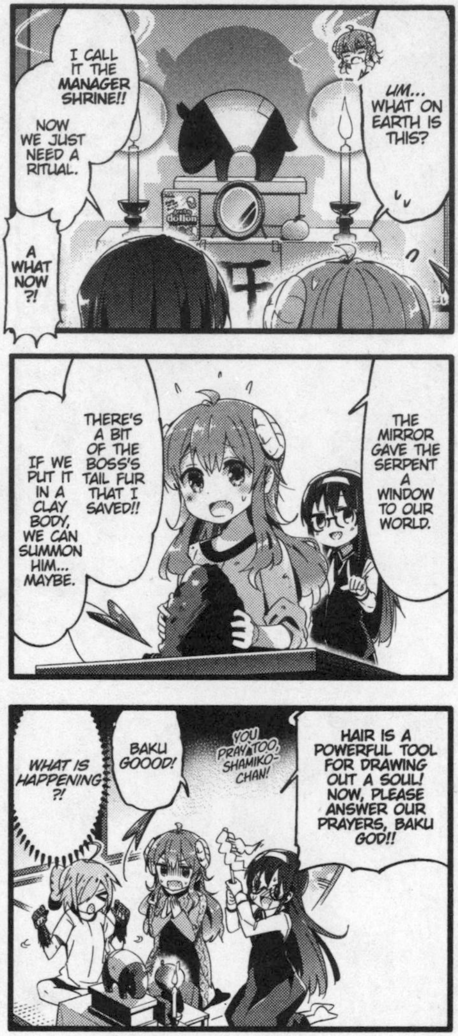
UM... WHAT ON EARTH IS THIS?
I CALL IT THE MANAGER SHRINE!!
NOW WE JUST NEED A RITUAL.
A WHAT NOW?!
THE MIRROR GAVE THE SERPENT A WINDOW TO OUR WORLD.
THERE'S A BIT OF THE BOSS'S TAIL FUR THAT I SAVED!!
IF WE PUT IT IN A CLAY BODY, WE CAN SUMMON HIM... MAYBE.
HAIR IS A POWERFUL TOOL FOR DRAWING OUT A SOUL! NOW, PLEASE ANSWER OUR PRAYERS, BAKU GOD!!
YOU PRAY TOO, SHAMIKO-CHAN!
BAKU GOOOD!
WHAT IS HAPPENING?!
AAH!!
WHERE IN THE WORLD ...
OH MY! SCARY!!
BAKU GOOOD!
YOU'RE SCARING ME, YUKO-KUN!

COMES WITH A MONEY-BACK GUARANTEE

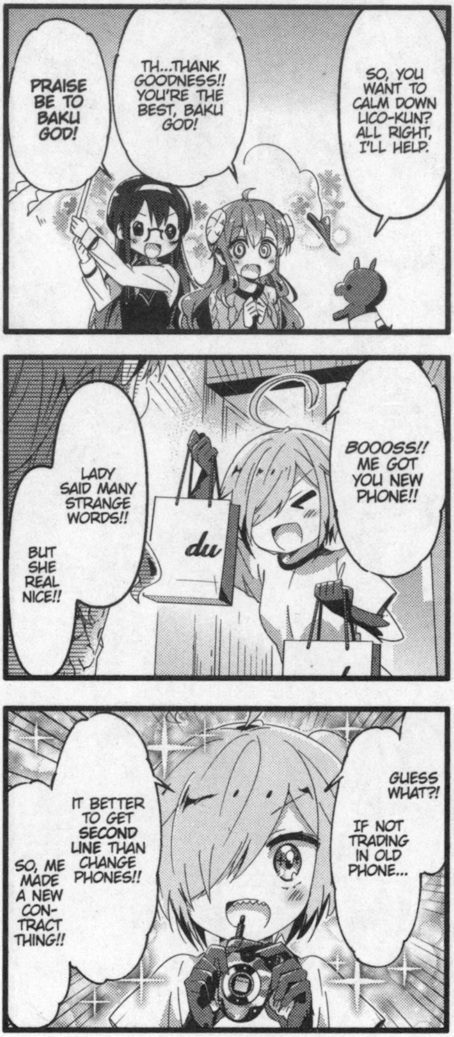
SO, YOU WANT TO CALM DOWN LICO-KUN? ALL RIGHT, I'LL HELP.
TH...THANK GOODNESS!! YOU'RE THE BEST, BAKU GOD!
PRAISE BE TO BAKU GOD!
BOOOSS!! ME GOT YOU NEW PHONE!!
du
LADY SAID MANY STRANGE WORDS!!
BUT SHE REAL NICE!!
GUESS WHAT?!
IF NOT TRADING IN OLD PHONE...
IT BETTER TO GET SECOND LINE THAN CHANGE PHONES!!
SO, ME MADE A NEW CONTRACT THING!!
ME RAN FIRST ERRAND EVER!! ME GOOD FAMILIAR!!
AWW! WELL DONE, UGALLU-CHAN!
GREAT!! YOU DID GREAT!!

DEVOUT FAITH

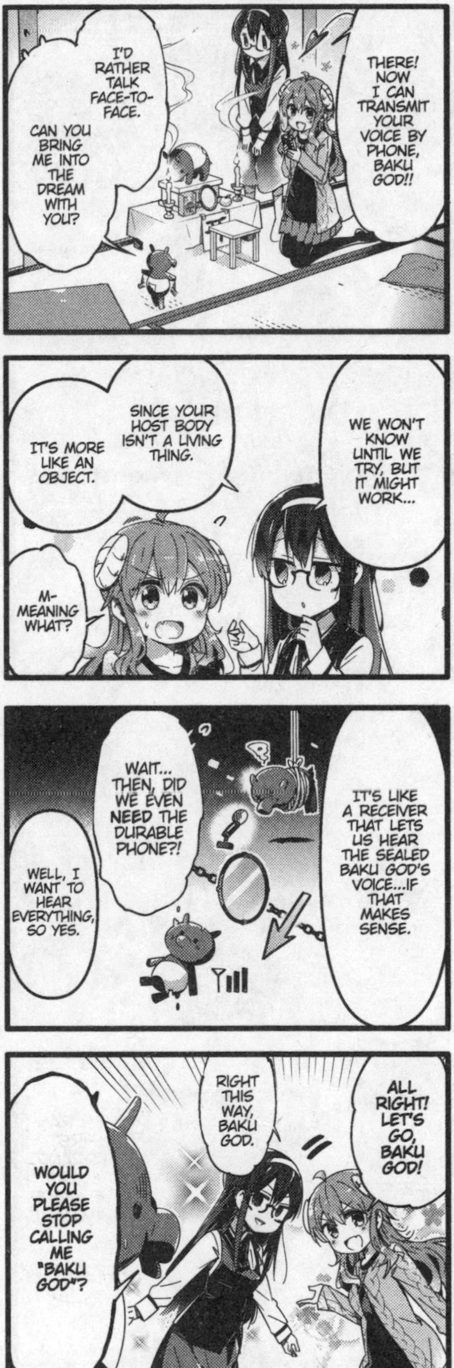
THERE! NOW I CAN TRANSMIT YOUR VOICE BY PHONE, BAKU GOD!!
I'D RATHER TALK FACE-TO-FACE.
CAN YOU BRING ME INTO THE DREAM WITH YOU?
WE WON'T KNOW UNTIL WE TRY, BUT IT MIGHT WORK...
SINCE YOUR HOST BODY ISN'T A LIVING THING.
IT'S MORE LIKE AN OBJECT.
M-MEANING WHAT?
IT'S LIKE A RECEIVER THAT LETS US HEAR THE SEALED BAKU GOD'S VOICE...IF THAT MAKES SENSE.
WAIT... THEN, DID WE EVEN NEED THE DURABLE PHONE?!
WELL, I WANT TO HEAR EVERYTHING, SO YES.
ALL RIGHT! LET'S GO, BAKU GOD!
RIGHT THIS WAY, BAKU GOD.
WOULD YOU PLEASE STOP CALLING ME "BAKU GOD"?

IT'S CALLED TOUGH LOVE

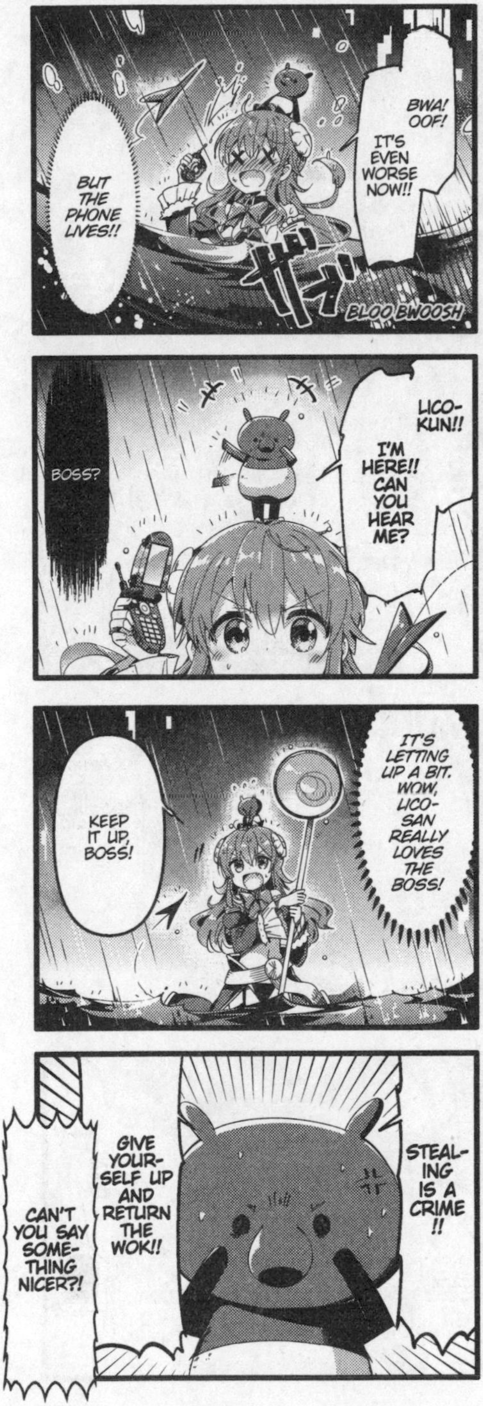
BWA! OOF!
IT'S EVEN WORSE NOW!!
BUT THE PHONE LIVES!!
BLOO BWOOSH
LICO-KUN!!
I'M HERE!! CAN YOU HEAR ME?
BOSS?
IT'S LETTING UP A BIT. WOW, LICO-SAN REALLY LOVES THE BOSS!
KEEP IT UP, BOSS!
STEALING IS A CRIME!!
GIVE YOURSELF UP AND RETURN THE WOK!!
CAN'T YOU SAY SOMETHING NICER?!

LONER LOGIC

ISSUE #5

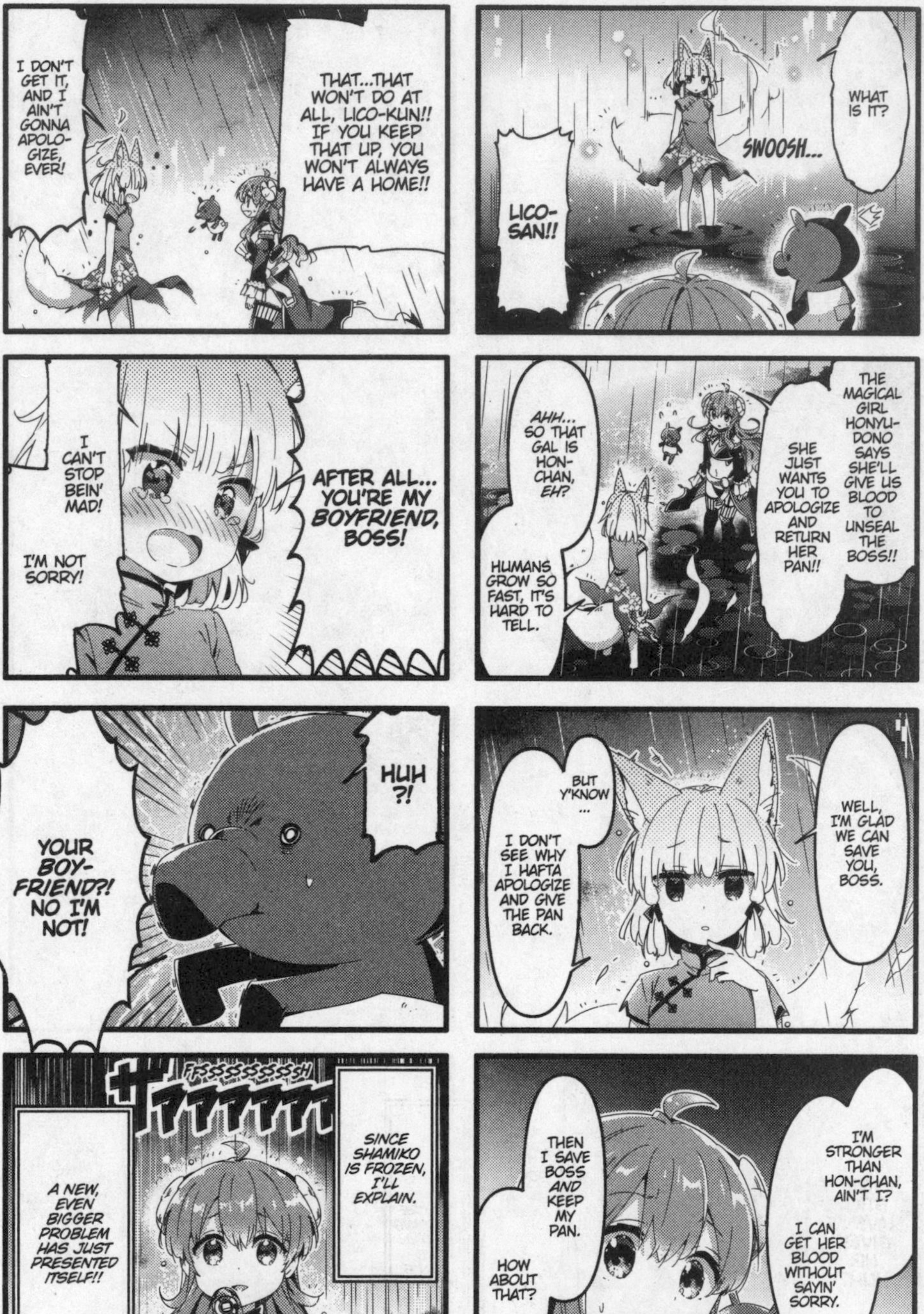
WHAT IS IT?
SWOOSH...
LICO-SAN!!
THE MAGICAL GIRL HONYU-DONO SAYS SHE'LL GIVE US BLOOD TO UNSEAL THE BOSS!!
SHE JUST WANTS YOU TO APOLOGIZE AND RETURN HER PAN!!
AHH... SO THAT GAL IS HON-CHAN, EH?
HUMANS GROW SO FAST, IT'S HARD TO TELL.
WELL, I'M GLAD WE CAN SAVE YOU, BOSS.
BUT Y'KNOW...
I DON'T SEE WHY I HAFTA APOLOGIZE AND GIVE THE PAN BACK.
I'M STRONGER THAN HON-CHAN, AIN'T I?
I CAN GET HER BLOOD WITHOUT SAYIN' SORRY.
THEN I SAVE BOSS AND KEEP MY PAN.
HOW ABOUT THAT?
THAT...THAT WON'T DO AT ALL, LICO-KUN!! IF YOU KEEP THAT UP, YOU WON'T ALWAYS HAVE A HOME!!
I DON'T GET IT, AND I AIN'T GONNA APOLOGIZE, EVER!
AFTER ALL... YOU'RE MY BOYFRIEND, BOSS!
I CAN'T STOP BEIN' MAD!
I'M NOT SORRY!
HUH?!
YOUR BOYFRIEND?! NO I'M NOT!
FSSSSSSSSSSH
SINCE SHAMIKO IS FROZEN, I'LL EXPLAIN.
A NEW, EVEN BIGGER PROBLEM HAS JUST PRESENTED ITSELF!!

THE STORMY BATTLEFIELD OF LOVE

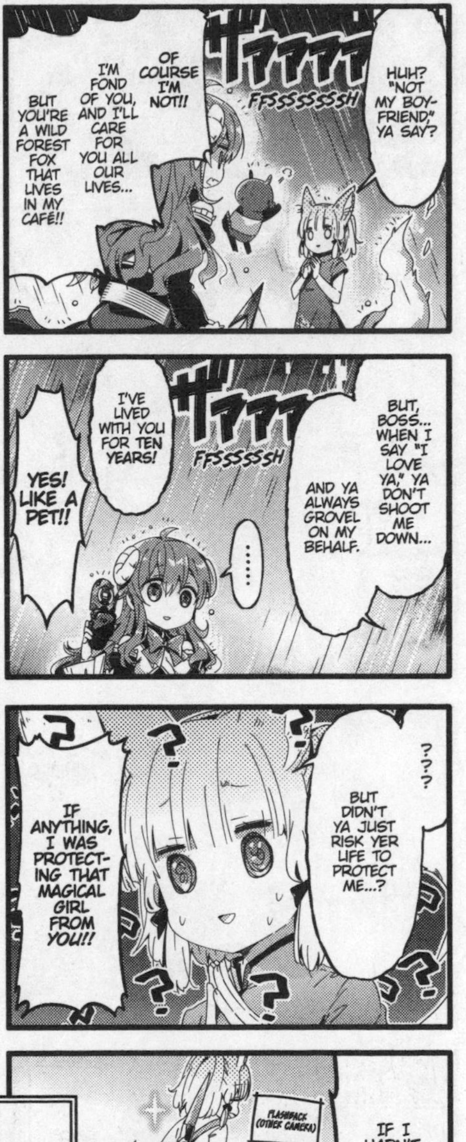
HUH? "NOT MY BOY-FRIEND," YA SAY?
ザァァァァ
FFSSSSSSSSH
OF COURSE I'M NOT!!
I'M FOND OF YOU, AND I'LL CARE FOR YOU ALL OUR LIVES...
BUT YOU'RE A WILD FOREST FOX THAT LIVES IN MY CAFÉ!!
BUT, BOSS... WHEN I SAY "I LOVE YA," YA DON'T SHOOT ME DOWN...
AND YA ALWAYS GROVEL ON MY BEHALF.
ザァァァ
FFSSSSSSH
I'VE LIVED WITH YOU FOR TEN YEARS!
YES! LIKE A PET!!
......
???
BUT DIDN'T YA JUST RISK YER LIFE TO PROTECT ME...?
IF ANYTHING, I WAS PROTECTING THAT MAGICAL GIRL FROM YOU!!
IF I HADN'T, WHO KNOWS WHAT YOU WOULD'VE DONE TO POOR HONYU-DONO!!
FLASHBACK (OTHER CAMERA)
I CAN'T LOVE SOMEONE WHO HOLDS A BUTCHER KNIFE BEHIND THEIR BACK!!
YOU'RE RUBBING SALT IN LICO-KUN'S WOUNDS HERE!!

FOX-O-DILE TEARS

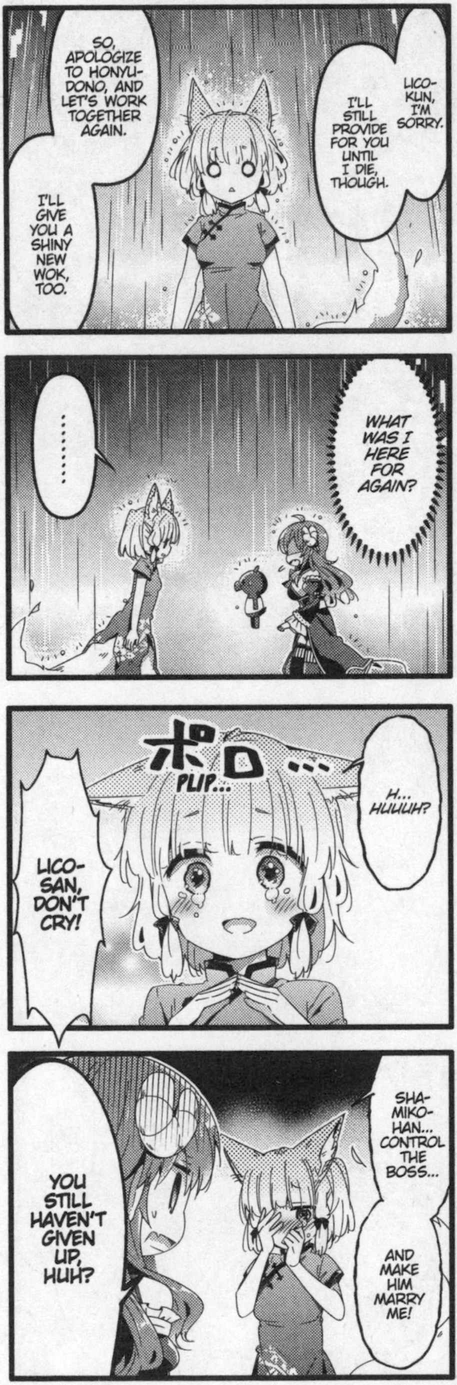
LICO-KUN, I'M SORRY.
I'LL STILL PROVIDE FOR YOU UNTIL I DIE, THOUGH.
SO, APOLOGIZE TO HONYU-DONO, AND LET'S WORK TOGETHER AGAIN.
I'LL GIVE YOU A SHINY NEW WOK, TOO.
WHAT WAS I HERE FOR AGAIN?
......
H... HUUUH?
ポロ...
PLIP...
LICO-SAN, DON'T CRY!
SHAMIKO-HAN... CONTROL THE BOSS...
AND MAKE HIM MARRY ME!
YOU STILL HAVEN'T GIVEN UP, HUH?

HOW TO USE DEMON POWERS, CONTINUED

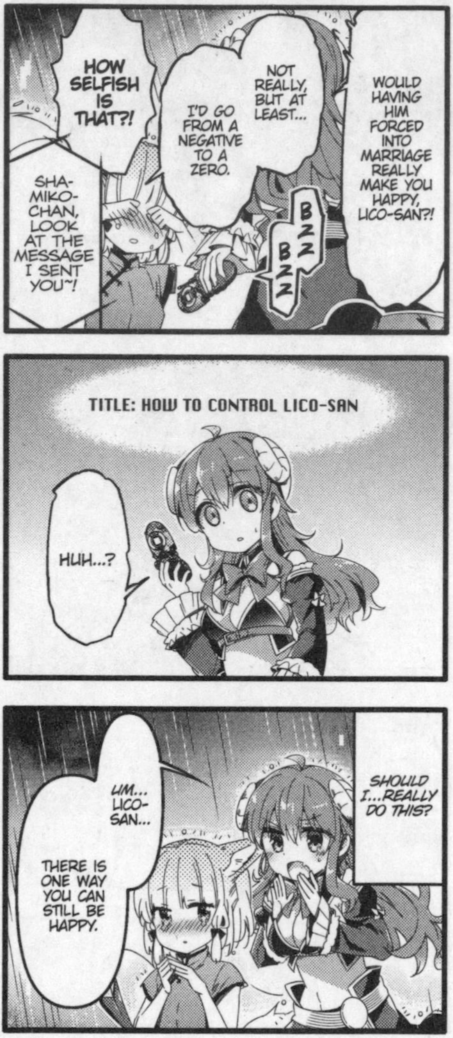
WOULD HAVING HIM FORCED INTO MARRIAGE REALLY MAKE YOU HAPPY, LICO-SAN?!
BZZ BZZ
NOT REALLY, BUT AT LEAST...
I'D GO FROM A NEGATIVE TO A ZERO.
HOW SELFISH IS THAT?!
SHA-MIKO-CHAN, LOOK AT THE MESSAGE I SENT YOU~!
TITLE: HOW TO CONTROL LICO-SAN
HUH...?
SHOULD I...REALLY DO THIS?
UM... LICO-SAN...
THERE IS ONE WAY YOU CAN STILL BE HAPPY.
IT'S EASY.
YOU JUST HAVE TO BE A "GOODY LICO-SHOES."

IT STILL HAS TO BE A TAPIR

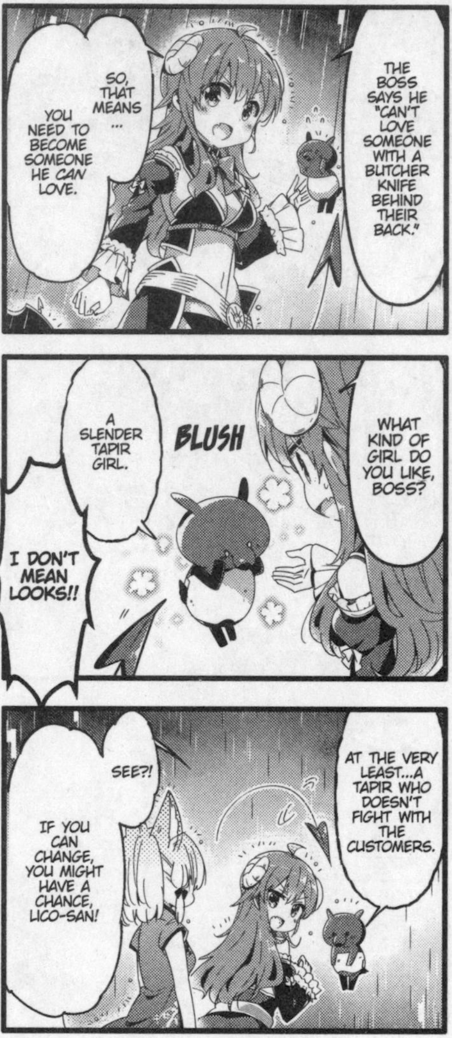
THE BOSS SAYS HE "CAN'T LOVE SOMEONE WITH A BUTCHER KNIFE BEHIND THEIR BACK."
SO, THAT MEANS ...
YOU NEED TO BECOME SOMEONE HE CAN LOVE.
WHAT KIND OF GIRL DO YOU LIKE, BOSS?
BLUSH
A SLENDER TAPIR GIRL.
I DON'T MEAN LOOKS!!
AT THE VERY LEAST...A TAPIR WHO DOESN'T FIGHT WITH THE CUSTOMERS.
SEE?!
IF YOU CAN CHANGE, YOU MIGHT HAVE A CHANCE, LICO-SAN!
SO, I OUGHTA TRANSFORM INTO A SKINNY TAPIR, EH?
NO, NO!
YOU SHOULD APOLOGIZE TO HON-SAN!

WE'LL WORK ON THE SPECIES THING

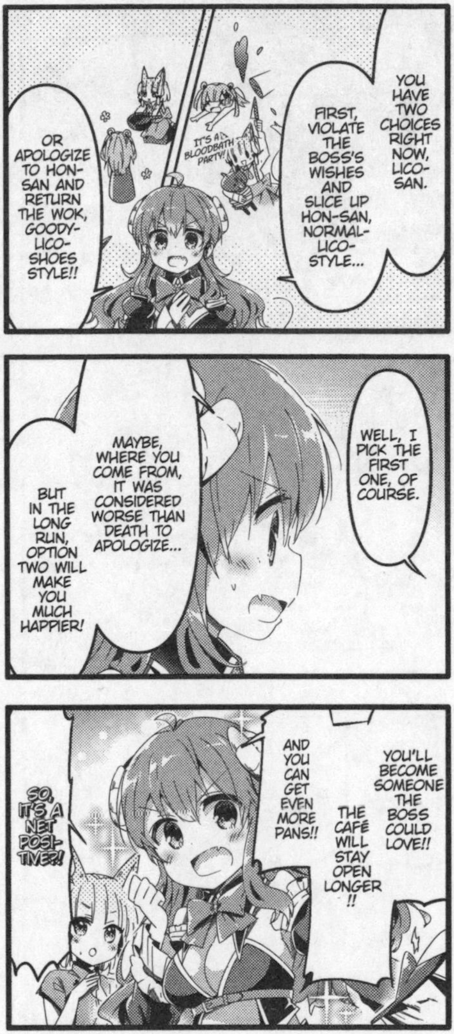
YOU HAVE TWO CHOICES RIGHT NOW, LICO-SAN.
FIRST, VIOLATE THE BOSS'S WISHES AND SLICE UP HON-SAN, NORMAL-LICO-STYLE...
IT'S A BLOODBATH PARTY!
OR APOLOGIZE TO HON-SAN AND RETURN THE WOK, GOODY-LICO-SHOES STYLE!!
WELL, I PICK THE FIRST ONE, OF COURSE.
MAYBE, WHERE YOU COME FROM, IT WAS CONSIDERED WORSE THAN DEATH TO APOLOGIZE...
BUT IN THE LONG RUN, OPTION TWO WILL MAKE YOU MUCH HAPPIER!
YOU'LL BECOME SOMEONE THE BOSS COULD LOVE!!
THE CAFÉ WILL STAY OPEN LONGER!!
AND YOU CAN GET EVEN MORE PANS!!
SO, IT'S A NET POSITIVE?!
THAT'S RIGHT!!
COMPROMISES LEAD TO BETTER PROSPECTS FOR THE FUTURE!!
SO, THE GOODY LICO-SHOES WINS OUT!!
I GET IT!! FINE, I'LL SAY SORRY!!
I STILL COULD ONLY LOVE A TAPIR, THOUGH.

REALLY, LICO-KUN?

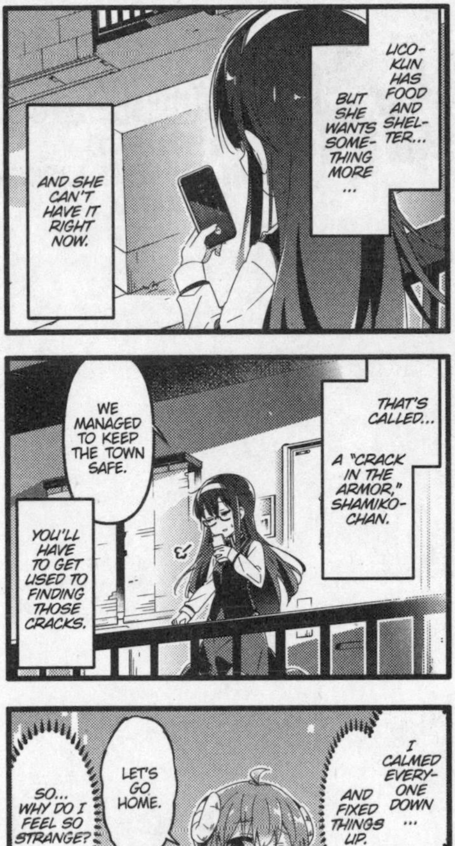
LICO-KUN HAS FOOD AND SHELTER...
BUT SHE WANTS SOMETHING MORE...
AND SHE CAN'T HAVE IT RIGHT NOW.
THAT'S CALLED...
A "CRACK IN THE ARMOR," SHAMIKO-CHAN.
WE MANAGED TO KEEP THE TOWN SAFE.
YOU'LL HAVE TO GET USED TO FINDING THOSE CRACKS.
I CALMED EVERYONE DOWN...
AND FIXED THINGS UP.
LET'S GO HOME.
SO... WHY DO I FEEL SO STRANGE?
SO, WHAT AM I APOLOGIZIN' FOR, EXACTLY?
?
FOR STEALING HER WOK!!!
I GUESS I GET ANXIOUS WITHOUT MOMO'S HELP.
I'LL TALK TO HER LATER.

SECONDS!!

DEMON GIRL NEXT DOOR

(CHAPTER 63) ~ WHAT YOU WERE LOOKING AT THAT DAY ~

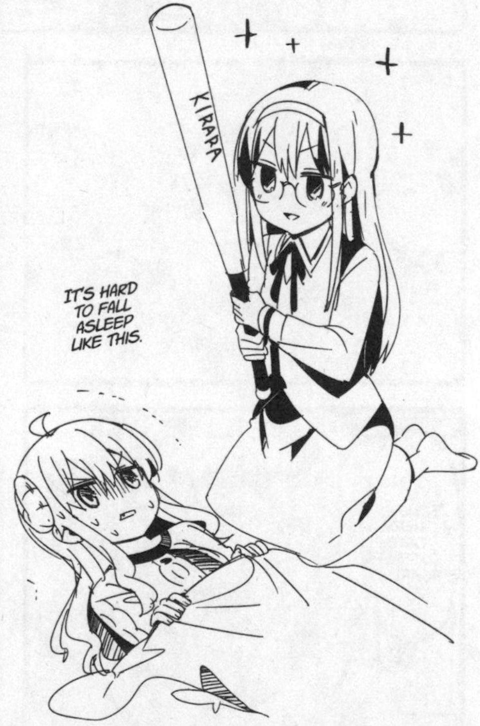
KIRARA
IT'S HARD TO FALL ASLEEP LIKE THIS.

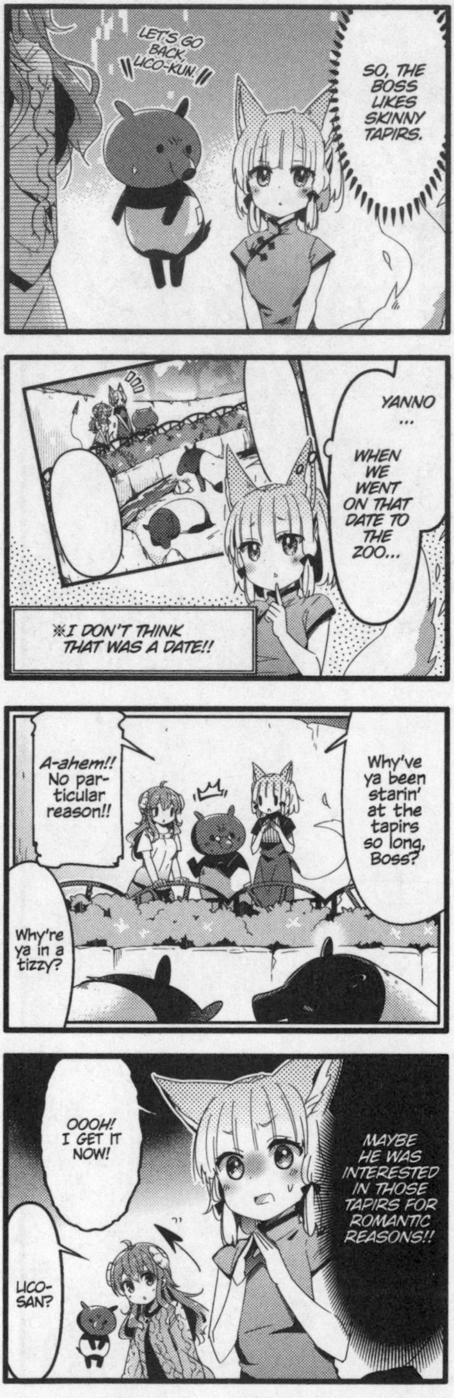
SO, THE BOSS LIKES SKINNY TAPIRS.
LET'S GO BACK, LICO-KUN!
YANNO... WHEN WE WENT ON THAT DATE TO THE ZOO...
※I DON'T THINK THAT WAS A DATE!!
Why've ya been starin' at the tapirs so long, Boss?
A-ahem!! No particular reason!!
Why're ya in a tizzy?
MAYBE HE WAS INTERESTED IN THOSE TAPIRS FOR ROMANTIC REASONS!!
OOOH! I GET IT NOW!
LICO-SAN?

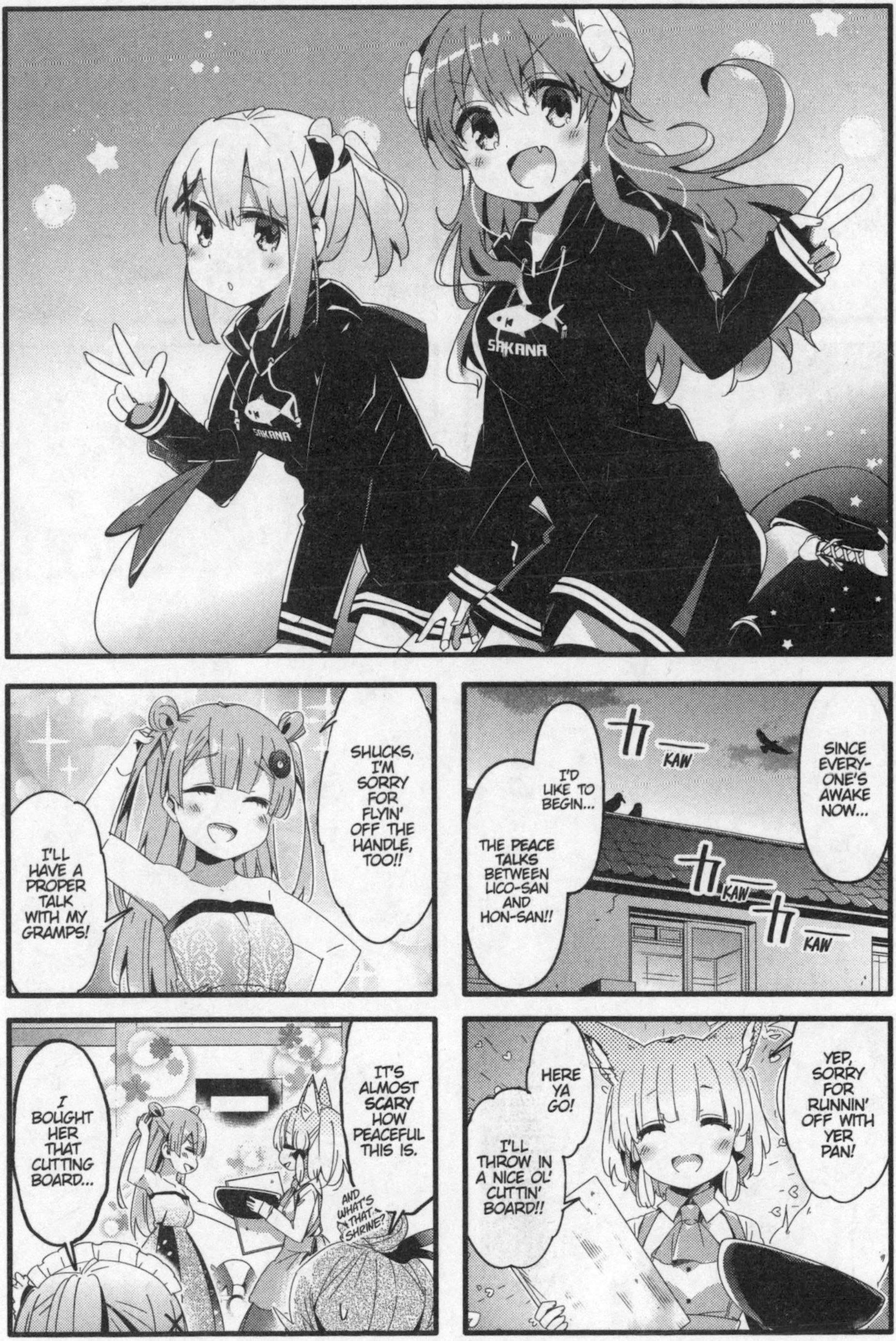
SAKANA
SAKANA
SINCE EVERYONE'S AWAKE NOW...
I'D LIKE TO BEGIN...
THE PEACE TALKS BETWEEN LICO-SAN AND HON-SAN!!
KAW
KAW
KAW
SHUCKS, I'M SORRY FOR FLYIN' OFF THE HANDLE, TOO!!
I'LL HAVE A PROPER TALK WITH MY GRAMPS!
YEP, SORRY FOR RUNNIN' OFF WITH YER PAN!
HERE YA GO!
I'LL THROW IN A NICE OL' CUTTIN' BOARD!!
IT'S ALMOST SCARY HOW PEACEFUL THIS IS.
AND WHAT'S SHRINE?
I BOUGHT HER THAT CUTTING BOARD...

THE SHARPER, THE BETTER, Y'KNOW

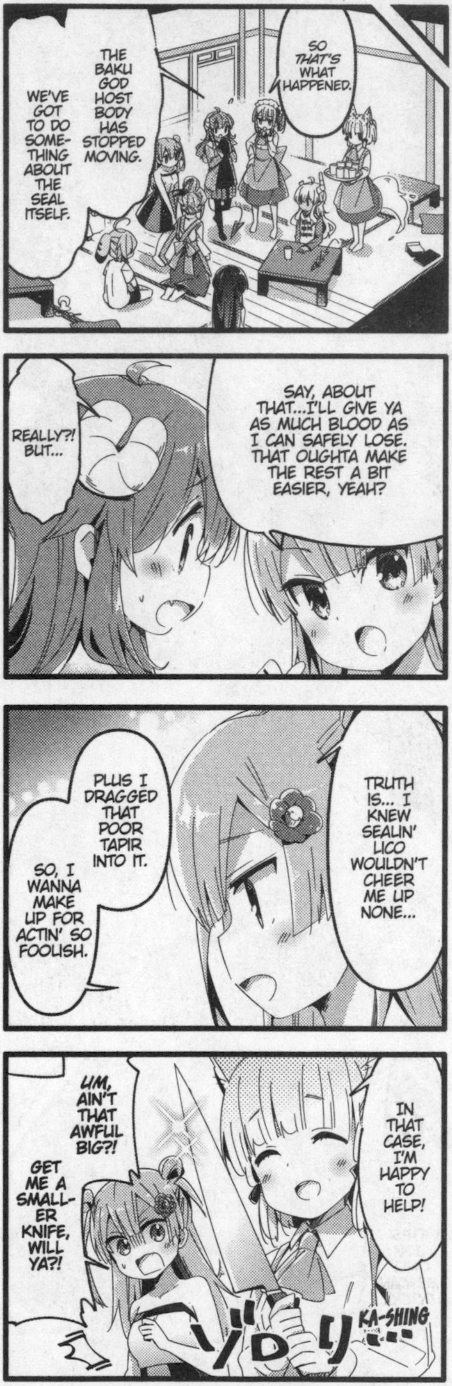
SO THAT'S WHAT HAPPENED.
THE BAKU GOD HOST BODY HAS STOPPED MOVING.
WE'VE GOT TO DO SOMETHING ABOUT THE SEAL ITSELF.
SAY, ABOUT THAT...I'LL GIVE YA AS MUCH BLOOD AS I CAN SAFELY LOSE. THAT OUGHTA MAKE THE REST A BIT EASIER, YEAH?
REALLY?! BUT...
TRUTH IS... I KNEW SEALIN' LICO WOULDN'T CHEER ME UP NONE...
PLUS I DRAGGED THAT POOR TAPIR INTO IT.
SO, I WANNA MAKE UP FOR ACTIN' SO FOOLISH.
IN THAT CASE, I'M HAPPY TO HELP!
UM, AIN'T THAT AWFUL BIG?!
GET ME A SMALLER KNIFE, WILL YA?!
KA-SHING

CARBONATION IS NICE AFTER A NAP

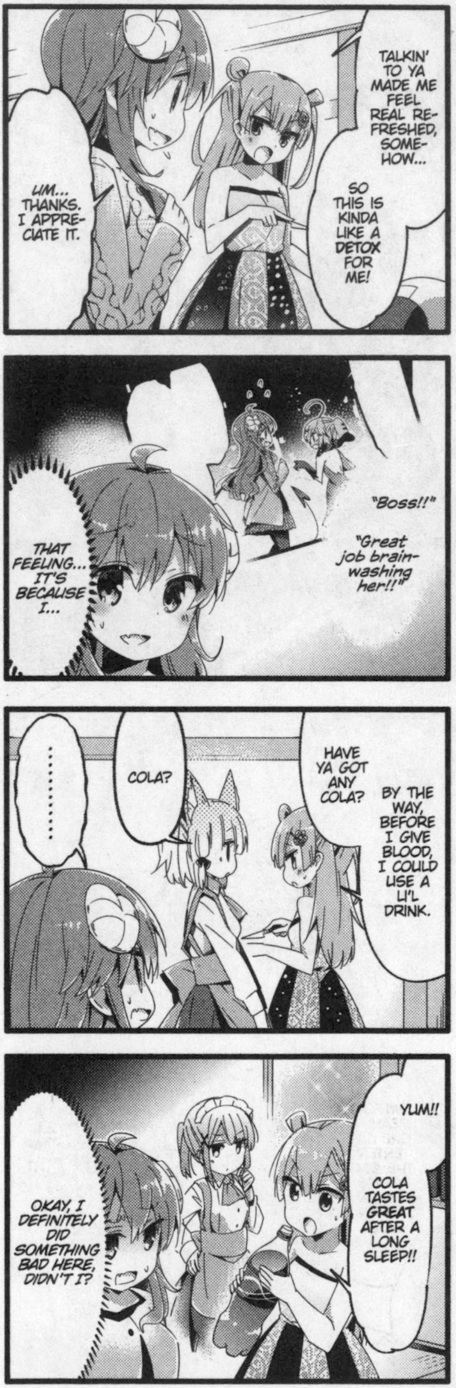
TALKIN' TO YA MADE ME FEEL REAL REFRESHED, SOMEHOW...
SO THIS IS KINDA LIKE A DETOX FOR ME!
UM... THANKS. I APPRECIATE IT.
"Boss!!"
"Great job brainwashing her!!"
THAT FEELING... IT'S BECAUSE I...
BY THE WAY, BEFORE I GIVE BLOOD, I COULD USE A LI'L DRINK.
HAVE YA GOT ANY COLA?
COLA?
......
YUM!!
COLA TASTES GREAT AFTER A LONG SLEEP!!
OKAY, I DEFINITELY DID SOMETHING BAD HERE, DIDN'T I?

SOMETHING ONLY I CAN DO

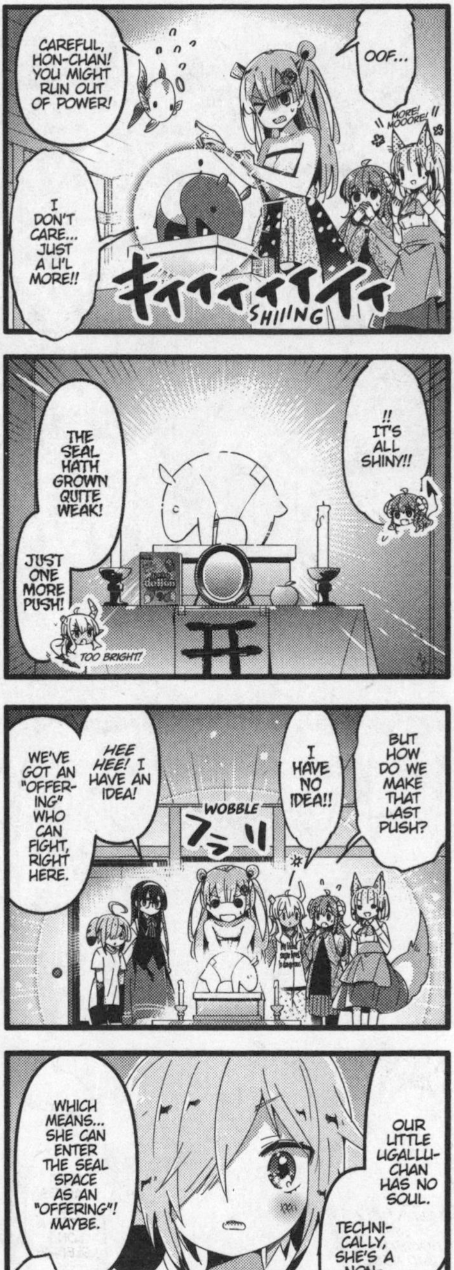
OOF...
CAREFUL, HON-CHAN! YOU MIGHT RUN OUT OF POWER!
MORE! MOOORE!
I DON'T CARE... JUST A LI'L MORE!!
キィィィィィィィ
SHIIING
!! IT'S ALL SHINY!!
THE SEAL HATH GROWN QUITE WEAK!
JUST ONE MORE PUSH!
TOO BRIGHT!
BUT HOW DO WE MAKE THAT LAST PUSH?
I HAVE NO IDEA!!
HEE HEE! I HAVE AN IDEA!
WE'VE GOT AN "OFFERING" WHO CAN FIGHT, RIGHT HERE.
WOBBLE
フラリ
OUR LITTLE UGALLU-CHAN HAS NO SOUL.
TECHNICALLY, SHE'S A NON-LIVING THING.
WHICH MEANS... SHE CAN ENTER THE SEAL SPACE AS AN "OFFERING"! MAYBE.
NNGAH!!

A TAPIR'S BIG PRINCESS-CARRY SCENE

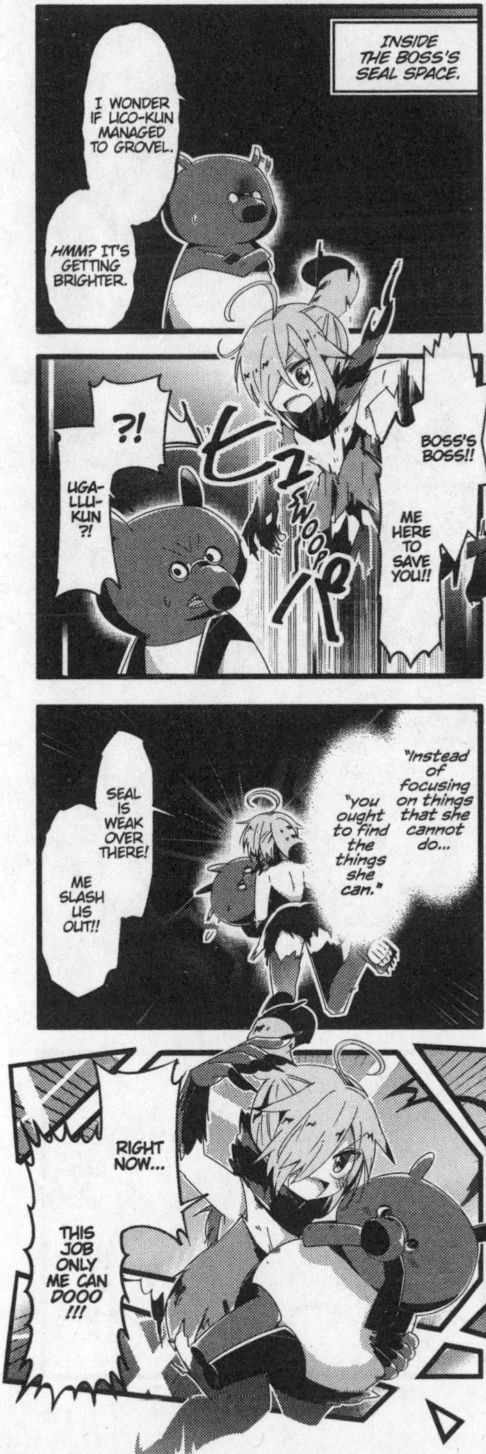
INSIDE THE BOSS'S SEAL SPACE.
I WONDER IF LICO-KUN MANAGED TO GROVEL.
HMM? IT'S GETTING BRIGHTER.
BOSS'S BOSS!!
ME HERE TO SAVE YOU!!
?!
UGALLU-KUN?!
"Instead of focusing on things that she cannot do...
"you ought to find the things she can."
SEAL IS WEAK OVER THERE!
ME SLASH US OUT!!
RIGHT NOW...
THIS JOB ONLY ME CAN DOOO!!!

STILL TURNING INTO A HANGOUT SPOT

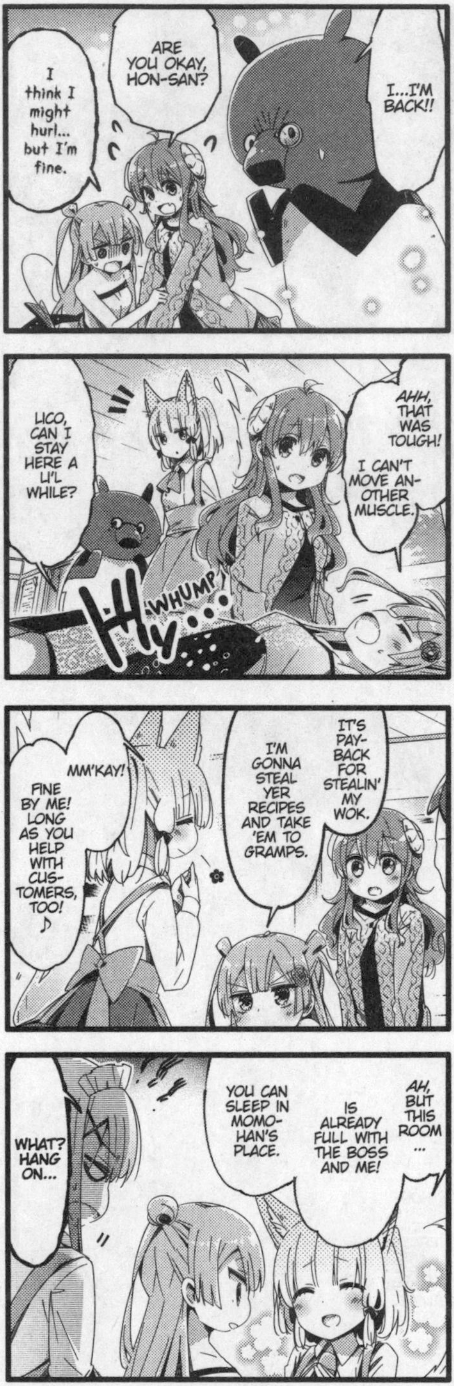
I...I'M BACK!!
ARE YOU OKAY, HON-SAN?
I think I might hurl... but I'm fine.
AHH, THAT WAS TOUGH!
I CAN'T MOVE AN-OTHER MUSCLE.
LICO, CAN I STAY HERE A LI'L WHILE?
WHUMP...
IT'S PAY-BACK FOR STEALIN' MY WOK.
I'M GONNA STEAL YER RECIPES AND TAKE 'EM TO GRAMPS.
MM'KAY!
FINE BY ME! LONG AS YOU HELP WITH CUS-TOMERS, TOO! ♪
AH, BUT THIS ROOM ...
IS ALREADY FULL WITH THE BOSS AND ME!
YOU CAN SLEEP IN MOMO-HAN'S PLACE.
WHAT? HANG ON...

MY BUFFET RAN AWAY

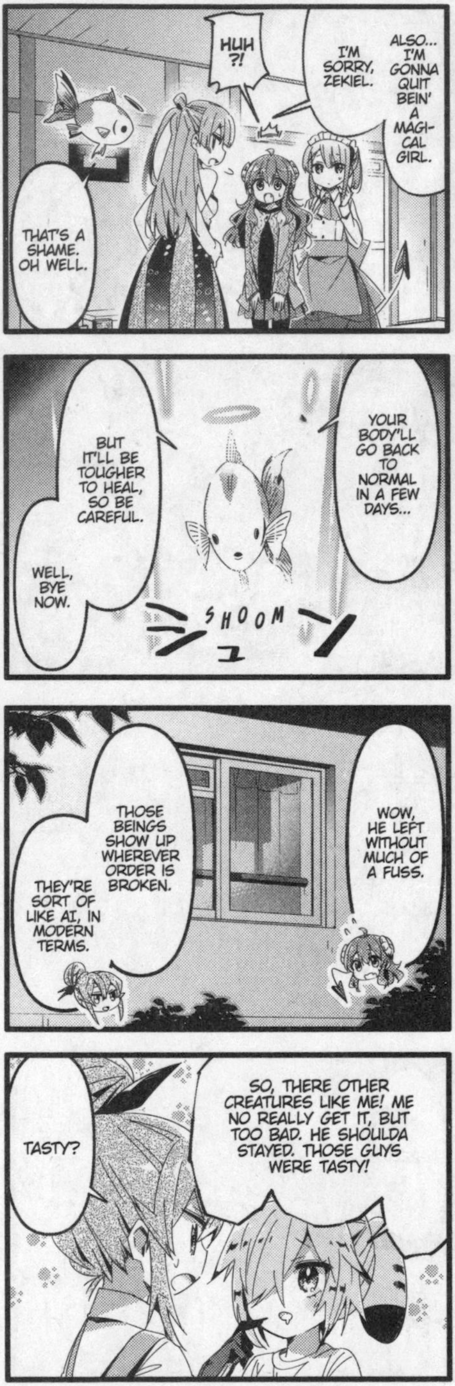
ALSO... I'M GONNA QUIT BEIN' A MAGI-CAL GIRL.
I'M SORRY, ZEKIEL.
HUH ?!
THAT'S A SHAME. OH WELL.
YOUR BODY'LL GO BACK TO NORMAL IN A FEW DAYS...
BUT IT'LL BE TOUGHER TO HEAL, SO BE CAREFUL.
WELL, BYE NOW.
SHOOM
WOW, HE LEFT WITHOUT MUCH OF A FUSS.
THOSE BEINGS SHOW UP WHEREVER ORDER IS BROKEN.
THEY'RE SORT OF LIKE AI, IN MODERN TERMS.
SO, THERE OTHER CREATURES LIKE ME! ME NO REALLY GET IT, BUT TOO BAD. HE SHOULDA STAYED. THOSE GUYS WERE TASTY!
TASTY?

CHAOS IN THE FIELD HOSPITAL

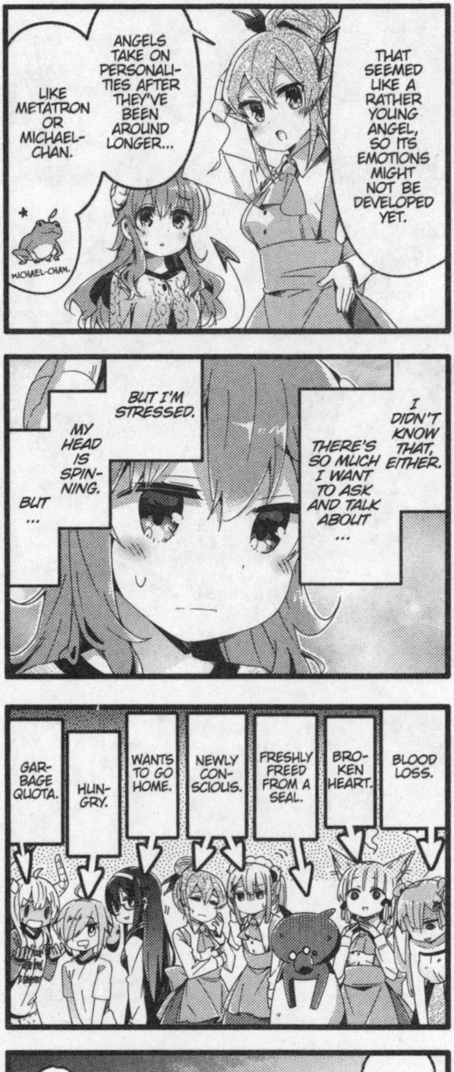
THAT SEEMED LIKE A RATHER YOUNG ANGEL, SO ITS EMOTIONS MIGHT NOT BE DEVELOPED YET.
ANGELS TAKE ON PERSONALITIES AFTER THEY'VE BEEN AROUND LONGER...
LIKE METATRON OR MICHAEL-CHAN.
* MICHAEL-CHAN.
I DIDN'T KNOW THAT, EITHER.
THERE'S SO MUCH I WANT TO ASK AND TALK ABOUT...
BUT I'M STRESSED.
MY HEAD IS SPINNING.
BUT...
BLOOD LOSS.
BROKEN HEART.
FRESHLY FREED FROM A SEAL.
NEWLY CONSCIOUS.
WANTS TO GO HOME.
HUNGRY.
GARBAGE QUOTA.
WE SHOULD CALL IT A DAY...
AND TAKE CARE OF THE REST ONCE WE'VE RECOVERED.
AGREED.

HOW TO USE DEMON POWERS, "RE-CONTINUED"

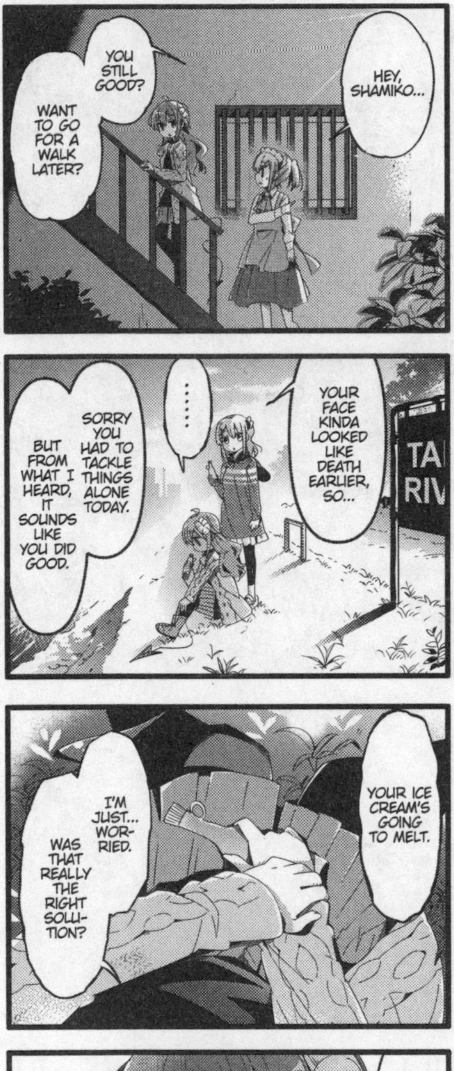
HEY, SHAMIKO...
YOU STILL GOOD?
WANT TO GO FOR A WALK LATER?
YOUR FACE KINDA LOOKED LIKE DEATH EARLIER, SO...
......
SORRY YOU HAD TO TACKLE THINGS ALONE TODAY.
BUT FROM WHAT I HEARD, IT SOUNDS LIKE YOU DID GOOD.
YOUR ICE CREAM'S GOING TO MELT.
I'M JUST... WORRIED.
WAS THAT REALLY THE RIGHT SOLUTION?
I FEEL LIKE I MADE PEACE...
BASED ON FALSE PRETENSES.
I TWISTED AROUND...
HON-SAN'S BITTERNESS AND LICO-SAN'S LOVE.

THERE ARE A LOT OF WEIRDOS IN THIS TOWN

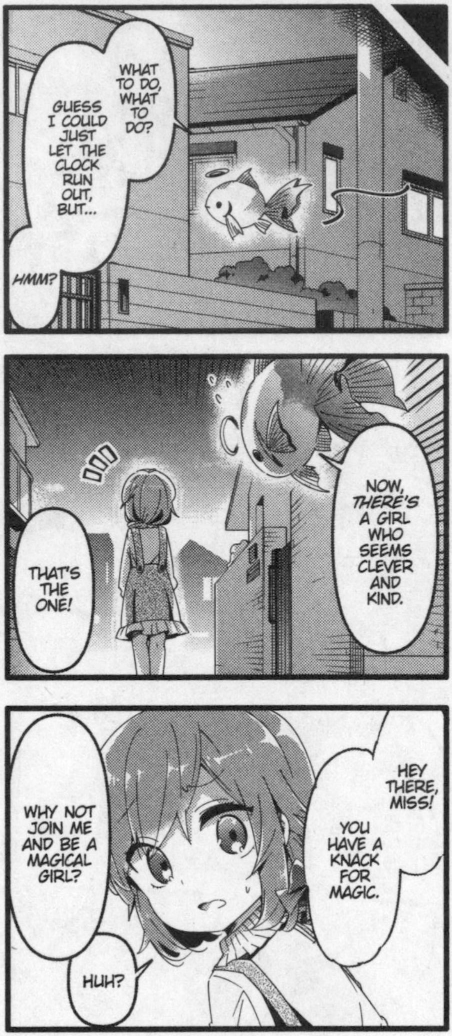
WHAT TO DO, WHAT TO DO?
GUESS I COULD JUST LET THE CLOCK RUN OUT, BUT...
HMM?
NOW, *THERE'S* A GIRL WHO SEEMS CLEVER AND KIND.
THAT'S THE ONE!
HEY THERE, MISS!
YOU HAVE A KNACK FOR MAGIC.
WHY NOT JOIN ME AND BE A MAGICAL GIRL?
HUH?
SORRY, BUT NO, THANK YOU.
C'MON, JUST HEAR ME OUT. IT'S A GOOD DEAL.
YOU'RE NOT SURPRISED? I'M A TALKING FISH.

ZEKIEL-CHAN AND THE FIELD OF LANDMINES

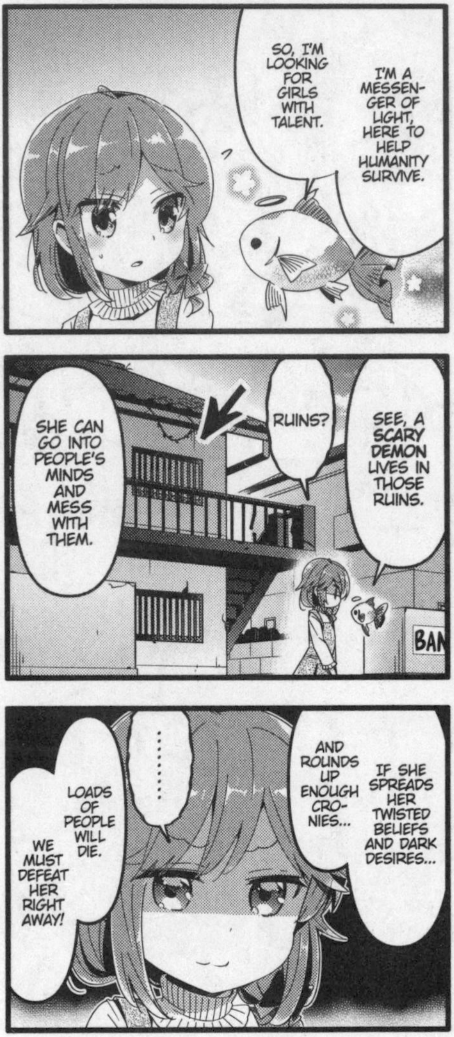
I'M A MESSENGER OF LIGHT, HERE TO HELP HUMANITY SURVIVE.
SO, I'M LOOKING FOR GIRLS WITH TALENT.
SEE, A **SCARY DEMON** LIVES IN THOSE RUINS.
RUINS?
SHE CAN GO INTO PEOPLE'S MINDS AND MESS WITH THEM.
BAN
IF SHE SPREADS HER TWISTED BELIEFS AND DARK DESIRES...
AND ROUNDS UP ENOUGH CRONIES...
LOADS OF PEOPLE WILL DIE.
......
WE MUST DEFEAT HER RIGHT AWAY!
YOU CAN GET POINTS FOR BEATING DEMONS.
SAVE 'EM UP, AND YOUR WISHES CAN COME TRUE!
UH-HUH...
STILL NO REACTION? IT'S MAGIC!

TRACKED BY A TRAIL OF COLA

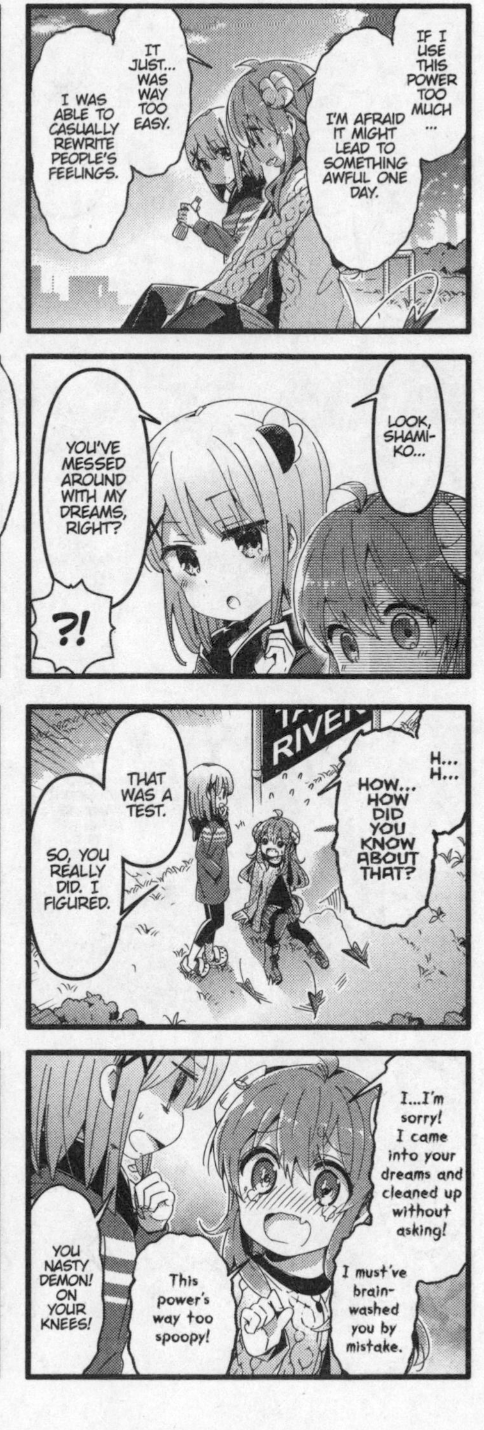
IF I USE THIS POWER TOO MUCH...
I'M AFRAID IT MIGHT LEAD TO SOMETHING AWFUL ONE DAY.
IT JUST... WAS WAY TOO EASY.
I WAS ABLE TO CASUALLY REWRITE PEOPLE'S FEELINGS.
LOOK, SHAMIKO...
YOU'VE MESSED AROUND WITH MY DREAMS, RIGHT?
?!
RIVER
H... H...
HOW... HOW DID YOU KNOW ABOUT THAT?
THAT WAS A TEST.
SO, YOU REALLY DID. I FIGURED.
I...I'm sorry! I came into your dreams and cleaned up without asking!
I must've brain-washed you by mistake.
This power's way too spoopy!
YOU NASTY DEMON! ON YOUR KNEES!

BECOME A MAGICAL GIRL WHO CAN SHARE HER FEELINGS

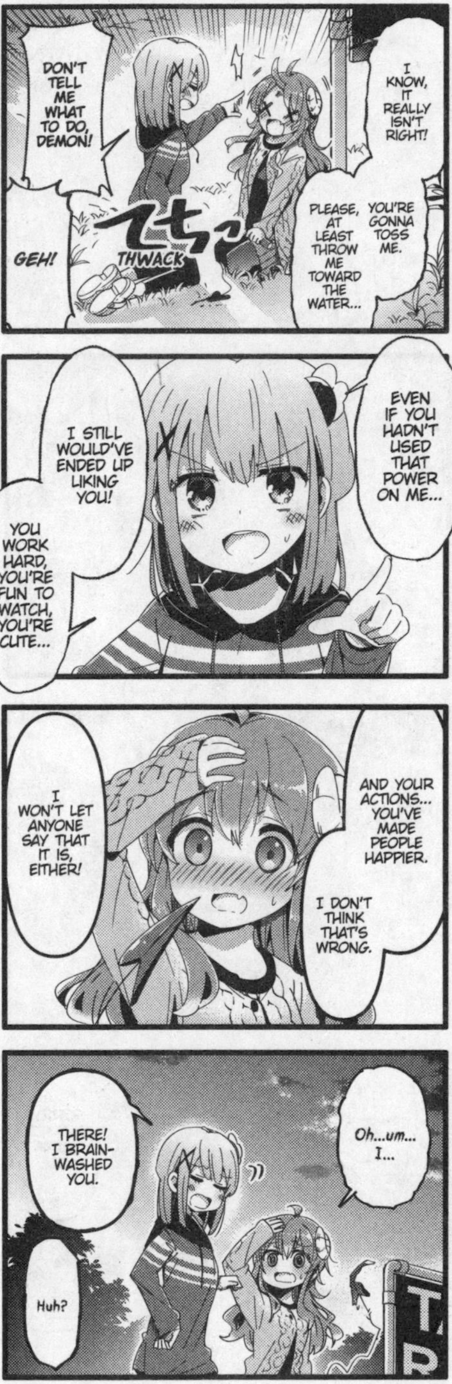
I KNOW, IT REALLY ISN'T RIGHT!
DON'T TELL ME WHAT TO DO, DEMON!
YOU'RE GONNA TOSS ME.
PLEASE, AT LEAST THROW ME TOWARD THE WATER...
THWACK
GEH!
EVEN IF YOU HADN'T USED THAT POWER ON ME...
I STILL WOULD'VE ENDED UP LIKING YOU!
YOU WORK HARD, YOU'RE FUN TO WATCH, YOU'RE CUTE...
AND YOUR ACTIONS... YOU'VE MADE PEOPLE HAPPIER.
I DON'T THINK THAT'S WRONG.
I WON'T LET ANYONE SAY THAT IT IS, EITHER!
Oh...um... I...
THERE! I BRAIN-WASHED YOU.
Huh?

DON'T TOY WITH A DEMON'S EMOTIONS

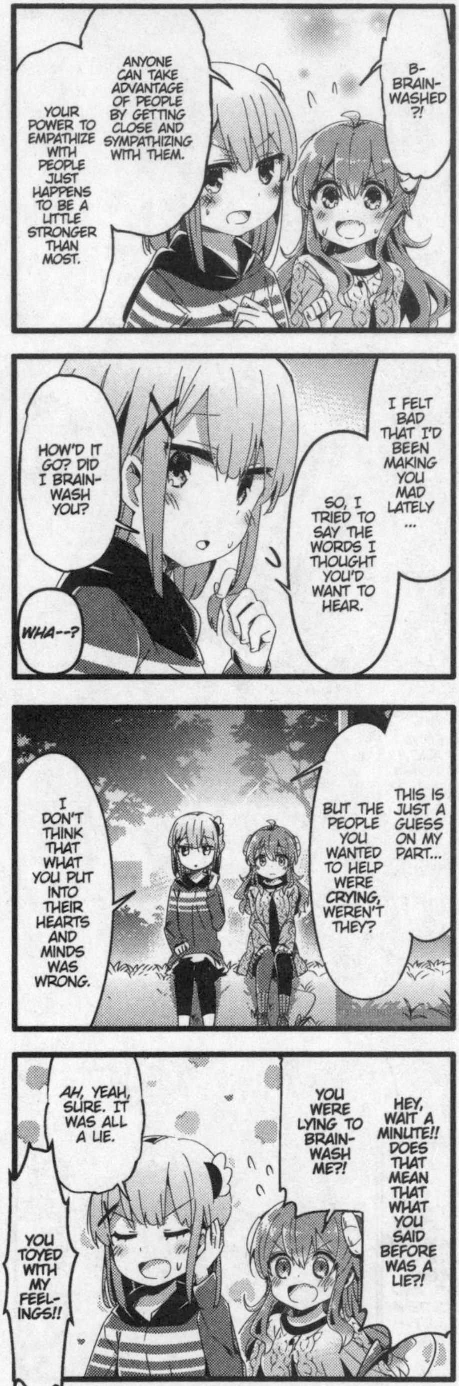
B-BRAINWASHED?!
ANYONE CAN TAKE ADVANTAGE OF PEOPLE BY GETTING CLOSE AND SYMPATHIZING WITH THEM.
YOUR POWER TO EMPATHIZE WITH PEOPLE JUST HAPPENS TO BE A LITTLE STRONGER THAN MOST.
I FELT BAD THAT I'D BEEN MAKING YOU MAD LATELY ...
SO, I TRIED TO SAY THE WORDS I THOUGHT YOU'D WANT TO HEAR.
HOW'D IT GO? DID I BRAINWASH YOU?
WHA--?
THIS IS JUST A GUESS ON MY PART...
BUT THE PEOPLE YOU WANTED TO HELP WERE CRYING, WEREN'T THEY?
I DON'T THINK THAT WHAT YOU PUT INTO THEIR HEARTS AND MINDS WAS WRONG.
HEY, WAIT A MINUTE!! DOES THAT MEAN THAT WHAT YOU SAID BEFORE WAS A LIE?!
YOU WERE LYING TO BRAINWASH ME?!
AH, YEAH, SURE. IT WAS ALL A LIE.
YOU TOYED WITH MY FEELINGS!!

MORTAL ENEMY COURSE CORRECTION

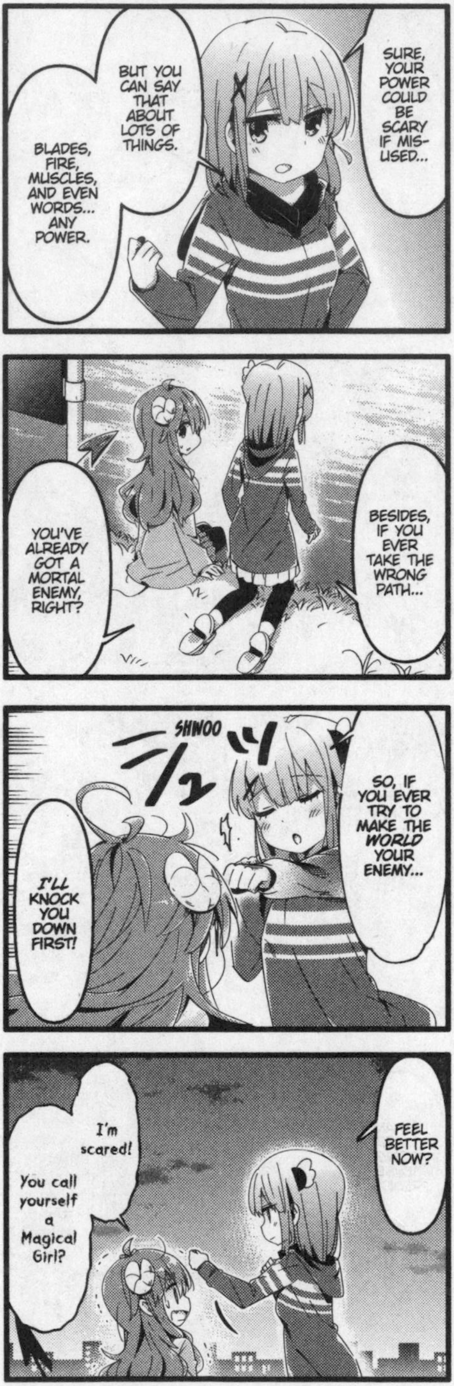
SURE, YOUR POWER COULD BE SCARY IF MISUSED...
BUT YOU CAN SAY THAT ABOUT LOTS OF THINGS.
BLADES, FIRE, MUSCLES, AND EVEN WORDS... ANY POWER.
BESIDES, IF YOU EVER TAKE THE WRONG PATH...
YOU'VE ALREADY GOT A MORTAL ENEMY, RIGHT?
SO, IF YOU EVER TRY TO MAKE THE WORLD YOUR ENEMY...
SHWOO
I'LL KNOCK YOU DOWN FIRST!
FEEL BETTER NOW?
I'm scared!
You call yourself a Magical Girl?

PROBLEMATIC FISH VS PROBLEMATIC GIRL

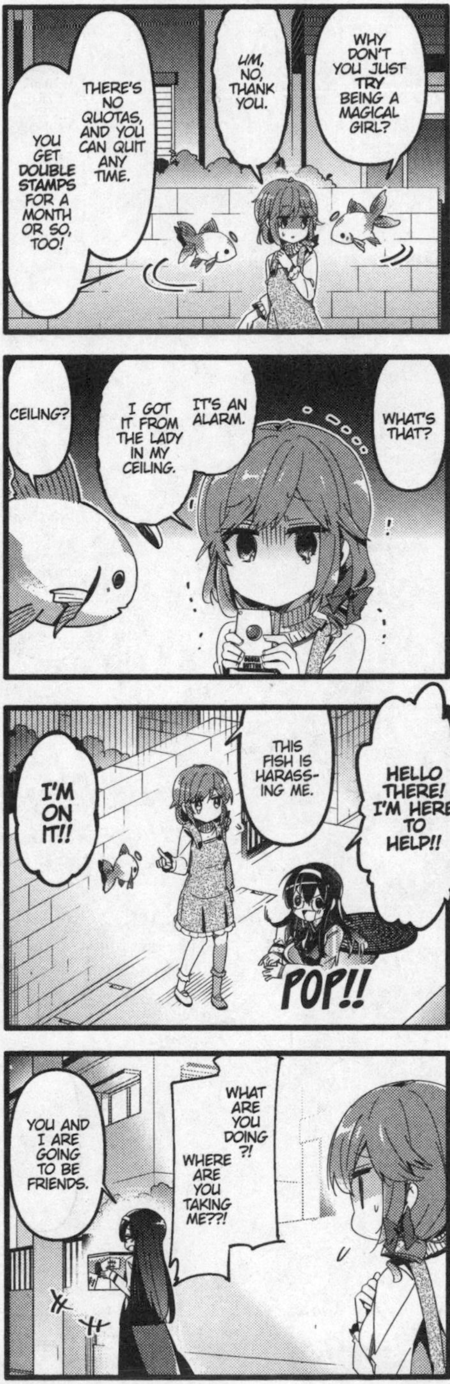
WHY DON'T YOU JUST TRY BEING A MAGICAL GIRL?
UM, NO, THANK YOU.
THERE'S NO QUOTAS, AND YOU CAN QUIT ANY TIME.
YOU GET DOUBLE STAMPS FOR A MONTH OR SO, TOO!
WHAT'S THAT?
IT'S AN ALARM.
I GOT IT FROM THE LADY IN MY CEILING.
CEILING?
HELLO THERE! I'M HERE TO HELP!!
THIS FISH IS HARASSING ME.
I'M ON IT!!
POP!!
WHAT ARE YOU DOING?!
WHERE ARE YOU TAKING ME??!
YOU AND I ARE GOING TO BE FRIENDS.

A NEW NIGHT BEGINS

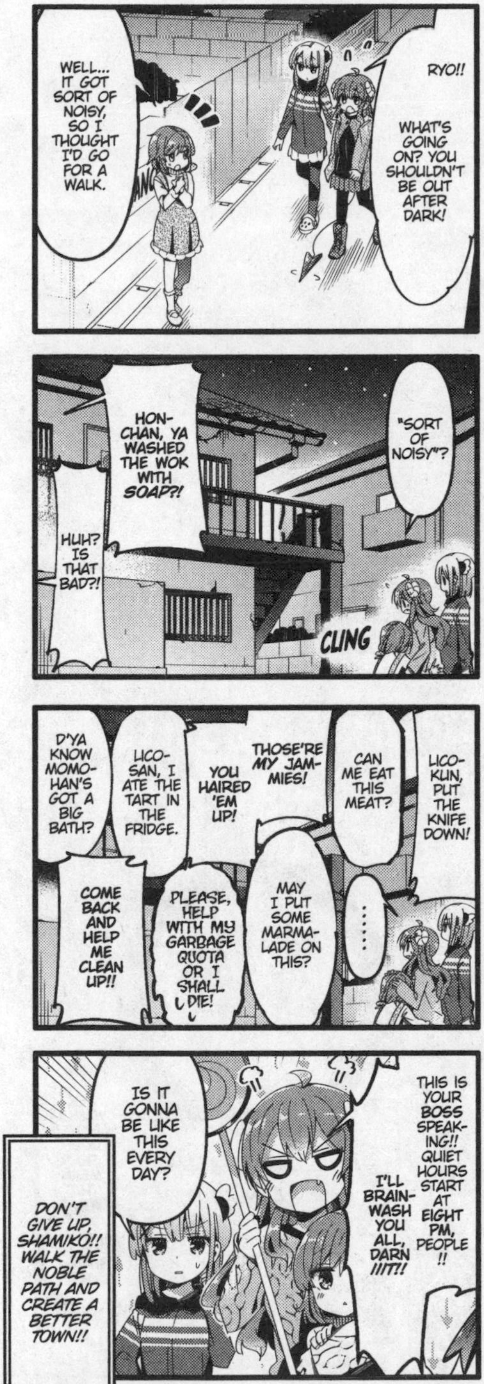
RYO!!
WHAT'S GOING ON? YOU SHOULDN'T BE OUT AFTER DARK!
WELL... IT GOT SORT OF NOISY, SO I THOUGHT I'D GO FOR A WALK.
"SORT OF NOISY"?
HON-CHAN, YA WASHED THE WOK WITH SOAP?!
HUH? IS THAT BAD?!
CLING
LICO-KUN, PUT THE KNIFE DOWN!
CAN ME EAT THIS MEAT?
THOSE'RE MY JAMMIES!
YOU HAIRED 'EM UP!
LICO-SAN, I ATE THE TART IN THE FRIDGE.
D'YA KNOW MOMO-HAN'S GOT A BIG BATH?
......
MAY I PUT SOME MARMALADE ON THIS?
PLEASE, HELP WITH MY GARBAGE QUOTA OR I SHALL DIE!
COME BACK AND HELP ME CLEAN UP!!
THIS IS YOUR BOSS SPEAKING!! QUIET HOURS START AT EIGHT PM, PEOPLE!!
I'LL BRAINWASH YOU ALL, DARN IIIT!!
IS IT GONNA BE LIKE THIS EVERY DAY?
DON'T GIVE UP, SHAMIKO!! WALK THE NOBLE PATH AND CREATE A BETTER TOWN!!

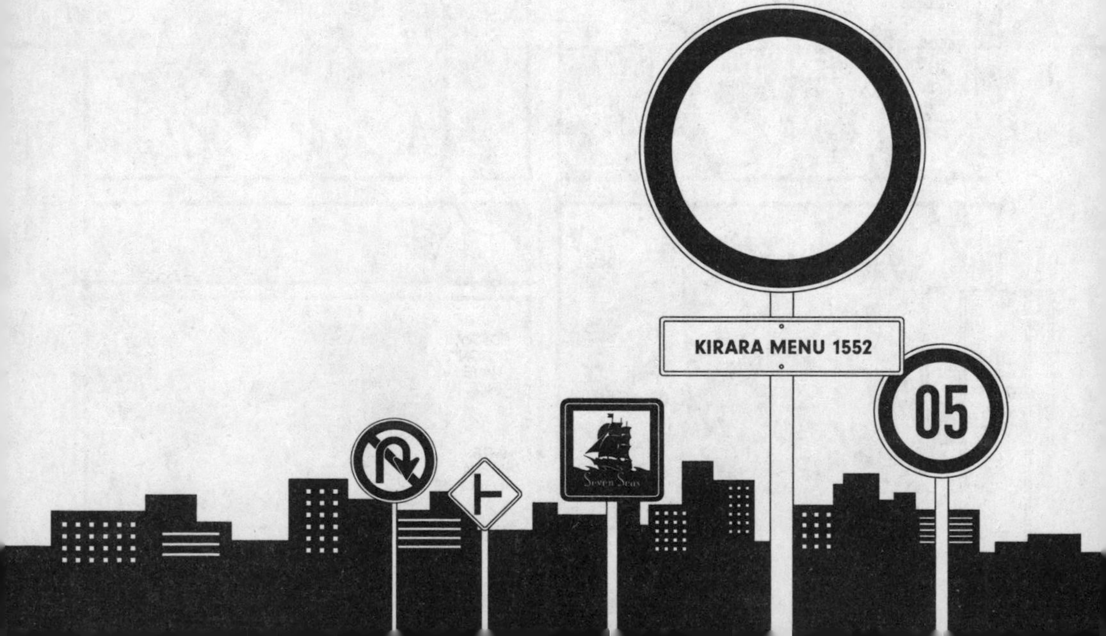
KIRARA MENU 1552
05
Seven Seas

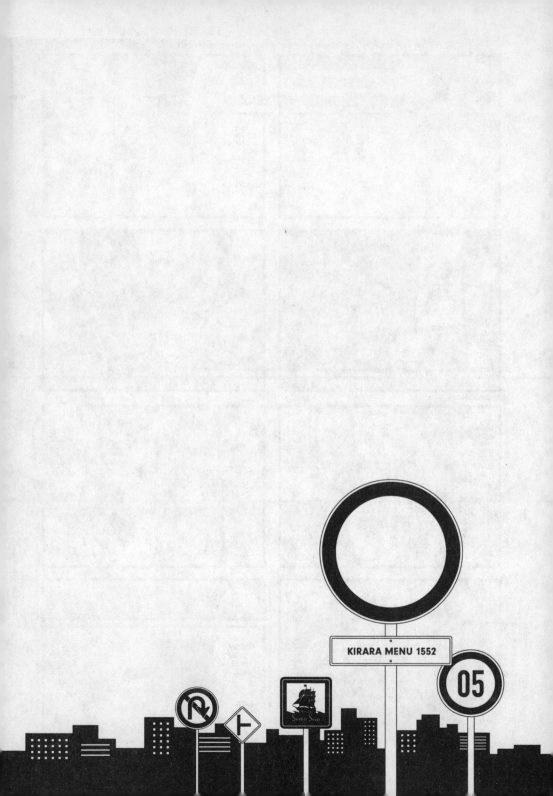

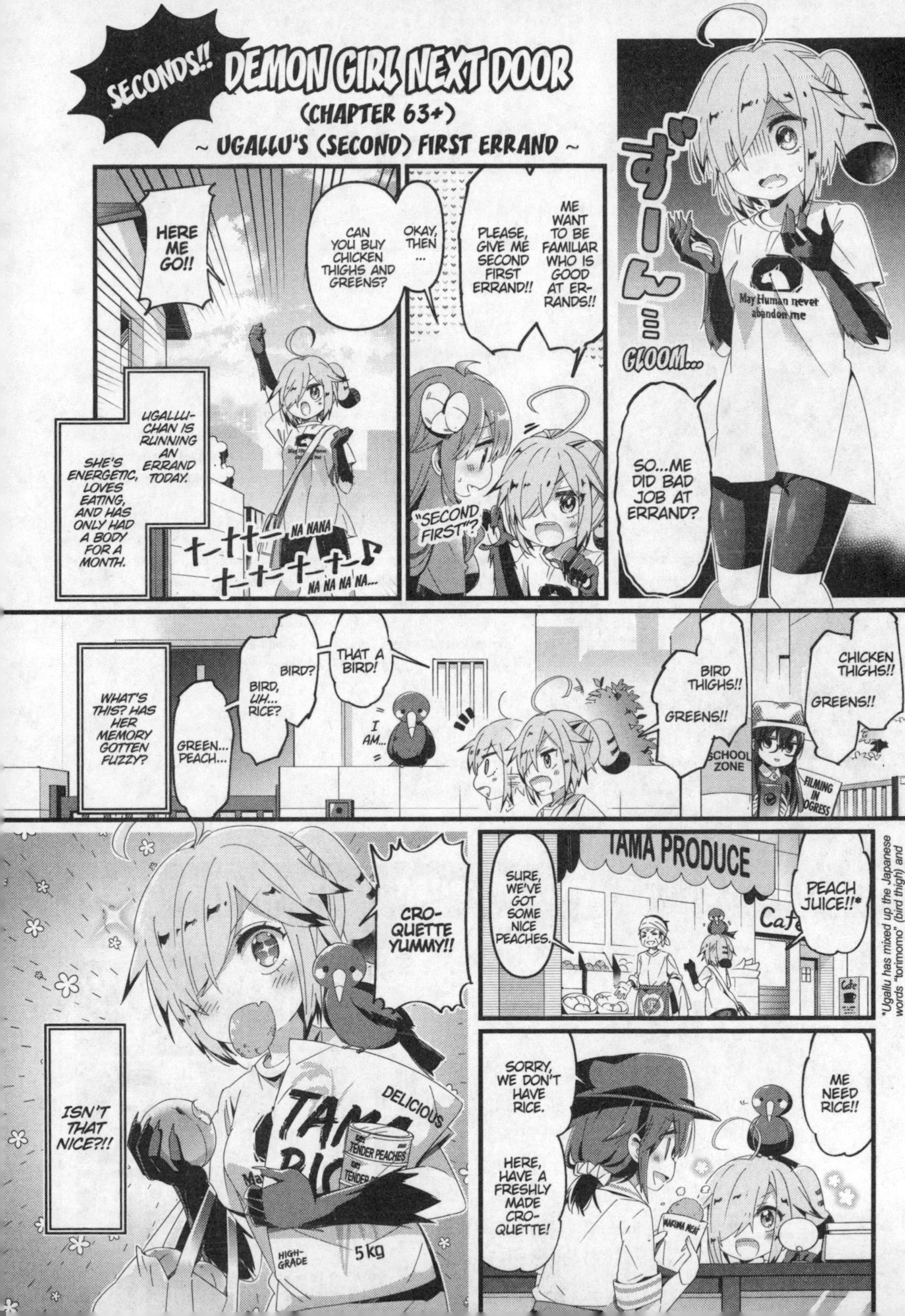
SECONDS!!
DEMON GIRL NEXT DOOR
(CHAPTER 63+)
~ UGALLU'S (SECOND) FIRST ERRAND ~
ずーん…
GLOOM...
May Human never abandon me
SO...ME DID BAD JOB AT ERRAND?
ME WANT TO BE FAMILIAR WHO IS GOOD AT ER-RANDS!!
PLEASE, GIVE ME SECOND FIRST ERRAND!!
OKAY, THEN ...
CAN YOU BUY CHICKEN THIGHS AND GREENS?
"SECOND FIRST"?
HERE ME GO!!
UGALLU-CHAN IS RUNNING AN ERRAND TODAY.
SHE'S ENERGETIC, LOVES EATING, AND HAS ONLY HAD A BODY FOR A MONTH.
ナーナナー
NA NANA
ナーナーナーナー♪
NA NA NA NA...
CHICKEN THIGHS!!
GREENS!!
BIRD THIGHS!!
GREENS!!
SCHOOL ZONE
FILMING IN PROGRESS
I AM...
THAT A BIRD!
BIRD?
BIRD, UH... RICE?
GREEN... PEACH...
WHAT'S THIS? HAS HER MEMORY GOTTEN FUZZY?
PEACH JUICE!!*
TAMA PRODUCE
SURE, WE'VE GOT SOME NICE PEACHES.
Cafe
ME NEED RICE!!
SORRY, WE DON'T HAVE RICE.
HERE, HAVE A FRESHLY MADE CRO-QUETTE!
CRO-QUETTE YUMMY!!
TAMA
DELICIOUS
TENDER PEACHES
HIGH-GRADE
5kg
ISN'T THAT NICE?!!

*Ugallu has mixed up the Japanese words "torimomo" (bird thigh) and "momotare" (peach sauce).

SEVEN SEAS ENTERTAINMENT PRESENTS

The Demon Girl Next Door

story and art by IZUMO ITO — VOLUME 5

TRANSLATION
Jenny McKeon

ADAPTATION
Kim Kindya

LETTERING AND RETOUCH
Rai Enril

COVER DESIGN
H. Qi

PROOFREADER
Danielle King, B. Lillian Martin

SENIOR EDITOR
Shanti Whitesides

PRINT MANAGER
Rhiannon Rasmussen-Silverstein

PRODUCTION MANAGER
Lissa Pattillo

EDITOR-IN-CHIEF
Julie Davis

ASSOCIATE PUBLISHER
Adam Arnold

PUBLISHER
Jason DeAngelis

Machikado Mazoku Volume 5
© IZUMO ITO 2019
Originally published in Japan in 2019 by HOUBUNSHA CO., LTD., Tokyo.
English translation rights arranged with HOUBUNSHA CO., LTD., Tokyo,
through TOHAN CORPORATION, Tokyo.

Seven Seas press and purchase enquiries can be sent to Marketing Manager
Lianne Sentar at press@gomanga.com. Information regarding the distribution
and purchase of digital editions is available from Digital Manager CK Russell
at digital@gomanga.com.

Seven Seas and the Seven Seas logo are trademarks of
Seven Seas Entertainment. All rights reserved.

ISBN: 978-1-64827-797-9

Printed in Canada

First Printing: April 2022

10 9 8 7 6 5 4 3 2 1

FOLLOW US ONLINE: *www.sevenseasentertainment.com*

READING DIRECTIONS

This book reads from **right to left**, Japanese style.
If this is your first time reading manga, you start
reading from the top right panel on each page and
take it from there. If you get lost, just follow the
numbered diagram here. It may seem backwards at
first, but you'll get the hang of it! Have fun!!

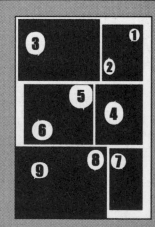